MANITOWAPOW
ABORIGINAL WRITINGS FROM THE LAND OF THE WATER

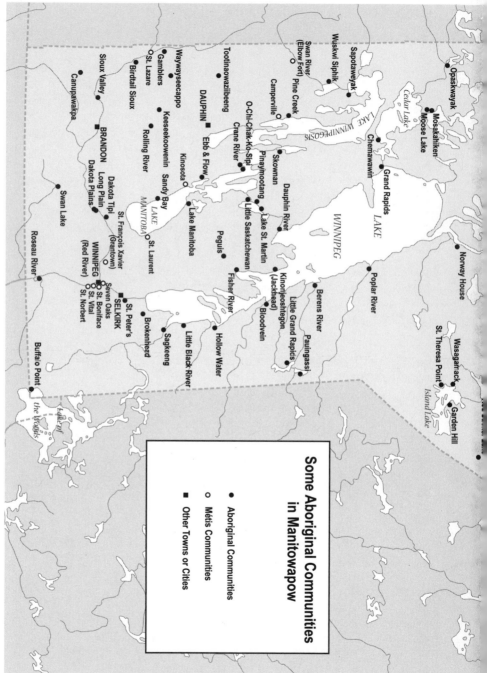

Some Aboriginal Communities in Manitowapow

- ● Aboriginal Communities
- ○ Métis Communities
- ■ Other Towns or Cities

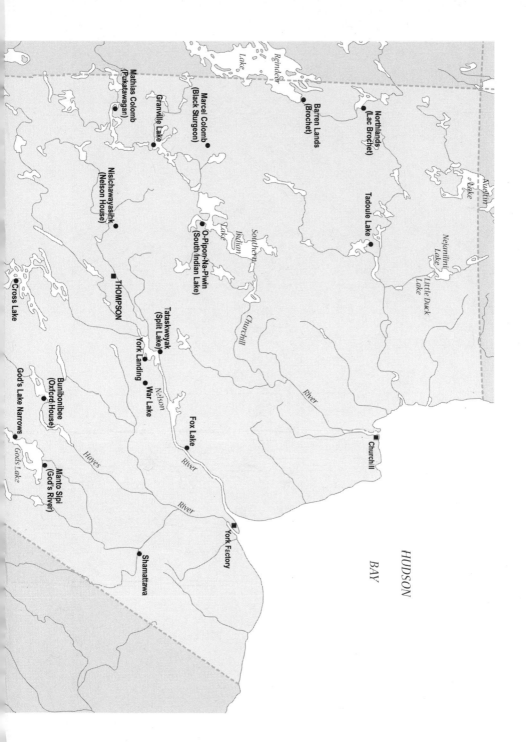

Reindeer Lake

Barren Lands
(Brochet)

Northlands
(Lac Brochet)

Nueltin Lake

Mathias Colomb
(Pukatawagan)

Marcel Colomb
(Black Sturgeon)

Granville Lake

Tadoule Lake

Nejanilini Lake

Little Duck Lake

Nisichawayasihk
(Nelson House)

O-Pipon-Na-Piwin
(South Indian Lake)

Southern Indian Lake

THOMPSON

Churchill River

Cross Lake

Tataskweyak
(Split Lake)

York Landing

Nelson

War Lake

God's Lake Narrows

Bunibonibee
(Oxford House)

Fox Lake

Churchill

Hayes

God's Lake

Manto Sipi
(God's River)

River

York Factory

Shamattawa

HUDSON

BAY

MANITOWAPOW
ABORIGINAL WRITINGS FROM THE LAND OF WATER

NIIGAANWEWIDAM JAMES SINCLAIR
AND WARREN CARIOU, EDITORS

FOREWORD BY BEATRICE MOSIONIER

HIGHWATER
PRESS

HighWater Press gratefully acknowledges the financial support of the Province of Manitoba through the Department of Sport, Culture and Heritage and the Manitoba Book Publishing Tax Credit, and the Government of Canada through the Canada Book Fund (CBF) for our publishing activities.

Proceeds for this book will be donated to the Emerging Aboriginal Writers' Fund, administered through the Centre for Creative Writing and Oral Culture, University of Manitoba.

HighWater Press is an imprint of Portage & Main Press.
Printed and bound in Canada by Friesens
Design by Relish New Brand Experience
Cover Art: *The Creation of the World* by Daphne Odjig. ©The Manitoba Museum, Winnipeg, MB. Used by permission of the artist.

LIBRARY AND ARCHIVES CANADA CATALOGUING IN PUBLICATION

Manitowapow : Aboriginal writings from the land of water / edited by Niigaanwewidam James Sinclair and Warren Cariou.

Includes bibliographical references and index.
Also issued in electronic format.
ISBN 978-1-55379-307-6

1. Canadian literature (English)--Native authors. 2. Canadian literature (English)--Manitoba. 3. Native peoples--Manitoba-- Literary collections. 4. Canadian literature (English)--21st century. I. Cariou, Warren, 1966- II. Sinclair, Niigaanwewidam James

PS8235.I6M347 2012   C810.8'089707127   C2011-908336-1

23 22 21 20   3 4 5 6 7

THE DEBWE SERIES

The Debwe Series features exceptional Indigenous writing from across Canada.

Series Editor: Niigaanwewidam James Sinclair, PhD

Titles in this series:

A Blanket of Butterflies, by Richard Van Camp
Fire Starters, by Jen Storm
The Gift Is in the Making: Anishinaabeg Stories, by Leanne Betasamosake Simpson
Indigenous Writes: A Guide to First Nations, Métis & Inuit Issues in Canada, by Chelsea Vowel

Perception: A Photo Series, by KC Adams
The Stone Collection, by Kateri Akiwenzie-Damm
Surviving the City and *From the Roots Up*, by Tasha Spillett
Three Feathers, by Richard Van Camp

HIGHWATER PRESS

www.highwaterpress.com
Winnipeg, Manitoba
Treaty 1 Territory and homeland of the Métis Nation

FSC
www.fsc.org
MIX
Paper from
responsible sources
FSC® C016245

For all who have experienced the power of this place.

Contents

Foreword

As a publisher at Pemmican Publications in the 1980s, I realized that there was a desperate need to have Aboriginal educational materials available for school curriculums. With the success of my first novel, *In Search of April Raintree*, with students, came the next realization—educational materials must be able to engage students and teachers, too. In early 2010, Niigaan and Warren told me about their plan for an anthology and what it would include. Listening to them, I thought of all the students I'd met at school visits who hungered for more knowledge of the Aboriginal experience. This would be a book that would feed their hunger. As teachers, writers, activists, and visionaries, Niigaan and Warren were the ideal editors. I believed in their vision and I believed in them. The proposed anthology would include excerpts from Aboriginal writers of Manitoba, from those who lived before our times to the writers of today. All together, they would tell the story of our province, known by many as Manitowapow.

More than a year after my initial meeting with Niigaan and Warren, I received their manuscript. One glance at the cover artwork, *The Creation of the World* by Daphne Odjig, promised me that within would be pages and pages containing a collection of rich, colourful, diverse stories written from our perspectives. The care taken to find and choose this perfect artwork is the same care taken to find and choose the collection within.

Because the excerpts in this book were compiled by Niigaan and Warren, I hungrily absorbed each piece, and by the time I reached the last page, it came to me that I had just read a memoir of Manitowapow. This collection of Aboriginal writings made me want to read on, read more—and it made me want to write! Imagine that. It aroused my emotions for as many different reasons as there were stories. It made me laugh; it made me cry; it brought joy; it brought anger. Most of all, it renewed my pride in my community. In spite of so many setbacks in their lives, consecutive generations maintained their sense of generosity, perseverance, compassion, and, of course, that wonderful sense of humour, evident in both the early and more recent stories.

This unique collection opens with early Aboriginal writings of Manitoba, including illustrations of petroforms, rock paintings, and birchbark scrolls. The excerpts that follow are organized chronologically, and each section is preceded by an invaluable brief biography of each contributor. Because this book is rich with prose, poetry, and historical events, it will be invaluable in Native studies, literature, and history courses, as well as for the general reader.

Another feature is the diversity of the collection. It's a gathering of recollections, songs, legends, speeches, plays, poetry, and a graphic-novel excerpt. Some are told in the languages of our people.

Once, at an Aboriginal writers' conference, I heard a writer say that if you are born Aboriginal, you are born political. There is a political thread throughout the offerings. As the oppressed, we are on an ongoing quest for social justice. Watching newscasts of the historical event at Oka, one 12-year-old, who became the activist Clayton Thomas-Müller, became inspired. He writes: "Our greatest power as the peoples of Mother Earth is in maintaining our sacred responsibility to protect her and to speak to those animal and plant relations that cannot speak for themselves."

On the light side, there's even a recipe for bannock—yummy!—with a story on the side. So much food for thought and—well, I keep thinking of food—yet, all these excerpts are served like a feast at a potlatch, all complementary to one another, and with enough choices to satisfy different appetites. You can even go back for seconds.

I share a vision that the editors and the writers have brought to life. *Manitowapow: Aboriginal Writings from the Land of Water* will bring an understanding of the Aboriginal experience, which readers can take with them into the future. They will learn from one another, put aside distrust, shun the erroneous misconceptions of the past, and embrace our humanity and compassion. They will know why the Aboriginal person values the land, the waters, the animals, the plants above material wealth, because if our Mother Earth is not healthy, nothing else will matter. I relish the words of Elijah Harper, one of our well-known leaders: "There needs to be a healing of the land and the people. There needs to be reconciliation, restoration, and restitution. Because of our relationship with the Creator and this land, this is a spiritual process. A nation without a vision has no hope. A nation without a vision has no future. We now embark on this journey together for the benefit of all people in Canada."

—*Beatrice Mosionier*

Preface

This project was intentionally ambitious. It is the first anthology to try to capture the range and scope of Aboriginal writings in Manitoba. In many ways this is an impossible task, but we attempted it nonetheless. It was also a labour of love. The many hours spent researching, compiling, and editing—as well as repeating all of these tasks—cannot be counted. Most of all, this project was incredibly exciting and inspiring. We hope that it will be a few more steps in a long and storied path of creativity in our Aboriginal communities.

When we were seeking out the narratives, poems, and plays that make up this volume, we were continually amazed by the variety and power of the writings we encountered. Some of the work by well-known writers and leaders such as Tomson Highway, Beatrice Mosionier, Louis Riel, and Phil Fontaine was not new to us, but we found that placing their justly famous works in the context of the other wonderful voices in this anthology brought out new resonances, new possibilities of meaning. It was also a great pleasure for us to reread the works of our friends and colleagues, such as the members of the Aboriginal Writers Collective of Manitoba and other writers whose words have inspired us over the years. In this process, we saw their work in new ways, too, and we are grateful for the chance to revisit all of their published writings in order to choose some for republication here.

In addition to these expected pleasures, we also discovered many extraordinary writers and texts we had never read before—even though we are supposed to be experts in the field of Aboriginal literature. Discovering these previously unheard voices was an incredible thrill for us, and we are so excited to be able to share some of them with a wider audience through this book. Some of our "discoveries" include the 19th century Cree Elder, Kuskapatchees, the participants in the Dene Elders Project of the 1970s, as well as work by the famed Oji-Cree painter Jackson Beardy. We have included stories by anonymous Aboriginal inmates at Stony Mountain Penitentiary, and excerpts from the short-lived but politically crucial Aboriginal community newspaper, *The Prairie Call*. We also learned that several celebrated writers who are not usually associated with Manitoba (such as Charles Eastman, Joanne Arnott, and Gregory Scofield) produced extraordinary writing about their experiences here. In addition, we found new work by many young Aboriginal writers who are bringing a new generation's sensibilities to the question of what it means to live here in Manitowapow in the early part of the 21st century. These emerging writers have dazzled us with their creativity, as well as with their interests in the traditions and histories of this place. The future of Aboriginal writing and storytelling in Manitowapow is in very good hands.

There was only one disappointment for us in the creation of this book: the realization that we could not possibly fit even a fraction of the best work into our allotted space. Our first collection of texts for this volume ran over 1800 pages, and even in that version we felt we were leaving out excellent material. Later, we constantly discovered and heard about more published material as we shared the book with Elders and community members. We were presented with unpublished manuscripts that writers and family members of writers wanted us to include. To create a book that would be a manageable size, we had to make some difficult decisions. Our primary criteria for these choices were artistic excellence, historical significance, and representation of the diversity of Aboriginal voices in Manitowapow—with a focus on the different cultures, languages, generations, gender identities, and physical locations of our writers.

The question of "who is a Manitoba writer?" was at times a complicated one for us, since writers, like other people, are mobile, and, of course, traditional Aboriginal territories do not conform to contemporary colonial political divisions. Still, we wanted to collect works that resonated with some connection to the place that is Manitowapow, whether the writers lived all of their lives or spent only a few years here. We tried to respect the fluidity of belonging, but at the same time we tried to maintain our geographical focus. This, unfortunately, meant that we had to leave out many extraordinary stories and writers. But we hope that *Manitowapow: Aboriginal Writings from the Land of Water* will be a first step in a larger movement that will bring all of those other amazing works of literature back into circulation. We will continue working to ensure that many other readers can discover the writings we have been so fortunate to encounter in our research. If any readers of *Manitowapow* have suggestions of published stories, poems, plays, or nonfiction work by Aboriginal writers that should be considered for future collection in another volume, we would be very glad to hear from you. We envision this book as one among many.

There are so many individuals and communities who have laid the groundwork for this work that one could spend an entire book thanking them. First and foremost are the authors of Manitowapow, whose support for this project never seemed to end. We've had a great deal of help behind the scenes, especially from our dedicated and brilliant research assistants Barbara Romanik, Andrea von Wichert, and Ryan Duplassie. Their work and their vision were indispensable, and we simply could not have done this book without them. Beatrice Mosionier was our inspiration, advisor, and confidante during the editing process and we cannot thank her enough for her enthusiasm and her beautiful foreword to the book. In addition we were very fortunate to have the guidance of an entire group of extremely dedicated and knowledgeable readers and colleagues who offered us advice on the manuscript: Nichola Batzel, Jennifer Brown, Rebecca Chartrand, Renate Eigenbrod, Craig Charbonneau Fontaine, Jean Friesen, Lorne Keeper and others at the Manitoba First Nations Education Resource Centre, Mary Jane McCallum, Duncan Mercredi, Katherine and Leo Pettipas, and Katherena Vermette. In terms of images, we were guided by knowledge keepers Edward Benton-Benai, David Courchene, Jim Dumont, Charlie Nelson, Sherry Farrell Racette, and Murray Sinclair. We are very grateful to these experts for their wise and detailed responses, and also for their willingness to work within our tight deadlines. Any mistakes or omissions that remain in the text are, of course, entirely our own.

We are also very thankful for the support of the University of Manitoba, which has provided us with many resources through the Centre for Creative Writing and Oral Culture, as well as to the departments of Native Studies and English, Film and Theatre. Migizii Agamik (also known as the Aboriginal Student Centre at the University of Manitoba) provided a venue in which we met with many authors and did work on the text. Financial support from the Canada Research Chairs Program, the Social Sciences and Humanities Research Council of Canada, the National Aboriginal Achievement Foundation, and the Canadian Council of Aboriginal Business have also been crucial for this project. Niigaan was also supported as a student by the Peguis First Nation Educational Authority during part of the assembling of this project and wishes to acknowledge Rhonda Olsen, William Spence, and Kim Sinclair.

There are also many other individuals, organizations, and publishers who directly or indirectly supported this publication and deserve special acknowledgment: Kateri Akiwenzie-Damm and Kegedonce Press, the staff and administration at the Manitoba Archives and Hudson Bay Archives, Joanne Arnott, Marie Annharte, Heather Beattie, the family of Jackson Beardy, Alison Calder, The Canadian Copyright Licensing Agency, the family of Dave Courchene Sr., Rosanna Deerchild, Paul DePasquale, Supt. Ray Derksen and Frontier School Division, Shayla Elizabeth, Lorena Fontaine, Phil Fontaine, Vanda Fleury and the Braiding Histories Initiative at the Manitoba Museum, Cate Friesen and the cast and crew at CBC's *Scene* and *The (204)*, Rainey Gaywish, Val Georges and the teachers and staff who consulted with us from Winnipeg School Division No. 1, Trevor Greyeyes, Anita Olsen Harper, Catherine Hunter and the University of Winnipeg English Department, the Indian and Métis Friendship Centre of Winnipeg, Kathi Kinew, Tina Keeper, Emma LaRocque, the Manitoba Museum, the Manitoba Historical Society, Dorene Meyer and the authors in the *Northern Writers* series, Le Musée de Saint-Boniface, Tracey Nepinak, Patricia Ningewance, the Ogamas Aboriginal Literary Festival, Pat Opitz, Julie Pelletier and the University of Winnipeg Indigenous Studies Department, Terry Price and the Manitoba Teacher's Society, Scott Richardson, David Robertson, Shirley Delorme Russell and the Louis Riel Institute, John Ralston Saul, Gregory Scofield, Helen Settee and the Aboriginal Education Directorate, Ruth Shead, Jocelyn Shedden, Gord Shillingford, Colleen Simard, Cindy Singer, Joan Sinclair, Theytus Books, and Jessica Woolford. We'd also like to acknowledge Kelly Hughes and David Robertson, who helped co-organize the *2010 Manitowapow Aboriginal Writers Series* at Aqua Books—an instrumental part of the initial stages of this project. Thanks also to Monique Woroniak and the Millennium Library for featuring this book and its authors in the Fall 2011 "Featured Writers" series. If we have forgotten or neglected to thank anyone we apologize. And, of course, we would like to recognize our families—for without them none of our work would be possible.

Last but not least, we want to register our enormous gratitude to Annalee Greenberg, Catherine Gerbasi, and the rest of the team at HighWater Press and Portage & Main Press. Their commitment to this project and their extraordinary work on the complex layout of the book has been awe-inspiring. It is an honour to partner with them, and we are so proud to be working with a publisher that has such a long and successful history of publishing Manitoba's Aboriginal writers. We are also happy to announce that Manitowapow will be the first book in a new series of Aboriginal writing, The Debwe Series from HighWater Press.

Because we want to give back to our local Aboriginal communities that have so deeply inspired us with their words, we have chosen to donate our proceeds from this book to a special fund administered through the Centre for Creative Writing and Oral Culture at the University of Manitoba. This fund will be used to support literacy and creative writing initiatives among Manitoba's Aboriginal youth, and we hope it will play a part in sparking new creativity in the next generation of Aboriginal writers of Manitowapow. Many of our authors and copyright holders have also joined us in this initiative by donating their fees to help make this project possible. We are deeply grateful to all of them for believing in the project and for their commitment to the future of our people's words, languages, and imaginations in this storied place.

Introduction

In 1971, Potawatomi/Odawa artist Daphne Odjig was commissioned to create an artwork to honour the province of Manitoba's centennial. The result was the ten-by-twelve-foot mural titled *The Creation of the World*, installed on a steeply curved wall at the entranceway to the Earth History Gallery in the Manitoba Museum. A remarkable work, it still stands there today and is viewed by thousands of visitors yearly. We are honoured that Odjig and her family gave permission for it to adorn the cover of *Manitowapow: Aboriginal Writings from the Land of Water*.

In *The Creation of the World,* a studious Nanabush is focused, working with a mound of earth on the shell of a turtle. From the earth, he creates land, hills, and mountains that run off the painting, from left to right.[1] This "new" earth is full of rich layers and colour, with part of it morphing into a female face whose eyes are closed and who appears to be in an act of prayer or thought. Around Nanabush and the turtle are three animals: a beaver and an otter, who both gaze at Nanabush, and a dead muskrat with outstretched paws. Water encompasses the bottom and left side of the frame, with large (and somewhat threatening) waves emerging throughout. Sun rays and waves of turbulence encompass the sky and meld into the landscape, blending together land, water, and air. Above all of the images, a thunderbird watches the happenings of the world below. The scene suggests a cacophony of everlasting and dynamic movement.

Like many of the writings in this book, *The Creation of the World* is a story full of other stories. The most evident one is the famous Anishinaabeg Flood Story, which tells of the covering of the world by water and the recreation of it by Nanabush after a heroic muskrat dives and sacrifices himself to get a paw-full of earth. Another is a version of the geography and history of Manitoba itself. During the last Ice Age, between 10,000 and 30,000 years ago, Manitoba was the bottom of an enormous glacier that covered most of North America. As this body of ice melted, it became a huge body of water—the great Lake Agassiz—that eventually drained into the world's

---

1   Known also as Wenabozho, Naanabozho, and other names in Anishinaabeg communities, Nanabush is a half-spirit, half-human being of aadizookaanag, sacred stories. We use "Nanabush" here to refer to Daphne Odjig's usage, also available in her 1971 series of children's books, *The Nanabush Book Series*. For more on these texts, how to order them, and other information about Odjig see: <www.daphneodjig.com>.

oceans and formed parts of local ecology (for instance, Lake Winnipeg, Lake Winnipegosis, and Lake Manitoba are remnants). Literally, as ice and water receded and carved out the environment, land formed. Another story in the work involves Odjig's innovation of Anishinaabeg art and aesthetics. As has been well documented, she worked tirelessly to bridge traditional Anishinaabeg iconography (as found in media such as birchbark scrolls and rock paintings) with her knowledge of Pablo Picasso, cubism, and other European artistic traditions.[2] There are also many stories about relationships throughout the mural; tales that explain ties between Nanabush and animals, spirits and land, and water and life—to name just a few.

This leads to some of the most interesting stories in *The Creation of the World*. While it is hardly a stretch to pinpoint certain cultural images and aesthetics in Odjig's art, critics often ignore the context in which her work emerged, her interests in activism and advocacy, and her commitment to Aboriginal historical and intellectual traditions. For instance, what cannot be forgotten is the time period in which this mural was produced—in 1970s Canada, when Aboriginal people from all walks of life were actively (and somewhat fiercely) advocating for themselves and their communities, often called the "Red Power" era. For Odjig, it was crucial that Aboriginal people be exposed to and learn their stories in order for cultural revitalization to be possible. As she stated in a 1968 interview: "If you destroy our legends you also destroy our soul."[3] The themes of constant movement and "creating a world" are reminiscent of the history of the Anishinaabeg, too. In the Anishinaabeg Creation Story, it is recounted how their ancestors travelled from their original homelands in the East across North America and eventually segmented into communities of Ojibway, Potawatomi, and Odawa—while trading, warring, and eventually settling with communities such as the Sioux and Cree along their path.[4]

This brings us back to where the work was created, where it stands, and where it continues to live: in Manitoba. As the works in this anthology also suggest, Manitoba has always been a place of activity, change, and struggle—movements that illustrate the harshness and beauty of life. From

---

2   For excellent studies of Odjig's use of Anishinaabeg aesthetics and cultural traditions see: R.M Vanderburgh and M.E. Southcott's collaborative book (written with Odjig), *A Paintbrush in My Hand* (Toronto: Natural Heritage, 1992), and Bonnie Devine's edited collection, *The Drawings and Paintings of Daphne Odjig: A Retrospective Exhibition* (Ottawa: National Gallery of Canada, 2007).

3   As quoted in Vanderburgh and Southcott, 17

4   For a version of the Anishinaabeg creation story, see: Edward Benton-Benai's *The Mishomis Book: The Voice of the Ojibway* (Minneapolis: University of Minnesota Press, 2010).

time immemorial, ancestors of Aboriginal communities now known as Anishinaabe, Assiniboine, Cree, Dene, Inuit, Métis, Oji-Cree, and Sioux inhabited, migrated to, and settled throughout these lands. They made homes, held ceremonies in sacred spaces, and forged relationships amongst themselves and with beings throughout the environment. They established traditions that extend into today. Much of this involved an intricate use of oral and written expressions that changed and adapted with the environment over time—a handful of which are included in this book.

Activity, change, and struggle have particularly been evident over the past two centuries in Manitoba, embodied by contentious relations between Aboriginal and non-Aboriginal peoples. Manitoba has been the scene of some of the most oppressive moments in Canadian history, featuring a flood of brutality and violence. A short list of the events that have created the province include exploitation by settlers and traders, unfulfilled treaty promises by governments, repression of the Red River Resistance and the murder of Louis Riel, many illegal and illegitimate removals (including citizens at St. Peter's/Peguis and the Sayisi Dene), dozens of Indian residential and day schools, some of the worst examples of the aptly named "Sixties Scoop," and countless unsolved "disappearances" of Aboriginal women and children. This is not to forget the many instances of flooding that takes place in First Nations communities due to poor drainage, industrial development, or the mistreatment of water. In fact, as we write this in 2011, over 2,100 flood evacuees from eight Manitoba First Nations communities—many of them children—have been unable to return to their homes for over six months and reside in Winnipeg.[5] This history obscures the myriad instances of cultural and political exchange, trading, and sharing that have made Manitoba into a collective mosaic of people and communities. And, while there are many strong and interdependent Aboriginal and non-Aboriginal communities here, there is indeed a long way to go in creating a healthy, positive relationship between Aboriginal and non-Aboriginal Manitobans.

Odjig directly references her own experiences of Manitoba in *The Creation of the World*. While her artistic interests began as a child, it was not until she moved to Manitoba in 1964 with her husband, Chester Beavon, that her professional career emerged and expanded. In 1966, as a governmental community development officer, Beavon was assigned to work in northern Manitoba with the Chemahawin Cree at Cedar Lake; they had been removed to Easterville after a hydroelectric dam at Grand Rapids flooded

5   See: "First Nation evacuees get Sally Ann space." <cbc.ca/news/canada/manitoba/ story/2011/11/08/mb-flood-school-salvation-army-winnipeg.html>.

their territory. Odjig, accompanying her husband in his travels, witnessed the devastating effects of this removal on the community and saw how a way of life drastically altered could lead to cultural and political atrophy, poverty, and substance abuse. She also saw how this community resisted, adapted, and demonstrated incredible perseverance. With her experiences at Easterville fresh in her mind—and particularly the floods of devastation and the floods of resilience she witnessed there—Odjig was unquestionably influenced by Manitoban history.

This gestures to arguably the most important story of all in *The Creation of the World:* the creation of a respectful and dignified home. As one can see, it takes a tremendous amount of constant and tireless work. It involves creating a place full of possibility, built through sustainability and equitable relationships involving people, animals, spirits, and the landscape. It involves being honest with one's history, truth-telling, and talking about the complicated parts—even if that inspires discomfort and disagreement. It involves recognizing and understanding that many have sacrificed much to provide others with opportunities. It involves constant motion, eternal change, and a commitment to balance, cooperation, and mutual responsibility. It involves acknowledging that life is complex, that it is all around us, and that we are a part of it. Many more stories exist in the mural of course, but this one—of the creation of a home full of opportunity, integrity, and including all diverse parts—is the most poignant. *The Creation of the World* is about the struggle that is Manitoba, or as it was historically called by many Aboriginal peoples, Manitowapow.

Manitowapow has always been a powerful place. This is embodied in one of the stories of the original name of this place, in its very name. While many alternate and legitimate versions and claims exist,[6] the most common explanation of the name is that it originated in the Cree words *Manitou* (Great Spirit) and *wapow* (sacred water), or in Ojibway, *Manito-bau*. From the Narrows of Lake Manitoba, where waves dashed against the rocky shores of Manitou Island, these sounds were thought to be sacred beats that dashed

---

6   There is considerable dispute when it comes to how Manitoba received its name. For instance, some Aboriginal communities claim that the petroforms of Manito Api are where the name Manitoba came from (see our description of this place in this anthology). Meeting Assiniboine communities near Lake Manitoba, French explorer La Verendrye heard the name "Mini-tobow," which he re-named "Lac du Prairies" ("Lake of the Prairies") and used to refer to all lands in and around the region. Others cite alternative originating words and stories. For a detailed survey of potential origins of the name, see: Frank Hall, "How Manitoba Got Its Name." *Manitoba Pageant* 15.2 (1970) <www. mhs.mb.ca/docs/pageant/15/ manitobaname1.shtml>. Without disputing the legitimacy of these other claims of origination, we offer "Manitowapow" as one version among many.

throughout Creation and created beauty, definition, and meaning. This is the voice of the Great Spirit, Manitowapow.

Settlers who came to Manitowapow also noted these sounds, often likening them to chimes or church bells. In 1867, Thomas Spence, leader of a growing settlement at Portage la Prairie, was the first to "officially" use the term, after forming a council and declaring the settlement the *Republic of Manitobah*. The republic collapsed, and Spence would later join Louis Riel's Métis Council.

In 1870, a delegation from the Council went to Ottawa to negotiate with Canada over the jurisdiction of the growing and lucrative Red River settlement, The territory was known as Assiniboia. but Riel never liked the name. On April 19, 1870, he sent the following letter to delegate Father Noël-Joseph Ritchot:

> The name of the country is already written in all hearts, that of Red River. Fancy delights in that of "Manitoba," but the situation seems to demand that of "North-West." Friends of the old government are pleased with that of Assiniboia (but) it is not generally enough liked to be kept. Choose one of the two names "Manitoba" or "North-West."

In 1870, the Canadian parliament passed the *Manitoba Act*. The traditional name of Manitowapow, which morphed through speakers of other languages into "Manitoba," became the name citizens of the province recognize and use today.

Alphabetical writing, of course, was first imported to Manitoba by Europeans, but the stories and the names existed long before the newcomers arrived, and Aboriginal people quickly adapted their expressive forms to this medium of text. This has resulted in an extraordinarily rich body of literature produced by Aboriginal writers in Manitoba over the last two centuries and more—a tradition that is presented uniquely in this book. The stories, poems, speeches, and nonfiction gathered in this collection present an analogue to Odjig's *The Creation of the World*. The writings draw upon the complex traditions of the many Aboriginal communities they come from and comment on the present day concerns of each writer in his or her time and cultural context. The writings are about spirituality, geography, migration, politics, and colonialism, yet they are also about hope and life and the importance of humour; beauty itself. They represent a broad history that encompasses many incredible struggles, but they also give voice to Aboriginal cultural values of community, sharing, respect for the land, and honour for the ancestors. They open us up to Aboriginal understandings of what has happened in this place over time, but many of them are also contemporary, urban, and experimental. They are, in a sense, nearly uncategorizable in their variety. What the writings do have in common is that they are the most moving, dynamic, and important works of literature that we found in our many months of research into archives, libraries, and other collections of Aboriginal stories. They are also all responses to this place, Manitowapow, in its many manifestations.

In July 1885, while imprisoned by Canadian forces, Louis Riel famously said: "My people will sleep for one hundred years, but when they awake, it will be the artists who give them their spirit back." It is our belief that he was not only speaking of Métis artists but also of other Aboriginal artists of the past, the present, and to come. Riel was speaking of the sounds of Manitowapow, resonances that have the ability—as Odjig demonstrates—to create our world. We honour this work. Whenever we hear someone speak the word *Manitoba*, we hear the echo of these stories. We hear, feel, and experience Manitowapow. We hope they will do the same for you and that you enjoy the beauty of these expressions.

Traditional Systems of Writing in Manitowapow

Systems of writing have been used in Manitowapow since time immemorial. Often employed alongside oral traditions, these texts record interactions among people and express connections to animals, spirit beings, and other creatures. Though they date from long ago, these writing systems have evolved over the generations as Aboriginal communities have changed and grown. Their intellectual and spiritual value is immense, and they provide a foundation on which all literature in Manitoba has been built.

Figures 1, 2, and 3 show the rock petroforms of Manitou Api in Whiteshell Provincial Park, a place that has hosted ceremonies for thousands of years. Manitou Api is often translated as "The Place Where Creator Sat" and is

Figure 1   *Figure 2*

Figure 3

considered by some Elders to be another source for Manitoba's name. The
images at Manitou Api document much knowledge: constellations, traditional teachings, and the unique ties Aboriginal people share with animals
and the spirit world. These images of a Turtle and a Snake express important teachings about politics, ceremonies, and belonging—important parts
that make up a healthy and vibrant community. The Path of Life symbolizes the choices human beings face throughout life. Echoing images found
on birchbark scrolls, it illustrates the physical and spiritual journeys taken
in life and death, as well as the many things that influence us along the way.

The next two images (figs. 4 and 5) are rock paintings, often called pictographs. Many can be found throughout Manitoba, usually near water and
on shorelines. These images represent the complex ecological and spiritual
systems embedded in particular places. They also illustrate a network of intellectual and physical pathways Aboriginal people travelled and how the
trading of stories and information took place alongside goods and resources.
The painting in figure 4 can be found in the northeast, on a rock facing Knee
Lake. It shows a figure with hands raised, likely gesturing to the home of
the mysterious and powerful *memegwesiwak* (little people of Anishinaabe

Figure 4

Figure 5

and Cree tradition), who live in rocks and hold medicinal and spiritual knowledge. The one in figure 5 is located in the southeast, on the shores of Sassaginnigak Lake (in Atikaki Provincial Park) and shows a human holding a medicine bag in one hand and a bow and arrow in another. Emanating around the figure are waves of power and beauty, likely referencing the actions (such as travelling and hunting) and ceremonies that take place there.

In April 1847, an Aboriginal leader named Wetus was among a group of Anglican converts near what is now The Pas. After a sermon by the Rev. Henry Budd, the missionaries demanded that any who wished to convert must give up their traditional ways, take a Christian name, submit their ceremonial materials, and be baptized. Wetus (subsequently named Louis Constant) gave Budd a Midéwiwin (Grand Medicine Society) scroll, written on birchbark (fig. 6). It passed through several hands and was later reproduced in an 1851 book in England. Under the interpretive direction of Three Fires Midéwiwin Lodge leader and teacher Edward Benton-Benai, this scroll has been interpreted to be a meme version of a complete scroll. It is an outline for Midéwiwin practitioners to use when teaching and explaining traditional philosophies of creation, life, and history. The scroll depicts several interconnected lodges, locations of members, and objects within, and how they all relate to the world. These are more than just images; they constitute an entire spiritual path and perspective. For many reasons, the specific information within the scroll is sacred and contextual to Midéwiwin practitioners (often never shared with non-Midéwiwin). But by viewing this small piece, one can get a sense of the immense body of knowledge that Wetus handed to Budd that day—and to future Aboriginal students and researchers.

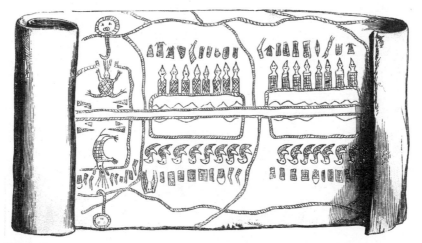

Figure 6

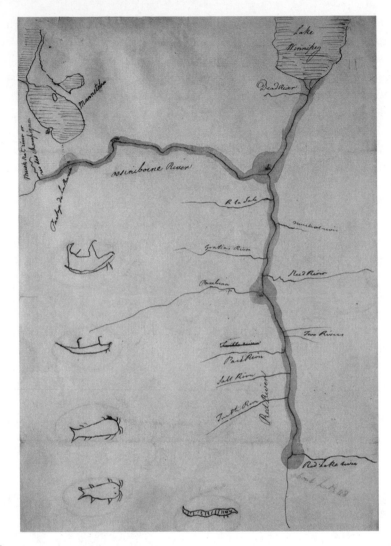

Figure 7

"The Selkirk Treaty" (fig. 7) is an 1817 land agreement treaty signed by Chief Peguis and four other Aboriginal chiefs with Thomas, Earl of Selkirk, indicating a land transfer along the Red and Assiniboine Rivers. The chiefs signed using their totems, which indicated their community affiliations. The images of bear, catfish, and other animals therefore also represent land claims, laws, and forms of government in the diverse communities they represented.

Figure 8 is a "Letter from a Seioux Indian" from 1822. It shows traditional forms of mapping (indicated through canoe and bodies of water), locations of communities, and the writer himself (who is also represented by his clan

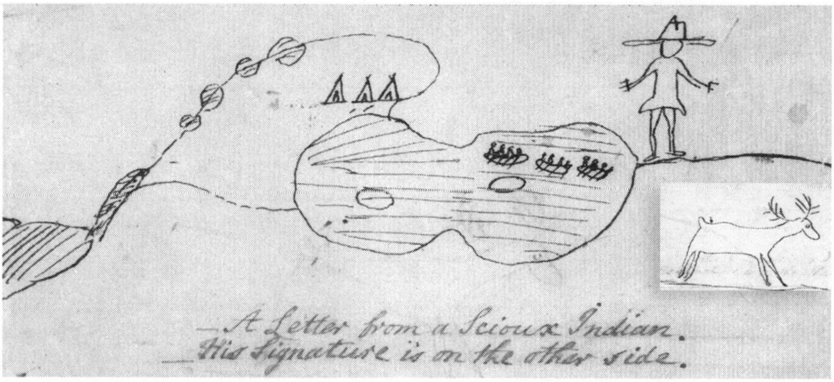

Figure 8

"signature" on the back). It tells a story about communication, travel, and a community on the move.

The Métis have created a rich body of non-alphabetical writing in Manitowapow, and a large hooked rug (fig. 9) created by Marie Grant Breland, the daughter of Cuthbert Grant, is one example. Images of earth and home drawn from her diverse heritage map a complex journey. Arranging tipi shapes, the prairie rose, "catalogne" rag weaving from Quebec, Anishinaabe diamonds, and pinwheel quilt patterns, the elderly artist tells a story that returns to where it begins in a constant cycle.

Figure 9

Figure 10

Aboriginal clothing represents many systems of expression. This northern Cree coat (fig. 10) is made from a single moose-hide that wrapped around the wearer's body. Lines and circles were pressed or carved into the surface of the hide, and paints made from natural pigments were applied to depict shapes. The finely tanned hide, the painted symbols, and the porcupine quillwork were visual conversations with the animals to assure them that their sacrifice would be honoured and every part of their body would be carefully used and made beautiful.

Figure 11 illustrates an excerpt of a story told by Elder John C. Courchene (1914–1984) of Sagkeeng First Nation and written in Anishinaabe syllabics. It is taken from a book entitled *Sagkeeng Legends: Sagkeeng Aadizookaanag*, edited by his grandson, historian Craig Charbonneau Fontaine. Syllabic systems represent the specific sounds and pronunciations of Aboriginal languages. This short excerpt, from the story "Aadizokaan Niish," introduces us to the two main characters, a young man and woman, and their families. Growing up together, we learn how they fall in love and are torn apart—setting the stage for a lifelong relationship that will carry them through separation, death, and eventually rebirth.

These ancient writing systems in Manitowapow, rich in history, tradition, and thought, are the foundation on which later English writing has been built. On their own, they are rich and dynamic expressions worth reading and listening to. We invite you to enjoy, appreciate, and learn from them.

```
      ⊲ᠤᢏ  ᒫᐧᐊ ᐁᐧᐄ ᑕᠧᒪ·ᑊ, ᐸᠷᐧᑸᑌᑊ ⊲ᠤᢏ ᑊᑭ ᑊᒥ
  ⊲ᑌᘘ·ᐃ·⊲ᑊ ᒥ ·ᐁᑊ ᐸᠷᐧᑸᑌᑊ. ⊲ᐧᑊ ᑊᑉᘘᠤ·⊲ᑊ ⊲ᠤᢏ ᑊᐃᠷᐅᑊᠷᐧ⊲ᑊ
  ᒥᠷ·ᐁ ᑊᐅᠷ ᑊ·ᐁᑌᠤᑊ, ᐅᑊᐱ⊲ᠤᑊ, ᐣ·⊲ᠤᑊ, ᠷ·ᑊ ⊲ᑺᠤᑊ ᑊᠷ ᑊᐅᠷ·⊲ᑊ. ᒥᠷ·ᐁ
  ᑊᐅᠷ·⊲ᑊ ⊲ᠤᢏᐁᑊ. ᒥᠷ·ᐁ ᑊᐸᠤ ⊲ᠤᢏᐁ ᑌ·ᐃᠤ.
      ᒥᑊᠤ ⊲ᠤᢏᐁᑊ ᑊᑭ ⊲·ᐃᑕ·⊲ᑊ ⊲ᒪ, ᠤᢏᠤ ᑊᑺᠷᑭ ·ᐃᑊᑸ·⊲ᑊ, ᠤᢏᠤ
  ᐃᠤᠤ·⊲ᑊ ᑊᐃ ᐃ·᠙·⊲ᑊ ᑊᠷ ·ᐃᑊᑸ⊲·⊲ᑊ ᑊᑺᑌᐅᠷ·⊲ᑊ. ᒥᐃᠤᐁ ⊲ᐧ ᑊᑊᠤᠤ·ᠤᑭ
  ⊲⊲ ᐧᠷᑊ ᐃ·᠙ᠤᐁ ᑊᑺᑺᠤ ᠷ·ᑊ ⊲·ᐁᑊ ᐧᠷᑊ ·ᑊ·ᐃᠤᐁ ᑊᑺᑺᠤ. ᒥᑊᐃ
  ⊲ᐃᠤᠷ ᐁᠷ·ᐃ·⊲ᑊ ᑌᑯ ᑊ·⊲ᠷ·⊲ᑌᠤ·⊲ᑊ ᐃᠤᠤ ᑊᑸᠤ ᑊ·⊲ᠷ·⊲ᑌᠤ·⊲ᑊ ᐃᠤᠤ ᑊᑸᠤ
  ·ᑊ·ᐃᠤᠤ, ᐃᠤᑊ ⊲ᠤ ᒥᑌᑌ·⊲ᑊ, ⊲ᑭᠤ ᐃᑊ ᑊ·⊲ᠷ·⊲ᑌᠤ·⊲ᑊ ᐃᠤᠤ ᑊᑸᠤ
  ᑊᑺᠷᠤᑊ·᠙ ᠷ·ᑊ ᑊᑺᠷᠤᑊ ᠷ·ᑊ ᒥᑊ·ᐁ ·ᑊ·ᐃᠤᠤ ᑊ·ᐃᠤ ᐃᑊ ᑊᠤ·ᐸᑊ·⊲ᑊ
  ᑊᐃᠷ⊲ᠤᠷ, ᑊᑊᑊᐸᠤᠷᠷᠤᑊᑊ ᐃᠤᑊ, ᑊ·ᐃᠤ ⊲ᐧᑊ ᠙ᑊ ᑊᑊ ᠙ᑊᠷᠤ, ᒥ·⊲⊲ ·ᑊ·ᐃᠤᠤ,
  ⊲ᐧᑊ ᐃᑊᠤ ᑊᑺᑊᐃᑊ·⊲ᑊ ᐃ·᠙ᠤᑊ ᠷ·ᑊ ⊲⊲ ·ᑊ·ᐃᠤᠤ.
```

Figure 11

Peguis

Anishinaabe (St. Peter's Reserve/Peguis First Nation) 1774–1864

Chief Peguis (also known as Be-gou-ais, Be-gwa-is, Pegeois, Pegouisse, Pegowis, Pegqas, Pigewis, Pigwys) was born about 1774 in the area known today as Sault Ste. Marie. Son of an Anishinaabe woman and likely a French fur trader, he led a community of Anishinaabe people to the Red River and settled at Netley Creek, south of Lake Winnipeg in Manitoba. There, he joined with a Cree and Assiniboine community decimated by disease. He became known as a great orator, leader, and mediator who led trade negotiations with the Hudson Bay Company and was one of the one of the five chiefs to sign a treaty in 1817 with Lord Selkirk for lands near the Assiniboine and Red Rivers that they would turn over for the usage of the white settlers. Though Peguis was presented with a medal and promised yearly presents, Selkirk never honoured this responsibility. In 1832 Anglican Missionary William Cockran (Cochrane) persuaded Peguis and some of his people to move and settle in St. Peter's Parish, a community north of present-day Selkirk. Soon after, and for political as well as spiritual reasons, Peguis was baptized and took the name William King—although he retained many of his Anishinaabe beliefs and practices. His descendants have chosen to use the last name Prince.

Peguis was witness to many trade and land disputes settlers brought to their new territory. Frequently Peguis was asked to intervene and, at times, provide protection—such as in 1812 when he was instrumental in supporting Lord Selkirk's settlers when members of the North West Company attempted to destroy their settlement. This was due to his abilities as a shrewd diplomat, peacemaker, and advocate for Aboriginal rights. These two selections illustrate these abilities. The first speech, recorded by land surveyor Peter Fidler, was Peguis's reply to Selkirk's settlers on June 25, 1815, after they asked for his help when men from the North West Company burnt down their settlement, demanding they leave the region. The second is an 1857 letter printed in The *Colonial Intelligencer* (in London, England) that was likely written down by one of his sons. It is a mini-history lesson, shaped as a formal complaint to the Queen's representatives, about the mistreatment his community endured and the responsibilities and relationships settlers hold with his kin.

A Reply to the Selkirk Settlers' Call for Help

We thank you for your speech. What is the matter with these People? You do not trade skins from us. Why then are they always quarrelling with you? They always had greedy hearts & jealous minds & always drove away those who brought us our necessaries. When your messenger came to our Tents he found my Brother Chief [Yellow Legs] and our young men assembled in order to come to your assistance as we had been told that the Canadians had carried off our Brother. We will offer these people the Pipe of peace and if they will not smoak with you, we will not restrain our young men more, but shall join them in the cry of War.

What do these people mean by driving you from these lands? Had we no other support than what they give us we might freeze in our tents die of want and be at the mercy of our enemies. Look round & you will see our young men defended from the Inclemency of the weather & tormented of the musquitoes by your means, and we have even a Pipe of Tobacco to smoak and a round of ammunition to support our families—nor have we forgotten how pitiful & poor we were before your arrival here. It seems our great father has two children and perhaps he loved one better than the other. He certainly did not tell one Brother to make war upon the other. For my part I have always loved the White people and have always taught my young men to be kind to them.

The people of the other house are always breaking my ears with complaints & telling stories about my lands, but these are not my Lands—they belong to our Great Father—for it is he only that gives us the means of existence, for what would become of us if he left us to ourselves. We should wither like the grass in the Plains, was the Sun to withdraw his animating beams.

The hearts of my young men are vexed & inclined to war; it is with difficulty we can restrain them. I hope to procure you Peace but if my lands must be reddened with your Blood, my Blood & that of my Children shall be mixed with yours & like a stone we will sink together.

—*1815*

An Open Letter to the Queen's Representatives

Many winters ago (in 1812) the lands along the Red River, in the Assiniboine Country, on which I, and the tribe of Indians of whom I am Chief, then lived, were taken possession of, without permission of myself or my tribe, by a body of white settlers. For the sake of peace, I, as the representative of my tribe, allowed them to remain on our lands, on their promising that we should be well paid for them by a great Chief who was to follow them. This great Chief, whom we call the Silver Chief (the Earl of Selkirk), arrived in the spring, after the war between the North-West and Hudson's Bay Companies (1817). He told us he wanted our lands for some of his countrymen, who were very poor in their own country; and I consented: on the condition that he paid well for my tribe's lands, he could have from the confluence of the Assiniboine to near Maple Sugar Point, on the Red River (a distance of 20 or 24 miles), following the course of the river, and as far Back, on each side of the river, as a horse could be seen under (easily distinguished). The Silver Chief told us he had little with which to pay us for our lands when he made this arrangement, in consequence of the troubles with the North-West Company.

He, however, asked us what we most required for the present; and we told him we would be content till the following year, when he promised again to return, to take only ammunition and tobacco. The Silver Chief never returned; and neither his son or the Hudson's Bay Company have ever since paid us annually for our lands only the small quantity of ammunition and tobacco which, in the first instance, we took as preliminary to a final bargain for our lands.

This, surely, was repaying me very poorly for having saved the Silver Chief's life; for the year he came here Cuthbert Grant, with 116 warriors, had assembled at White-Horse Plain, intending to waylay him somewhere on the Red River. I no sooner heard of this than I went to Cuthbert Grant, and told him if he came out of the White-Horse Plain, where his warriors were assembled, I should meet him at Sturgeon Creek with my entire tribe, who were much more numerous than they are now, and stand or fall between him and the Silver Chief. This had the desired effect; and Mr. Grant did not make the attempt to harm the Silver Chief, who came as he went, in peace and safety. Those who have since held our lands not only pay us only the same small quantity of ammunition and tobacco which was first paid to us as a preliminary to a final bargain, but they now claim all the lands between the Assiniboine and Lake Winnipeg—a quantity of land nearly double of what was first asked from us. We hope our Great Mother will not allow us to be treated so unjustly, as to allow our lands to be taken from us in this way.

We are not only willing, but very anxious, after being paid for our lands, that the whites would come and settle among us, for we have already derived great benefit from their having done so—that is, not the traders, but the farmers. The traders have never done any thing but rob, and keep us poor, but the farmers have taught us how to farm and raise cattle. To the Missionaries especially we are indebted, for they tell us every praying-day (Sabbath) to be sober, honest, industrious, and truthful. They have told us the good news, that Jesus Christ so loved the world that he gave himself for it; and that this was one of the first messages to us, 'Peace on earth and goodwill to men.' We wish to practice these good rules of the whites, and hope the Great Mother will do the same to us; and not only protect us from oppression and injustice, but grant us all the privileges of the whites.

We have many things to complain of against the Hudson's Bay Company. They pay us little for our furs; and when we are old we are left to shift for ourselves. We could name many old men who have starved to death, in sight of many of the Company's principal forts. When the Home Government has sent out questions to be answered in this country, about the treatment of the Indians by the Company, the Indians have been told, if they said anything against the Company they would be driven away from their homes. In the same way, when Indians have wished to attach themselves to Missions, they have been both threatened and used badly. When a new Mission has been established the Company has at once planted a post there, so as to prevent Indians from attaching themselves to it. They have been told they are fools to listen to Missionaries, and can only starve and become lazy under them. We could name many Indians, who have been prevented by the Company from leaving their trading post and Indian habits when they have wished to attach themselves to Missions.

When it is decided that this country is to be more extensively settled by the whites, and before whites will be again permitted to take possession of our lands, we wish that a fair and mutually advantageous treaty be entered into with my tribe for their lands; and we ask, whenever this treaty is to be entered into, a wise, discreet, and honourable man, who is known to have the interests of the Indians at heart, may be selected on the side of the Indian, to see that he is fairly and justly dealt with for his land; and that from the first it be borne in mind, that in securing our own advantages we wish also to secure those of our children and their children's children. I commit these my requests to you as a body well known by us to have the welfare of the poor Indian at heart; and in committing this to you on behalf of myself, do so also on behalf of my tribe, who are as one man in feeling and desires on these matters. Will you, then, use the proper means of bringing before the great Council of the nation (Parliament) and through it to our Great Mother (the Queen), who will shew herself more truly great and good by protecting the helpless from injustice and oppression than by making great conquests.

I give you, at the end of this, such certificates of character as I hold, from the Silver Chief (Lord Selkirk) and the Governor of Rupert's Land (Sir George Simpson). I have also a British flag and valuable medal, from our Great Mother (the Queen), which I treasure above all earthly things.

Wishing that the Great Spirit may give you every good thing, and with warmest thanks for your friendship,
I remain
Gentleman Your true friend Peguis or Wm King
Chief of the Saulteaux Tribe at Red River
X His Mark.

—1857

Pierre Falcon

Métis (Elbow Fort) (1793–1876)

Pierre Falcon was born near what is now called Swan River, Manitoba, to a French-Canadian father who worked for the North West Company and an Aboriginal mother who is believed to have been Cree. He was sent to L'Acadie in Lower Canada as a child, where he learned to read and write French. At age 15, he returned to the Red River settlement and began work as a North West Company clerk. In 1812, he married Mary Grant, daughter of Cuthbert Grant Sr., and, in 1825, the family moved with Mary's brother, Cuthbert Grant Jr., to the new Métis settlement of Grantown, where Falcon served as a justice of the peace.

During his lifetime, Falcon was well known as a poet, composer, and singer of songs documenting the Métis way of life. His songs were performed by many Métis, including voyageurs, throughout much of the 19th century. While the lyrics of many of these songs have been lost, several have been preserved and collected in M.A. MacLeod's *Songs of Old Manitoba* (1960). Falcon's songs about the 1816 Battle of Seven Oaks remain very popular as documents of a crucial time in Métis history. Falcon himself participated in the Battle of Seven Oaks, a fight in which a group of Métis fur traders repelled an attack by Hudson's Bay Company men. After this battle Lord Selkirk travelled toward Red River to quell the unrest, and on his way there he seized control of the Métis fur traders' fort. As in many such conquests at the time, Selkirk's first act after seizing the fort was to hold a dance for the traders in order to gain their sympathies. Falcon's song "Li Lord Selkirk au Fort William" gives us a fascinating picture of that dance, at which the Métis men are, in a sense, asked to dance to the tune of their colonizer. The men participate in the dance, but at the same time they undermine it by insisting on dancing and playing music in their own traditional ways, despite Lord Selkirk's objections. The result is an ironic dialogue that shows the Métis asserting their own autonomy in the face of a colonizing presence. The Michif-French language version of the song presented here was created by Métis writer and professor Paul Chartrand for his book *Pierriche Falcon: The Michif Rhymester*.

Li Lord Selkirk au Fort William

A HERALD:

1. Allons, vite, accourez.
   Rats musqui, bois bruli.
   Au Fort William un Milord fait regal.

2. Allons donc, dépêchi!
   Vous saut'ri, vous dans'ri.
   Y a musique; y vous aurez beau bal!

3. McNabbs, que McGil'ore,
   Parmi nous autres sa sont assi.
   Ji veux qu'ils brillent en ce fameux regal.

4. Avec lui, retenez.
   Vous saut'ri, vous dans'ri.
   Y a musique, vous aurez beau bal.

5. Allons gai, McKenzi.
   Vini di si coti,
   Vous prendri part a s' p'chi regal.

6. Y puoi si vous l'vouli
   Vous saut'ri; vous dans'ri.
   Y a musique vous aurez beau bal.

7. Oh ça! Docteur, entri.
   Icit vous assayeri.
   Pas d'humeur somber en ce joyeux regal!

8. Docteur vous chanterez.
   Vous sauteri, vous dans'ri.
   Y a musique; y vous aurez beau bal!

9. Belle Troque! Avanci!
   Ah! Fraser! Un tel ni,
   Y ben cilooui d'aen courier de regal

10. Ça, morbleu, vous booayri!
    Pi aprez vous dans'ri.
    Y a musique; y vous aurez beau bal!

11. Ça, Meurons, accordez.
    Priludi, commenci,
    Y joez-nous quelqu' air aen peu jovial.

12. Messieurs li bois bruli,
    Vous saut'ri; vous dans'ri.
    Y a musique vous aurez beau bal.

LES BOIS-BRÛLÉS:

13. Qui vois avez d'bonti!
    Milord! D'honnêteti!
    Quand pourrons-nous vous rendre un tel regal?

HIS LORDSHIP (SELKIRK):

14. Allons! Vous vous moqui!
    Dansi Matchicotis!
    Y a musique; y vous aurez beau bal.

LES BOIS-BRÛLÉS:

15. Allons! Pas tant d'facon.
    Sautons donc, dansons donc.
    Que l'dgiabl emport Milord et son regal!

16. Qu'avec vous tous si Meurons,
    Sur leurs maudits violons,
    Cent ans durent il dans un pareil bal.

The Dance of the Bois Brûlés   *[translation]*

A HERALD:

1. Come on, hurry, run.
   Muskrats, Bois-Brûlés.
   At Fort William M'Lord gives a ball.

2. Come on then, hurry up!
   You will hop, you will dance.
   There is music; you will have a great time!

3. McNabb, as well as McGilor',
   Among us are seated.
   I want them to shine at this famous ball.

4. With him, stay there.
   You will hop, you will dance.
   There is music; you will have a great time.

5. Come on gaily, McKenzie.
   Come this way,
   You will take part in this little ball.

6. And, if you please,
   You will hop, you will dance.
   There is music; you will have a great time.

7. Hey there! Doctor, come in.
   Here you will sit.
   No somber mood at this happy ball!

8. Doctor you will sing.
   You will hop, you will dance.
   There is music; you will have a great time!

9. Good Trader! Come on up!
   Ah! Fraser! Such a nose,
   Belongs to someone who frequents balls.

10. Ah! Bloody murder!
    You will drink!
    And after you will dance.
    There is music; you will have a great time!

11. Ah Meurons, come together.
    Start playing something,
    And play us a jovial air.

12. Bois-Brûlés, gentlemen,
    You will hop, you will dance.
    There is music; you will have a great time.

LES BOIS-BRÛLÉS:

13. How much goodness you have!
    My Lord! And honesty too!
    When could we give you such a ball?

HIS LORDSHIP (SELKIRK):

14. Come on! You are mocking me!
    Dance, move your legs!
    There is music; you will have a great time.

LES BOIS-BRÛLÉS:

15. Come on! Never mind these airs!
    Let us hop, let us dance.
    May the devil take M'Lord and his ball!

16. That with all these Meurons,
    on their damn violins,
    For one hundred years may he dance such a ball.

    —*1816; trans. Paul Chartrand*

Cuthbert James Grant and the Sioux Chiefs

Métis (Fort de la Rivière Tremblante, SK) 1793–1854/unknown

In the 19th century and especially in the early 1840s, the emerging Métis Nation was involved in periodic conflicts with the Sioux over territory and access to bison herds. During this period, the Sioux were traditional enemies of the Cree and Anishinaabe—who were often the parents and grandparents of the Métis—so the conflicts had a cultural inflection as well. In 1844, these tensions came to a head when violence erupted between the Métis and the Sioux after an attempted peace conference, leaving several men dead on both sides. After the violence, the leaders of the two communities conducted a series of diplomatic negotiations in the form of the letters reproduced here. The Sioux were represented in this exchange by several chiefs, including Wa Nen De Be Ko Ton Money ("La Terre Qui Brule"), In Yag Money ("The Thunder that Rings"), Etai Wake Yon ("The Black Bull"), and Pin E Hon Tane ("The Sun"). The Métis were represented by Cuthbert Grant, Jr., who had also led the Métis in struggles against the Hudson's Bay Company in earlier years.

This series of letters, translated by Alexander Ross in his 1856 book *The Red River Settlement: Its Rise, Progress, and Present State*, gives a unique glimpse into the diplomacy between Aboriginal Nations in this period of Plains history. The highly structured and poetic rhetoric on both sides reveals a sense of the solemn and ceremonial importance of these communications. The resolution of the conflict is reached through the Sioux chiefs' traditional request that their lost warriors be symbolically replaced by the Métis men who had killed them. This kind of diplomacy was not intended as a punishment of enemies, but rather as a complete cessation of conflict, so that the former enemies become adopted members of the family. Despite these gestures toward peace, there was still considerable conflict between the Sioux and the Métis in the following years.

Letter from the Sioux Chiefs to the Métis

White Bear's Lodge, 14th November, 1844

Friends,—We hang down our heads; our wives mourn, and our children cry.

Friends,—The pipe of peace has not been in our council for the last six days.

Friends,—We are now strangers. The whites are our enemies.

Friends,—The whites have often been in our power; but we always conveyed them on their journey with glad hearts, and something to eat.

Friends,—Our young men have been killed. They were good warriors: their friends cry.

Friends,—Our hearts are no longer glad. Our faces are not painted.

Friends,—You owe the Sisitons four loaded carts, they were our relations; the half-breeds are white men: the whites always pay well.

Friends,—The four Yanktons did not belong to us: but they are dead also.

Friends,—Tell us if we are to be friends or enemies? It is to be peace or war? Till now our hands have always been white, and our hearts good.

Friends,—We are not frightened; we are yet many and strong. Our bows are good; but we love peace: we are fond of our families.

Friends,—Our hearts were not glad when we left you last; our shot pouches were light, our pipes cold; but yet we love peace. Let your answer make our wives happy, and our children smile.

Friends,—Send Langé with your message, his ears are open; he is wise.

Friends,—We smoke the pipe of peace, and send our hearts to you.

Friends,—Tell Langé to run, he will eat and rest here. He will be safe, and we will not send him off hungry, or barefooted.

Signed by the chiefs.

Wa Nen De Be Ko Ton Money	X	La Terre qui Brule
In Yag Money	X	The Thunder that Rings
Etai Wake Yon	X	The Black Bull
Pin E Hon Tane	X	The Sun.

Letter from Cuthbert Grant to the Sioux Chiefs

Grantown, 8th December, 1844

Friends,—The messenger which you sent to us, found us all sad as yourselves, and from a similar cause: a cause which may give a momentary interruption to the pipe of peace; but should not, we hope, wholly extinguish it.

Friends,—You know that for half a century or more, you and we have smoked the pipe of peace together; that during all that time, no individual in your nation could say, that the half-breeds of Red River lifted up their hands in anger against him, until the late fatal occurrence compelled them in self-defense to do so; although you well know, that year after year, your young men have killed, and, what we regard worse than death, scalped many belonging to us. Not that we were afraid to retaliate; but because we are Christians, and never indulge in revenge. And this declaration, which may not be denied, brings us more immediately to notice and to answer the several points in your message to us.

Friends,—You say your people have been killed: we believe what you say, and sincerely regret it; but at the same time, you forget to express your regret that our people were killed also: the one fact is as well known to you as the other; and they were killed first. You forget to notice, that whilst La Terre qui Brule and party were in the midst of our friendly camp, smoking the calumet of peace in all confidence and security, your people at that moment were treacherously murdering our friends within sight of that very camp! You forget to mention that our dead were brought into the camp, the bodies yet warm, and laid before your eyes! Till then, never did it enter into the head or the heart of a Red River half-breed to seek in revenge the blood of a Sioux.

Friends,—You state that our people have often been in your power: we acknowledge what you say; but you must likewise acknowledge, that your people have often been in our power and we sent them off with glad hearts also. Even on the late fatal occurrence, when our dead were before your eyes, and when a hundred guns pointed with deadly aim threatened La Terre qui

Brule and party with instant death, yet more were for you than against you; so you were safe; La Terre qui Brule and party were safe in the camp of the half-breeds. The brave are always generous.

Friends,—You state that when you last left us, "your shot pouches were light and your pipes cold." There is a time for everything; was it a time to show you special kindness when murdering our relations? You demand from us four loaded carts for the four Sisitons: we never refuse paying a just debt, never consent to pay an unjust one. Let us see how far we are liable. In the first place, then, you know your people were the first aggressors. You, La Terre qui Brule, saw with your own eyes our dead, and you knew that none of your people were then killed, and we gave up all thoughts of retaliation, still clinging with fond hopes to that peace and friendship which had so long cheered our intercourse together; but the very next day after you left our camp, a party of your people were discovered rushing upon one of our hunters who happened to be a little on one side and alone; the alarm was given, when the first at hand scampered off at full speed to the rescue of their brother, and in the onset your people were killed. Four, you say, were Yanktons. The demand you make we cannot comply with, either for Sisitons or Yanktons, be the consequences what they may: because we consider it unjust. We may give a pipe of tobacco or a load of ammunition voluntarily; but we will submit to no unjust demand.

Friends,—You put the question, "Shall we be friends or enemies, or shall there be peace or war?" We leave yourselves to answer the question. They who would have friends must show themselves friendly. We have violated no faith, we have broken no peace. We will break none. We will not go to find you to do you harm. We will always respect the laws of humanity. But we will never forget the first law of nature: we will defend ourselves, should you be numerous as the stars, and powerful as the sun. You say you are not frightened: we know you are a brave and generous people; but there are bad people among you.

Friends,—We are fond of you, because you have often showed yourselves generous and kind to the whites: we are fond of you from a long and friendly intercourse, and from habits of intimacy. To sum up all in few words, we are for peace, peace is our motto; but on the contrary, if you are for war, and you raise the tomahawk in anger, we warn you not to approach our camp either by day or night, or you will be answerable for the consequences.

Friends,—You have now our answer; we hope you will take the same view of things, and come to the same conclusion we have done. Langé will lay this before the great chiefs; may your answer be the sacred pipe of peace.

Put your decision on white man's paper. And may that peace and friendship, which has so long knit our hearts together heretofore, still continue to do so hereafter.

Signed, Cuthbert Grant,
Chief of the Half-breeds,
and Warden of the Plains.

Letter from the Sioux Chiefs to the Métis

White Bear's Lodge, 12th Feb. 1845.
Friends,—Langé is here, and your message is now spread before us in council. Ne-tai-ope called for the pipe; but Wa-nen-de-ne-ko-ton-money said no: all the men were then silent; but the women set up a noisy howl out-doors. Nothing was done till they got quiet. The council then broke up. Next day it was the same. The third day the council received your message as one of peace. We now send you our answer. Langé promises to run.

Friends,—I, the afflicted father of one of the young men killed by you, wish that he who killed my son should be my son in his stead. He had two feathers in his head.

Ne tai Opé.

Friends,—Among the young men killed by you, I had a nephew. He who killed him I wish to be my nephew. He was the smallest of all the unfortunates.

Friends,—You killed my son, he was brave, San-be-ge-ai-too-tan. He who pointed the gun at him, I wish to be my son. He had a feathered wand in his hand. I send it by Langé to my adopted son.

Tah Wah Chan Can.

Friends,—I wish the brave who killed my brother, should be my brother. He had a gun and many feathers in his head. He was young.

Hai To Ke Yan.

Friends,—I am old and bowed down with sorrow. You killed my brother-in-law. He was braver than the bear. Had three wounds, and a scar on the face. Whoever killed him, I wish him to be my brother-in-law for ever. He was bareheaded. Hair painted red. Many bells and beads on his leggings. He was tall and strong.

Tah Tan Yon Wah Ma De Yon.

Friends,—My cousin never returned. He is dead. Whoever deprived me of his friendship, I wish him to be my friend and cousin. He had been wounded before, and had a crooked hand. His feathers were red. He had garnished shoes.

Wah Ma De Oke Yon.

Friends,—You killed my father last summer. I wish him who made me fatherless, should be my father. He was a chief, a Sisiton warrior, had a gun and a bow, had been scalped young, His feathers reached the ground. Whoever will wear those feathers, I will give him a horse. I will be proud of him.

Friends,—You killed my uncle, Thon-gan-en-de-na-ge. I am sad. The man who was so brave, I wish to be my uncle. He was a Yankton. My face is always painted black. He had on cloth and leather leggings, and one feather.

Kan Tan Kee

Signed by the chiefs.

Wa Nen De Ne Ko Ton Money.	X	La Terre qui Brule.
In Yag Money	X	The Thunder that Rings.
Etai Wake Yon	X	The Black Bull.
Pin E Hon Tane	X	The Sun.

—*1844–1845*

Peter Jacobs (Pahtahsega)

Anishinaabe/ Mississauga (Credit) 1807–1890

Born in Upper Canada and named Pahtahsega, Peter Jacobs converted to Methodism at a young age after meeting missionary Reverend William Case. Later, and believing that God understood only English, Jacobs despaired that his English was not yet adequate but was reassured by fellow Anishinaabe convert-turned-missionary Peter Jones that God "understood" all languages. Jacobs began preaching to Indians in 1836. In 1840 he helped found the Rossville Mission near Norway House, Manitoba, before establishing his own base at Fort Alexander. In 1842, he journeyed to England for ordination at Centenary Hall, and returned to Hudson Bay the following year, establishing missions and proselytizing throughout the region. He journeyed west again in 1852 before returning to Ontario to hold intermittent postings.

The following are excerpts from Peter Jacobs' 1853 *Journal* in which he recollects the summer of 1852, when he travelled by canoe to investigate the success of various Aboriginal missions and settlements across much of what is now called Ontario and Manitoba. The reader gets a sense of the adventure and peril experienced by Jacobs and his fellow travellers, as they come close to drowning on a stormy lake, are upset in rapids, and encounter large bears. Overall, Jacobs was pleased with the progress of Aboriginal communities, often commenting on Christianization, construction of farms, and adoption of technology. His journals also interestingly document some subtle resistance to his mission of Christianization his travels.

From *The Journal of the Reverend Peter Jacobs*

Friday, [June] 11th [1852].—Early this morning we started off, with a strong current in our favor, and soon came to, and ran down the Dalles. Here the men bought some sturgeon from the Indians. I also bought a young porcupine for my own breakfast; I gave a little tobacco for it. The flesh of this animal is excellent, and I shared it among a few of my choice friends—the Iroquois. After breakfast, the wind being strong and fair, and the current being strong, all in our favor, we hoisted sail, and soon passed through a chain of lakes, and at half-past ten o'clock arrived at the grand discharge, the commencement of a succession of short portages, the three principal of which are a quarter of a mile in length, and two or three more smaller ones: and all these lay within four miles of each other. At one o'clock P.M. we arrived at the White Dog, where I met with Mr. Kennedy, who is in charge of a newly established mission station of the Church of England; and here we took our dinner. I here had a long conversation with the Indians on religious subjects. I was especially desirous to impress their minds on the happy results of becoming Christians in earnest, bringing as a proof of my remarks the happy condition of the Indians in Canada, who are Christians, and are rapidly advancing in civilization. I told them that I had been over the great waters to England, and had seen the *Great Female Chief* eight times during my last visit. They inquired how she looked; I told them that she was very handsome; that she lived in houses or castles like mountains; was surrounded by many great men, soldiers and great guns, so that no one who intends evil to the great female Chief can come near her. I told them also that England was a wonderful and a very rich country; everything wonderful was there to be found—steamboats and carriages which go by steam, running very fast on iron roads; and the whole land is filled with people, like the multitudes of musquitoes in their own country.

...

Thursday, [June] 17th.—At ten o'clock this morning the wind abated, and at one o'clock we reached the Big Stone Point. Here, unexpectedly, I met my son Peter, in a small canoe, on his way to Fort Alexander to meet me. I thank the Lord for sparing the life of my son, and mine, and permitting us once more to meet each other. Our meeting was, therefore, a joyful one. My son and his crew consisted of one young Mr. McKenzie and three Indian boys; their provisions, a piece of ham, half a loaf of bread, half a pound of tea, one pound of sugar. Each had a tin cup. They had a small kettle, but no plate nor knife; and it was well for them that they had not to spend a night by themselves. They, of course, returned from here, and passed the Broken

Head River; came to a point of marsh in the neighborhood of the mouth of Bed River, and encamped for the night.

Monday, 28th June—Left the Grand Rapids, where my son and I boarded in a private house. Mr. and Mrs. M., our hosts, were very kind to us while we staid with them. Went then to Stone Fort for my voyaging provisions. I was not a little disappointed when I could not get a pound of butter. I was grieved at the conduct of one Mr. Lane, a clerk. Before he came into the shop, I had got some biscuit and a ham; and evidently, by his behavior, I would not have got these had he been by when they were put down. I cannot believe that times in Red River are so hard as that a passer by cannot purchase a pound of butter for his voyage. I am sure had J. Black, Esquire, been here he would have given everything necessary. He assured me on last Saturday that I would get anything I required at the Stone Fort for my journey. When Mr. Ross, a retired chief factor, heard that I had been refused a pound of butter, he cheerfully, with his usual kindness, gave me two or three pounds from his own stock, gratis. I owe this gentleman many thanks for kindness shown me and my family by him, when I was at Rossville, at the commencement of that mission. May he ever live before the Lord!

At one o'clock we went down, and had the pleasure of dining with Rev. Mr. and Mrs. Cockran at the Indian Mission station. After, dinner I parted with my son, who is engaged with the Bishop of Rupert's Land to teach one of his principal schools during the coming year. Having hired two men and a canoe, I made a start, and only went to the mouth of the Red River.

Tuesday, June 29th.—At day-break, some unknown, evil-minded Indian fired a gun through my tent with shot. The report of the gun made me jump up from my bed; and I asked my bowsman if he had killed a duck or a goose, supposing that he must have fired at something of the kind; but he asked if I had killed anything by firing, he thinking I was the person who had fired the gun so near the tent, as he was, like myself, asleep, but was only awakened by the report of the gun. But, on examination, I found that five grains of shot had passed through my tent. I suppose that the unknown enemy fired at the tent to frighten us away from our encampment, so that in the hurry of our departing we might leave something for him to pick up. I could not imagine that he intended to kill any of us, as he did not know who we were, not having seen any one during the previous evening.

...

Thursday, [July] 8th. ... At five o'clock arrived at Norway House. This is one of the principal establishments of the Hudson's Bay Company, in these parts, being central, and an inland depot where all the brigades of the northern department (except McKenzie's River) meet on their way down to York Factory.

G. Barnston, Esquire, a chief factor, is in charge, who kindly received me on my arrival, and invited me to tea, which I readily accepted, and after which proceeded down to the Rossvile Mission Station, which is about one and a half miles below, where I found Mr. and Mrs. Mason and family, all well. I, just coming from Europe, and through Canada, they, of course, expected every information relative to the civilized and Christian world; and, as a matter of course, I cheerfully gave them such information as I possessed concerning men, with matters and things.

Sunday, [July] 11th.—At seven o'clock this morning Mr. Mason began reading the Sunday service of the Methodists, and a few of the Indians responded. After the lessons, collects, and prayers, he then read a sermon translated into the Indian, written in the syllabic characters. He performed the whole of the service well, and read his sermon well; but I am not a competent judge of this mixed language of Ojibway, Cree, and Swampy. The Cree and Swampy are nearer kin to each other than either to the noble and majestic Ojibway; and that is the language I profess to understand.

We went over to the company's fort, where Mr. Mason read the English service, and after which I preached in English to a respectable congregation, who paid marked attention to my discourse. I trust some good has been done to the edification of some of my hearers. The service being over, Mr. Barnston kindly invited us to dine with him. I find this gentleman is of high and polished education; and the best of all is, that he loves and fears God.

At three o'clock this afternoon we held another service in the mission church, which was quite full, as many of the fort people came down to join our afternoon worship. Mr. Mason read the hymns in the Cree. I prayed, and had a tolerable good time in preaching to my native brethren. Once or twice I reminded the congregation of the many precious seasons we had together in the house of God eleven years ago, and some of the old members caught the spirit of this; and I have reason to thank God that they were encouraged to go on their way rejoicing, and that they were edified. The men and women of this congregation were respectably clad, and sung well. The church, at both morning and afternoon service, was well attended; and I am informed by Mr. Mason, that when the men belonging to this village, and passing brigades stopping for the Sabbath, the church at such times is crowded to overflowing, as it occurred again on the following Sunday.

...

Wednesday, [July] 14th. … On our sixth day from Oxford House we arrived at the general depot, York Factory. Here are extensive warehouses, wherein English goods are stored, imported from England, and are intended for the whole of the northern department of the Hudson's Bay Territories; not that there is a factory at York where goods are manufactured, as people would naturally think by the word *factory*. At the time the ship arrives from England, the place is quite lively, like some seaports in the civilized world.

At York Factory there are numerous small white whales, which come up the river to the wharfs of the establishments, and the people kill them to feed their dogs upon. Seals also are found here. The polar bears are also very plentiful, and walruses along the coast from either of the factories. In the seasons of spring and autumn, it is said, geese and ducks are very numerous; and the company send out hunters in those seasons, who kill them by hundreds, and then salt them, which they serve out as rations to their people. I have not seen any of the Esquimaux here, but they are at Church Hill, where they trade. This is an out-port of York Factory, in the northern direction from the factory. The Esquimaux are of a white complexion and in their mode of living they are exceedingly filthy. None of this people trade at the factory.

On the arrival of Mr. Mason and myself at York Factory, we were kindly received by W. McTavish, Esquire, the governor of the fort. We stayed there a fortnight, and baptized over thirty persons, which number, added to those baptized at Oxford Mission, make over sixty. Let the friends of missions rejoice! Even in the Hudson's Bay Territories, where the cause has to contend with opposing influences existing, perhaps, nowhere else, it is progressing. How attentive to the spoken word are the Indians of these territories! In the congregations there is no coughing, no going out and in, no sneezing with a whoop, that in the woods would make an Indian dodge behind a tree, and look to his gun; but every one is as quiet and still as they would wish those to be to whom they themselves were speaking. Were gold as plenty as lead, a guinea would be of the same worth as a bullet, did it weigh as much. The people of Canada do not, nor the people of England, value the preached word as they should. Did they, as the Indians of Hudson's Bay, hear a preacher perhaps only once a year, they would be quiet and still enough during service.

…

The following, the remainder of the Journal of my Journey from the Hudson's Bay Territories, is written from memory, as the original papers were lost in Lake Winnipeg.

On Tuesday [August 31, 1852], ten o'clock A.M., the people assembled at our canoe, and we had a prayer-meeting. Then, parting with Mrs. Mason and friends, we proceeded to Norway House, which is in sight of the mission, and dined with the gentleman in charge. He was very kind to us, and gave me some things for the voyage. The afternoon was calm and beautiful; and as we had had a good rest and were apprehensive of head winds, we pulled all that night. At sunrise next morning we attempted to land and breakfast, but the water was so shoal [shallow] we could not, without having to wade a distance. The beach was of bright sand, and the sun was about two hours up, when I saw an object moving on shore. It appeared to be a man; and as we neared it, it appeared to make gestures to us. We were wearied and hungry, but, nevertheless, thinking the stranger was in danger or suffering, we pulled on toward him. Judge our surprise when we found him to be an enormous bear. He was seated on his hams, and what we thought his gestures were his motions in raising himself on his hind legs to pull berries from a high bush, and, with both his paws filled, sitting down again. Thus he continued daintily enjoying his fresh fruit, in the position some of our ladies' lap-dogs are taught to assume when asking a morsel from their mistress. On we pulled, and forgot our hunger and weariness. The bear still continued breakfasting. We got as close in shore as the shoal water would permit, and John taking my gun, a double-barrel, leaped into the water and gained the beach. Some dead brush-wood lay between John and the bear, hiding the bear from his sight. From our position off shore we could see both John and the bear. He now discovered us, and advanced toward us; and John not seeing him for the dead brush, ran along the beach toward him. The weariness from pulling all night, and being so long without breakfast, and the reaction produced by seeing the bear, probably destroyed my presence of mind, for I remembered now that the gun was loaded with heavy duck-shot only, and you might as well meet a bear with peas. John was in danger, and we strained at our paddles; but as the bear was a very large one, and we had no other fire-arms than the gun John had, we would have been but poor help to John in the hug of a wounded bear. The bear was at the other side of the dry brush on the beach. John heard the dry branches cracking before the brute, and dodged into a hollow, under a thick bush. The bear passed the dry brush, and was coursing along the sand; but as he passed by where John lay, bang went the gun. The bear was struck. We saw him leap through the smoke on to the very spot where we saw John last. We held our breath; but, instead of the cry of agony we expected, bang went the gun again! John is not yet caught! Our canoe rushed through the water. We might yet be in time. But my paddle fell from my hand as I saw John pop head and shoulders above a bush, and with a shout point to the side of the log he stood upon. "There he lies—dead enough!" We were indeed thankful to the Preserver. The man who was somewhat scared at a corked bottle of ginger-beer could meet alone, with duck-shot only, a large, old bear, and kill him too.

Here I learned for the first time how to preserve meat without salt for a month, and have it then good and fresh as when killed. The men having to return to Norway House, their home, dug a hole in the swamp, about two and a half feet deep, put in the bottom a few dry boughs, then, putting in the bear's skin and about half the meat, covered all up. When they returned, they would take it home with them. We took about half the bear along with us, all the canoe would carry.

...

We were nearly two miles from shore when a wave struck us, and over we went. When I rose to the surface, I found the canoe bottom up, and John astride on its stern. I struck for the stern, and grasping it in my arms hung on. The old man, my bowsman, hung on somewhere about the midships. He had the worst hold of us three, and from his being more frequently under the waves than John or I, he would be the first to give out. I said to John, "We die now." "Yes," John replied, "we certainly die now." I advised the men not to attempt swimming to shore, as the water was so cold they would get faint and drown, but to hold on to the canoe, and we would drift ashore some time. They promised to do so.

I now saw that the bowsman was getting exhausted: his efforts to resist and rise with the heave of the wave appeared to be more and more feeble. I asked him if he were prepared to meet his God? He said: "I have prayed to him long, long ago." He was ready to die. Both the men were good Christians, members of the Norway House Mission. The old man's eyes were closing, when John reached forward his hand, and taking him by the hair, at the risk of loosing his own hold, placed the old man's chin upon his knee, and kept it there, thus keeping his mouth out of the water. We thought that the old man was dead; but John, a hero, would not let his head drop, determined, if we should get to the shore, to bury his companion on the beach.

I now felt getting weak, and that all hope was over. I committed my soul and my family to God. I told John that I felt I was drowning, and that he must, if he could, save his own life. He replied, that he had no wish to live. If we were drowned that he would drown too. The poor fellow's heart was like to burst, not for himself, but for the old man and me. When I thought of home, and the wants of the work, I did wish to live. If my work was done, I would die; if not, all the water in the lake could not drown me. God's will be done! I was perfectly resigned. I prayed; and as I prayed, suddenly hope of being saved, hitherto lost, filled my mind. I felt an irresistible impression that we would not drown, that we would all be saved. Nothing that I saw had occurred to cause this, but I felt assured of its truth. The wind blew, the waves heaved, and we, like floating leaves, were tossed about as the storm willed. It was He who rules the winds, the waves, and the hearts and strength of men—from him did we get our hope and our strength. I felt so much revived that I began to paddle with my arm; and just as the waves threw a paddle almost into John's hand, the bowsman's eyes opened. I now felt merry; not that I could laugh, but very, very happy—thankfulness to God being the uppermost feeling.

We neared the shore, and several times I let my feet drop to sound; but no bottom. Still we neared the shore, and again and again did I sound, and at last found the bottom, but a few yards from the beach.

The old man was our first care—he could not walk up-right. John and I returned to save the canoe, and, on turning it up, found of all we had only my bedding. God was indeed good to us in this; for we would have suffered much from cold during the night had the bedding not been restored to us. We knelt down on the beach and returned Him thanks. We now felt ourselves so much exhausted that we had to lay down on the beach, wet and cold as we were, and rest.

We picked up a few things that came ashore, among others a bag of biscuit, and about four pounds of pemmican. Our misfortune lost to me my double-barreled gun, all my clothing, money, and the goods I had to pay my voyagers, amounting to over £80 sterling.

...

[Tuesday,] September 14. ... After dinner we proceeded. Along the sides of the river were fine marshes having good wild hay, extending for miles together. During the afternoon we made several little portages, and at five o'clock we made the last little portage in this river, and soon reached the main river again. A laughable incident took place while making the last-mentioned portage. We were too lazy to carry the canoe on our backs, so we tried to pull it up over the rapids with a cord. The rapids had not a rise of more than four feet, and were not more than thirty or forty feet in length. We were on the south side on a smooth rock nearly perpendicular, and nearly five feet high. After the canoe was hauled up to the water above, we came down the rock of nearly perpendicular height to go in the canoe, but as I was about to step in, my foot slipped on the smooth rock, and in falling down into the water, knocked over one of my men, who, in turn, knocked over the other; so we all three splashed in the water by the canoe. We could not prevent ourselves from going in. Luckily at this place the water was not more than four feet deep. We struggled and soon came up to the surface, with our heads and shoulders alone out of the water. One of my men, who was nearest to the canoe, which was already approaching the rapids, plunged in that direction and laid hold of the canoe, and kept it from going down the rapids which we had just passed. All this took place in a moment. We gave vent to our mirth, and laughed at ourselves on account of our misfortune. We waded right over to the opposite shore, and landed on a level spot of ground. Our clothes were, of course, all wet; but this was of no consequence, as we had our traveling dress. Perhaps my readers would like to know what my traveling dress consists of. I generally wear a wide-awake hat, a striped colored shirt, a girdle and corduroy trowsers, without a handkerchief, coat, vest, shoes, or socks. The men, or regular voyagers, wear a cap, a colored shirt, a girdle, and common linen trowsers. This is all they wear. Our wading in the water so often easily accounts for our not wearing shoes; besides, we get warm enough without putting on more clothing. We suffer, however, in one respect, for wearing no neckerchief. Our enemies, the musquetoes, take advantage of us while our necks are exposed. We do not care much for them in general, as each one takes such a very small portion of blood; but when thousands come and take away much blood, then there is no fun in it. Millions of these annoying musquetoes wait for passengers at the landing of the portages in this country, and very politely escort them through the length of the portages, against the will of the passengers, and for their trouble, they take their pay in blood. It was from wearing my voyager's dress that I lost all my fine suits of clothes in Lake Winnipeg, when my canoe was upset. I always wear my common dress in voyaging, as I work as well as my men. I might go like a passenger, as gentleman, but I seldom do.

—*1853*

Henry Budd (Sakachuwescam)

Cree (Norway House) 1812–1875

Sakachuwescam ("Going Up the Hill") was raised in Norway House, Manitoba until the age of eight, when Reverend John West brought him to the Anglican Mission in Red River to be educated. There, Sakachuwescam was baptized and named Henry Budd. A gifted student, he went on to become a missionary at The Pas Fort in 1840 and, in 1852, he became the first Aboriginal person ordained as a priest in the Anglican Church. He also worked as a farmer, teacher, clerk, and trapper for the Hudson's Bay Company, travelling through much of what is now Manitoba and Saskatchewan. He was known for his diligence, dedication to his work, and eloquence in both English and Cree. Although he lived a life marred by many family tragedies (including the deaths of his wife, five sons, and a daughter) he maintained his Christian faith throughout his life. He was also very active in his efforts to convert his fellow Cree people to Anglicanism, even as many resisted his attempts. Still, he taught many to read and write Cree syllabics and was attuned to the social and physical needs of his people in his interactions with them.

A meticulous writer and thinker, Budd recorded his observations and ideas in letters, church records, and journals. In these writings, he articulated his belief that Christian conversion and a move from hunting and fishing to farming were the only options if his Aboriginal brethren were to survive in a rapidly changing northern landscape. He also recorded his many travels and reflected on the success or failures of his sermons. From Budd's personal journal entries below, written during one of the last years of his life, the reader can see that he was very familiar with Cree traditions, and he maintained a strong affection for the people he worked with, even if he sometimes felt differently about their ancestral traditions and spiritual paths.

From *The Diary of Henry Budd*, 1870–1875

December 18, Sunday [1870; Cumberland House]. The Indians having all come in now, I prepared for the morning Service betime. Immediately after breakfast over I assembled them in the large Hall. All the Indian families, and the people of the Fort were present. The Service commenced and was in the Native language as best understood by the hearers. I enjoyed the Service very much, and I trust my fellow worshippers enjoyed it also. May the Lord cause His blessing to rest on his holy Word and make it bring forth in us the fruit of good living to the praise and glory of his holy Name. Early in the Afternoon we assembled again around the Table of our Lord and partook together of the Holy Communion. There were in all 35 Communicants present. Thus, have we given up ourselves, our souls and bodies, to be a reasonable, holy, and lively sacrifice unto God. In the evening held a baptism, a little Infant belonging to one of the people.

...

December 25, Sunday [Devon Mission, the Pas]. Christmas day. A nice fresh morning but very cold. The Church Stove will have to do its work today. It was being heated early in the morning. At 10 A.M. we were all in Church which was well filled. Had the pleasure and privilege of again addressing the Congregation on the subject of Christ's birth. May the Holy Spirit of God condescend to bless the Word spoken in much weakness, and cause it to grow in each of our hearts until we bring forth fruit even a hundred fold to His own glory.

December 26, Monday. As is usual when a Crowd of Indians are here, we had a great many visitors today. The people have had their Xmas only today as yesterday was Sunday, and they had to attend Church. It usually was always a bustling time, but they have kept very quiet. They all came over to see me in the morning, and then were away to invite each other to a dinner in each of their houses. Thus the day past in a quiet friendly manner. In the

evening the men held a consultation among themselves and bound themselves to cut and have the firewood for the Church & School house, to serve
all the winter to collect Timber for building purposes, cut and haul fence &
Picquet[7] for their farms, and that they will strive when the spring comes to
put more seed in the ground than they had the last spring. Poor people. I
wish they had the means of doing all they propose of doing.

...

January 9, Monday, [1871]. In School all the forenoon, and writing all the
Afternoon, but Oh what interruptions, the Indians constantly wanting something or another.

...

Wednesday, January 18. Sent off 3 Sledges more this morning for another trip
of fish. The weather is extremely cold. When the School had been dismissed
I went over to another of the Indian houses & collected them for prayers.
This, I think, with the blessing of God is doing some good among the people;
and if my visits to them could be more frequent. It would help them greatly
to understand more of what they hear from the Pulpit. Indeed it is the only
way to know and sound the depth of their experience in the Christian life,
for when we have them in their own ground, they are not so shy to speak
out their mind freely, as they generally are before company.

January 20, Friday. The Indians have many of them gone off for their fish at
the Lake; but I fear that some of them are gone for the last of their fish, and
when they have done with those then they will have to take to the fishing in
the river which I fear is not at all productive.

...

January 28, Saturday. I fear the Indians have not caught fish enough for their
dinner tomorrow. They have now done with all the whitefish they laid up at
the Lake. Their only resource is to fish in the Saskatchewan [River]. The fish
in this river do always fail about this time, and all the next month.

...

February 4, Saturday. The weather is really very cold and the poor Indians
have to go out and fish notwithstanding, & very few fish he will get for his
pains. Some arrival of Indians for the Sunday. They are much the same as
these at th[is] place, they cannot find much of any thing to live on, and as for
their hunting furs and any thing in that line. They are doing nothing, they
cannot find any thing to kill.

---

7   A pointed wooden stake that is driven into the ground for fencing or for
     tethering horses

...

February 15, Wednesday. I fear the people are not catching so many fish as they did now for a long time, & some of them must be in want. The School have now gone on regular without interruptions since the Xmas holidays, and the two upper classes are evidently improving. Having been in the School all the forenoon we called the people together for the Weekly Lecture. We commenced the meeting by singing a hymn & asking God's blessing on the portion of Scripture to be read. A few verses are then read and expounded and a second prayer offered up by one of the Indians present and conclude with benediction.

February 18, Saturday. I went out to see the people fishing, some of them were visiting their nets and the rest were angling with the hook. Really they have not taken many, nothing like enough to serve their families. I very much fear they will soon be badly of[f] for food. They will have to run to the lake again, and try to pass the remainder of the winter out there. Only few of those who have made their fall fishing have any of the fish now, they are all done. I think most of the Indians see and feel the benefit of going out as we do to the Lake when the season for the fish is come, and lay by hundreds and thousands of them in a few days. I expect that the next fall [there] will be more nets and more people at the Clear water Lake in the month of October.

...

March 3, Friday. The weather much milder, and the fish are sometimes catching better. I trust the poor families may yet get through the winter tolerably. Our own fish will be out before we can get fishing in open water.

...

March 19, Sunday. We have attended to the usual Services today and endeavoured to worship God in his house of Prayer but Oh! what a worship we have rendered him! Full of sin and imperfections! The best of our performances not worthy to appear in His presence. How justly He might reject us and our prayers too. Lord wash our very prayers in the blood of thy dear Son.

...

March 24, Friday. An accident happened today which gave us all such a shock, but which through the mercy of God did no[t] much harm. The Stove pipes of the Mission House caught fire, and the wind strong, drove the flame between the planking and the shingles and was burning away before it was perceived. When it once got vent with such a wind, and every thing so very dry, the fire soon burnt rapidly through the planks and shingles and made such a gap in a very few minutes from the time it was first perceived. Through kind Providence however, there were men on the spot who had just come with a trip of Picquets, and other men were coming as fast as they could, the ladder was standing at its place reaching up to the roof of the House, so that the men were on the roof in a minute carrying up water and snow which soon put out the fire. I congratulate myself that my house and the goods upstairs, was spared from being burnt down to ashes, and thanked God for His great mercy.

...

April 8, Saturday. More arrivals of Indians for Easter. Many of them have come from a long way off, through all the cold snow and mud and water up to their knees; I wonder it does not prove their death! I could not expect many could come to the Village for Easter, as they had travelled a long way hunting these little animals, at this season; but contrary to my expectations we shall have a large number tomorrow (please God). Held a meeting in the School room with all the Communicants for prayer for God's blessing on His Ordinances. When prayer was over the men consulted among themselves how they were to subscribe for our Sacrament wine, once this settled and we dismissed.

...

May 13, Saturday. A pretty sight, I thought, to see all the Indians busy working this morning preparing their ground for the seed. "A pretty sight" I repeat; to see them working at the soil, when I had almost despaired of ever seeing them to do so. I am sure, my predecessors at this Mission, never expected that the Indian here could be induced to trouble the soil. Could they have seen them this morning as I did from my front garden, some of them hoeing away at the ground, others carrying away the Stones, and the rest finishing their fence, they would have said with me—"It is a pretty sight."

...

May 28, Sunday. Having held our Morning prayers we had to start to get to the Nepowewin if possible, by the end of the month, and try to get back again to Cumberland to meet the Indians before they disperse. Camping at the foot of the Rapid, called "Thoburn's Rapids" we camped here. We held our evening prayers after taking our supper and the men laid down.

...

October 8, Sunday. The old man waited at his door to welcome me in. After resting some time I went out to my own tent which was now ready, and having got a fire lighted I told the headman I wanted to see all the people, to make known to them what I had come for. Accordingly he sent a message to all the Tents and summoned them all before my fire. Then, I began to tell them the object I had in view for Coming to see them was, to make known to them the Gospel message of our Lord and Saviour Jesus Christ. I was not come for the object of Trade, or any suchlike but as there were some among their people who have been baptized by us, we consider them as belonging to us, and we wish to make known to these the Xtian Religion into which they have been baptized and I had come also with a view to encourage them in their temporal pursuits; such as growing some vegetable for their support. They sat for a long time and listened attentively to the Word of God which I endeavoured to impress their minds with. It was late before they retired to bed and left me to get into my cold tent under the blankets.

October 9, Monday. I had been so encouraged by the quiet hearing the Indians have to the Word last night, that I resolved to see them again for a little while. Two of the men one of them my own were obliged to go off early in the morning down to the Lake to be shooting some ducks for our dinner. The rest of the men came to my Tent, and I spoke to them again for a little while. Then there was a stir among them getting their horses and putting down their tents. I waited till the old man was ready to go and went in company with him & his old woman. He very kindly got his Son to take all my things down to the lake as he had taken them up. We all went off with the last horses; and kept the company of the old man and his old woman. We came to their camp on the Carrot River, and halted. Our man brought us the ducks and one of the women commenced to clean and cook them for our dinner. After our dinner taken, we came off and left this party for the other camp at Shoal Lake towards our way home. We reached this camp late in the evening. Here we spent the night proposing to start to-morrow for Devon.

...

October 19, Thursday. It is really cold and we cannot do without fire now. Cold work for the poor Ind[ia]ns wading through the water and the cold mud going after the ducks.

...

October 23, Monday. The cold weather continues, and the Snow that has fallen has not been thawn yet. Married two Couples today, being our own young people.

...

November 7, Tuesday. In school all the forenoon, Charles has the little ones with the Cree Syllabic, and I take the first classes, some learning the English.

...

November 13, Monday. Now that the ice has taken in good earnest the Indians will have to run about and try to get their advances paid up. One advantage they have of there being many muskrats this fall. Some of the men have gone away today to hunt them.

...

December 2, Saturday. Dreadfully cold the whole of the week, and blowing with it. Hard work to keep the houses warm.

...

December 17, Sunday. The cold was excessive tho' the wind was in a great measure down. Got all the people and assembled them for the Morning service. A large Congregation came from all parts. After dinner assembled the people again and administered the Sacrament of the Lord's Supper to all the Communicants, after which held two Baptisms, and an Evening Prayers. Held a consultation for a little while as to how the Congregation have to get some wine for the next year for their own use.

...

December 25, Sunday*[sic]*. Xmas. Very cold morning. Two full Services held today. A large number of Communicants, may our blessed Lord and Saviour be in our midst.

—*1870–1871*

Louis Riel

Métis (Red River) 1844–1885

Louis Riel was a great political and spiritual leader of the Métis people in the 19th century, and today he remains the most influential Métis in Canadian history. While generally acknowledged as the founder of Manitoba, Riel was a controversial figure in his day, deeply beloved by his own people but generally despised in English-speaking Canada and abroad for his many efforts to consolidate Métis control over their homeland. In 1869–1870, as president of the Métis provisional government, Riel called for the Canadian government to recognize Métis sovereignty. However, less than a year later, the provisional government fell when a Canadian military expedition was sent to Red River. Over the subsequent decade,

Riel spent time as an exile in the United States and Quebec and as a patient in a mental hospital. However, by the early 1880s, he began a new life in Montana, where he got married, started a family, and became active in state politics.

A group of Métis led by Gabriel Dumont came to Riel in 1884 and asked him to return to Manitoba and lead the struggle for Métis self-determination and Aboriginal rights. He agreed and went on to become the political leader of the Métis Resistance, culminating in battles between the Métis and Canadian soldiers at Duck Lake and Batoche in 1885. Assuming he would be treated as a military leader negotiating a peace treaty, Riel surrendered himself to Canadian authorities after the Métis were defeated. Instead, he was imprisoned and charged with high treason. After a sensationalized trial, Riel was convicted and sentenced to death. He was executed on November 16, 1885.

Though Riel's political leadership and tumultuous life have garnered the most attention from historians and artists, he was also a gifted orator and writer. His skills made him an effective politician and leader, as can be seen in the "Declaration of the People of Rupert's Land and the North West," reproduced here. Created in 1870, just before the establishment of the provisional government, it eloquently spells out Métis grievances to the Canadian government and gives constitutional reasons why the Métis people created their own government. In Riel's later essay, "Metis of the North West," published shortly before his execution, he elaborates on the theme of Métis self-determination, this time from a much more personal perspective. Riel also wrote poetry for most of his adult life, and his poems offer a powerful glimpse into his complex view of the world. "La Metisse," written in 1870, celebrates the establishment of the Métis government and the creation of the *Manitoba Act* by presenting readers with the voice of a young girl, who represents the future of the Métis Nation. "Palpite, Ô Mon Esprit" was written while Riel was awaiting execution, and it gives us a devastating picture of his state of mind in this terrifying situation.

Declaration of the People of Rupert's Land and the North West

It is admitted by all men, as a fundamental principle that the public authority commands the obedience and respect of its subjects. It is also admitted that a people when it has no Government is free to adopt one form of Government in preference to another to give or to refuse allegiance to that which is proposed. In accordance with the first principle the people of this Country had obeyed and respected that authority to which the circumstances surrounding its infancy compelled it to be subject.

A company of adventurers known as the "Hudson's Bay Company" and invested with certain powers granted by His Majesty (Charles 2nd) established itself in Rupert's Land. AND IN THE NORTH-WEST TERRITORY for trading purposes only. This Company, consisting of many persons, required a certain constitution. But as there was a question of commerce only, their constitution was framed in reference thereto. Yet since there was at that time no government to see to the interests of a people already existing in the country, it became necessary for judicial affairs to have recourse to the officer of the Hudson's Bay Company. This inaugurated that species of government, which, slightly modified by subsequent circumstances, ruled this country up to a recent date.

This government thus accepted was far from answering the wants of the people, and became more and more so as the people increased in numbers, and as the country was developed, and commerce extended, until the present day, when it commands a place amongst the Colonies.

Ever actuated by the above mentioned principles, this people generously supported the aforesaid government, and gave to it a faithful allegiance: when, contrary to the law of nations, in March 1869, that said Government surrendered and transferred to Canada all the rights which it had or pretended to have in this territory, by transactions with which the people were considered unworthy to be made acquainted.

It is also generally admitted that a people is at liberty to establish any form of government it may consider suitable to its wants, as soon as the power to which it was subject abandons it, or attempts to subjugate it without its consent, to a foreign power; and maintain that no right can be transferred to the foreign power.

1st. We, the Representatives of the people in Council assembled at Upper Fort Garry, after having invoked the God of nations, relying on these fundamental moral principles, solemnly declare in the name of our constituents and in our own names before God and man, that from the day on which the Government we had always respected abandoned us by transferring to a strange power the sacred authority confided to it, the people of Rupert's Land and the North West became free and exempt from all allegiance to the said Government.

2. That we refuse to recognize the authority of Canada, which pretends to have a right to coerce us and impose upon us a despotic form of government still more contrary to our rights and interests as British subjects than was that Government to which we had subjected ourselves through necessity up to recent date.

3rd. That by sending an expedition on the 1st of November charged to drive back Mr. William McDougall and his companions coming in the name of Canada to rule us with the rod of despotism without a previous notification to that effect, we have but acted conformably to that sacred right which commands every citizen to offer energetic opposition to prevent his country being enslaved.

4th. That we continue and shall continue to oppose with all our strength the establishing of the Canadian authority in our country under the announced form. And in case of persistence on the part of the Canadian Government to enforce its obnoxious policy upon us, by force of arms, we protest beforehand against such an unjust and unlawful course, and we declare the said Canadian Government responsible before God and men for the innumerable evils which may be caused by so unwarrantable course.

Be it known, therefore, to the Canadian Government, that, before seeing our country coerced into slavery, we shall employ every means of defence that Divine Providence has placed at our disposal. And that it is not to see our country which we have so often defended at the price of our best blood against hordes of barbarians (who have since become our friends and allies) invaded by the stranger.

That meanwhile we hold ourselves in readiness to enter into negotiations with the Canadian Government, which may be favorable to its aggrandisement and our good government and prosperity.

In support of this declaration relying on the protection of Divine Providence on oath we mutually pledge ourselves, our lives, our fortunes, and our sacred honor to each other.

—*1869*

From "The Métis of the North West"

The Métis have as paternal ancestors the former employees of the Hudson's Bay and North-West Companies and as maternal ancestors Indian women belonging to various tribes.

The French word *Métis* is derived from the Latin participle mixtus which means "mixed"; it expresses well the idea it represents.

Quite appropriate also, was the corresponding English term "Half-Breed" in the first generation of blood mixing, but now that European blood and Indian blood are mingled to varying degrees, it is no longer generally applicable.

The French word *Métis* expresses the idea of this mixture in as satisfactory a way as possible and becomes, by that fact, a suitable name for our race.

A little observation in passing without offending anyone.

Very polite and amiable people, may sometimes say to a Métis, "You don't look at all like a Métis. You surely can't have much Indian blood. Why, you could pass anywhere for pure White."

The Métis, a trifle disconcerted by the tone of these remarks would like to lay claim to both sides of his origin. But fear of upsetting or totally dispelling these kind assumptions holds him back. While he is hesitating to choose among the different replies that come to mind, words like these succeed in silencing him completely.

"Ah! bah! You have scarcely any Indian blood. You haven't enough worth mentioning." Here is how the Métis think privately.

"It is true that our Indian origin is humble, but it is indeed just that we honour our mothers as well as our fathers. Why should we be so preoccupied with what degree of mingling we have of European and Indian blood? No matter how little we have of one of the other, do not both gratitude and filial love require us to make a point of saying, "We are Métis." "

—*1885; trans. Elizabeth Maguet*

La Métisse

1. Je suis Métisse et je suis orgueilleuse
   D'appartenir à cette nation;
   Je sais que Dieu de sa main généreuse
   Fait chaque peuple avec attention.
   Les Métis sont un petit peuple encore
   Mais vous pouvez déjà voir leurs destins;
   Être haïs comme ils sont les honore,
   Ils ont déjà rempli de grands desseins.

   Refrain:
   Ah! si jamais je devais être aimée,
   Je choisirais pour mon fidèle amant
   Un des soldats de la petite armée
   Que commandait notre fier adjudant.
   Je choisirais un des soldats
   Que commandait notre fier adjudant.

2. Quand ils ont pris Schultz avec sa phalange,
   Le sept Décembre au soir, il fit bien beau;
   Notre soleil couchant, beau comme un ange
   Veillant sur nous, retira son flambeau
   Seulement quand Schultz eut rendu les armes.
   Le lendemain fut splendide pour nous:
   Le huit Décembre, entouré de ses charmes,
   Vit les Métis triompher à genoux.

3. N'ai-je pas vu, moi qui suis jeune fille,
   Le Fort Garry plein de soldats Métis?
   Huit cents Métis dans le fort et la ville,
   Je les ai vus, défendre le pays
   Avec autant d'amour que de vaillance.
   Que c'était beau de voir ces hommes fiers,
   Courbant le front, prier la Providence
   De leur aider à garder leurs foyers.

4. Un saint pasteur, un pretre inébranlable
   Partit un jour du cote d'Ottawa
   On l'entoura d'un bruit épouvantable
   Mais pour passer le Bon Dieu l'appuya.
   Il s'en revint avec notre Province
   Heureusement faite en six mois de temps,

Et McDougall, un moment notre prince
Resta confus de tous ses mauvais plans!

Song of the Métis Maiden *[translation}*

1. I am a maid of the small Métis nation
    And with great pride this heritage I share;
    I know that God when He shaped His creation
    Made every race with equal love and care.
    Though the Métis are not many in number,
    Great is the destiny which they command;
    Proud of the hate that the world heaps upon them,
    Yet they have played a great role in this land.

    Chorus:
    Oh! If some day perchance I should be courted
    Gladly I'd love without shame or demand
    A soldier brave from the little detachment
    So proudly led by our chief-in-command.
    Gladly I'd love a soldier brave
    So proudly led by our chief-in-command.

2. When on that night, the seventh of December,
    They captured Schultz and his troop all in one,
    The fading sun, like a guardian angel,
    Hung in the sky until the task was done.
    Then morning came on the eighth of December,
    One never saw a day so bright and fair;
    And the Métis in their moment of triumph
    Fell to their knees in a heart-warming prayer.

3. Have I not seen, I, a timid young maiden,
    The Métis troops in the Fort and the town,
    Eight hundred strong in defence of their country,
    Risen as one with no thought of renown?
    Oh! wondrous sight to behold our proud soldiers,
    Sons of the plain where man is free to roam,
    With their heads bowed in a most humble gesture
    Praying for help to save their land and homes.

4. Then a fine priest, a brave and saintly pastor,
    For Ottawa set out one morning bright
    At every turn he met with disaster

But he had God aiding him in his fight.
Six months of toil had given us a Province
Happily wrought of his faith and his dreams;
While McDougall who envisioned a kingdom
Had to forgo all his devilish schemes.

—1870; trans. L. Verreault

Palpite, Ô Mon Esprit

Palpite! ô mon esprit! ô mon ame! tressaille!
La paix vous ouvre un champ et plus libre et plus beau
Que la campagne ouverte ou le champ de bataille.
La paix et ses fruits font reculer le tombeau!

L'heureuse paix du coeur dans les plus grandes luttes
Toute seule vaut mieux que tous les autres biens.
Les revers, avec Elle, ont 1'air d'être des chutes
D'abord; pour devenir ensuite des moyens.

O mes amis! La paix que Jésus-christ nous donne
Produit sous tout rapport d'admirables effets.
La paix qui vient du monde est précieuse et bonne
Mais tous ses résultats sont bornés, imparfaits.

Ayons la paix de l'âme! Et l'Infini nous ouvre
Des apperçus nouveaux, gais à chaque moment.
Avec la paix de Dieu, le bonheur se découvre
      À nos yeux Merveilleusement.

Faire la volonté de Dieu nous rend plus calmes
En face du danger, plus paisibles que l'eau
Sans aucun courant d'air. Ouvrons bien les deux palmes
Des nos mains vers le ciel. Renaissons de nouveau!

Sainte Vierge, obtenez qu'un torrent dc lumières
      Vienne éclairer le genre humain.
Saint Joseph! priez Dieu qu'un fleuve de prières
En Jésus-christ nous sauve aujourd'hui pour demain.

Shudder, My Spirit *[translation]*

Shudder, my spirit! Quiver, my soul!
Peace opens a vista more free and lovely
Than open countryside or battlefield.
Peace and its fruits will repel even death!

A peaceful heart in the greatest battles
is better than anything in this world.
Our trials might seem like failings at first
but with time they show us the way.

O my friends! The peace of Jesus Christ
Creates such beauty under everything.
The peace infusing the world is precious and good
But its earthly appearance is shrunken, imperfect.

Let us have peaceful hearts! And the Infinite will open
For us new visions, joyful in each moment.
With the peace of God, that goodness unfolds
            Brilliantly before our eyes.

Giving our thoughts over to God calms us
In the face of danger, more peaceful than water
Without a breath of wind. Let us open our palms
Toward the sky. Let us be reborn anew!

Blessed Virgin, create a torrent of light
            Come illuminate humanity.
Saint Joseph! Pray to God for a flood of prayers
For Jesus Christ to save us, today for tomorrow.

—*1885; trans. Warren Cariou*

Gabriel Dumont

Métis (Red River) 1837–1906

Gabriel Dumont was a celebrated military and community leader of the Métis during in the late 19th century. Born near the Red River settlement, his family moved to Fort Pitt (in what is now Saskatchewan) when he was two years old. As a young man, he became well-known as a horseman, buffalo hunter, guide, and interpreter. He was also fluent in six languages. A natural leader, he was elected chief of his Métis community in 1862. In 1868, his community established a settlement near Batoche on the South Saskatchewan River. During the Métis resistance of 1885, Dumont was a military leader, working with Louis Riel. He earned great renown for his strategic knowledge and bravery on the battlefield.

After the defeat of the Métis by Canadian forces at Batoche, he travelled to Montana Territory, where he joined Buffalo Bill's Wild West Show in 1886. He travelled widely with the show, receiving top billing. In the summer of 1886, the Canadian government granted him amnesty; however, he did not return permanently to Canada until 1893, when he moved home to Batoche.

According to historians, Dumont could not read or write, nor did he speak English. Instead, he often sought out friends to transcribe letters for him in French, some of which included autobiographical accounts. In 1902–1903, he was interviewed by a member of the *Union Métisse de St. Vital*, and, in French-Michif dialect, he gave a detailed story of his life. These accounts were collected and translated into English by Michael Barnholden in the book *Gabriel Dumont Speaks* (1993), excerpted here. In these autobiographical stories, Dumont reveals his natural storytelling ability as well as his keen political and military insights.

Episodes of My Life

Once I killed a Blackfoot when I was fighting for the Cree. This Blackfoot was more daring than the rest: he came toward us all alone. I rode down on him. I had a good runner and managed to turn him, but he got away—so I chased him just like a buffalo, going from side to side. When I caught up to him I stuck the barrel of my rifle in his reins and fired. He fell forward onto the neck of my horse. At full gallop the surprise made him rear violently and almost threw me off backwards. The Blackfoot pony stayed right beside me. I passed my leg over the neck of my horse and jumped to the ground catching the riderless pony's bridle. Then I returned to check the Blackfoot. He was dead, and that caused me some pain because he had never done anything to me.

But you want to know why I killed him? This is why. Six or seven Métis tents were camped near a Cree camp. We were on good terms with them. One day when I was not there, a Cree came to my tent and took a good horse I had left chained and locked. He wanted my horse to fight the Blackfoot who were in the area, so he demanded the horse from my wife. She said no. So the Cree said, "If you don't open the lock I will kill the horse."

My wife did as he told her. When I got back and found this out I was very angry. That same night the Cree were having a war dance. I went into the lodge and stood among the women and didn't say anything. When they finished dancing I jumped up and joined the warriors and asked to speak.

"Friends, I have done this and I have done that. I will fight beside you here and now to show my courage. Then when I finish the enemy and they fear me, everyone will say that I am the best with a horse and rifle. But today you have done something to offend me. When I wasn't even there, you took my horse. It was not brave to scare my wife. Since I married her we have always been together, and what is done to my wife is done to me. I have told you what has happened. I will not let it pass."

The Cree said that this was not done to offend me, but that it was their law. Friends and allies were obliged to supply their best horses when they went to war.

"I do not follow your law," I said. "If you want me to go to war with you, there will be no one in front of me when we ride against the enemy. If it was any other way you could come and take my horse. But as long as I am always first to go up against the enemy, then nobody should touch my horses when I am not there."

The next day the Cree fought the Blackfoot and I went to battle with them. That is what led me to chase down the Blackfoot and kill him. I had to show the Cree that I was the best and that they should respect me.

My Wound at the Battle of Duck Lake

I suffered through the whole war, from Fish Creek to Batoche, shouting all day long. My head bled all night. When I arrived in the States, the wound started to bleed again. I tried to fix it myself. There was a cut two inches long and three-quarters of an inch deep, right on the top of my head. It was lucky I had a very thick skull or I would have been killed. The doctors told me a main artery had been cut. I had many accidents right after the war. When I coughed hard it was like being hit over the head with a hammer, and many times I lost consciousness and fell. But most of the time I would fall and recover right away. One day in a blacksmith's shop I fell face first on top of a pile of angle iron and marked up my whole face. Since then the accidents haven't happened much. The circulation has no doubt been restored by the nearby arteries growing little by little to replace the cut one.

I WAS SUPPOSED TO have been in France with Buffalo Bill. It is not true! I worked for Buffalo Bill, but only in America, and that was before 1889. During his trip to Europe, Buffalo Bill was going to pass through England and I did not have my amnesty so I could not go.

With Buffalo Bill in France were Michel Dumas, Ambroise Lepine—brother of old Maxime Lepine, general in the 1870 rebellion, but no part of the "rebellion" of 1885—Jules Marion, son of Edouard Marion, and Maxime Goulet, brother of Roger Goulet—lately the head of the land bureau in Winnipeg. Michel Dumas and Ambroise Lepine did not stay long with Buffalo Bill. They were almost always drunk and were shown the door. Lepine pretended that he had been mistaken for Buffalo Bill and that it was jealousy that got him fired. They were out on the streets, so they went to knock on the door of the Canadian consul in Paris. That is when Dumas tried to pass for me. M. Pierre Fourrin, a secretary at the Canadian consulate, was asked to present them to the mayor of the Commune of Neuilly where Buffalo Bill's show was set up.

"General," said Fourrin, "I wish to present to you Generals Dumont and Lepine of the Army of the Métis Rebellion in Canada."

The General took an interest in them as he would show good will to any brother-in-arms. It was because of his intervention with the Canadian consul that Michel Dumas returned to Canada as me, Gabriel Dumont.

Ambroise Lepine was brought back by the son of Adolphe Ouimet, a Montreal lawyer. Goulet was also shown the door by Buffalo Bill. His brother sent him the money to come home. Jules Marion, who was hired to drive a dog team, stayed his full time.

I went to France once in 1895 for one year and never left Paris. I got my amnesty in the winter of 1886, one year after the others.

My Story

Around 1880 or 1881, the Métis of Batoche and St. Laurent got very tired of having to pay for wood they cut for planks and firewood. I led the discontent. I could not understand why this was happening, since it was still wild country.

* * *

Around this same time we also saw that the Métis of Edmonton were being pushed off their land by new settlers. When they reported this to the police they were told that nothing could be done. The Métis were the first to live there, and claimed squatters' rights. There were about thirty Métis families who had been forced out, and they decided to get justice for themselves. They accused the government of ignoring their rights to the land which had been signed over to these new occupants, whom the government represented. They threatened to pull the small houses of the settlement down with their horses and some ropes. The settlers naturally became very irritated. But the Métis did not leave soon, and came very close to spilling blood.

The Métis of the Saskatchewan learned of their fate and feared that the same might happen to them. The problems we were having with the government and the wood superintendent were not good signs. We did not want to have to fight for our rights which had been won in the rebellion of 1870. But we were resolved to demand our rights from the government.

During 1882 or 1883 we were greatly occupied with this issue. We had meetings that were my idea, along with Charles Nolin and others, at Batoche, St. Laurent, and just this side of Prince Albert. We petitioned the government but never got an answer. The last meeting in this period was held at the home of my father, Isidore Dumont. He had become discouraged, and only wanted to know how we could quickly and easily obtain our rights. An English Métis named Andrew Spence answered, "There is only one man who can help us now: Riel."

Everyone agreed. Riel was the only one who could intervene between the Métis and the government in 1870, and that negotiation had made those rights a reality. It was quickly decided to bring Riel back to the Saskatchewan to help us draw up petitions, and use his contacts and abilities. We wanted a treaty like the one he had negotiated with the government. (Riel's papers were found by Baptiste Rochelot after the battle. He left them with a priest from Winnipeg named Campo, who was originally from Montreal and had come to Batoche with Lemieux after the rebellion.)

Jimmie Isbister and I were asked to go and find Riel. The people would look after our families while we were gone. Moise Ouellette and Michel Dumas volunteered to go with us because they wanted to meet Riel and would beg him in case he did not want to come back. Lafontaine and Gardupuy were going to Lewiston to look for Lafontaine's mother. They came with us part of the way. I had a small simple wagon. Moise and Jimmie each had two hitch wagons.

It was my first trip to Montana, but somehow I knew exactly how long it would be to the Mission of Saint Pierre. So I said before I left, "The fifteenth day after we leave here, you will know we are getting close."

In fact, we left on the nineteenth of May and on the morning of June fourth we arrived. Riel was teaching there with the Fathers. It was exactly 8 o'clock when we entered the courtyard of the Mission. Mass had just begun. We waited in a small house that Jimmie Swan lived in. We asked him where Riel was and he told us that Riel was helping with mass, as he did every day. I then spoke to an old woman named Arcand who said she would go and speak to Riel right away, and let him know that there were some people who wished to speak to him right away.

Riel left the chapel and came toward Swan's house. When I saw him I went out to meet him with my hand outstretched. Riel took my hand and held it in his and said to me, "You are a man who has travelled far. I don't know you, but you seem to know me."

"Yes," I answered, "and I think you might know the name Gabriel Dumont."

"Of course, quite well," answered Riel, "I know it well. It is good to see you but, if you will excuse me, I am going to hear the rest of the mass. Please go and wait for me at my home, over there, the house near the small bridge. My wife is there and I will be there shortly."

After returning from mass, Riel asked why we from the Northwest had come to see him and what we wanted. He seemed surprised and flattered by what he heard. As he answered us I knew that I would always remember his words: "God has helped me understand why you have made this long trip, and since there are four of you who have arrived on the fourth, and you wish to leave with a fifth, I cannot answer today. You must wait until the fifth. I will give you my answer in the morning." We were not in too great a hurry—we could wait one day before leaving. So we would wait until the morning for an answer. The next day, as he promised, Riel gave his answer: "It has been fifteen years since I gave my heart to my country. I am ready to give it again now, but I cannot leave my little family. If you can arrange for them to come I will go with you."

"Good," we answered. "With our three wagons we can make room."

Riel had his wife, a son about four years old, and a two-year-old daughter. "But," added Riel, "I cannot leave for eight days. I am employed as a teacher here and I would like to make arrangements to leave properly." We waited, as he asked, during this delay, and on the eighth day we started our trip.

After a few days we arrived at Belton, Montana. Riel took mass and afterward he went to the priest to ask for his blessing. The priest told him that he didn't see why he should give his blessing. Nevertheless, since we were stopping for twenty-four hours to rest the horses, the next morning, Riel went to mass again. After mass the priest came to find him and told him, "Yesterday I answered you as I did because I didn't think my blessing would be useful. But since I see you still want it, I will give it to you."

Riel accepted and left to find us because he wanted all of us to receive the priest's blessing. I was the only one who wanted to go to the church for this. Riel also brought his wife and children. All five of us kneeled at the communion table to receive the blessing Riel had asked for. Immediately after we left and were back on the trail, I made up a commemorative prayer for this blessing. It just came out of my mouth: "Father, give me courage, and my belief and my faith in the holy blessing I have received in Your holy name, in order that I will remember it all of my life right up to the hour of my death. Amen."

The twenty-second day after we left the mission of St. Pierre we arrived at Fish Creek, where sixty Métis had come to meet us. That night we camped at my place, some in the house, the rest nearby in tents. It was the fifth of July, 1884. The next day we left for Batoche. I went ahead to get Father Moulin to prepare the church where Riel was to make a speech. But so many wanted to hear him, when he got there he realized that the church was too small. So he spoke to the crowd which had followed him, outside behind the church. He spoke of rights, treaties and other matters.

Riel stayed first at Moise Ouellette's. Then he went to Charles Nolin's with his family and stayed there until the rebellion. (I don't know whether Riel ever bought the Prince Albert Journal, as Caron reported.) The summer and winter passed, and during this time many meetings and petitions were made. One of the last meetings was held at Joseph Arcroix's in February, 1885. None of the old petitions, all addressed to the government in Ottawa, were ever answered. In the end, Riel and the other leaders of the movement were losing patience, and one day he let the words slip: "They should at least answer us, either yes or no. And they cannot say no, since we are only asking for what has already been promised. If they don't give us our rights we will have to rebel again."

After that the word *rebellion* was on the tongue of every Métis, along with the tragic meaning it had already acquired. We all remembered the rebellion of 1870 which had been very passive and there had been only one victim. Scott got what he deserved for his extreme fanaticism. This time the Métis who were talking about rebellion felt that a noisy threat would bring them their rights. These were the memories that were held in everyone's minds. No people in the world are as strong and good as the Métis. Given a choice between riches and their rights, they would choose their rights and everything would be right in the end.

But then there was still Clarke, the representative of the townspeople of Fort Carlton, who had returned from Winnipeg by way of Qu'Appelle. When he passed through Batoche he asked those who were there, "Have you had more meetings? What have you been doing all this time? Did you get your answer?"

Then Clarke told them, "Good, good—it won't be long now. There are eighty soldiers coming. I saw them at Humboldt, and tomorrow or the next day Riel and Dumont will be taken."

Naturally everyone was excited. The next afternoon we had a general meeting at the church. Riel and I addressed the crowd. I told the crowd the latest news: "The police are coming to take Riel." I also asked the people, "What are you going to do? Here is a man who has done so much for us. Are we going to let him slide through our hands? Let us make a plan."

Riel then spoke: "We send petitions, they send police to take us—Gabriel Dumont and me. But I know very well how this works. It is I who have done wrong. The government hates me because I have already made them give in once. This time they will give up nothing. I also think it would be better for me to go now. I must leave you and I feel I should go now. Once I am gone you may be able to get what you want more easily. Yes—I really think that it would be better if I went back to Montana."

The whole crowd interrupted and told him "No, we won't let you go. You have worked hard for our rights and you can't quit now."

"Then," said Riel, "If I must I will desert."

"If you desert, we will desert with you."

I answered them: "It is for the best that we go and cross the line. We will not be insulted and made prisoners."

"We won't let that happen. Don't be afraid of that," answered the crowd.

"So what will you do?"

"When they come, we will take up arms and no one will lay a hand on you!"

"What are you saying?" I asked. "You talk of taking up arms. But what arms do you have to battle the government? And how many of you are there?"

"Yes!" They answered as one. "We will take up arms if you want us to."

Riel would not say whether he would stay. So I continued: " 'Yes,' you say. I know you well, I know all of you like my children. I know how much you are all for taking up arms. It is good to be firm, but not everyone is. So I ask again, how many will take up arms? All in favour of taking up arms raise your hands."

Instead of only raising one hand, the whole crowd rose as one. There were cries of joy and they yelled, "If we are to die for our country, we will die together."

I was frozen. Even though I was the most enthusiastic one there and capable of any heroism in the face of danger, I tried to remain calm and take judgment into account. I said again, "I can see that you have made your decision, but I wonder if you will become tired and discouraged. Me—I will never give up, but how many will be there with me? Two or three?"

"We will all be with you, right to the end!" answered the whole crowd.

"Good then," I said. "This is good, if you really want to take up arms, I will lead you as I always have."

"Good then. If you will lead us, that is good—to arms, to arms."

It was done. The armed rebellion had begun.

—*1902–1903*

Harriette Goldsmith Sinclair Cowan

Métis/Cree (Red River) 1832–1926

Harriette Goldsmith Sinclair Cowan was a member of the Red River fur-trading elite, daughter of the Hudson's Bay Company Chief Factor William Sinclair and the remarkable Cree woman, Nahoway (Margaret Sinclair). Educated in Point Douglas at the Red River Academy, Cowan travelled across the United States with her family to attend college in Illinois in 1848. She returned to Canada in

1850 and married physician William Cowan in 1852. They had four children and together made a formidable political couple, with William eventually posted to Upper Fort Garry as second in command in 1862. Harriette was a networker who worked with many Indian and mixed-blood women throughout the area, an important skill given that the future of the Red River Colony was unstable. This instability came to a head on November 3, 1869, when the Métis (led by Louis Riel) took control of Upper Fort Garry and held the Cowans as prisoners for two months. Escaping to England, the family eventually returned to Winnipeg, where Harriette was interviewed about her life by W.J. Healy for the book, *Women of Red River* (1923). She died in 1926 and is buried in St. John's Cemetery in Winnipeg.

The following are four excerpts from these interviews. In the first piece, Cowan recounts the struggles of her father and how the Hudson's Bay Company would not let him expand his trade business (which set the stage for a later revolt against the company). Next is Cowan's interesting depiction of a magician's show and the underground economy of the Red River settlement. In the third account, she details the devastating 1850 Manitoba flood and how she witnessed heroism, feared for certain Aboriginal communities, and struggled to return home. The last narrative recounts her capture by Riel, her impressions of him, and her courageous choice to stay with her husband (and, later, escape with him). These accounts illustrate Cowan's class, political views, keen sense of detail, and fondness for story.

On My Father

My father was a busy man, and was often away on his journeyings, by dog trains in the winter, and by Red River cart trains in the summer over the plains. He used to take his furs to St. Peter's, on the Mississippi. He was the first to send furs from Rupert's Land to England independently of the Company. Often he went to St. Louis. Year after year Sir George Simpson tried in every way to get my father to join the Company, but my father preferred to be independent. At the same time, he was in perfect accord with Sir George about Oregon. They both felt strongly the importance of colonizing that territory with British settlers, so as to hold it under the British flag, and in the winter of 1840 they persuaded twenty-three Red River families to move to Oregon, with all their belongings, including their horses and cattle. Starting out in the spring of 1841, my father led them across the plains and through the mountains. I often heard him tell of the happenings on that long journey. None of the writers on the early history of the West have ever done justice to it. When my father came back from that first visit to Oregon, where he entered into business relations with John Jacob Astor, he continued in the fur trade more actively than ever. But after 1844, when some United States traders actually came to Red River, and everybody in the settlement who had any means began to be engaged in the fur trade, the Company decided to put an end to all that.

The "Evil One"

The McDermots let [a magician] use their kitchen for his entertainment. I can see yet the kitchen table behind which he stood. It had a cover with red and white checks, and on one corner of it were the buffalo sinews which were the price of admission. Each person who came to the entertainment had to pay one buffalo sinew on coming in. Most of all I remember his dark eyes and short brown beard, and his bold adventurous look. He was a buffalo hunter—Desjarlais was his name. I remember how I clung to Mary's hand, the servant in whose charge I was allowed to be taken to see the "magician." The kitchen was full of people. But Desjarlais was the only one I had eyes for. He smiled down at me as Mary laid two buffalo sinews on the table, and I clung all the harder to Mary's hand. When the "magician" put a watch under his hat, and then took up the hat and showed that the watch had become a potato and then pulled an immense quantity of coloured ribbons from the hat, and did other things no less marvellous, I was lost in amazement and delight. It was like a fairy book coming true. I am not sure that some of the more simple-minded of the grownup people weren't doubtful whether Desjarlais had had dealings with the Evil One.

The 1850 Manitoba Flood

I remember that on the way from Galesboro, we saw at Galena in Illinois a railway track which had just been built—the first I ever saw. But there was no railway train there for us to see, as we had been hoping there might be. As we came northward through Minnesota we found a great deal of the country flooded, and we had to come by a different route from the one we had travelled two years before. At Red Lake river, and again and again in order to cross other rivers and streams, rafts had to be made with branches of trees and the wheels of the Red River carts tied together and covered with oiled sheets of canvas. The wheels were made in dish shape, for that purpose; and the dish shape made them go better along uneven and slippery roads and prevented the carts from toppling over. James McKay, the best plainsman of that time, who was afterwards in the Legislative Council of Manitoba, was in charge of our party. I remember that when a horse in trying to draw a cart across a swollen stream stuck in the middle helpless, James McKay unhitched the horse and got between the shafts himself and dragged the cart across. We had to keep on the lookout for the Indians, not the fierce Sioux of the prairies, but the Chippewas, who lived in the northern part of Minnesota, where there were lakes and forests. They were usually called the Pillagers. For several days we never lit a fire for fear they would see our smoke. At Pembina the water extended two miles out from the hill where Mr. Kittson had built his house. We stayed there four days, and then Mr. Kittson sent us in boats to Fort Garry. The expanse of water over which we voyaged from Pembina was in places eight miles wide. At night we had to tie up the boats to the trees, as it was not safe to go on in the dark.

On Being Captured by Riel

Riel told me I might go, but I decided to stay with my husband. There was a back door to our house, which Riel's men did not know of, and James Anderson, the storekeeper at the Fort, used to manage to come to it at night and tell us the news during that terrible winter. I was never afraid of Riel until after he shot Scott, early in March. Donald Smith and I stood at a window of our house and saw poor Scott led out blindfolded, to be shot. Soon after that Riel ordered us out of our house, where Donald Smith lived with us, and we had to go to more crowded quarters in another house within the walls of the Fort. Governor McTavish,[8] who was a dying man, was at Fort Garry. He wanted to go to England, and to have my husband go with him. Riel was willing to let the Governor go, but refused to let my husband leave Red River. The Governor and Mrs. McTavish went to England; he died two days after their landing in Liverpool, in July. It was in July that my husband and I, who were then living at the Stone Fort,[9] made our preparations for escape. Governor McTavish had prevailed on Riel to let us move down there. My husband went up to Fort Garry two or three times a week; I never knew whether he would be allowed to come back. Mounted men were stationed near the Stone Fort by Riel. When we had all our preparations made and a York boat loaded, we started off for Lake Winnipeg as fast as our crew could row. One of Riel's mounted men galloped off to Fort Garry, to tell him of our escape, but before we could be overtaken we were out on the lake and on our way northward to York Factory. We had one child with us. When we got to York Factory we had to wait a few weeks until the ship sailed in which we crossed to England. That was my third voyage across the Bay and through the Strait. When we returned from England two years later, we came on a ship that brought us to Montreal.

—1923

---

8   Governor William MacTavish

9   Lower Fort Garry

Charles Alexander Eastman (Ohiyesa)

Santee Sioux (Minnesota) 1858–1939

Ohiyesa, later known as Charles Alexander Eastman, was born near Redwood Falls, Minnesota, to a Santee Sioux father and a mother of mixed Sioux and English heritage. He was educated at Dartmouth and at Boston University Medical School. He spent most of his youth as a refugee in Manitoba after his father and other Sioux warriors were captured after warring with the United States government over land and resources. Eastman was one of the first Native American writers to achieve a mass popular audience through his books and in his magazine accounts of Indian life and customs. Eastman is best known for having witnessed, as a government physician at Pine Ridge in South Dakota, the Wounded Knee Massacre in 1890—an event that would profoundly affect him for the rest of his life. Eastman's influence has been felt most acutely through his autobiographical writing. His book, *Indian Boyhood* (1902), describes his traditional upbringing and experiences up to the age of 15, when he was sent to mission school. In *From the Deep Woods to Civilization*

(1916), he describes his experience of colonialism, stresses the contribution of Indians to American society, and articulates a powerful criticism of the United States government for its indifference toward the suffering of the Sioux people.

Much of Eastman's work can be read within the complex context of his roles as a cultural translator and a popular writer. It was with the knowledge that most of his audience was not Native American that he described and shared his understanding of and appreciation for Aboriginal traditional culture, rituals, and customs. This excerpt from *Indian Boyhood* illustrates how an annual celebration, the "feast of maidens," functions to distribute wealth, preserve traditions, and strengthen allegiances and relations in an eclectic community of Sioux, Crees, Assiniboines, and Hudson's Bay Company employees. Eastman's prose pays particular attention to the aesthetics of tribal customs, dress, and dance, and he is able to vividly capture the beauty and joy experienced by those participating in the event.

The Maidens' Feast

There were many peculiar customs among the Indians of an earlier period, some of which tended to strengthen the character of the people and preserve their purity. Perhaps the most unique of these was the annual "feast of maidens." The casual observer would scarcely understand the full force and meaning of this ceremony.

The last one that I ever witnessed was given at Fort Ellis, Manitoba,[10] about the year 1871. Upon the table land just back of the old trading post and fully a thousand feet above the Assiniboine river, surrounded by groves, there was a natural amphitheatre. At one end stood the old fort where since 1830 the northern tribes had come to replenish their powder horns and lead sacks and to dispose of their pelts.

---

10   Actually, Fort Ellice, near St. Lazare, Manitoba.

In this spot there was a reunion of all the renegade Sioux on the one hand and of the Assiniboines and Crees, the Canadian tribes, on the other. They were friendly. The matter was not formally arranged, but it was usual for all the tribes to meet here in the month of July.

The Hudson Bay Company always had a good supply of red, blue, green, and white blankets, also cloth of brilliant dye, so that when their summer festival occurred the Indians did not lack gayly colored garments. Paints were bought by them at pleasure. Short sleeves were the fashion in their buckskin dresses, and beads and porcupine quills were the principal decorations.

When circumstances are favorable, the Indians are the happiest people in the world. There were entertainments every single day, which everybody had the fullest opportunity to see and enjoy. If anything, the poorest profited the most by these occasions, because a feature in each case was the giving away of savage wealth to the needy in honor of the event. At any public affair, involving the pride and honor of a prominent family, there must always be a distribution of valuable presents.

One bright summer morning, while we were still at our meal of jerked buffalo meat, we heard the herald of the Wahpeton band upon his calico pony as he rode around our circle.

"White Eagle's daughter, the maiden Red Star, invites all the maidens of all the tribes to come and partake of her feast. It will be in the Wahpeton camp, before the sun reaches the middle of the sky. All pure maidens are invited. Red Star also invites the young men to be present, to see that no unworthy maiden should join in the feast."

The herald soon completed the rounds of the different camps, and it was not long before the girls began to gather in great numbers. The fort was fully alive to the interest of these savage entertainments. This particular feast was looked upon as a semi-sacred affair. It would be desecration for any to attend who was not perfectly virtuous. Hence it was regarded as an opportune time for the young men to satisfy themselves as to who were the virtuous maids of the tribe.

There were apt to be surprises before the end of the day. Any young man was permitted to challenge any maiden whom he knew to be unworthy. But woe to him who could not prove his case. It meant little short of death to the man who endeavored to disgrace a woman without cause.

The youths had a similar feast of their own, in which the eligibles were those who had never spoken to a girl in the way of courtship. It was considered ridiculous so to do before attaining some honor as a warrior, and the novices prided themselves greatly upon their self control.

From the various camps the girls came singly or in groups, dressed in bright-colored calicoes or in heavily fringed and beaded buckskin. Their smooth cheeks and the central part of their glossy hair was touched with vermilion. All brought with them wooden basins to eat from. Some who came from a considerable distance were mounted upon ponies; a few, for company or novelty's sake, rode double.

The maidens' circle was formed about a cone-shaped rock which stood upon its base. This was painted red. Beside it two new arrows were lightly stuck into the ground. This is a sort of altar, to which each maiden comes before taking her assigned place in the circle, and lightly touches first the stone and then the arrows. By this oath she declares her purity. Whenever a girl approaches the altar there is a stir among the spectators, and sometimes a rude youth would call out: "Take care! You will overturn the rock, or pull out the arrows!"

Such a remark makes the girls nervous, and especially one who is not sure of her composure.

Immediately behind the maidens' circle is the old women's or chaperons' circle. This second circle is almost as interesting to look at as the inner one. The old women watched every movement of their respective charges with the utmost concern, having previously instructed them how they should conduct themselves in any event.

There was never a more gorgeous assembly of the kind than this one. The day was perfect. The Crees, displaying their characteristic horsemanship, came in groups; the Assiniboines, with their curious pompadour well covered with red paint. The various bands of Sioux all carefully observed the traditional peculiarities of dress and behavior. The attachés of the fort were fully represented at the entertainment, and it was not unusual to see a pale-face maiden take part in the feast.

The whole population of the region had assembled, and the maidens came shyly into the circle. The simple ceremonies observed prior to the serving of the food were in progress, when among a group of Wahpeton Sioux young men there was a stir of excitement. All the maidens glanced nervously toward the scene of the disturbance. Soon a tall youth emerged from the throng of spectators and advanced toward the circle. Every one of the chaperons glared at him as if to deter him from his purpose. But with a steady step he passed them by and approached the maidens' circle.

At last he stopped behind a pretty Assiniboine maiden of good family and said:

"I am sorry, but, according to custom, you should not be here."

The girl arose in confusion, but she soon recovered her self-control.

"What do you mean?" she demanded, indignantly. "Three times you have come to court me, but each time I have refused to listen to you. I turned my back upon you. Twice I was with Mashtinna. She can tell the people that this is true. The third time I had gone for water when you intercepted me and begged me to stop and listen. I refused because I did not know you. My chaperon, Makatopawee, knows that I was gone but a few minutes. I never saw you anywhere else."

The young man was unable to answer this unmistakable statement of facts, and it became apparent that he had sought to revenge himself for her repulse.

"Woo! woo! Carry him out!" was the order of the chief of the Indian police, and the audacious youth was hurried away into the nearest ravine to be chastised.

The young woman who had thus established her good name returned to the circle, and the feast was served. The "maidens' song" was sung, and four times they danced in a ring around the altar. Each maid as she departed once more took her oath to remain pure until she should meet her husband.

—1902

Kuskapatchees

Swampy Cree (Nelson House) 18??–19??

There is little documented information about Kuskapatchees except for what she reveals in the brief story of her life (below). She was probably born sometime in the mid-19th century within the proximity of Nelson House, Manitoba, near Three Point Lake, or what she refers to as Three Capes in a Lake. When Kuskapatchees was young, she was known as *Mamao*—pileated woodpecker. As a young woman, she fell in love with a white man, possibly a Hudson's Bay Company employee. When he was reassigned to another post, the couple ran away together. They travelled east down the Burntwood River, past Manasan Falls, and came to a place called Bright Stone Lake. There, Kuskapatchees and her lover encountered a group of Swampy Cree, and with them they established their home and wintered. Their happy cohabitation came to an end when the man drowned in an accident.

In her old age and through an interpreter, Kuskapatchees shared her stories with non-Native researcher Charles Clay in exchange for gifts of tobacco. Clay published Kuskapatchees' 20 tales in *Swampy Cree Legends* (1938). In his preface, Clay explains that he tried to repeat Kuskapatchees' own words literally and to retain the flow of her language. However, he says that he omitted certain phrases that had sexual or controversial implications—as he states, he found many of her stories more suitable for adult listeners. Many of Kuskapatchees' tales deal with the Cree trickster figure, Wesukechak, a being possessing mystical and magical powers but also capable of many human failings and vices. Wesukechak's appearance in Kuskapatchees' own story about her name also point to a complicated and intensely personal relationship between this figure, animals, the universe, and the Cree.

While Kuskapatchees' Wesukechak stories included here have separate titles and are ordered, it is an order and naming imposed by Clay in editing rather than by Kuskapatchees. Clay writes that "the good reciter of [Wesukechak stories] can keep on telling story after story for many, many days and nights." And so—at any given time—it would have been Kuskapatchees who would have chosen which story to tell, how to tell it, and why. As evidenced here, she was a remarkable storyteller, thinker, and grandmother.

Kuskapatchees: The Smoky One

Nosesim—which being interpreted means "my grandchild"—the story you ask me to tell, of how I got my name, goes back a long, long time. I am old now. Many winters' snows have blown around my aged head. But there was once a time when many beavers' lodges were to be found in this country, when the deer roamed in herds, and when the Indians lived in bark and skin Meekeewaps and dressed in rabbit-skin clothing. In that time I was a young girl.

I was handsome then. My eyes were black and shiny; my hair hung in long raven braids; I was straight and supple. My reflection in still water told me I was very beautiful. But the smoke of many Meekeewap fires has made my eyes red and watery; my hair is like the inner bark of dead poplar trees; I am bent and stiff. The children shrill at me for my ugly face. But it was not always thus.

In those distant days we saw little of the white man. But once a year we followed down the rivers to Bitter Water, which is the Ocean, where the white men had built large houses. And there we would trade our furs. We bought axes and knives, powder and shot, guns, cloth, beads, flour, salt and tea. We would watch the white man and his strange ways of living. Sometimes we would see great canoes with large white sails on them.

Then we would pack our goods in our birch-bark canoes and go back to our forest homes. It was a long, hard journey. In summer we would roam from place to place following good hunting; and in winter we would wander with the deer, building our bush wigwams, called Sitteewaps, as we moved from place to place.

Then the white men moved to our country. They built big houses here at Nistwiyase—which is to say at the Meeting of Three Capes in a Lake. Then we didn't have to make the long journey to Bitter Water each year.

Many years have gone by. Now we too build houses like the white man. We do not roam as much as we used to, except in winter when we go to our distant trapping grounds. We wear the white man's clothes and eat the white man's food and use the white man's tools. Life is very much changed now.

In those long years ago, my name was not Kuskapatchees, the Smoky One; it was Mamao, which means pileated woodpecker. I was named thus because I flitted in and out among the trees so nimbly. Now I am wrinkled Kuskapatchees, the Smoky One; and this is how I got my name:

When the white men came to the Meeting of Three Capes, there was one among their number that looked on me with warm eyes. He was young, but little older than myself, and he was tall and strong and handsome. And we loved each other very much. But the white men he was with did not like that we should love each other, and we would meet in secret in the moonlight. Though we couldn't talk much together, we understood each other. And then one night he told me he would have to go away. His white brothers were sending him back to Bitter Water. My heart was very full with sorrow. So we parted, I thought forever. But Wesukechak, the Great Spirit and Brother of the red man, came to my help, and in the heart of my lover he put the great desire.

That night, as I lay on my couch of furs I heard a scratching on the bark wall of my father's Meekeewap and my name whispered, Mamao! It was my lover. I rose softly and slipped out into the starlight. He took me in his arms and whispered to me—would I flee with him to the country beyond Laughing Lake this very night? He would not leave me for Bitter Water, for he loved me greatly. And then my heart was filled with joy, and I thanked Wesukechak.

I stole back into my father's Meekeewap and picked up my loon skin bag of needles and sinew and prepared skin; I added a knife that was lying on the brush floor, and stole out again. Around the camp-fire were lying our pots and pans; I picked up two and joined my lover. I was ready for our great adventure.

He led the way to the lake shore where he had a small birch-bark canoe ready. We stepped in, and each with a paddle moved out across the lake to the river's mouth. My heart was beating very fast, but I was happy, for I was going to the country beyond Laughing Lake with my lover.

It was daybreak ere we came to the first waterfall, the Manasan. We carried our goods over. That early autumn morning was beautiful, and as we stood on the cliff top overhanging the falls the sun rose up into the sky. Standing there in its first bright beams, our faces to the east, we held hands, and gave our hearts to the Great Spirit and had them made as one. And I was happy at that moment.

And then to show our thankfulness we threw some tobacco leaves into the swirling water. Our hearts were light as we paddled onward. It took us many days to reach Laughing Lake, and then we turned up a river and travelled many more days. Thus we came to the deer country.

On the shores of Bright Stone Lake we found a small camp of my people, and there my lover and I built our Meekeewap. We would stay the winter there. I made fish nets from the inner bark of the willows and set them in the waters of the lake. I tanned the skins of deer he brought home. I made moccasins and clothes for each of us. We were very happy indeed. My lover went hunting with the other men, and he learned very rapidly, and all my people were proud of him.

And then one day, he set off alone to gather water-lily roots, for we had to lay in a winter's store of dried roots to grind for flour. He was away all day and at night did not return and my heart grew heavy and tight.

The next morning the men found him. His foot had gone through the bottom of the canoe, and it had turned over, and he was drowned. When they brought him home I fell senseless. And for many days I was in the power of an evil spirit. My beauty fled, my heart went cold, my limbs heavy; I was no longer light and happy, I was dull and sad.

I sat all day over the fire and crooned to myself—I thought of our happiness together, of the things I had made for him but would make no more, of the things he had done for me but would do no more. And so the years have gone by. I sit over the fire and dream of those long-ago days. I sit and smoke all day long and croon and my eyes fill with visions of my lover.

No longer am I Mamao the fleet and the beautiful. My eyes are red and watery, my limbs are bent and stiff, the children shrill at me for my ugly face. I am Kuskapatchees, the Smoky One.

How the Flood Came

Metunne kiyas—which being interpreted means "very long ago"—long before the white man came, and all the animals were Wesukechak's brothers, a great flood arose. And this is how it came about.

Wesukechak, the Great Spirit, lived a carefree life in the forest with one of his brothers, the black Wolf. Wesukechak did not have to work, for the black Wolf worked. He killed animals every day, and Wesukechak hung the meat up to dry for future use.

But the other animals were angry to be preyed upon by the black Wolf, and they called a big council for advice. And at last it was arranged that the Sea Lion would try to take the black Wolf away from Wesukechak.

Now Wesukechak soon learned the the animals were plotting against him, and he warned his brother, the black Wolf. He said:

"O my brother, you must never go near water. You must never jump over a creek, but always walk a pole across it. You must never follow a Deer into water, but go around the shore."

And the black Wolf said he would do that.

But one day when he was chasing a Deer, the Deer came to a lake with an island in it, and began to swim to the island. And the Wolf jumped after it, because he forgot what Wesukechak had said. Now the Sea Lions lived on this island, and as soon as the Wolf was in the water, they made it boil and toss, for they had that power, and the Wolf was not able to swim, and he floated to the island, and the Sea Lions killed him.

Wesukechak waited till night, and all night till dawn, without sleeping. But the black Wolf, his brother, did not return. So Wesukechak followed his trail. He saw where the Deer had jumped into the lake, and he saw where the Wolf had jumped in after it, and he suspected what had happened.

Then Wesukechak looked about him and he saw Okiskemunisu,[11] the Kingfisher sitting on a tree, and he asked:

"Okiskemunisu, what do you see?"

"Fish," answered the bird.

"Not so," said Wesukechak, "for you are looking at that island."

"I want some fish, and I have broken my beak," said the Kingfisher.

"Come to me," ordered Wesukechak, and he fixed the bird's beak and gave it a white necklace as well. And the bird soon caught a fish.

"Now, what do you see on the island?" asked Wesukechak.

"I see Sea Lions playing with a wolf's tail," answered Okiskemunisu, and he flew away. And Wesukechak knew that his brother was dead, and he vowed to punish the Sea Lions.

So Wesukechak made a big raft. Amisk, the Beaver, cut down trees; Muskwa, the Bear, rolled the trees to the water; Nehkik, the Otter, and Wuchusk, the Muskrat, pushed the logs to Wesukechak, and Wesukechak fastened the logs together with the bark of the willow which he made into ropes. And food was gathered and put on the raft. And Wesukechak made a long spear, and tipped the point with the sharp prong of a Deer's horn. And when all was ready he waited for night. And then he sailed across to the island and when dawn came he was standing like a stump on the shore of the island.

In the morning the Sea Lions saw this stump, and they thought it strange they had not seen it before, and they jumped at it. But Wesukechak stood firm and did not flinch or fall down, and the Sea Lions were assured it was only a stump. So after their breakfast they lay down to sleep. And then Wesukechak took his spear and speared them. And the Lions flopped into the lake and it boiled and hissed and the waters rose so fast that Wesukechak had to run to his raft.

---

11   Note from Charles Clay: "*Okiskemunisu* means, 'he has a file', and the Kingfisher is so named for the curious rasping noise it makes."

Soon all the land was covered, and the animals were in danger of drowning, so Wesukechak told them to climb on his raft, for he was the one who had caused the flood by avenging his brother's death.

How the World Was Made Again

For many days and for many nights the animals drifted about on Wesukechak's raft, and in those long-ago times the nights were very dark since there was no moon. But the animals were brave, because Wesukechak was with them. Only Maheekun, the grey Wolf, who is a great coward, grumbled.

The raft drifted for so long that all the food gave out, and even Wesukechak despaired, for he thought the waters would not go down and the land reappear in time and thus all would starve. The days and nights dragged by as slowly as the snail walks, and still the waters did not go down. And Wesukechak cried out aloud in his distress, and said:

"O little brothers, have I only saved you from drowning to let you die from hunger? If I had some dirt, even a little mud, I would make you another world."

When Wesukechak spoke thus, Maheekun, the grey Wolf, howled. But Wuchusk, the Muskrat, said:

"O brother Wesukechak, let me help. Tie a thong around my leg and I will dive down for some mud."

So a thong was tied around Wuchusk's leg and down he dove—down, down, down. But he could find no bottom, and he came back gasping, half-drowned, and very unhappy because he had not succeeded. And then spoke Amisk, the Beaver:

"O good my brother Wesukechak, I can swim somewhat better than Wuchusk. Let me try." So a thong was tied around Amisk's leg and he too dove down, down, far into the water; and he was away a long time; and at last he came back, but he had no mud. When Maheekun saw that Amisk failed, he howled louder than ever. But Nehkik, the Otter, spoke: "O my brothers, let us not despair yet. I am an old and tried swimmer, and stronger than Wuchusk or Amisk. Tie the thong to my leg, brother Wesukechak, and let me try." So the thong was tied around Nchkik's leg, and he dove into the water; down, down, he went, swimming his best, and Wesukechak let out the thong quickly. Many feet of it followed Nehkik. And then it disappeared more slowly, and still more slowly, and finally it stopped, and was very slack.

The animals waited. It seemed a long time. But Nehkik did not reappear, and Wesukechak got anxious lest Nehkik drown. So he pulled on the thong, and he could feel something on the other end. And he pulled and pulled. And finally Nehkik was pulled to the top. He was limp and nearly dead, but under one of his paws was a little piece of mud which he had succeeded in scratching from the bottom before he lost his senses.

And Wesukechak took this piece of mud quickly, and he rolled it between his hands, and he blew on it four times, and the piece of mud grew into a ball, and Wesukechak rolled faster and blew louder, and the ball grew bigger and bigger. And finally when it grew too big for Wesukechak he blew a very loud blast and sent it spinning into the air, where it expanded into an enormous ball too big to see over.

And all the animals went ashore. And Wesukechak said to Kehkawwahkeen, the Wolverine:

"Run and see how big the world is now."

And Kehkawwahkeen ran around the world in a week, and he said:

"The world is too small, Wesukechak."

So Wesukechak blew some more. And the Wolverine was twenty days in going around the world.

"It is too small yet," said the Wolverine, and the other animals agreed.

Then Wesukechak blew and blew a great deal. And Kehkawwahkeen said as he ran off once more:

"If I do not return in forty days you may quit blowing."

The Wolverine did not come back, for the world was big enough. And these experiences made Kehkawwahkeen a great wanderer.

Then Wesukechak told the snakes to make rivers. And Maheckun, the grey Wolf, jumped about with his big feet in the soft earth and made hollows that formed lakes. And he pushed up big piles of mud with his nose, and mountains were made.

And Wesukechak ordered trees and grass to appear, and they appeared, for he had the power.

And that is how the world was made again.

Why the Moose's Skin Is Loose

Long, long ago, when the rivers were young, the animals of the world had neither fur coats nor horns. They were all the same colour, grey; and being without vanity they lived much together, as one big family. Nehkik, the Otter, was a good friend of Pisseu, the Lynx; Wapoos, the Rabbit, and Sakwaseu, the Mink, were often seen together; even Atik, the Deer, and Maheekun, the grey Wolf, were on speaking terms.

But all the animals suffered during the cold winter months; and after one especially long and chilling winter, Muskwa, the Bear, called a great council. Thus he spoke:

"O my brothers of the wilderness, this has been a hard winter. We have all suffered greatly. Our coats are not warm enough. Let us ask the Keche Manitoo to give us warmer ones."

The animals thought this to be a very good idea indeed, and wanted it acted on at once. Kakwa, the Porcupine, who is a very vain fellow, said:

"Muskwa has spoken well. I should like to add that we also ask for horns while we are at it. I think horns would be a good thing."

So Muskwa, and Kakwa, and Atik were chosen by the council to see what could be done, and they went at once to see Wesukechak. And Wesukechak said he would take the matter up with the Keche Manitoo.

Now the Keche Manitoo had seen what a hard winter all the animals had had, and he was quite agreeable. So Wesukechak called Muskwa, Kakwa and Atik to him and said that the Keche Manitoo thought it good to give them warmer coats, and Wesukechak asked if they had any ideas about what kind of coats.

And Muskwa said he thought there should be a variety to choose from, of different colours. And Atik said that he for one would like horns. And Kakwa said that he wanted a special coat made, of which there should be none like it. So Wesukechak appointed a day in the coming autumn when all the animals should search out a certain cave and choose their new coats.

This was very satisfactory. Muskwa and Atik and Kakwa returned with this message, and Wesukechak set about at once to make the new coats. He worked hard all summer, and by autumn had a great store of them all ready, of many shapes and colours. He also made a small number of horns. And for Kakwa he made a special coat.

The appointed day slowly drew near, and the animals began to collect near the cave. They came from many parts of the country, and they all wondered what their new coats would be like. Only one animal was not in a flutter, and that was Mooswa, the bull Moose, and he was very greedily eating water-lily roots in a nearby stream. Even when the animals all went to the cave he was not worrying much, but continued eating.

At the cave, however, there was great excitement. The animals were very busy selecting their coats. Wapoos, the Rabbit, picked out a creamy white one, saying no one would be able to see him in the snow with such a coat. Pisseu, the Lynx, chose a handsome yellow coat, with little tufts on the ears. Atik, the Deer, liked a pretty fawn coat, and picked a pair of fine horns to go with it. Kakwa, the Porcupine, found a special package for him, and when he put on his quill coat, and heard it click when he walked, he was so proud he would talk to no one.

And as the animals chose their coats they went away. And Mooswa, who was busily eating all this while, saw them, and he left his precious water-lily roots and hurried to the cave. But, alas! when he got there, for he had to stop twice to eat some succulent twigs, only a great loose coat was left. Mooswa put it on, and it hung in floppy folds, and did not fit at the neck at all. It was far too big, but there was no other coat. The cave was bare, except for one pair of horns, a large flat pair, and not at all beautiful. Mooswa put those on, too, and sadly left the cave. But he was soon hungry, and he forgot all about his loose coat in a little while, because he was busy pulling up water-lily roots.

And that, Nosesim, is the story of the Moose's loose skin. The other animals, in their new coats, became so vain they wouldn't speak to each other for a long time, and some of them don't speak yet.

Why the Loon Has a Flat Back

Long ago, Nosesim, Mokwa, the Loon, was a tall and handsome bird. He could walk like Niska, the grey Goose, walks. But now he is squat and deformed. His back is flat. His thighs are short and bent so that he cannot walk at all. And this is how it came about.

At the end of a winter which had been cold and many moons long, Wesukechak was glad to welcome spring. Because many snows had fallen, the hunting had been bad, and Wesukechak had had to live on dried meat. And he was very hungry for fresh meat. So he went abroad in the soft spring air to see what he could find.

And he came to a large lake, which was covered with numerous geese, and ducks, and all kinds of waterfowl. But Wesukechak had no weapons, so he began to plan how he could kill some geese for himself by cunning.

And he went into the forest and gathered up a big bundle of muskeg moss and put it on his back and began to walk along the shore of the lake.

All the birds saw him walking, and they cried to one another, "That is Wesukechak!"

And they called out to him, "What is that you are carrying?"

"It is a dancing song," Wesukechak answered, for he knew that the waterfowl loved to dance.

"Good, good!" cried all the birds flapping their wings, "Let us dance to it!" And the geese honked and the ducks quacked with pleasure at the idea.

Then Wesukechak agreed, and threw down his load of moss, and gathered poles, and began to build a great dancing Kinnookumik, or tent. He covered the sides with moss. He covered the top with bark. And he covered the floor with the tips of spruce boughs. And soon all was ready. And Wesukechak's mouth watered, for he thought he soon would feast on fresh goose meat.

So Wesukechak stood in the door of the Kinnookumik and called out:

"Come, O my waterfowl brothers, to the dance I have prepared for you. The songs I have are so fine that you will dance with joy when you hear them."

And all the birds flocked into the tent.

"Now, my brothers," cried Wesukechak, "dance and sing with me. Sing the tune I sing, and dance. And do what the song says."

Then Wesukechak began to sing:

Close your eyes,
Close your eyes,
Close your eyes:
Lie over on your backs,
Lie over on your backs,
Lie over on your backs.

And the birds sang, and did as the song said, and Wesukechak reached out and quickly wrung the necks of the geese.

But Mokwa, the Loon, did not shut his eyes when he was singing. And he saw what Wesukechak was doing, and he called out loudly:

"Wesukechak is killing the geese! Wesukechak is killing the geese!"

And all the birds opened their eyes and jumped up and saw Wesukechak's trap and started to rush outside. Then Wesukechak was very angry, and when Mokwa tried to escape through the door Wesukechak stamped on him and broke his back.

And ever since then the Loon has not been able to walk. He does not go about on land, but keeps to the water and air. He makes his nest near the shore, and drags himself to it by using the elbows of his wings.

—1938

William Berens (Tabasigizikweas)

Anishinaabe (Berens River) 1866–1947

William Berens (or Tabasigizikweas, "Sailing Low in the Air After Thunder") was born in 1866 at Berens River, Manitoba. He came from a long line of political and religious leaders of the influential Moose clan. His father, Jacob Berens, facilitated the entry of the first Methodist mission into their community, but William was also raised around Anishinaabeg Midéwiwin (Grand Medicine Society) ceremonies and learned about the power of the *memengwesiwag* (little and powerful human-like creatures that live in forests and dwell in rocks). He was a hunter, trader, and interpreter for surveyors and Indian agents, which gave him many opportunities to meet and share knowledge with outsiders. He served as chief of Berens River from 1917 until his death. In this position, he oversaw his community's transition to agricultural production and negotiate with governments and church organizations to lift restrictions placed on Native commercial fishing on Lake Winnipeg. Berens collaborated with anthropologist A. Irving Hallowell throughout the 1930s, sharing his people's history, culture, stories, myths, and philosophies, allowing knowledge from Berens River to reach a wide audience. Though criticized by some for urging pacifism in his community during World War II—he felt it wrong to kill people with whom his people had no quarrel—he contributed to the war effort by recruiting Aboriginal people to work on farms in order to quell wartime labour shortages. He died two years after the war's end.

Berens was fluent in Anishinaabeg traditions and beliefs. He understood the power of dreaming and story. These are illustrated in the three selections below, which were transcribed by Hallowell. In the first two examples of *dibaajimowin* (contemporary or modern narratives), Berens relates to Hallowell powerful dreams he had, and he shows how these dreams influence his decision-making processes and illustrates how dreams are gifts of knowledge and insight. Both excerpts are interesting historical commentaries on the radical changes taking place around him as well (such as the introduction of Catholic beliefs). The third piece is an *aadizookan* (a traditional or sacred myth), which Berens heard from his grandmother. In it are details of the birth of the four winds, how earthquakes came to be, and the birth of Misabos (The Great Hare). It is a creation narrative that explains the nature of the world and the forces within it.

The Boy in the Red Tuque

I was walking along and came to a house. I went in. There was no furniture in the room I entered. All that I saw was a small boy with a red tuque. He said to me, "Oh, ho, so you're here." "Yes," I replied, "I'm here." This boy had a bow in his hand and two arrows. One was red and the other black. "Now that you've found me," he said, "I'm going to find out how strong you are." I knew that if he ever hit me that would be the end of me. But I went to the middle of the room, as he told me, and stood there. I filled my mind with the thought that he would not be able to kill me. I watched him closely and, as soon as the arrow left the bow, I dodged. I saw the arrow sticking in the floor. He had missed me. Then he fitted the other arrow to his bow. "I'll hit you this time," he said. But I set my mind just as strongly against it. I watched every move he made and he missed me again.

"It's your turn now," he said and handed me the bow. I picked up the two arrows and he went to the middle of the room. Then I noticed a strange thing. He seemed to be constantly moving yet staying in the same place. He was not standing on the floor either, but was about a foot above it. I knew that it was going to be hard to hit him. I let the black arrow go first and missed him. I made up my mind that I was going to hit him with the red arrow and I did. But it did not kill him.

He took the bow from me, tied the arrows to it and laid it aside. "You have beaten me," he said. I was very anxious to know who it was but I did not wish to ask. He knew what I was thinking, because he asked, "Do you know who you have shot?" "No. (I will tell you who I really am. You remember those little flies like a bee.) I am a fly."

Then he told me to walk along the road to a tent and go in. I walked and came to the tent. There was a man in there with a gun. I had no sooner stepped in than he pointed his gun at me and shot at me. But I felt no bullet. This proved right then and there how I had been blessed.

Told my wife I would not be killed if I went to war. She asked how I knew. I told her it was none of her business.

The Priests and the Furnace

I had this dream before the Catholics started their mission here. I had four or five children at the time. I dreamed that I was close to the place where the woodpile of the Hudson's Bay Company now stands. Two Catholic priests were holding me, one on each side. Another Indian was there too. One of the priests took his head off. There he stood without a head.

I was fighting them but they dragged me off towards where the Catholic mission now stands. We came to a big furnace and these priests tried to push me into it. At the same time there was an old man who stuck his head out of the flames and tried to pull me in. But they were not able to get me in.

I kept on fighting them and they dragged me to another place where there was another furnace. Here the same thing happened. An old man stuck his head out and tried to pull me in while the priests tried to push me in. This old man had a spear. I got pretty close to the flames that time. Then I woke up.

The Birth of the Winds, Flint, and the Great Hare

Long ago the Indians were all gathered together in a camp such as you see here now. One old man had a very beautiful son. He was very proud of him. So he determined to make a great man of his son. He told the boy that he must go into the woods to fast and dream so that he might be blessed. The old man made a fine *wazïsan*[12] for his son in a tree. Here the boy went and stayed alone.

One morning he found his blanket wet. It had not rained during the night and there were no clouds in the sky. The next morning the blanket

---

12   nest

was wet again. He found this very strange and said to himself, "I won't sleep here tonight." So he took up his bow and shot an arrow from it with all his strength, holding tight to the end of the arrow. Where it dropped he landed on the earth again. (Of course, by this time no one knew where the boy was.) He lay down to sleep that night as before under his blanket. Once again he found it wet in the morning. This time he said to himself, "I will stay awake tonight and see what happens." About midnight he saw a woman come sneaking towards where he lay. She stood alongside of him. Then she put one leg over him and pissed on his blanket. Up he jumped, but the woman ran away and disappeared in the bush. He recognized her at once, however. She was a woman from his camp but one who was not highly thought of. Instead of returning to the camp and telling his father what had happened, which would have brought great shame upon him, the boy resolved to tell no one. "I'll hide so this woman cannot find me," he thought. So he counted the scales on a white spruce. When he had finished he said, "Let one of you hide me." But the woman found him nevertheless and the same thing happened. (She was just as powerful as he.) The next day the boy started out to find some other hiding place. He came to a swamp with lots of cattails growing in it. He requested one of the downy (bractless pistillate?) flowers to carry him far up among the clouds. Here he thought he would at last be free of the woman. He succeeded for although she was powerful enough to follow him aloft on another cattail down she failed to find him. But she had already borne a girl-child (magically sired by the boy.) This child grew with unusual rapidity. She was soon running around. Her mother had made their camp on a high piece of ground. She put up a hide-covered tipi. On the outside it was painted in several colors.

While sailing about in the sky, the boy saw this dwelling below. "I wonder who lives there," he thought. So he came down to earth again and walked up to the tipi. As soon as he stepped inside he recognized the woman but it was too late to escape then. The little girl was playing about and he watched her. "Give your father a drink," said the woman. The child ran and filled a dish with water and handed it to him. The woman watched him closely. As soon as he started to drink she pushed the dish into his mouth and said, "Let the earth swallow you up." The boy immediately sank into the ground, but he had sufficient power to keep his head from sinking below the surface of the soil. "You'll stay there for good," the woman said. That day she moved the camp to another spot some distance away.

As soon as the woman was out of sight the boy tried to release himself from the earth. He used all the power he had. He called on all his dream helpers, but he failed to escape. "This is the end of me," he said to himself.

Then he thought of one thing more. He said, "I wish my head to turn into a blueberry patch." And so it happened.

One day the little girl walked around to see the place where their old camp had been. She saw the blueberry patch and when she went home mentioned this to her mother. The woman said, "Don't you go near those blueberries. They might be your father's head!" But the little girl wanted to eat some of the blueberries. So she sneaked back to the old camping place again and started to pick some blueberries. The boy wished the girl to come closer and little by little she did come closer. Then he wished that her arse be turned towards him. When she was in the right position he blew into her arse and said, "Now you'll have some kids." The girl was so scared that she ran back to their tent crying and told her mother what had happened. "I told you not to go near that blueberry patch," her mother said.

Soon the girl was heavy with child. Then her time came and she gave birth to a boy. As soon as he was born he could speak and walk. But it was an easy birth. "My name shall be *Wabanasi* [13]" he said, "I shall be fairly kind to human beings." Then another boy was born. He was partly grown, too, and took his place beside the first one born. "*Änicinábek* [14] shall call me *Cauwanasi*, [15]" he said, "I'll be very good and treat human beings well, as long as any exist on this earth." The third child born spoke and said, "Human beings shall call me West Wind. I'll be a little rough on them but I'll never be wicked. Be easy on our mother," he went on, as another boy popped out. This one said. "Human beings shall call me *Kiwetin*. [16] I'll have no mercy on any human being. I'll treat them just the same as the animals."

"How do you expect human beings to exist if you are going to treat them like that?" his brothers asked. Then another child stuck its head out of the girl's womb. "Be easy on our mother," the other children said. "Easy, nothing," this one replied, and as he jumped out of his mother's body it was torn to pieces. "My name is *Piwának*, [17]" this child announced. His whole body was made of the hardest kind of stone. The girl's mother cried when she saw her daughter in pieces, but she picked them all up and carefully put them in a bark rogan. [18]

One morning the woman heard a noise in the rogan. It sounded as if something alive was moving around in it. So she picked it up and looked

---

13 East Wind

14 human beings, Aboriginal people, or Anishinaabeg people

15 South Wind

16 North Wind

17 flint

18 basket

inside. There she saw a little hare. "Ah, my poor *nozis*,[19]" she said. But when she looked again, there was another boy. This one said, "Human beings shall call me Misabos.[20]"

Shortly afterwards the brothers decided that they could not all remain together any longer. The East Wind said, "'I'll go to live in the east." The West Wind said, "'I'll sit opposite to you, at the other end of the earth." The South Wind said, "'I'll go to the southern end of the earth," and the North Wind said, "I'll go to the north end." Then flint said, "I'll go down into the *sóskŭtciwanank*[21] of the water." But Misabos said, "My brothers, I see that all of you have already made your choices. I'm going to remain here with my grandmother for awhile. I will not make my choice yet." Then all of the other brothers went off to the places they had chosen and Misabos stayed with his grandmother.

Misabos did not know whether or not he had a mother. So one day he said to his grandmother, "Grandmother, how did I come into this world?" The old woman did not answer. Misabos asked her again. Then she told him what happened—"One of your brothers, the youngest one. He it was who destroyed your mother." Misabos was mad when he heard this. He knew Flint was strong but he wondered whether there was anything which was powerful enough to break him in pieces. He made up his mind to find out. He thought the best way was to discover what Flint was afraid of. So Misabos paid a visit to his brother. He said to him, "You have a strong body. Are you afraid of anything at all?" "Nothing!" replied Flint. So Misabos went home disappointed.

Then he paid a second visit to Flint and asked him the same question. And he got the same answer. So he was disappointed again. When he got home, he said to his grandmother, "I wonder how I can make my brother tell me something." But she said nothing. So he thought to himself, "Perhaps if I wait awhile and ask a third time, he will tell me something. He may forget what he said before." So after some time had passed he got ready and started off again to visit Flint. Misabos asked his brother the same question he had asked before. This time Flint replied, "An arrow made of steel. That's the only thing I'm afraid of." But as soon as he had said this, Misabos noticed a change in the expression of his face. He knew that Flint was sorry he had said what he did. It was Flint's turn now and he said to Misabos, "What are you scared of?" "Of an arrow made of a cattail stick with a head of white spruce cut like a spear," said Misabos.

---

19   grandchild

20   The Great Hare, also known in some Anishinaabeg communities as *Naanaboozhoo*, *Wenabozho*, *Nanabush*

21   swift current

Then Misabos went home. But now Flint knew his brother was after him, and that things would not be easy for him. So he went out and collected cattails and spruce bark and made some arrows. Misabos got busy, too. He made a lot of arrows with steel heads. In a few days he said to his grandmother, "I'm going to see my brother Flint again. I'm going to fight him." So off he went. When Misabos reached Flint's camp he did not go in. He shouted for him to come out. Flint came out and the two brothers started to fight. Every time Misabos hit his brother with one of the steel arrows you could see a spark of fire.

When Flint shot Misabos, the bark heads of the arrows just broke off. That was all. No harm was done. But every time Flint was hit, a piece of his body broke off. He got smaller and smaller as the fight went on, and more and more pieces broke off. Then Misabos said to himself, "He's small enough now. He's had enough." And to Flint he said, "Those pieces broken from your body may be of some use to human beings some day. But you will not be any larger so long as the earth shall last." Then he left and went home.

Not long after, Misabos said to his grandmother, "I'm going to leave you now. I'm not going to stay on the earth any longer. I'm going above. But every human being will know it when I visit this earth. They will call it *kwingwan*,[22] earthquake.

—*1930–1933*

Maurice Sanderson

Cree (Fairford First Nation) 1877–?

Reverend Maurice Sanderson was born in 1877 at the Fairford Indian Reserve in Manitoba. His father was originally from Cumberland House, Manitoba, and his mother came from Moose Factory, Ontario, on James Bay. He attended the mission school in Fairford until he was 12 years old, then left home to attend an Indian industrial school near Winnipeg. He studied printing and worked at this for six years. While looking for a printing job in Winnipeg, he ran into a member of the clergy he had known as a boy, and the man invited him to join the ministry. He entered St. John's College in the

fall of 1896 and was ordained, in 1902, in the ministry of the Anglican Church in St. John's Cathedral.

Sanderson was an avid contributor to the *Manitoba Pageant*, the magazine of the Manitoba Historical Society. The following are excerpts from three of his articles. The first is a fond recollection of a gristmill in his community—a community in transition from hunting and fishing to farming, with all of the economic, social, and political changes this brings. The next is Sanderson's reminiscences of his industrial school experiences. Most interesting are the images he uses to

---

22 Some translations claim this word also means a comet or a meteorite hitting the ground.

describe his educational journey, the Indian children who "break new land" with oxen, the introduction of printing, and the growth of trees. Last, Sanderson speaks about his first days of being a missionary, encountering (and breaking) stereotypes regarding Aboriginal people, and the perils and dangers of being a missionary to Aboriginal communities. What is unique in all of these passages is the way Sanderson describes himself, his path through life, and his work as constant struggles against change, time, the environment, and the weather.

Mill Stones at Fairford

When I was a boy, a good many years ago now, there stood on the bank of the river at Fairford, Manitoba and on a piece of ground a little higher than the rest, a grist mill.

When the early missionaries of the Anglican Church began the Mission among the Indians at Fairford, they not only looked after the spiritual welfare of the people, but also encouraged them to work for themselves, to help out their meager way of living by hunting and trapping. They got them to clear land and break the ground to plant gardens. The only tools the Indians had were the grub hoe, or matlock, and the spade. As they cleared more land, a plough was brought in and their missionary showed them how to use it to break up more land, then how to sow grain. In those days, and in what was then remote country, they didn't have the machinery farmers have now. The grain was scattered by hand. When the grain was ripe, it was cut with a sickle, and threshed with a flail. Many a time I watched my father use these tools.

It wasn't easy to get flour at Fairford in those days. When the Indians grew enough wheat to warrant it, the missionary got a man who knew how to build a grist mill, and a mill to grind wheat into flour was built on the mission grounds. It had two large flat rounded granite stones, between which the grain was ground, and it was driven by the wind. Near the top it had what we called sails to catch the wind, and these sails were adjustable. If the wind was light, the sails could be opened out to catch all the wind there was; or if it was strong, they could be adjusted so that they wouldn't catch the full force of the wind. This was to regulate the speed of the grinding stones. An old man once told me that when he was a boy, as he passed by the mill one day, he saw that the sails were not turning as fast as they might be in the high wind that was then blowing, so he opened them out to full capacity, and away they went at full speed. Of course, that turned the stones at high speed, which caused much friction and heat and when the man whose grain was then being ground came to get his flour, he found—not flour, but something like dough.

As transportation became easier and supplies could be brought in without too great a cost, there was not the same need for the mill. Better flour could be bought than could be ground in the old mill, and gradually it went out of use. And there the old mill stood, abandoned, but still a great land mark.

When I was a boy, it was still standing intact. I went off to school and when my schooling was over, I took up work elsewhere. When I went back to Fairford after fifty-five years, there was nothing left of the old mill, except the two stones lying half-buried in the ground.

Quite a large number of men and a few women from Fairford had enlisted in the two great wars, some never to come back. Other places had built memorials to their honoured dead but as yet Fairford had none, so we determined that we must not be behind others. After much consideration we decided on a stone cairn, and what was better or more appropriate for this purpose than the old mill stones. At first we tried to think of a way to use them just as they were, but no satisfactory way occurred to us. We had an old country stone mason, who was living in the district, break them up and build them into a cairn.

It was a great day for us at the unveiling. The veterans paraded to church, and Lieutenant-Colonel Alex Cairns, Secretary of the Manitoba and North Western Ontario Command, Canadian Legion, B.E.S.L., gave the address. The Honourable Stuart Garson, who was then Premier of Manitoba, did the unveiling, and William Bryce, Member of Parliament in the Federal House, Fairford being then in his constituency, laid the wreath. It bears a bronze plaque kindly donated by Mr. Garson.

And there, on the bank of the Fairford River, the cairn stands, just inside the cemetery gate in front of the church, on a solid concrete base, and built of stone that ground flour a hundred years ago for the people at Fairford.

There is history, as well as sentiment, built into that cairn.

—1958

Reminiscences of St. Paul's Industrial School

It was always the policy of the Anglican Church (and other Churches) to encourage education and to undertake teaching as part of their missionary work, so whenever a mission was opened among the Indians, a school soon followed. At first this work was undertaken by the Church itself, but when the government made a treaty with the Indians, it took over the responsibility and made certain arrangements with the Churches.

As time went on it was felt by those interested in the Indians that, because of changing conditions arising from the settlement of the country, the Indian way of making a living, by hunting and trapping, would have to give way to something different. In order to prepare them for the change, it was felt that an opportunity should be given the young to learn some other occupation.

With that in view, larger schools for Indian children were built here and there throughout the country, away from the Reserves, where children might be taught not only the three R's but also some trade or occupation.

One such school was in the parish of St. Paul, Middlechurch, Manitoba, a few miles north of Winnipeg, and was called Rupert's Land Indian Industrial School. Later, when the government took over full responsibility, it was known as St. Paul's Industrial School. The building had been finished in 1889 and opened at the beginning of 1890. The first pupils began entering during the early part of January of that year.

As different trades and occupations were taught, buildings were put up and equipped for the purpose, but these were added only as funds became available. However, as it was necessary to provide for the common needs of such an institution as soon as possible, stables for cows and horses were built. The cows provided milk and the horses were used to work the farm for the growing of vegetables.

An old flour mill, long since in disuse, stood on the bank between the other buildings and the river. Because of its many angles and coves, that building provided a favourite place to play hide-and-seek and other games. When summer came the machinery was taken out and the building was divided by a partition, one part being fitted up for a carpenter shop and the other for a blacksmith shop.

In those years oxen were still used for the heavier work such as breaking new land, and at the School there were two oxen, one red and the other white. I don't remember correctly what we called the red one, but I think it was "Buck," and the white one was soon dubbed "Wab," this being the first syllable of the Indian word meaning "white." He was quite a rangy animal, not like Buck who was low-set and heavy, and he could certainly run. Besides, being quiet and gentle, he didn't mind being ridden. He seemed to be particularly tolerant of a little fellow named "Shorting," and when Shorting was on his back he acted like a thoroughbred. No ox in the neighborhood could touch him in a race; nor was a picnic complete without an ox race, if there were any to challenge him. Of course, Shorting and Wab always came in first. I am sure Wab enjoyed the fun for he seemed to know what was required of him.

Some time later, printing was added to the line of trades taught. There was no building on the school grounds in which to set up the outfit, but across the road on the parish grounds there stood St. Paul's rectory, old and unused, but still in pretty good condition. Under proper arrangements, this was fitted up for a printing shop, and continued to be so used until a more suitable place was found.

At the school there were about the same number of girls and boys, and they were trained in the useful homemaking duties, such as laundering, sewing, cooking and housekeeping.

There were, of course, the classrooms where every child had to attend until they reached a certain age, when each was assigned to the kind of work he seemed adapted for, or wished to take up. They worked for half the day, and spent the other half in the classrooms.

The first Principal was the Reverend (later Canon) W. A. Burman who was quite a noted botanist. He later became Lecturer in Botany at St. John's College, Winnipeg and a leader in the formation of the first Horticultural Association in Manitoba. So it is not surprising that, when he came to live on that bare piece of land at the School, he soon had a garden laid out, and trees planted. The large trees standing now on the grounds of the Old Folks' Home at Middlechurch are the ones planted at that time—sixty-seven years ago.

Children came from Indian Reservations near and far, and with the increase in enrollment the original buildings had to be enlarged or new ones built. In order to provide more classroom space, a large hall was built near the main building; the lower floor was used for recreation and the upper for classrooms.

Some years later this building was destroyed by fire and never rebuilt. This meant the closing of the School. Few institutions, I suppose, turn out one hundred percent perfect graduates, and that cannot be claimed for the School, but it can be truthfully said that in that old School was laid the foundation that set many on the way to a useful life.

After standing idle for a number of years the remaining buildings were taken over by the Welfare Society of those days and turned into an Old Folks' Home. And there it stands, on the same grounds, and in its original outward form, surrounded by flower plots, and shaded by trees that were planted by Indian boys. I know, for I planted some myself, sixty-seven years ago.

—*1958*

Recollections of an Indian Missionary

I met with a rather amusing incident the first Sunday after my ordination. Some preparation had to be made before I left for my first appointment and this made it necessary for me to spend another week in town, and the Sunday between I was sent to take service at a small church in the country. Just before the service began, two young men came in and sat in one of the back pews. There was nothing strange about that, but what I did find strange was the way they kept their eyes fixed on me all through the service. It pleased me, of course, to think that I was making some impression and holding the attention of at least two of my congregation. After the service I took the opportunity of having a word or two with the congregation as they left. My two attentive friends were the last two to go, but they stopped and asked if I had time, would I go over and see them at their own home. It was just a one-roomed house, and they had made it very comfortable and home-like, but what struck me when I went in was the number of weapons that decorated the walls—shotguns and rifles and revolvers, and even a sword or two. I didn't ask them, but I wondered why so many deadly weapons. Then they told me the story.

They were two English boys, who, after much thought, had decided to seek their fortune in a new country, and chose Canada in which to make the venture. They knew very little about the country, but when they decided on Canada, they read up on what they could find about it, and among their reading was some wild and woolly stuff that told of painted warriors and scalping Indians, always on the war-path and brandishing tomahawks and scalping knives. Truly a fearsome country for peace-loving people to try and make a home. So they must come prepared to sell their precious lives as dearly as possible in case some marauding Indians made a raid on their poor unsuspecting selves. What interested them was that the first Indian they saw in Canada was a clergyman of their own Church, and I don't think he gave them any cause for alarm.

...

I did most of my travelling by snowshoe and dog-team in winter, and by canoe and paddle in summer, but also by train and car and gas boat wherever possible and latterly by plane when that mode of travel came into more general use. The latter was a quick and convenient way to travel where there were no railways or motor cars, but even with the planes, there were still places I had to visit that called for the old way of travel, that is by snowshoe and canoe.

In so much travelling over wind-swept lakes and through forest trails, and through blinding blizzards in winter, across rough and stormy lakes, and running foaming rapids in frail canoes in summer, it was inevitable that things did not always run as smoothly as one hoped. I don't think I ever took any fool-hardy chances, and if I did take any risks it was from necessity and I always came safely through them.

I remember once travelling across a large lake—many miles across—when a blizzard struck when I was still ten miles out. There were times when I couldn't even see my lead dog. Then night came on, no sign of stars or moon to guide me and I was all alone with only my dogs for company in that howling, shrieking blizzard and blinding snow. Just before darkness fell, I came to a crack in the ice that ran right across my way, and stretched for miles on either side. I spent a lot of valuable time looking for a safe place to cross, but at last I found a place where I thought I might be able to make it. There was just a thin sheet of ice over it, and this was one time when I had to take a chance. Even the dogs seemed to sense the danger, but I persuaded them by cracking of whip and voice to make a dash for it. We made it all right, but I could see the water coming up behind me as we passed over the thin ice. I was on the toboggan, of course, which acted like a plank when one ventures on dangerous ice.

At long last I began to feel the snow getting deeper under me. That told me that we were getting near the shore where the snow began to pile up, and sure enough, a little farther and we hit land. By following the shore and keeping in the lee of the bush, we came to the Indian village that I was making for and all was well.

On another occasion, I had to make a trip of some distance rather late in November, and took a man with me in case I met with some difficulty at that season of the year, and we sure had lots. On our way back, the weather that up to that time had remained fine, turned bad. Thick clouds began to gather, and the wind shifted to the north. We were still twenty miles from home when we made camp that night. During the night the storm broke and when we woke up in the morning we found ourselves covered with a thick blanket of snow. I never carried a tent except in the summer as a protection from rain. For three days the storm raged with the high winds that whipped the lake into wild high waves. At the end of the third day, we ate the last morsel of food we had, though we had tried to make it last out as long as possible. But we still had tea. We rolled in our bedding that night hoping that the storm would blow itself out, but when we awoke next morning it was still blowing, though the snow had stopped. All we had for breakfast was tea. There was not a sign of any living thing around, though we sought them in the bush, not even a squirrel or a whiskey jack. We couldn't stay there without food, and besides, when the wind went down the Lake might freeze, and to wait several days without food for the ice to get strong enough to travel on, offered a poor prospect. There was only one other thing to do, and that was to get away from there as quickly as possible. Loading our stuff into the canoe, and with one more mug of hot tea, we launched out. How that frail canoe bounced about on the rough waves, but it began to get heavy as the splashing water froze on to it as it fell. The same thing happened to me as I was at the bow of the canoe and got every splash. Travelling under those conditions was hard work, and of course we were just paddling—no outboard motors in those days. Empty stomachs made it a lot harder. About every two hours we would land and "boil the kettle." Though we made a round in the bush there was nothing to be seen that would serve for food. The storm had driven everything under cover. Then we came to a deep bay running many miles inland, but only three miles across. We decided to risk the three miles of rough water. We had been travelling on rough water before, but were near land all the time, but in this case it was crossing a deep bay with no land near, and if the water got too rough there was no shelter to run to.

It was getting late in the short autumn afternoon when we got across without mishap, and on rounding the point—there in a little sandy cove lay a birchbark canoe, and nestling among the shelter of pine trees a birchbark wigwam, with a little curl of blue smoke coming out at the top. What a pleasant sight and feeling, for even my hunger didn't seem so acute when I saw that. There was also a dog that gave warning to the inmates that strangers had arrived.

When I pushed my way through an opening that had a piece of canvas hanging over it to serve for door, and stood inside, the good lady of the wigwam uttered an exclamation of surprise. Her first words were, "What happened?" for I was just about covered with ice. I ignored her question and said, "We're hungry."

After a good meal of boiled whitefish and potatoes and bannock, we set out again, only this time we had several large whitefish that our kind friends supplied in case we had to stop on the way for a meal, for we still had ten miles to paddle before we reached home. Towards evening, the wind began to calm down, and the clouds cleared away. We knew the lake would freeze, so we kept on going till we came to the end of our journey long after midnight. As we paddled along, we could see that ice was beginning to form on the water, but let it freeze, we were just about home. When I looked at the lake later that morning, it was covered with ice. We got home just in time.

—*1959*

Alex Grisdale

Anishinaabe (Brokenhead First Nation) 1896–?

Alex Grisdale was a traditional storyteller from Brokenhead First Nation, Manitoba, who wrote stories throughout his life. His first manuscript of old stories and legends burned in a tent fire in 1915 and his second in a school fire in 1932. Still, he continued to write even as he worked on construction projects and for lumber companies, often recording stories he heard during his travels. In the 1960s, he met and recounted several historical and traditional Anishinaabe stories to researcher Nan Shipley, who published them as *Wild Drums: Tales and Legends of the Plains Indians* (1972). In her foreword to *Wild Drums*, Verna. J. Kirkness described Grisdale as a "sincere, dedicated man" to whom we are all beholden for revealing to us "much of Indian culture, the thinking and the values of our ancestors."

In the first two of these stories from *Wild Drums*, we learn much about traditional Anishinaabe society and economy, and in the third piece, Grisdale tells a story about a neighbouring Assiniboine community. While men appear to hold powerful leadership positions in families and in the community at large, all three stories illustrate the courage and cleverness of women. In Grisdale's stories, women are the heroes who defeat enemies, defy oppressive authority, and befriend the Little People (also called *memengwesiwag*). Most important, Grisdale teaches us that stories live everywhere and in all places throughout the land—a fact that tells a great deal about Aboriginal life in Manitoba.

Death Island

There was a band of Indians camped near Lake Winnipeg and one of the headmen was very cruel. His name was Red Stone and when his daughter refused to marry the old man her father had chosen for her, he beat her with his heavy buffalo-hide belt.

The girl, named Shadow, was not afraid like her mother and she defied her father. "It is up to me if I want to be married. I will choose my own man!"

People walked away ashamed when they saw Red Stone beat his only child so hard. But everyone was afraid of him because they knew that by bad herbs and secret medicine he had killed many people. Even the girl's mother was afraid to talk to Red Stone. She just cried for her poor daughter.

"Someday I will kill him," Shadow said. "Someday soon."

When Red Stone saw that he could not make his daughter marry the old man, he thought he would give her a very bad scare then she would do as he said, for the old man who wanted Shadow had promised Red Stone many horses and robes.

"You get ready. We are going to paddle very far!' Red Stone shouted angrily.

Shadow's mother began to cry. "He is going to take you to Death Island in the lake and leave you there. No one has ever come back from that evil place!"

Yes, Shadow knew the story of this strange island, how many persons had gone there—sometimes with her father—and they had never returned. When searchers went on the island in great numbers to look for the missing man or woman all they found were human bones as if wild animals had killed and devoured them.

Shadow was paddling up front, and Red Stone sat in the rear, steering the canoe towards Death Island. Shadow looked at the strange place with fear. The beach was sandy with big rocks in clusters and the ground was covered with thick bush. She counted only ten trees.

Red Stone with a mighty thrust of his paddle shoved the canoe up onto the island. "Get off!" he shouted.

"No! No!" Shadow cried clinging to her paddle.

The man roared at her then threw Shadow out of the canoe and vowed, "You will die here tonight!"

She got slowly to her feet still clutching her paddle and turning her eyes westward prayed to Manitou. "You help the weak and helpless. Oh. Great Spirit save me from this death!"

When the canoe was about a hundred yards from the shore Shadow heard a sharp crack, and she saw that her father's paddle had broken. Quick as a flash she thrust her own out of sight among the rocks.

Red Stone used his hands to push the canoe around and headed back for the island, and when he was on the sand he shouted, "Give me your paddle."

Shadow told him, "I threw it in the bushes," and she began to run along the beach when her father got out of the canoe. What could he do but go into the bushes and look for that paddle. It was a long way back to camp.

When Shadow saw him disappear into the bush she ran back to the rocks for her paddle and jumped into the canoe.

Red Stone heard the grating sound of the canoe moving over the sand into the water. By the time he ran out to the beach. Shadow was far out on the lake.

"Come back! Come back!" he begged. "Pity me. Do not leave me here to be killed by wild animals!"

"You will get no help from me," she called back. "You will see how it is when night comes to Death Island."

It was almost dark when Shadow paddled close to her camp. At first the people, seeing only one passenger, were very sad. Red Stone had left another one of them on the fearful island. They went into their tepees and fastened tight the door flaps for none would dare to question or criticize the evil Red Stone.

Shadow called to her mother, "I have ended our bad times and nights of terror. I have left Red Stone on Death Island."

All the people jumped up and ran from their tepees to gather about Shadow. They listened to her story and saw the broken paddle in the bottom of the canoe. They made a big bonfire and the drums began to beat as the singers and dancers circled about the brave girl.

Her mother said, "Tomorrow I will burn Red Stone's medicine-bag and we will smash his canoe and that will be the end of him."

The chief and the headmen praised Shadow for what she had done which no other was brave enough to do. Everyone hated Red Stone but in those days people did not interfere when a man was cruel to his wife and children, and nobody had lived to come back from Death Island to tell what had happened to them.

Now all fear was gone, and the camp was happy. Shadow and her mother did not need a man to hunt and provide for them so many presents were laid at their tepee door.

Niskesis and the Little People

Long ago there lived a little girl named Niskesis, which is Little Goose, with an Indian band camped close to a northern river. "Go to the water's edge and gather dry firewood," her mother said.

Niskesis took her time this fine summer day and watched the leaves and bits of bark that floated lazily on the current. Suddenly she saw riding quite close to the riverbank, a tiny canoe no longer than her finger. It was paddled by one of the Little People—a very small man dressed all in green. Niskesis was so excited she forgot that the best thing one can do is to pretend not to see these Invisible Ones. But no, she waded out into the water and picked up the little canoe and laughed happily at the little man.

He did not enjoy being taken from the water and was so sulky that he would not speak at all to the girl. Niskesis ran home calling to everyone to come and see what she had found.

Her parents were shocked at Niskesis' rash act and they cried in alarm, "Go and put him back where you found him. Put him back at once before ill-luck strikes all of us!"

Niskesis was very disappointed but she realized that she had done a foolish thing and perhaps offended the Little People. "I meant you no harm," she whispered to the green man as she carried him back to the river. "If I have done wrong please forgive me and do not punish the people at camp. Truly, I meant you no harm. I think you are a very clever person to make such a beautiful little canoe and a paddle no bigger than a pine needle." Gently she set the canoe back in the water at the exact spot where she had found it.

For a moment it seemed as though the little man would speak but he said not a word and paddled away in silence.

The summer days passed swiftly and in the Autumn Moon or September when the deer rub their horns, Niskesis went with three young friends to gather highbush cranberries along the riverbank. The girls carried baskets made of birchbark hung from their necks on deerskin thongs, but other pickers had been here before them.

"The berries hang bigger and redder on the other side of the river," one of the girls said. "What a pity we have no canoe to cross over."

Niskesis sighed, "I wish my little green man would come. It was right at this spot where I last saw him."

"Bold Girl! Bold Girl!" a small voice called. "I will take you and your friends to the other side of the water."

"There he is!" Niskesis exclaimed. "And he has brought four friends in their canoes!"

"Step into my canoe and I will take you to the other side of the river," the little man said to Niskesis. "My friends will take your friends also."

Niskesis moved forward but the other girls laughed knowing that the moment she placed her foot on the canoe she would crush it to dust. But Niskesis had great faith in the Little People's power. Even as she put her foot forward she was not sure that the small man was going to punish her for what she had done one day in the summer. If this was his plan then she must obey him to save her family and friends from his revenge.

Niskesis' moccasin touched the little canoe and lo, she became as small as the Little People and settled down feeling quite safe. "Do as they say," she called back to her friends for now she knew they meant her no harm.

The Little People paddled the girls across the river and the moment that Niskesis and her friends placed their feet on the ground they grew to their normal size. The girls knelt down on the riverbank to thank the Little People and watched the tiny canoes glide away with the current and out of sight.

It was almost dark when men from camp found the girls and took them back to camp with overflowing berry baskets. When they asked the girls how they had crossed the river without canoes, none of them would say.

The men shrugged. "It is a woman's story and they will never tell any man."

The Torch Woman

Many years ago before the white man came to this country a band of Indians set up their tepees by the Assiniboine River near where Brandon city now stands. These were Stone Roasters, people who dropped hot roasted stones into water to make it boil. This tribe is called the Assiniboine.

The band made their camp near a cut bank where the land dropped fifteen or sixteen feet over the rocks into the water. The chief chose this place because it was safe. Enemies could not approach by river.

There was a widow in this camp, and because she was young and child-less she was expected to look after herself. Her husband had been killed by the Sioux and she was still in mourning for him when the scouts rode in to report a large herd of buffalo about a day's ride out on the plains. At once the people prepared to break camp and move closer to the hunt.

"I will remain here until you return," the widow said.

Her friends were alarmed. "What will you do if the enemy comes while you are alone? We will be gone for the days of one hand."

She shrugged and continued to scrape fat from a buffalo hide with her sharp flint stone scraper. "If this happens then I shall surely die."

When the chief saw that the woman was determined to remain in her tepee by the river, he ordered that three other lodges remain standing. This might deceive any spies into believing several families were here instead of a lone woman.

The people rode away to the buffalo hunt and the widow slept one night without fear. Only the sound of the river and far away coyotes disturbed the dark stillness. But she knew that if enemy scouts were about and had seen the departure of the band they would lie patiently watching the four tepees to count the men who went in and out. It would not be long before they would discover that she was alone. But she was prepared to die, for her husband had been dead two moons and she still grieved for him. To live or to die was of no consequence to her.

She performed her work as usual about the quiet camp. Even when the sun set and there was nothing for her to do, the widow carried her tanning frame into her tepee to work by the light of her fire and the birchbark cone she had thrust into her beaded headband, like a torch.

As she scraped the hide, the widow became aware of strangers just out-side her lodge. A moment later the door flap was raised and six Sioux war-riors entered. They carried bow and arrows and tomahawks in their belts. She knew she must die.

"Sit down and eat before you slay me," she said quietly.

Without a word the men sat down, three on each side of the entrance. The widow's invitation was not strange. Many warriors facing death com-mitted an act of supreme courage or service, and it was the custom to per-mit those doomed to die, a last request.

The woman with the torch on her head set fresh meat and berries on birchbark platters. She passed these to the men seated on the ground. When their hands were full she darted from the tent and ran towards the river.

The torch on her head made it easy for the Sioux to follow her and the warriors were right behind, shouting and yelling their rage. When the widow came to the edge of the cut bank she tore the torch from her headband and threw it ahead, and then dropped to the ground crouching low.

The Sioux chasing the light plunged over the cut bank to their death on the rocks below.

The woman listened to their cries for a time to see if all had really fallen and she was safe. Now she was too frightened to spend the night in her own tepee so she began to run westward where she knew her band would be camped in readiness for the big buffalo hunt.

She ran all through the night and it was sunrise when she saw the familiar lodges in the distance. The guards had seen the lone figure and rode out to discover who it was. One was waving his blanket in a friendly signal. They were certainly surprised to see the widow.

The people of the camp listened in disbelief as she told her story. Could a lone woman outwit six cunning Sioux? Was she telling this wild story to win honour for herself?

The chief ordered a fast pony for the widow and he with twenty of his men rode back to the four tepees by the Assiniboine River. As the men peered over the edge of the cut bank and saw the six bodies they knew that the woman's story was true. They made their way down to the rocks below and the six scalps were taken as proof of what had happened.

The widow rode back with the chief, his men following, all singing the Hero Song to let the women in camp know that they must prepare a feast in the widow's honour. That night all sat around the campfire and watched as she who was now called Torch Woman danced and enacted the story of her experience.

The chief proclaimed the widow a heroine. "Had our enemies killed her they would have hidden in our lodges there and waited our return and killed us all. Truly this woman is one of the great hero-queens to be honoured for all time."

Torch Woman was greatly admired for all her life after that. She received many gifts and many offers of marriage.

—1972

The Dene Elders Project

Dene (Wollaston Lake and Brochet)

Traditionally, the Dene (or Chipewyan as they were called by the Cree and later, by Europeans) followed herds of caribou in a cycle of hunting and trapping throughout the Northwest Territories and the northern regions of Manitoba, Saskatchewan, and Alberta. The Dene often gathered in seasonal communities, sharing stories and performing collective ceremonial practices such as the giveaway dance, where possessions changed hands several times. Many of their stories emphasized the beauty of life in a challenging, cold north and described the competitive relations with other communities over land use.

The Dene Elders Project originated in 1977 through an initiative by Saskatchewan Education. Interested in gathering details about the lives and stories of the Dene people of Saskatchewan, researchers spent two and a half years living with, learning from, and interviewing Dene Elders throughout northern Saskatchewan. The project recorded many fascinating stories and accounts in a combination of English and Dene. Unfortunately, it was abandoned due to a lack of money. However, in 1999 the taped interviews were located and transcribed. The following excerpts are from interviews with Elders from Wollaston Lake, Saskatchewan (who spent time

travelling throughout northern Manitoba), and Reindeer Lake (modern-day Brochet). These communities' contact with settler-Canadians came later than that of many Aboriginal communities in the south. When a Hudson's Bay Company post opened in 1859, however, the arrival of missionaries to their communities become a regular occurrence. These two events introduced radically different economic and spiritual practices that merged with historical events and traditional beliefs, creating narratives that show a rich history of change and cultural reconciliation—sometimes difficult, sometimes less so. Although the communities have undergone much change, they are still places where Dene culture and language continue to thrive through the many legends, stories, and songs that are shared by the people.

Marisis Aze

Born in either 1904 or 1905, Marisis Aze was raised near Nueltin Lake. It was not until she had two children that she travelled south by canoe to Brochet for the first time. In one of her stories, she recalls

tuberculosis and influenza epidemics that devastated her people. She also tells the story of Thanadelthur, the legendary Dene heroine who helped her people establish their first contact with Europeans.

Early Life

I was the only child in the family because all of the others died. The sickness came a long time ago. And they all died. The people used to die one every day.

The very first time I remember the sickness, I was a teenager. The body of a sick person was all red and they were covered with red spots. If a person gets cold, they die when the spots disappear. If you don't get cold and the spots stay, you survived. It has come three times since. I took care of the bodies. I dressed them up for burial and then the bodies were sent back to Brochet. When the first sickness came I did not get sick. But the second sickness, I just about died. Many children died from that second sickness; some adults too.

One old man in Black Lake is called Crippled William[23] because he walks with a cane. His parents and all his siblings died. It was Crippled

23   According to the Dene Elders Project, this man's real name was William Dadzene.

William that took care of all the dead bodies. He said there was a man who was chopping wood. Then as he was walking back to his house, he fell down dead. There are many stories similar to this one. One old woman was hauling water when she died. It must have been very bad because it was said that dead bodies were found outside where they fell down. Some people died in this area, but not as bad as in the Athabasca, around Black Lake and Stony Rapids.

Dreamers

I was born after our people were baptized. How can you be a dreamer if you were baptized?

Still, there were some people who could do ɪkǫ́zɪ[24] when I was young. And I have heard stories about it. This is the reason why our people exist today. These people helped us to survive.

Even after the white man found the Dene, even when they made friendship between the Dene and the Cree, there were still people killing us. This is where Hǫk'ǫdelo helped the people. He was named after a small bird that cries out, 'ha un lic, ha un lic'. He saved the people by ɪkǫ́zɪ. He dreamed winter. He brought the cold north wind. He did this to kill the enemy by freezing them. After winter was over the Dene looked for survivors. When they found them, they killed them. But one survivor went back home and reported what had happened. He said, "The Dene are strong people. From now on you must not fight them anymore." This is how our people survived.

The Story of Thanadelthur

Thanadelthur is the reason we exist today. Before she found the white men, different tribes were killing our people. One day the Cree raided a Dene village and killed everyone except Thanadelthur. She lived with the Cree for many years. Every time the Cree went to the trading post they would tell Thanadelthur to stay behind in hiding. This went on for many years. The Cree were telling the traders at the post that they needed shells to kill off the animal-like creatures in the barrens.[25] One day, Thanadelthur thought to herself, "I might as well die if it is meant to be, since all my people are killed. Next time they go to the rock-like shelter I will follow."

So next time the Cree went to the post, Thanadelthur followed them. The traders saw her as she walked past the window. They quickly went outside,

---

24 Traditional Dene practices of healing and medicine

25 Aze likely means here fellow Dene or other Northern Aboriginal communities.

before the Cree could stop them. The traders asked Thanadelthur who she was and where she came from. Thanadelthur told them that she had been captured and forced to live with the Cree after her people were killed. She said that this was the fourth time the Cree had come here while she waited up by the rocks.

The traders brought Thanadelthur inside the post and told her that they would look for her people.

When they were ready to leave on this journey, Thanadelthur was told to wear red clothing so she could be seen from far away. She asked if she could make a dress for herself and the traders agreed so she made a long, red dress.

There were many white people that were going to look for her people and they brought with them many gifts. When the Dene were spotted, Thanadelthur was told to meet them first. The Dene ran away but Thanadelthur kept on walking after them. It looked to the Dene like a big blob of blood was coming.

Then an old woman said, "Why are we running away when only one person is coming after us? We should wait and see why this is happening. Besides, one person cannot kill all of us." One old man and an old woman stayed behind while the other Dene waited further up ahead. It must have been a very tense wait, not knowing what the outcome would be.

When Thanadelthur caught up to the old people, she said, "I have found white people and they are bringing many things for you to survive."

Axes became available with Thanadelthur. The people were very happy to get axes. They went to a big hill with many trees and they started chopping them down. When they finished chopping, one side of the hill was bare.

My grandfather Casimir told me this story.

—2003

Bart Dzeylion

Barthelemy Dzeylion was born in 1922, the youngest of 10 children. He was raised in the Brochet/Wollaston Lake area (around the Manitoba-Saskatchewan border) and died there in 1999. His family was fiercely independent and refused to take treaty payments from the Canadian state, instead making their living through hunting and trapping. Dzeylion followed suit, establishing himself as a renowned trader. In the excerpt below, Dzeylion shares traditional knowledge used by the Dene to locate caribou and people, as well as how ɪk̓ǫ́zɪ—traditional practices of healing and medicine— were used.

Using Bones

The shoulder blade of a caribou—*ehgǫ́lá*—is taken out and prepared for something, not to eat, but for *bé k̓ë̓ʔɪzɪ*.[26] This is used to locate people.[27] When someone is gone somewhere for a long time and has not come back when he said he will, this marking is used. What you do is this, you write the days of the week on the shoulder blade. You mark an X for Sunday. Then you put this *ehgǫ́lá* in front of the stove hole.[28] *Ehgǫ́lá* is placed there by the stove to heat it. When a marking appears on any days of the week, this person is expected to be back on that day. For example, if the mark is on Wednesday, this person should be back by Wednesday. This was used long ago by our people because there was no radio or phones. If this technique is not used, they are in the dark about this person. This works because the person could be back a day before or a day after the weekday that was marked.

Another thing is about *dzagór tsóé*.[29] It is used to locate caribou. Sometimes the caribou will not come for a long time and it was very hard to know how far they are. You cut off a bear's knee bone until all the meat is off the bone and place it on a very hot stove. Then you say to the *sas dzagór tsóé*,[30] "Don't move if there is no caribou. Move when the caribou are near." *Sas dzagór tsóé* will start moving a little and finally it will spin around. "Oh good, caribou will be here today, tomorrow, or the day after." Whatever direction the long bone points, that is where the caribou are. This is true because it was used many years ago and it was a very effective technique. Sometimes when there is no caribou *ɪk̓ǫ́zɪ* was used by dreamers to tell them where and how far the caribou are.

These techniques that the Dene used were the only way to find out when a person will return and if the caribou are near or if there is no caribou around. This was used many, many years ago by our people so it was passed down from generation to generation.

There used to be caribou all over the place here in Wollaston Lake. These caribou were here because they helped people to survive but now it seems people don't need them as much because they get rations and they get family allowance cheques. Maybe that's why the caribou are way up north now.

· · ·

---

26 "marking on something"

27 This practise, known as scapulimancy, is a common in many Indigenous traditions.

28 This is the draft hole on the front of old stoves.

29 kneecap bone

30 a bear's kneecap bone

When people used *ɬkǫ́zɪ* back then they didn't use anything except singing, with the sick people inside the skin tent. They didn't use medicine, they just sang over the person. Using *ɬkǫ́zɪ* is just like being an ordinary doctor. Sometimes people get well, sometimes they die. All the dreamers do is just sing. They don't talk to this sick person, they give them no medicine, they just use *ɬkǫ́zɪ*.

—*2003*

Helen Joseyounen

Helen Joseyounen was born in 1903 at Nueltin Lake on the Manitoba/Nunavut border. Her nickname was *Ts'u dłaghe* (Laughing Girl). Joseyounen raised nine children at Da lou Tué (Lac Brochet, Manitoba) with her first husband before moving to Wollaston Lake to be with her second husband. Helen Joseyounen's recollections shed some light on the complex role of women in Dene culture and the rituals around childbirth and courting among the Dene.

Childbirth

A long time ago, when a woman was ready to give birth, she would go to a place that was made ready for her. There would be a shelter made of trees. It was there that she would give birth to her child. Two or three midwives would be with her. The woman would put the newborn child against her skin, inside the caribou hide clothing.

But very, very long ago, a woman would give birth, clean up the baby, and right that instant the baby would follow the mother back to the camp. It was said that Dene people were like caribou.

Another thing, too. The woman that had given birth did not go into the tent through the doorway. She had to come in from the back of the tent because the doorway is where the food is brought in, so it was respected.

A menstruating woman faced some restrictions as well. She would follow the people on the trail but when they came across a frozen pond with a beaver house on it, a marker was placed so she had to walk all the way around the shoreline. No matter how big the pond was, she had to walk all around it. She could not walk across the pond with a beaver house on it.

More Than One Wife

In the past men would sometimes wrestle for women, or throw them back and forth in the tent. Because the tent was round, the men would be across from each other and they would pass the girl across, over the fire. Sometimes the girl would get dizzy, or pretend to get dizzy, and take hold of the man that she wanted. Then the other man could do nothing about it.

Long ago, when a young woman gave birth out of wedlock, the girl would say that the father of her baby would be whoever she wanted to marry. This happens even today. So instead of letting her marry the man she wanted, the young men would pass the baby around, when the baby was about a year old. If the baby peed on a young man, that young man is the one who lived with her. There were no marriage ceremonies performed. You would just go and live with that person.

When a man wanted a wife, the woman he wanted just moved in. He could do this many times.

A man would have two or three wives. It was said that when a man only had one wife, they would always travel around hunting. They would take all their belongings because the Dene didn't have that many things. They would be together, sharing whatever work needed to be done. They would do this if they didn't have children. They would live in one camp, travel for awhile, and then live in another camp. But if a man had two wives, they would live in a Dene camp until the camp moved. Then they would move with the camp.

—2003

Gabriel Tsannie

Gabriel Tsannie was born in 1904 in an area around Sunrise Lake. Recognized as a spokesperson and leader in the community, Tsannie offers an interesting take on the figure of Dátsątthı (Crowhead), one of the mystical figures of Dene stories. These narratives are fascinating in their ability to incorporate new ideas and experiences through time.

Stories of Crowhead

Crowhead (Dátsątthı) was from a long time ago, from a time before Jesus. People still think he's alive somewhere. No one knows what happened to him. No one has ever heard of him being dead. He could be on the other side of the land.[31] Elders from a long time ago think he was German because it was not known if he ever died or was killed. There were no witnesses.

Dene elders think Hitler was Crowhead because he was not known to have died. They think somehow he managed to go across the ocean. It was said that Hitler, the leader of the German people, could not be killed. No one knows what happened to Crowhead because, according to the elders, he did not die.

Crowhead was said not to be human because of his strange ways. He would be staying with the Dene, but sometimes he killed his own people. Yes, he killed even his own relatives.

---

31   Tsannie likely here means across the ocean, or in Europe

But he did not do the actual killing. He let the Cree kill them. He would say, "May the Cree kill you all!" Then the Cree would kill them all. When all the Dene were killed and the Cree had left, Crowhead would gather all the dead bodies into one huge pile. He would then sleep among them. Crowhead would be covered with *ghįnáí*.[32]

This is strange and hard to understand because then he would reverse the killings. Crowhead would then kill all the Cree by making them come back to the same site where they had slaughtered everyone. He then made all the Dene come alive again and live as if nothing had happened at a different campsite. Then he would go and live with them again.

. This probably happened up north because the Dene depended on caribou and at the time they used only bow and arrows. They would have had to live close to where there were a lot of caribou. And Crowhead lived with them, wherever they were.

Crowhead had a small boy that he raised as his grandson. People know these stories of Crowhead through his grandson. This grandson was tough too. He had to endure many hardships. His name was Erełkal, the one who has power from the wolves.

When Crowhead was still alive he would tell his grandson to watch for him while he slept among the dead people. His grandson would be hiding in the bush and would tell Crowhead when the Cree were approaching. Crowhead told his grandson to say, "The Wolverine has come!" if he saw canoes coming.

One time two canoes full of Cree were approaching where Crowhead was sleeping. The grandson saw them and said, "The Wolverine has come!". It was said that it was very hard for Crowhead to wake up when he was sleeping among dead people. He would sleep until the Cree would be almost upon him. Then he would wake up and grab his club, made from a flat antler of a caribou, and start hitting the Cree.

This time he did not kill them. He broke the bones in their arms and legs. The Cree were then helpless.

Crowhead then told his grandson to go around and cut off the penis of all of these Cree and put them in a bag. They then continued on their journey to join the people he had returned to life. He told his grandson, "If you see or hear anything, drop one those penises on the ground." This is probably how he got his *įkʼǫ́zį*.

Crowhead used to wear a blanket made of the skin from the heads of crows. The whole blanket was covered with them, with the beaks sticking out all over. Whenever he came back to camp he would say, "Who laughs at

---

32 maggots

my blanket?" Crowhead would know if someone made fun of his blanket and he would get very mad. He would then leave and go somewhere else for awhile. This is the time that the Dene would be killed, by other tribes or by the intervention of Crowhead.

—*2003*

George Barker

Saulteaux (Bloodvein & Hollow Water First Nations) 1896–c. 1980

George Barker was born on the Bloodvein Reserve in Manitoba and adopted by his maternal grandparents after a smallpox epidemic devastated his family and community. Most of his time was spent trapping and fishing with his grandparents, who later moved to the Hollow Water Indian Reserve on the eastern shore of Lake Winnipeg. After he left home at 16, he worked as a labourer and forest ranger. It was not long, however, before he became interested in politics. He returned to Bloodvein, where he was elected chief in 1926 (a position he held, with only one two-year break, until 1968). He witnessed countless legal and institutional practices of cultural and political assimilation by federal and provincial governments, and, as chief, was instrumental in resisting these and uniting Aboriginal leaders to fight for rights, land claims, and representation. It was primarily Barker's political will that resulted in a trapline registration in 1947 that protected the claims of Aboriginal hunters to their territories. In recognition of his long-standing dedication to wildlife protection, the Chief George Barker Wildlife Refuge was created in his memory.

Barker's life story, *Forty Years a Chief* (1979), gives fascinating and intricately detailed accounts of his youth, hardships, struggles, and political life. Two excerpts follow. The first is a rich account of Barker's early years and the many struggles his family faced during harsh seasonal travels and living with an oppressive *Indian Act*. The second is a theme that comes out consistently throughout Barker's stories: a desire that traditional ways not be forgotten, even in the face of seemingly insurmountable odds. In his description of the Midéwiwin, he relates tradition and ceremony to the life and existence of a community of active, thriving Aboriginal people. His words are reminders of the resilience and dynamic everyday nature of Aboriginal life in Manitoba.

My Early Years

When I was very young many of my people in Bloodvein died from smallpox. I remember quite well walking to a neighbor's log cabin. It was one of the few cabins around; most people, including ourselves, lived in wigwams. They had a large family. As I opened the door to enter I will never forget the odour. It smelled awful. I walked inside and everyone was still in bed. This was unusual because every other time I went there, the family would all be up. I didn't stay long. I ran back and told grandma. She scolded me and said, *"cou-cou-cou,"* which means "lost" or "dead." The whole family had died.

All the dead from that epidemic were placed in one large grave. Sticks were put on the bodies and then mud on top.

During the sickness no doctor came. It wasn't until only a few cases were left that the doctor and two policemen arrived. They burned all the clothing and blankets so the sickness would not spread. Some clothes and blankets were supplied by the government, but as most of the blankets in those days were handmade, the women were kept very busy making new ones for everybody.

Now was *tuck-wa-gin,* the time of the year when the leaves change colour. This was the time for my people to hunt and prepare for the cold winter ahead. My earliest memories are of those happy times.

Soon we must leave Bloodvein. Since we have only one old canoe, we must build two new ones, so that my grandparents and I, my uncles John and Peter Skye, and three cousins can go inland up the Bloodvein River to trap and hunt.

Grandfather was an expert at making canoes. Grandma had to gather the birchbark, the best she could find. She took her older son with her. Grandfather cut white spruce and spliced it to make the ribs. Everything was arranged just so. Starting from the centre, he placed them just right, first one side, then the other. Willows were used to fasten the ribs in place, doing the same for the bow and stern.

The gum was gathered from the white spruce to make the pitch. It was melted in an iron kettle. As the bark settled on the bottom the gum would come to the top. It was strained through an old jute sack, which the Hudson's Bay Company used to wrap pork in. Charcoal and sturgeon oil were put into the gum and mixed to the right texture. The ribs were arranged, and then glued in place.

Next, the birchbark was pierced and sewn to the gunnels. Small roots from spruce trees were used in sewing the bark together. These were split, the core removed and soaked in water. This made them flexible and easy to work with.

When he was sure everything was well made, grandfather turned the canoe over and checked that it was well pitched, using his own spit to smooth it over. He wanted a perfect job. This also prevented the glue from sticking to clothes. Finally, he took willow and boiled it until it was a thick brownish colour. With this he painted the canoes.

Now everything was ready and we prepared to leave. The sun was shining. The waters were still. Grandfather was pleased with his canoes.

We traveled up the Bloodvein. The site was chosen by grandfather, who made sure that there was enough dry wood for a few days. Three forked poles were cut for our tent and firmly staked to the ground. The tops were pulled together and tied, with a small space left for the smoke to escape. Our tee-pee was covered with animal skins.

When all the work around camp was finished, Grandfather Skye, with his sons John and Peter, went into the bush to hunt. They killed a moose. An overnight camp was set up near the place where the moose lay.

Grandma acted as the butcher. She carefully sliced the meat into long, narrow strips. The men built a rack of poles to hang the meat on. When the meat was dry, the hide of the moose was placed over a smooth flat rock, and with the use of a mallet, the meat was pounded into powder.

The bones of the moose were cut into small pieces and boiled to make grease. The powdered meat was put into this and boiled, and the mixture was then poured into a basket made of birchbark, and covered with a weight placed on top. In about six hours, the liquid was squeezed out. The white men called this pemmican. The Indians called it *pec-a-mee-ika-gon*. It has been claimed that it could be kept for ten years without spoiling, and it was light and easy to carry.

The bladder of the moose was cleaned and filled with oil for use when needed. A bone was used as a spout so that the oil would not spill. A thigh-bone from either a pelican or goose made a good spout. This was also handy for carrying, as it was not breakable.

It wasn't long before another moose was killed. This time the kill had taken place far from the river. The men had the tough job of packing the meat on their backs to where the camp was.

Four or five days later we would make another move. This time we stopped at the fork of the Bloodvein and Gammon Rivers. It was near the end of September. Grandfather went hunting again but killed only three bears. Again the meat and skins were carried in packs down to camp by his sons. The meat was processed in the same way as the moose.

It was here that grandfather speared seven beautiful sturgeon. The spear he used was made of bone which apparently had been left by other trappers. Grandma would have the task of filleting and drying them. The oil from the sturgeon was kept in the birchbark containers. It was good for patching the canoes, acting as a glue. Another way of getting glue was from the navel of a squirrel. It stuck well and was most useful.

Soon we went to Whiterock Lake on the Gammon River, and then had a day's portage of one and a half miles over rough and rocky ground to South Eagle Lake. From there we moved to North Eagle Lake to gather wild rice.

Every September we harvested the wild rice, filling many bags. It was dumped into a cache made of rocks placed in a circular shape like a big nest. Birchbark was placed on the bottom, then the rice poured in and covered with another layer of birchbark. A weight was placed on top so that wild animals could not destroy it. More rice was harvested which was placed in bags and carried with us for food. Whenever we ran out, we would go back to this cache for more.

The rice was processed by digging a hole in clay about two feet deep. Leather made from moosehide was placed in the hole and the rice poured on to it. Another piece of leather covered the rice and then someone danced on it, which separated the straw from the kernels. Even I was old enough to help with this.

By the time we left the rice fields it was near the end of October. We moved back towards White Rock Lake and camp was set up on a jack pine ridge. We chose to camp there because rabbits were plentiful for winter food. Grandfather and the two uncles would trap. By this time there was a lot of snow, which often had to be dug away with our snowshoes so that we could put up our wigwam. It was also quite cold now and wood was needed, which grandmother cut everyday.

Our supplies would be getting quite low by this time. The Hudson's Bay Company used to send a man out to supply those on the traplines. There was never any trouble finding the trappers because each one let the Company know ahead at what location he would be camped. If he had to move, he would tell a neighbouring trapper where he would be.

The supplies were bought with furs; there was never any cash involved. I liked the system of trading without cash because we always seemed to have something to eat without having to manage money.

During the winter we camped in many different places, but when spring came we made our way towards Lake Winnipeg, hunting as we went. When we arrived at the Bloodvein settlement our furs were sold to the HBC. This was our winter lifestyle. In summer my grandfather fished for sturgeon and sold it to old Louie Seymour at Bloodvein,

In the winter of 1903 my uncle John Skye took very ill and died at Muskeg Bluff. We had to leave his body where it was and walk to Hole River Reserve. There we told what had happened, and a Mr. Black and Mr. John Moneyas went by dog team to pick up the body. Grandfather told them to leave the wigwam since he thought we would return later. We never did. Grandmother did not want to see the place again.

After I started trapping I went looking for the place where the wigwam was left. This was about 1948. The wigwam had collapsed but the birchbark was still there.

Soon grandfather was too old to hunt any more. He spent his time fishing on the lake and trapping near home at Bloodvein. When I was about seven years old he and three other men went for supplies at East Doghead. On the way back grandfather fell through the ice and could not be saved. He drowned right there.

I had no idea how tough life was going to be for grandma and me from now on. There was no one to look after us, and in those days Indians had very little help from the government. Our monthly rations consisted of fifteen pounds of flour, five pounds of pork, and ½ lb. of tea. I knew we were going to be poor.

There is nobody now living in the present generation who has tasted such hardships.

Medicine Dance

The Medicine Dance, Mitewiwin (pronounced *me tay we win*), has been a revered ritual among the Indians for centuries. This is held only rarely these days, if at all. The last site in Manitoba where these ceremonies took place that I know of was at what is now known as Drumming Point, at the northern end of Black Island on Lake Winnipeg. I was fortunate to live close by so was able to attend, and take part as a servant. The head medicine man was David Black whose Indian name was Kakeivepit.

Mitewiwin was held annually during the early summer months, long before modern civilization. This special occasion was basically a healing one, new medicine men were ordained at this time who would then be given the power to heal the sick. But, like everything else, the ceremony has changed through the years.

The event lasted eight days, from sunrise to sunset. There was much preparation. A special shelter was erected, facing east and covered with birchbark. It was about 48 feet long and 12 feet wide. Another enclosure was built close by, of the same length and six feet high, but without a roof. It was in here that the actual ceremonies were conducted.

In the centre of this second enclosure was a big square pillar and a large boulder. This was the place of honour, where the head medicine man sat. He was dressed in buckskin and was the most important individual in the ritual. On top of the square pillar was a carved kingfisher, which also faced east. This bird would revolve with the sun as it moved from east to west. I could never find out how this bird revolved, but it seemed to turn automatically.

NO ONE WAS ALLOWED on these sacred premises at night. The Indians were warned against entering after sunset lest something very dreadful befall them.

One story was told about a man called Peter Bird and a woman named Mary Irving, who did not heed this warning. They wanted to see for themselves whether anything would happen to them. They entered the premises when they thought everyone had retired for the night. To their dismay, both fell to the ground and were unable to get up. Their arms and legs became weak, and they could not walk.

The head medicine man rescued them. He rubbed their arms and legs with black earth which he took from the ground. Only then were they able to get up and leave, to their consternation and shame. It was a lesson to all those in attendance, who now would not dare to come close to the area after sunset.

THERE WERE MEDICINE MEN on other Indian reserves, such as Jackhead, Bloodvein River, Fort Alexander and Scanterbury. When the time came, it was always the head medicine man who decided in which area the Medicine Dance would be held.

He would send his servants to the other reserves to pick up their head medicine men. The usual practice was to send birchbark canoes, three persons in each, and to command them to be back on a certain date. There was never any worry about the canoes encountering storms because, as curious as it may seem, those canoes always returned at the appointed time. The weather remained calm during their absence. Those responsible had much faith and prayed for their guests' safe arrival.

Undoubtedly, it will be hard for some to believe what the rest of my story will bring, but having been an eyewitness to one of these rituals; I will tell everything exactly as it happened.

Though it was not supposed to rain or blow while the Medicine Dance lasted, we once had an unusual experience with the weather. I recall one morning while the dance was beginning, that the sky grew overcast and it began to rain. The head medicine man said that this was very strange.

He had in his possession a small bag containing some substance unknown to us. He told the people that it had been promised to him that if it should ever rain during a medicine dance, all he had to do was to open this bag. This he did and immediately the rain stopped. Within ten minutes we started to see blue sky and within half an hour, there was not a cloud to be seen.

What I experienced that morning was shared by many, including our storekeeper, Mr. George Leyond, who was a whiteman.

MANY PEOPLE ATTENDED THE Mitewiwin, either because they believed in it, or were perhaps simply curious. Caribou were killed so there would be meat for all. No one was allowed to take this meat home; it had to be eaten there.

THE MEDICINE DANCE WAS performed for the benefit of the people, to keep them healthy, and to cure the sick. Very long ago, children were eaten as a sacrifice to the Great Spirit. In exchange for such a supreme gift, the parents of such children would be given the knowledge of medicine. With the advent of civilization, medicine men sacrificed dogs instead. During my time, if a dog should enter the area where the Dance was taking place, one of the servants would immediately kill it and it would be cooked and eaten; such a dog symbolized a bear. In return for the loss of his dog, the owner would be given enough medicine to cure any illness he or his family may have had.

Much of the ceremony for the new medicine men was secret, and those wishing to become ordained had to progress through four levels or degrees of initiation. Usually, the head medicine man's son was given the powers of healing when the father got too old. The candidates partook in various rituals with the head medicine man. A special spot was selected, one which had at least four or five different herbs growing on it. When this place had been chosen, an enclosure was built around it. The head medicine man would pray to the Great Spirit (Manitou), imploring him to reveal which illnesses could be cured from the roots of these herbs.

The healing properties of such roots were fantastic. Medicine men would travel far each year in search of specific herbs for curing certain illnesses. They were always careful to place tobacco where they pulled the roots out. This was important in order to appease the spirits.

AT THE TIME APPOINTED for healing, the servants of the medicine men would stand in a circle around the head. A servant was appointed to bring in the sick, one by one. The afflicted person would bring an offering to the medicine man of his choice, very much as in modern times when a person has the right to choose his own doctor.

One of the servants had a special drum for these rituals. The head medicine man would sing a drum song, and every time he changed from one song to another, the servant would hit the drum four times. This was repeated each time a sick person was brought in to be treated.

When all had been brought in and had chosen their doctors, the head man would arise, go to the post, and ask Manitou to give these Indian doctors the power to cure the people. Objects and animals were venerated because the Indian always saw Manitou in everything He has created.

The head medicine man would then lead a procession with each patient carrying a cut plug of tobacco, one inch square, which was placed on the boulder as payment.

A row of stones, placed from smallest to largest, was often used to aid the medicine man. These formed snakes of various lengths. The sick person was laid beside the snake, which would then begin to move. Often, this resulted in a cure. The stones also sometimes became turtles.

The rows of rocks, and those which formed snakes and turtles would move while the Medicine Dance was in progress. At the end of one row of stones, four rocks were placed to form a square. When the dancers came to the square, they would dance around it, making strange guttural sounds.

If a person was dangerously ill, he was taken to a special tent, called the Shaking Tent, and laid in the centre of it. The medicine man would call upon the spirits to send a specific animal to their aid. This was done by what we called conjuring. I have seen the head medicine man going into the tent to ask Manitou to help him find the animal needed to cure the sick person. When he knew, a hunter would be sent for that particular animal. The pelt was sprinkled with medicine, and rubbed on the naked body of the patient, and as surely as the sun rises on the horizon, the sick person was cured.

I remember when old Mr. Whitesand was lost in the bush. The head medicine man called upon Mr. Thickfoot, or Ga-Kap-A-Kisit, who had a pet bear, to go in search of Mr. Whitesand. The bear went ahead just the way a dog would be used. It wasn't long before the search party returned with Mr. Whitesand.

These men had great faith in their medicine—so great that they were actually able to make animals and even pelts do whatever they wanted them to do. It was fantastic. I believe strongly that if a person wants to be healed he can be with a strong faith. I have always felt that the reason why our Indian medicine men had such great powers was because our people had a strong faith.

WHEN THE CEREMONIES WERE over, the medicine men and those sick people who were now restored to health, proceeded to dance around the leaf enclosure where the rituals had taken place, and then to the original birchbark tent. This dance would last all night.

Those who could, sang the drum songs while they danced. These people were given the one-inch squares of tobacco which had been placed on the boulder, and also received more tobacco at the other tent if they sang and danced there. This was payment for their extra exertions.

The participants in these dances were usually given a steam bath, called *matotawin*. A small tent, about five by five feet and big enough for two people, would be erected. Stones were put into a fire to heat, and then dropped into a pan or pail half filled with water, which produced enough steam for the people in the tent.

While the dance was going on in the open enclosure, it was amazing to see the medicine men pick up live embers from the four bonfires which were burning. Using some powdery substance which they rubbed on their hands, they would hold those live embers and blow on them to keep them aflame all the while they were dancing around the circle.

I remember Kakeivepit would also rub the powder in his mouth and hold a live coal there while he was dancing. People had to witness these performances to believe they actually happened.

THERE WERE MANY LOCATIONS besides Black Island where the Mitewiwin was held. These included Kenora, Lac Seul and the Whiteshell. I urge those of you who have the opportunity, to visit one of these areas. Approximately one-half mile east of the Whiteshell River there is a sign which tells of this sacred place. You will still see some of the rocks that represented snakes and turtles. No doubt most of the visitors to this place will be wondering what it all means.

It has been observed that prairie chickens hold a dance which is similar to our Medicine Dance. I have witnessed such a dance myself, about 300 to 400 feet from the shore of the Gammon River, known as the Long Stretch, where they congregate for four to six days. I have not been there to watch for some years, but I am sure I could still find the area.

—*1979*

James Redsky (Esquekesik)
Anishinaabe (Shoal Lake) 1899–?

James Redsky was born and raised in the Shoal Lake area of Manitoba. He began his studies at a missionary school at the age of four and continued until he enlisted as a soldier in World War I in 1915. He fought in some of the most horrific battles of the Great War and returned home to dedicate himself to his community. Studying under his uncle Baldhead Redsky, James learned the stories, ceremonies, and other cultural practices connected with the Medéwiwin spiritual tradition of his people. He became widely known as a master of the Medéwiwin tradition, and became a custodian of eight ancient and sacred birchbark scrolls containing historical information, cultural stories, and ceremonies. In 1960 he was ordained an elder in the Presbyterian Church but this did not conflict with his Midé beliefs. Throughout his life Redsky maintained his knowledge and practise of Medéwewin traditions despite the Canadian government's many attempts to destroy Aboriginal spiritual practices. In his early seventies he published a collection of stories entitled *Great Leader of the Ojibway: Mis-quona-queb* (1972). Edited by anthropologist James R. Stevens, the book recounts in English many of the stories and insights that James had learned from his uncle Baldhead Redsky and retells narratives from the birchbark scrolls he inherited.

The first of two excerpts from *Mis-quona-queb*, "Eagle Feather," is a story about a legendary hero of the Shoal Lake Anishinaabe named Mis-quona-queb (probably an actual warrior from a period several generations before Redsky) and a young and courageous woman named Pennisk ("Eagle Feather"). It also illustrates some of the many confrontations that took place between the traditional enemies, the Anishinaabeg and the Sioux in Manitoba. The second story, "The Creation of Man," is based upon creation narratives of the Anishinaabeg found on Redsky's birchbark scrolls, and tells a small part of the vast intellectual knowledge described in those ancient texts.

Eagle Feather

When I was a young boy there was an old old woman with hair white like the snow of winter who lived on Silver Fox Island. Her name was Eagle Feather, or Pennisk in our language, and many stories were told about her bravery and beauty in the moons of her youth. I remember one story well; it goes this way.

Now the Ojibways never fought just for the pleasure of it. If our men went off to fight it was either for protection or revenge.

One time the Sioux raided an Ojibway village and took away some small children. Mis-quona-queb came to this village and he selected a beautiful Ojibway girl named Eagle Feather to go on the war party against the Sioux.

Pennisk was to be used as sexual bait for the Sioux. This beautiful young woman could speak the Siouan language because she had been captured by the Sioux as a young child and had lived with them for many seasons. When she travelled with the Ojibways she did not sleep with the men because it would take away from her power and she was a very fine woman.

After a trek of three days to the grassy lands, a large camp of Sioux was discovered at a place just east of what is now Portage la Prairie. Mis-quona-queb wanted to find out where the Sioux had taken the children, so Pennisk was sent into the Sioux camp under the darkness of the night sky. In the camp she saw one of the missing children. Pennisk bid the child to come to her and she told him to get the other children and walk quietly off to the east.

"Go straight east and don't zig-zag," Pennisk said, "and you will find your parents."

Then she searched for the teepee of the Sioux chief. Lifting the flap of the tent she saw the painted chief sitting there smoking his pipe. Quickly, Eagle Feather took out her leather bag which was full of round white pebbles. As she slipped back to the waiting Ojibway war party, Pennisk dropped the pebbles with every step leaving a well marked trail behind her. When she reached the Ojibway warriors she asked, "Have the children arrived yet?"

"Yes, they are here."

Mis-quona-queb told his men he would enter the Sioux camp and only one person need accompany him, the maiden Pennisk. Pennisk told Mis-quona-queb, "Just follow my white pebbles. They will lead you right to the chief's teepee. I will be following behind you."

Mis-quona-queb walked ahead of the beautiful woman, following the pebble trail to the Sioux chieftain's tent. In one quick movement Mis-quona-queb raised the buffalo skin flap and shot the chief in the chest, killing him.

When the Sioux people heard the shot, wild screams and howling resounded through their encampment. But Mis-quona-queb was a powerful man. He did not run away; it would have been a terrible thing for a head man to run away.

All of the Sioux warriors ran up to the chief's tent to discover Mis-quona-queb and Pennisk standing there. When they lifted the tent flap, they saw their fallen chief lying in his own blood.

The Sioux screamed angrily: "Kill him! Kill him!"

Then Pennisk spoke to the Sioux warriors. Her soft voice was entrancing. All the Sioux listened carefully to her words.

"Do not kill him," she said. "He is of no consequence to the Ojibways. The reason I ask for his life is that he is a half-brother of mine. Spare him and I will remain in your camp as a hostage."

Then she showed the men her body by removing her buck skins and the Sioux were entranced by her beauty. Meanwhile, Mis-quona-queb walked silently off to his warriors.

The next morning, Pennisk escaped and returned to the Ojibways.

There was another time Pennisk went with an Ojibway war party of about six hundred braves. There was an advance party of one hundred, a main party of four hundred and a rear guard of one hundred. They were all experienced warriors. The first night on the march they slept at Paskadipewisipeng, near Hadashville, Manitoba. When daylight appeared the men were whooping and hollering; they were anxious to meet the Sioux. The advance group went about a mile ahead, then the main party, and the rear guard marched about a mile behind the main fighting force. Mis-quona-queb and his leaders were with the advance party.

Pennisk had left before daylight; she was about five miles ahead of the main body of warriors. When she reached a place called Asadi Minaquang, or Poplar Grove, she looked out on the prairies and saw smoke rising into the sky about six miles away. She waited and could finally distinguish the movements of men coming toward her. When she was certain of what she saw, she raced back to warn the advance party that a large group of Sioux were coming straight toward them. When Mis-quona-queb learned of this he ordered the advance stopped. He sent Pennisk to the rear guard to tell them to halt and prepare an ambush. Mis-quona-queb went on with the advance party to the place where Pennisk had seen the Sioux. Hiding in the shrub bluffs at the edge of the prairies, Mis-quona-queb could not believe the sight in his eyes—there were great masses of Sioux right in front of them.

When the Sioux got closer, Mis-quona-queb went with four of his men to greet the Sioux chief, who sat proudly on his horse. The Sioux chief raised his stick as was the custom when one wanted to talk in a friendly manner. At the instant the Sioux chief was going to light from his horse one of Mis-quona-queb's men shot him in the chest with an arrow. It was accomplished so quickly and accurately that no one noticed where the arrow had come from. The Sioux chief fell to the ground in a heap—dead! When the Sioux saw their chief was dead some of them started to run away but the advance Ojibway party attacked and slew some of them. But by the time the main party arrived the Sioux had all fled. Some of the Ojibways gave chase but they could not catch them.

She was a great Ojibway, this Pennisk. They say she lived to be one hundred and twenty years old.

The Creation of Man

Now God thought He would make a human being. He spat on the ground and then picked up wet clay from the ground and held it in His fist until it became very warm. After a while, He opened his hand and there stood an Anishinabi.

God blew His breath on the Anishinabi and set him down on the ground. The Anishinabi stood there, made in the likeness of God. He measured the Anishinabi's height, twelve hands. The human's eyes were brown, the colour of clay, and they gleamed in the rays of the sun. The Anishinabi was stalwart and heavily built. He breathed strongly.

God spoke to him: "*Ke mi no a ya na*. Are you all right?"

The Anishinabi did not respond right away. When he spoke fire came out of his mouth and he said: "*Ke kit*. That's right."

Then God placed His hand on his head because he was too godly. He did not want the Anishinabi to have the power to go above Him, because then nothing in the world would work right. Then God saw a great shadow go over the man. This represented the many sins and mistakes that the Anishinabi would soon make.

God began to talk to His creation and He taught him every important thing in order to lead a good life. If the Anishinabi was going to live the wrong way in life he would lead the millions that would come after him the wrong way.

Immediately after this God told him: "Go now and find your wisdom and knowledge. I am sorry I cannot lead you all the time but I will watch over you at all times. When you are in trouble, just call upon Me and I will hear you.

"If you think I am not listening just go outside your home; wherever you look you will find Me because everything is My creation. And everything listens to Me: the trees and the grass; the air and the birds in the air; the earth and the creatures of the earth. Everything is so sensitive I can call them and I can place my ears on them and hear them.

"If I say to that hill: 'Move!' you will not see it the next day. If I say to the rough waters: 'Calm!' they will do so immediately. I have the power and the words in this scroll are My power. He that believes not My words should have his ears cut off and thrown into the deepest part of the lake to rest there, where nothing is heard, because his ears are useless unless attached to his head.

"Now, at this time, I am giving you a name. You will be called Okupeosadung, or Walker, because you will be walking day after day."

Then God took Okupeosadung down to a little creek and bathed him until he was absolutely clean. Then He let Okupeosadung go.

Then Okupeosadung started walking to explore the earth. As he walked along he saw a woodpecker climbing and pecking a tree to see if it was hollow. If the tree was hollow, then it was time for the woodpecker to give itself a headache by putting a hole in the tree to see if there were any grubs there to fill its little stomach. Now and then Okupeosadung would scare up a squirrel that would get annoyed until he walked away.

One day when he was eating handfuls of berries he sat down and saw a little snake. Just above him qui-qui-shee, the whisky-jack, sat. Okupeosadung stared at it until it flew away. Okupeosadung exclaimed: "*Uguchi. Kawin inundawenimigosi chi ka na wa pa mug.* Ashamed. He didn't want me to look at him."

Day after day he walked over the beautiful fields, beside the lakes and rivers.

—*1972*

Albert Edward Thompson

Cree/Saulteaux (St. Peter's Reserve/Peguis First Nation) 1900–1973

Chief Albert Edward Thompson was a great, great-grandson of Chief Peguis and was born in 1900 at St. Peter's Reserve. Educated on-reserve and at Elkhorn Industrial School, Thompson took an interest in politics from a very young age, having witnessed the removal of his community from St. Peter's to their current lands at Peguis First Nation in Manitoba's Interlake. When he was in his 50s, he was elected councillor and, later, chief at Peguis Reserve, a position he held until his death in 1973. Thompson was seminal in establishing the Manitoba Indian Brotherhood and was the organization's first president. He was known as a historian and storyteller, two skills that led him to write about the history of his community in *Chief Peguis and His Descendants* (1973).

The most influential event in Thompson's life was the St. Peter's removal. Having signed Treaty One in 1871, members of the St. Peter's Indian Reserve believed that their claims to their homeland on the banks of the Red River near Selkirk, Manitoba, would be protected. Land-hungry settlers and government agents, however, conspired to remove them from this rich and fertile soil. On September 23, 1907, officials arrived to hold a land "surrender" vote. Through bribery, whisky, and trickery, the illegal vote passed, and St. Peter's residents were ordered to move to Peguis Indian Reserve, a northern swampy area that was inadequate for farming, unsustainable for hunting, and prone to flooding. Some refused to leave, squatting on lands that were once their homes. Today, many continue to live in what is now the city of Selkirk. Named by one historian as Manitoba's example of "ethnic cleansing," Chief Albert Edward Thompson documents this brutal process here. In 1998, the Government of Canada acknowledged that the St. Peter's removal was illegal, and, in 2008, ancestors of the removal were paid $126 million in compensation.

From *Chief Peguis and His Descendants*

Many of the Indians protested. They declared that they had only been made aware of the proposal when four posters appeared on various buildings in town two days before the meeting was to be held. These read:

> To the St. Peter's Band of Indians—Take notice, that a meeting of the male members of this Band of the full age of twenty-one (21) years, will be held at the Treaty grounds of this Reserve on Monday the 23rd day of September 1907 at 11 o'clock a.m. for the purpose of considering, deciding, and assenting to the release and surrender of St. Peter's Indian Reserve on the terms to be set forth at this meeting. (signed) Chief William Prince.

It was utterly impossible for all the residents of the Reserve to be made aware of this meeting. Many men were miles away hunting. Many others could not read the notice, which was written in English and not Cree.

The meeting was held in a schoolhouse too small to hold the 200 men who turned out. This made it necessary for those within the building to make known the progress of the meeting through the open window to those standing outside.

Eye-witness accounts were given by various respected men of the community whose knowledge of English was perfect. One of the most intelligent letters was written to Ottawa by William Asham, a former Chief of the Band. Briefly he says—

The meeting was held in an old school-house on the Reserve, too small to hold more than half of those present. Those present representing the Government were Chief Justice Howell, Frank Pedley, Deputy Superintendent General of Indian Affairs, S. J. Jackson, M.P., E. Rayner of Selkirk, John Semmons, Inspector of Indian Agencies, J.O. Lewis, Indian Agent, and Dr. Grain.

When the meeting was called to order, Frank Pedley was selected to take the Chair, and I was called in from outside and requested by one of the gentlemen to act as Interpreter. This I declined to do stating I wanted a free hand, but William Henry Prince, one of the Councillors, acted as Interpreter and interpreted parts of the proceedings.

Mr. Pedley started to explain the condition of the surrender informing the meeting that he was sent by the Government to arrange for the surrender of the Reserve. Mr. Pedley explained to the meeting what the Government was willing to do if we would agree to surrender the Reserve. One proposition he made was that the Chief would receive 180 acres of land and each Councillor 120, and each Indian receive only 16 acres of land. I immediately demanded the reason why the Chief and Councillors should receive more land than the ordinary Indian. Mr. Pedley replied that they were getting the extra land for their recognition. I then stated the only recognition they had was the coat they wore and the extra money they receive annually. I also stated that they were not entitled to one acre more land than the ordinary Indian would receive but as the agreement of surrender was already prepared there was no change made at the time.

I further declared that at least two-thirds of the Indians present did not understand the conditions as stated by Mr. Pedley. I, understanding English, did most of the talking against the surrender of the Reserve and after talking several hours back and forward I demanded a vote to be taken. At this time there was no question that a large majority of the Band that were present were against the surrender, and expressed themselves loudly at times to this effect. Mr. Pedley and the Council and others interested refused to allow the vote to be taken that night and the meeting was adjourned until ten o'clock the next day at the same place.

William Asham's long letter continued to describe what took place the following day at the little school-house:

I was surprised to find that some of those who had supported me strongly against the surrender the day before had been changed during the night. What caused this change God only knows, I don't. We adjourned for lunch after a good deal of talking, and Mr. W.D. Harper, Councillor, asked me to have lunch with him at his home.

Mr. Harper was the son-in-law of the late Chief Henry Prince.

After lunch sitting in the school with the others Harper slipped a piece of paper into my hand with the following words written in lead pencil by himself to the effect "What would you think if you were to be made equal to a Councillor?" meaning of course that I would get as much land as a Councillor if I would agree to the surrender. I stated that I could not possibly agree. Before going into lunch, James Williams Councillor, came up to me and giving me a nudge whispered, "Go and see Chief Justice Howell. I replied "No, I will not go near him."

A moment later Asham was approached by the Member of Parliament S.J. Jackson, who drew the former Chief, William Asham, aside.

"Mr. Asham, you are strongly opposed to the surrender."

"Yes."

"What would you think if we were to make you equal with the Council? I will promise to get you a patent for the land within six weeks."

Asham rejected the offer:

I declared that if I had agreed I would have felt that I would be accepting a bribe to desert my friends who were protesting against the surrender. Now, soon after this, we were in the heat of a hot discussion in the matter regarding the surrender. Mr. Pedley during his speech at this time said "I have $5000 here," pointing to a satchel at his side. "If you agree to this surrender this money will be distributed among you, but if you don't agree to the surrender, I will take my satchel and go home and you won't get a cent." Then we were told the time had come to take a vote. Up to this time fully half of the Band present had not been able to get into the building and did not hear what had taken place. The building being too small to take the vote in, we were asked to go outside. Then Mr. John Semmons, the inspector of Indian agencies, spoke loudly in Cree saying—"All you that want $90 go to this side"—indicating where the Chief and Councillors were standing. "The others go to the opposite side." The crowd separated not knowing what they were doing. After they were separated some of them moved from one side to the other. Mr. Semmons and myself started to count the votes that were against but when we got through counting we turned around to count the other side. I was told then that the other side had been counted. I did not know who counted the other side, and they claimed they had a majority of seven. I was astonished to hear this, and sized up the two sides and satisfied myself that there were a larger number standing on my side (opposers) than there was with the Chief and Councillors, but I had no opportunity whatever of counting the number that stood by the Chief and Councillors. I protested to Mr. Semmons, saying that he should not have said "You who want the $90 go on one side" but you should have said "you that want to surrender the Reserve go to one side, and you that don't want to surrender the Reserve go to the other side," then the people would have understood what they were voting for.

William Asham declared the vote irregular, and objected to the fact that when Mr. Pedley read the surrender it was in English and too fast, and that even he who knew English well found it difficult to understand the terms of the surrender:

> This was not interpreted to the Band in their own language, consequently few, if any, understood the conditions of the surrender. I am satisfied that Mr. Pedley and the others came determined to secure the surrender. It was all prepared without any consultation with the Band, they brought the $5000 with them. Without this money on the ground I am satisfied that never could they have secured the support they did in favour of the surrender.
>
> Immediately after the vote was taken the treaty was signed, and they commenced paying the money out… I have never ceased to protest against what I consider to be an outrage and the disinheriting of the Indians and sacrificing my birthright.
>
> And I make this solemn declaration conscientiously believing it to be true and knowing it to be of the same force and effect as if made under oath and by virtue of the Canada Evidence Act.

When the stunned opposers to the surrender realized what had taken place gloom and depression settled on the homeless people. The educated Indians who understood the full implications of the matter, placed their grievances before G.H. Bradbury, Member of Parliament for the area. Armed with sworn statements and proof of trickery and bribery by Government officials and land-sharks, Mr. Bradbury spent two days in the House in Ottawa laying bare this miserable act of broken faith before the Government.

Four men were chiefly implicated in this fraudulent acquisition of Reserve lands, acquired at $2 per acre, and which they frequently sold for $20. No Government action was ever taken to rescind this illegal purchase of Indian Reserve land. No effort was made to adjust the low prices paid to the Indians.

After the surrender was made the people had to move north one hundred miles to where the Fisher River empties into Lake Winnipeg. Unlike long-established St. Peter's Parish there were no houses here, no broken land, neither school nor church.

After the signing of the surrender of St. Peter's Reserve on September 24, 1907, the Dominion Lands Surveyors through the Chief Engineer, Mr. McLean, supervisor, made preparations to survey our new Reserve to be called Peguis, and the people began to move from St. Peter's in 1909.

—1973

Thomas Boulanger

Cree (Oxford House) 1901–?

Tom Boulanger was a fur trader whose father died when he was 16. Alongside his brother, he was taken in by a minister and raised as a Protestant. He later moved to Berens River where he married his wife (Virginia McKay) in 1925 and spent his entire life on the land, trapping and fishing in northern Manitoba.

In 1971, Boulanger contacted Adam Cuthand of Peguis Publishers and presented him, in a hotel room, with a stack of papers "bound by fish cord." Among the papers were Boulanger's firsthand recollections, experiences, and stories about the changes he experienced as a fur trader in northern Manitoba during the 1920s and 1930s. The collection eventually became *An Indian Remembers: My Life as a Trapper in Northern Manitoba.* These excerpts, in Boulanger's unique writing style, describe his child's birth, his encounter with aircraft pilots who had crashed, and his detailed knowledge of animals. While this was, unquestionably, a time period marked by constant change, Boulanger's faith and good nature allow him to describe a rich and interesting life in Manitoba's north.

From *An Indian Remembers: My Life as a Trapper in Northern Manitoba*

I was married in 1925 in Berens River. I had a very wonderful time having a partner in trapping, always going with me every year. I always had a lot of fur.

Two years after I am going to tell you news. I never made my life exciting. We went up to a trapping ground named Charron Lake. When I was going up again to trap in the winter, I didn't know my wife was going to have a baby. We tried to come back to Berens River. We used a dog team. We started at the first of February. At the first of February we couldn't go because there was a big snowstorm. The only thing I did that day was, I put on my big snowshoes and tried to break the road about fifteen miles away. The next day we started home with a team of dogs. We made up to fifteen miles that day where I made the road, and there we made a camp. We had a little stove just about right in the cold weather.

It was about ten o'clock my wife started to be sick that night. Then we didn't know what to do. We were excited. Then I spread my fur all over in the tent and chopped up a lot of wood. When I was working outside I heard a baby crying. Then I went inside and my wife had a baby. Good thing I had everything. We had milk and things to use for the baby. After awhile we fixed the baby I went back to the old shack where we were before. I knew a trapper close by. Before I went to the old shack, I put a lot of wood in the tent where my wife could reach to keep on putting wood in the stove. I went away about three hours.

When I went in the old shack, I only saw a woman named Mrs. Pascal whom we knew. She gave me a cup of tea. Mr. Pascal was not home for he went to see his traps early in the morning. Mrs. Pascal told me that they would be behind, and to go and see my wife with the dogs. Finally I came back again to see my wife. I had a good snowshoe running that time. I met my wife again. She was all right with the baby too. That afternoon Mr. and Mrs. Pascal came to our tent with their dogs. Mr. Pascal made his camp beside our camp and he told me we had to stay a week at the same place so my wife could have a rest.

A week time I decided to go back at my trapping grounds where my old shack was. I made a sleigh carriole where I can take my wife back. We didn't have any cradle. Mr. Pascal told me that he was going to carry the baby himself. So he tied the baby in a big snowshoe and carried him on his back.

The baby's name was Wilson Boulanger. So we were glad to have a baby that time. We stayed there till open water. Later we came home to Berens River after trapping by a canoe trip.

When we returned to Berens River, we had a big time joining the old people, my wife's father and mother, Mr. and Mrs. J.J. McKay. This news is from 1931, the year Wilson was born on the second of February.

That's all the child I got in my life. My wife had an operation after awhile. So I now have a lot of grandchildren. Eleven all together; six girls and five boys. Wilson is quite busy to keep going. I was with Wilson on my trapping ground when he was sixteen years old, hunting. He killed a moose medium, about a quarter mile away in a bush. He also killed quite a few of fur that time.

We made an average about two thousand dollars worth of fur. It's a very good experience of hunting if a man knows what to do.

That time in 1932 I was trapping again. I was trapping on the north side of Charron Lake. It was freeze-up. The company's name was Canadian Airways. One day as we were coming home to our shack, across the lake walking, we seen two islands on fire. Then I saw two men walking on the east side of the shore. I thought it was game wardens from Ontario because the Ontario boundary is not far from there (about six miles), but it was not them. That was Old Canadian Airways two men.

Then I went to meet them. First they spoke to me if I can talk English myself. I said, "Yes, a little." They told me they landed on the lake just about dark. The ice was three or four inches thick in the lake. They were very heavy loaded. The engine was going down on the water. The wings just hanged it up on the ice, but these two men didn't drown. They saved themselves by making a fire in the bush all night. When I met them they asked me if I could save them, and I told them to go back where they made the fire and wait for me there. They had nothing to eat. They were supposed to be going to Island Lake, but it was too late to go that's why they landed.

I went home to my shack and I told my wife to clean up one little extra shack I had. We put a camp stove there and a little wood bed. It's a good thing I had a lot of grub at that time. So after while I bring them to my home. Then I fed them. I kept them about a week. They were watching every day for other planes to fly around. No sign. There were no radios that time or no sending wires, that's why they were waiting so long.

One morning they asked me I wonder if I can take them to little Grand Rapids to try to reach the company over there. So I didn't have much power, I only got three dogs. Another fellow I knew had three dogs near the place. I went to ask him to help me move these fellows. He promised he could help me. Then I told these men I could help them with the trip. Three dogs were pulling one sleigh and the other three were pulling another sleigh; six altogether. That's all I got. I told these men I was sorry they can't stay on a sleigh they have to themselves. Mostly the dogs carry dog food, bedding and our grub.

Charron Lake to Little Grand Rapids is about sixty miles. We travelled about four days. It was a very hard and slow trip. It was a very rough muskeg when we were travelling. The men were very tired at night. So we made it all right. As soon as we were in Little Grand Rapids we seen a big plane circling around on the south side of the lake. They were looking for the men. The pilot was glad to find them alive.

We stopped at the Hudson's Bay that night. The manager was Johnny Moore. That time a few days before Christmas it's the time they found them. Next morning the pilot took them home. These two men that were lost were the names John Foster from Labrador, engineer; the other one's name was McCluray from Winnipeg.

I went back home with another fellow. The pilot said to me we will go and see our boss about the plane that is hanging on the ice. So I waited and waited. They never bothered to save it. I think it is the plane insurance, that's why they never bothered with it. So when it was open water it sunk down. I should of save the plane to be a salvage with it. So I never bothered with it. I thought they were going to pick it up.

· · ·

I am putting a story about my mother. Before my mother died she told me a story about her life, about a dream she had. She saw in this dream one night a gentleman dressed in green standing in front of a large house at the south side where the door was. He called to her and opened the door and said, "Come into the house." He gave her a place to sit and when she looked around inside the house she saw all kinds of shelves filled with wild roots and medicines and he spoke and said, "My friend, on each side of the wall are medicines. Which will you choose. On the right are medicines that can save your people and on the left side are ones that do evil." She said, "I will take only the ones that can help my people." The man was pleased and took my mother by hand and put it in his and walked over to the right side where the good medicines were and showed her the many secrets.

When my mother woke from this dream she could remember all the words the man had spoken and the many medicines and roots she had seen. Many sick people were cured by the medicines that she had learned in the dream, and when she was old and passed these secrets on to her children that they may not be lost. Before she awoke the man told her don't give the medicines away for nothing, to give her something to eat first or little clothing, but no money. That's what she dreamed I think. I believe myself of God's Blessings helping different kind of people in different ways. That's all the news for my mother what she dreamed.

. . .

Here's another news from trapping and hunting in my life. My age is sixty-seven years old now. I have been hunting and trapping for fifty-one years. I am going to talk about big animals such as deer and moose. The first thing I am going to talk about is the moose. The easiest way to kill a moose in the summer time is sometime you would see him swim across in the water. In the middle of the summer time when there is a lot of flies, hot days, in evenings, early in the morning, that's the time he comes in the river and lake shores, coming to drink. He also comes and washes himself, because flies bother him much. That's what they do every day. That's why it's easy for the people to see him when they're hunting. The deer is almost the same.

In the winter time the moose is different when you're hunting for him. He's quite experienced and when you track the moose he knows you from a long distance, because there are no flies to bother him in the winter. When you track the moose in the winter time you have to step quietly and you have to pick up high places where you can see him good. Before he runs away you have to be quick and shoot him. If you're a good hunter you'll be happy lots of times and cow-moose is the best meat to eat in the winter time because its good meat.

The easiest way to skin a moose in the winter time, if its about two or three feet of snow and its quite heavy to try and skin a moose, what I do myself alone is I dig one side of the snow away, where the moose would lay down, then I turn it over easy and when its laying upside down, then I tie up the legs on trees and I got a good chance now to skin him. You have to have a sharp knife to skin him. After you cut him to pieces and lay down the meat good and you shove the meat into the snow about four inches thick. You put brush on top. After you put the brush then you put a big pile of snow on the top. Then you go home for a few days and then the rabbits don't bother it. But if you want to leave the meat for a long time you have to hang it in the trees and cover it good with the brush. Then the wolves don't bother it.

There's only one animal I know who spoils the meat when you hang it up and it's very dangerous too, and it is the wolverine. When he finds the meat he eats it up a lot, after he had a big meal he tramps it all over, he scratch it up, he spoils it and wets it. It's very smart and also very hard to catch him in the trap. When you set him a trap and make a hole, he always digs at the back side trying to find a bed but he won't go near the trap. There is not many wolverines in the north country. Since I have trapped in Charron Lake I just trapped one. He spoiled my moose meat, too. One good thing from a wolverine is his hide. Good for a trim on a parka in a cold weather, no frost gets in, not the same as in the other kind of fur. I don't know the price of the fur. That's as far as I know about the wolverine.

The moose and deer are almost the same, only the deer is always travelling, never stay in same place.

—*1971*

Norway House Elders

Cree (Norway House)

These personal recollections, legends, and accounts of local history were told by Norway House Elders and recorded in the 1980s by Byron Apetagon, a Cree language teacher living in Norway House, Manitoba. The following excerpts come from the first two volumes of *Norway House Anthology: Stories of the Elders Vol. 1 & 2* (produced by Frontier School Division in 1991 and 1992). They document fascinating Aboriginal intellectual traditions and the many rich experiences in a rapidly changing north over the past century.

Irene Muswagon

Irene Muswagon was born in 1909 and spent most of her life learning about traditional medicines and sharing this knowledge in her community. Here, she shares various home remedies for common ailments and serious illnesses, all the while showing her tremendous knowledge of the connection between human beings and the land.

Red Willow Crystals

The red willows produce sugar-like crystals in the spring. Usually the crystals form from a sugary substance which seeps through the pores of the willow bark. This substance becomes hard once it is on the outer bark.

Herbalists collect red willows, scrape off the crystals, and wrap then in a cloth bundle. Such crystals are collected and stored in large amounts. Later these crystals are pounded into a powdery substance.

This produces a medicine used to soothe teething pains for smaller infants, and for other tooth and gum complications.

The crystals are divided into smaller bundles which are then moistened in water and rubbed along the infected areas of the gum and teeth.

Usually the rubbing will cause the child to salivate. Sometimes the child will swallow the saliva which allows the medicinal element to enter the internal system.

Rubbing with the crystal bundles is repeated until the patient shows improvement.

Muskeg Leaves

Kákiképakwa means "forever leaves" in Cree. *Kákiképakwa* plants grow in areas where there is plenty of water and muskeg.

The plant usually has a stem which can grow as high as thirty-five centimeters. The leaves are narrow and grow as much as five to seven centimeters in length.

The leaves never all die off at once, regardless of what season it is or what the weather is like. This is the reason why they are called "Forever Plants" in Cree. They can be collected in all seasons, including winter.

These plants are used for medicinal purposes. They soothe and heal internal pains and digestive complications such as those relating to the intestine. Other uses include soothing and curing ulcers, gall stones, and pains in the diaphragm.

The muskeg plants are collected, then tied and bound together in bundles. They are usually stored like this until they are needed for applications.

The leaves are boiled in a large container for some time. As they boil, they give off a bitter odour and the water becomes very dark-colored like strong tea. After the liquid has cooled, it is used as a drink for stomach pains and complications.

It is said this drink was used to remedy diseases like tuberculosis and reduce cancer symptoms. It was also used to ease diarrhoea as well as menstrual problems in women.

Ginger Roots or *Wíhkés*

The ginger root, better known as *wíhkés*, is found in marshy areas where cattails and bulrushes grow. One can quickly find the roots in marshy areas.

A sense of smell is important here because, in areas where *wíhkés* grow, a strong sweet odour is given off.

This root is used for medicinal purposes. It soothes toothaches, headaches, stomach ulcers, indigestion, and stomach cramps. There are several ways to apply *wíhkés*. It can be chewed directly and placed over the toothache, or it can be kept in the mouth to treat headaches and colds.

The *wíhkés* can also be boiled and later the steam from the boiling *wíhkés* is inhaled to soothe and cure headaches.

Sometimes *wíhkés* is mixed with warm water and consumed in the same way as citron. This soothes stomach ulcers and internal body cramps.

—1991

Tommy York

Tommy York was born in 1908 at Sipastikok, near Norway House. He witnessed the last days of the Hudson's Bay Company's York boats and was present when the first airplane arrived in Norway House. His recollections describe many of the great technological changes occurring in northern Aboriginal communities during the 20th century.

Treaty Days

Treaty days were a main attraction long ago. I recall when they were held at Rossville. People and families came from all over to join in the festivities and collect treaty payments.

Treaty Days were usually held around August 16 every summer. When people arrived at Rossville, tents were set up near where the Hudson's Bay store, Lakeside Restaurant, and the cemetery are now. The tents were all lined up in long rows.

In those days a big boat filled with tourists, pedlars, and Indian agents arrived at Norway House. I remember a man was hired to be an informant. Whenever these people were about to arrive, the informant went around Rossville shouting and telling people the Indian agent had arrived. Then the celebrations would begin.

A big tent was set up where the treaty payments were to be distributed to all the recipients. When the Indian agent finished his preparations, the man who had been hired as an informant told everyone it was time to collect the treaty monies in Rossville. Only the father or the headman of a family went to see the Indian agent. Each reported the number of people he had in his family.

While the treaty people collected their money, the pedlars laid out goods, food, and other merchandise which the people purchased from them.

The pedlars came from around Selkirk and Winnipeg. They usually followed wherever the Indian agents went to distribute the treaty annuities.

I remember things were inexpensive in those days. A twenty-five pound bag of flour sold for a dollar, sugar and tea were five to ten cents a pound. Lard was ten cents a pound, and salt pork was under fifty cents a pound. Once I remember my father bought flour, sugar, tea, and salt pork for less than five dollars.

Rations

Just before the treaty days were over, the event began for which everyone had been anxiously waiting. This was the giving of winter provisions, better known as "The Ration."

A large table with goods and merchandise was laid out on the open grass where the Lakeside Restaurant now stands. Once everything had been carefully sorted out, people sat around the table forming a large circle. The people who gave out rations stood at the centre of the circle.

One by one, the families received their rations according to the size of their families. The main necessities were the only items distributed. They included flour, tea, sugar, lard, salt pork, and white beans.

The flour was given out in portions determined by family size. Tea and sugar were also given in scoops by the pound. I remember the salt pork was thick and had plenty of meat. Beans were also given out in portions by the pound. Bullets and shells were provided and were again given according to size of family. Both parents received one bullet and one shell each. Other items distributed were thread for fish nets and rope for each family.

Whenever there were leftover goods and merchandise, they were stored away. Later these supplies were used at community events.

Just before the treaty days ended, the pedlars lowered prices on their goods and merchandise. People purchased more necessities they might use later. Before leaving for home, the pedlars usually sold all their goods to the local people.

York Boats: The Tail End of an Era

I vividly remember seeing them arrive at Rossville Lake. We used to hear them coming from the mouth of the Nelson River—moaning, thumping sounds beating in rhythm. Some time before the big boats actually appeared, everyone prepared to go down the bank to see them pass by. Sometimes there were two, three, four, five, and even six boats—all in a line. We could see the men pulling and heaving on the oars. It was quite a remarkable sight to see.

In those days, we lived at York Village. It is about three miles across the lake from Rossville. Many families lived there before it became deserted in the 1940s. It was there I remember seeing the York boats. I was just a small boy but it was something I could not forget. When the boats came into the open waters past Hope Island, they went on the north side of Long Island and Forestry Island. Once the wooden boats hit the open lake and caught a tail wind, they used their sails to go across.

Sometimes the York boats dispersed to the Hudson's Bay Fort, to Hyer's Point where the RCMP detachment is now, and to the Indian agency at Rossville. The boats usually stayed for one to two days. They were unloaded, loaded up again, and would leave one by one. Some headed towards the south and others to the north, all returning to where they had come from before.

Sometimes the York boats met here in Norway House. The people who worked on them were fed and accommodated at the Hudson's Bay Fort.

The First Airplane I Ever Saw

My father began to shout, "Here it is!…Look to the West!…You can see it!" We all looked towards the western horizon, and clearly I saw a strange looking spectacle. We all looked with curiosity and were quite uneasy.

The day was Sunday. It was late afternoon, very peaceful and calm. A loud thundering sound was heard all over the silent lake. It sounded like it was going to storm, but all that noise was coming from the airplane. As it came closer and closer, the noise increased and the airplane got bigger. It flew over the lake, lowered its altitude, circled over Drunken Island, hovered over Fifty Cent Island, and landed on the waters passing Bull Island. It sped over to Forestry Island where it docked safely.

In the meantime, people jumped into their boats and canoes and paddled to Forestry Island. Some went very close; many others watched from their boats in the open waters off the Island.

This was the first airplane to arrive in Norway House. It came during the summer of 1920 or 1921. In the winter of 1924–25, two more airplanes landed at Norway House. They were heading somewhere to the North. After that, several other airplanes arrived occasionally.

Because airplanes were not generally available for transportation, dog teams and canoe brigades were still used for hauling and carrying goods. Later people began to use horses to deliver freight and mail to Wabowden.

—*1991*

Ruby Beardy

Ruby Beardy is the wife of Donald Beardy of Cross Lake, Manitoba. She shares a story told to her by her husband of a fire at the residential school at Norway House in the 1940s. Her husband and his friend helped the students escape the fire that began in the middle of the night.

Residential School Burns, May 29, 1945

The fire started at 2:30 during the night. Donald was awakened by a burning sensation in his nose. When he opened his eyes, the dormitory was filled with smoke. Donald jumped out of his bed and ran towards the window which had been left partially open. He pushed the screen out and looked down onto the ground. He could see flames gushing out from the wood bin in the furnace room. Instinctively, he woke up his friend, Oliver Sinclair, who was sleeping in the bed next to his. Oliver leaped up and obediently followed Donald's orders.

The two young boys quickly woke up everyone, telling each one to make much noise. All the boys began to bang and hit the beds. They did this to wake up the little girls who were sleeping in another dormitory just below their floor.

Donald ran out of the dormitory to wake up the boys' supervisor, Mr. Organ, who then went and rang the fire alarm. Mr. Organ told Donald to go outside and catch the girls as they came flying down the fire escape pillars. Meanwhile, Oliver was catching the boys at their fire escape.

Less than a half hour later, all the children were out of the building and secure in the care of local people who had run to the burning building to help. The matron of the school lined up all the children and head-counted each one. All were saved, including the staff members. Most of the children were wearing only their night clothes and socks. Donald had his pants and socks on. Within an hour after Donald and Oliver had awakened everyone in the school, it was completely demolished by the raging flames.

The principal, Mr. Jones, had gone south a day before the school burned down. He was travelling on the *Keenora* to Winnipeg. Local authorities managed to contact him at Berens River.

The next morning, most of the children had breakfast at the hospital. The students from Norway House returned to their homes with parents, guardians, or relatives.

Donald and his sisters were taken to Douglas McIvor's place and stayed there for almost four days. Then Donald, Alice, and Christina went home to Cross Lake. Six canoes travelled to Norway House to pick up the Cross Lake students. The paddlers included Jimmy Magnus Ross, Jimmy Muswagon, George Mason, and Zacheus McKay among others.

Before Donald went home to Cross Lake, he was promised verbally by Indian Affairs in Norway House that he would be given a house to reward his quick thinking and brave actions. However, to this day, Donald Beardy still has not received the promised reward. Ironically, he has not even received an official "Thank-You" from anyone for saving one hundred or more people.

—*1991*

Betsy Muminawatum

Betsy Muminawatum was born in Norway House in 1921. Her recollections vividly describe the life of northern Cree families as they move cyclically and attempt to negotiate life over a single year in northern Manitoba. They echo a steady stream of near-constant work and a variety of visitors and tasks that made for a satisfying life.

The Winter Setting at Máhtawak

Long ago many families used to move to the winter camps in the surrounding lands of Norway House. Some families remained behind but because our fathers were trappers, fishermen, and hunters we went with them to the winter camps.

My father's winter camp was at a place called Máhtawak. It is around the Molson Lake area. Ever since I can remember we always went there for the winter. Sometimes people left in groups to go to the winter camps. My father always left earlier than other families; we usually travelled by ourselves. Sometimes our grandparents accompanied us. We did not travel at the quickest pace. My father hunted and fished along the way. By the time we arrived at Máhtawak, we had some food stored for the winter. Not long after we arrived at the winter camp other families and relatives began to arrive. They had hunted and fished along way also.

Upon our arrival at Máhtawak, we lived in a tent temporarily. There was much work to be done before the cold winter perched upon us.

The men and the older children gathered and collected dry wood. Once there was plenty of wood, all cut and neatly piled, the men left us behind with our mothers to go hunting. They hunted for moose mainly. Sometimes the men were gone for many days. Later they arrived home with plenty of wild meat.

While the men were gone, we still had many tasks to do. Everyone including the younger children hauled moss and muskeg to the cabin. These were used to fill in the cracks between the layers of logs on the houses. They were excellent insulators and kept the cold winds from entering the interior. After all the cabins were insulated we hauled dry wood for use as firewood.

Sometimes the men built a new log house before they went hunting. They would only built a new house if one was getting too old, or if more people had joined our group.

The cabin we had at Máhtawak had a clay stove in it. I remember once our mother was roasting some meat using this stove. The meat hung from the roof on a string. She would twist and turn the meat until it became a nice brown color. Everything was cooked on the clay stove. There were fish, rabbit, and moose meat meals. These were all delicious meals which we never got sick of eating.

I can remember there were at least five to six families at Máhtawak. Everyone trapped, fished, and hunted until the lakes and rivers froze over. Freeze-up did not prevent the men from trapping for the fur bearing animals.

The Travelling Stores of the Fur Buyers

I remember the fur buyers used to come to Máhtawak at least twice a month. One of the regular fur buyers was Donald Houle who worked for one of the fur traders at Norway House. I can remember there were at least three stores at Rossville. These were the Hudson's Bay Company, Trappers, and Mr. Sunde's. All three stores stood side by side adjacent to where the present band hall now stands. I can remember that when customers entered the stores, a counter separated them from the storekeeper. The customers asked for the things they needed. The storekeeper fetched all the supplies and recorded everything. Things were cheaper in those days.

Earlier in the summer my father would take us to one of the stores. There he would purchase all the things we needed at Máhtawak. He bought salt pork, white beans, tea, rice, lard, flour, and some sugar. He also bought other things which we needed for trapping and fishing. That was the only time we went to a store. The next time we saw a store was a travelling one brought by a dogteam which moved from camp to camp.

When the fur buyer's dogteam arrived at our camp, I remember he would bring in all his goods and merchandise. Everything was all laid out on the floor. My father and mother would do all the selecting while all the children looked on. In the end, most of the supplies were food goods. I rarely saw my father buying things he did not need and I also remember he did not give all his furs away; he kept some furs for the next fur buyer to come knocking on our door. I cannot recall seeing any money when the trades were made.

Before the fur buyer went away on his journey to his next stop, we always had a little treat from our father. He would make some sweet biscuits. We each got one biscuit and didn't get any more until a few days later.

I also remember the children did not drink tea often. When we were given some, water was always added. There was sugar that was sold in cubes and only adults used it.

We used sugar when we became older. We had flour to make bannock. There were times when we did not have enough flour. Flour had many uses. We also had some lard but it was available in limited quantity. We always had plenty of rice. I got tired of eating rice day after day.

Off to the Spring Camp

On the verge of the spring season when the weather became much warmer, all the families moved away to their spring camps. My father took us to his spring camp when there were plenty of muskrats and beavers.

After we had stored all our winter equipment and supplies, we took things we needed at the spring camp.

Spring trapping was the best time for everyone to trap. Everyone, even the small children, were allowed to set muskrat traps. There were plenty of muskrats where we trapped. In those days there was no such thing as registered traplines or licenses. Everyone trapped alongside each other without much bitter envy or resentment.

The hustling and bustling about in the spring camp was always evident. The men and women were skinning and stretching muskrat skins. The girls were washing dishes and clothes, or cleaning up around the spring camp. The boys helped in everything. My brothers learned to skin and stretch muskrats.

Everyone worked all day long. When evening came our parents would call us in for prayer. (We were not allowed to make noise after sunset.) We always said prayers in the morning and evening, as well as before meal time. My father valued prayer. This is how each family lived long ago.

I remember when our parents got up in the morning, all the children had to get up too. If one slept in, it meant missing a meal. That was the rule my father gave us. I also remember my parents always told us to eat when it was time for everyone to have a meal. We hardly ever ate between regular meals.

The spring season brought a change of diet. We had ducks, geese, and fish daily. As the spring hunt came to an end, we journeyed back to Rossville. We had more wild food along the way. We were always excited to see our old friends once again.

Homemade Jeans and Woolen Socks

My mother Annabella had expertise in sewing, beadwork, and knitting. Being a girl I was taught all these things so I could use them when I went on my own.

Rarely did we have store-bought clothes. Most of our new clothing were made from old clothing. We used to be very happy and excited when our mother made us new clothes.

I remember the old stores used to provide jean cloth material. My father and mother used to buy the material and later my mother would make new jeans for my brothers.

My mother knew how to treat and tan hide. My father was a good hunter. We always had enough hide. My mother made new moccasins for us. I learned how to make moccasins and slippers from her. Sometimes when there was enough money, she would buy some silk to make other clothing wear.

Once I remembered my grandmother had an old woolen sweater. She had received it in a trade with another old woman. In those days the older women exchanged old clothes for old clothes. Anyway after she received the sweater, she took the whole thing apart to make yarn. Later when the yarn was rolled into a ball, she took her needles and made woolen socks for us. My, we were so happy to get new socks from a very old sweater.

I also wore rabbit skins on my feet. We all did. The rabbits were the warmest socks one could have in those days. We wore the rabbit skins when we played, worked, and when we went into the bush to haul and carry wood. Our footwear was always moccasins. We did not see anything fancy like the runners, joggers, and oxfords of today. We also had the moccasin rubbers which we wore constantly during the spring seasons.

I remember we used to have a large rabbit fur blanket. It was a blanket made from rabbit skins collected and sewn together. I guess the blanket was used as a comforter. I helped my mother make one. They are very warm, especially on cold nights.

—1992

David Courchene Sr.

Anishinaabe (Sagkeeng First Nation) 1926–1992

David Courchene Sr. was a renowned orator and advocate for Aboriginal people in Manitoba and Canada. Educated by his grandparents and later at Fort Alexander Residential School, Courchene worked as a hunter, trapper, and heavy-machine operator until turning to politics in order to challenge the systemic discrimination and oppression that Aboriginal communities—and particularly youth—were experiencing. His inspirational speeches, tireless work ethic, and hopeful outlook inspired many; he was elected chief at Sagkeeng in 1965 and was the first Grand Chief of Manitoba's First Nations when the Manitoba Indian Brotherhood (MIB; later, the Assembly of Manitoba Chiefs) was formed. Under Courchene, the MIB published *Wahbung: Our Tomorrows* (1971), a response to Prime Minister Pierre Elliott Trudeau's "White Paper," which advocated Aboriginal assimilation and the erasure of treaties. Courchene received many awards throughout his career, including an honorary doctorate from the University of Manitoba and induction into the Order of Canada. His words, actions, and legacy continue to be felt throughout all segments of Manitoba.

The following "Message of the Grand Chief" appeared at the beginning of *Wahbung* and is Courchene's message to Canadians—and Trudeau's government in particular. It speaks of the power and resiliency of Aboriginal people in Manitoba and calls for an end to assimilationist practices and policies as well as demands for a full recognition of Aboriginal rights and self-determination. The second piece is an excerpt from an essay Courchene wrote in 1973 entitled "Problems and Possible Solutions." Written in honour of the hundredth anniversary of the signing of Treaties One and Two (which resulted in the province of Manitoba), Courchene examines the problems Aboriginal people have endured since "the coming of the white man": the failure to honour treaties, violence through colonial policies and practices, and a lack of respect. While fierce and motivated by injustice, in both these pieces most notable are Courchene's unwavering belief in hope, change, and possibility in Manitoba.

Message of the Grand Chief

We, the first people of this land now called Manitoba, are a people of indomitable will to survive, to survive as a people, strong and creative.

During the centuries in which we lived on this land, we faced many times of struggle, for the land is not always kind, and our people like any other people had to find ways to adapt to a changing environment.

These last one hundred years have been the time of most difficult struggle, but they have not broken our spirit nor altered our love for this land nor our attachment and commitment to it. We have survived as a people.

Our attachment means that we must also commit ourselves to help develop healthy societies for all the peoples who live upon this land. But we will not be able to contribute unless we have the means first to develop a healthy society for ourselves. Since the signing of the Treaties one hundred years ago, we have been constantly and consistently prevented from doing so.

Three fundamental facts underlie this paper and are reflected in all aspects of it.

First, we are determined to remain a strong and proud and identifiable group of people.

Second, we refuse to have our lives directed by others who do not and who can not know our ways.

Third, we are a 20th-century people, not a colourful folkloric remnant. We are capable and competent and perfectly able to assess today's conditions and develop ways of adjusting positively and successfully to them.

Other Canadians must recognize these three facts.

We ask you for assistance for the good of all Canada and as a moral obligation resulting from injustice in the past, but such assistance must be based upon this understanding. If this can be done, we shall continue to commit ourselves to a spirit of cooperation.

Only thus can hope be bright that there might come a tomorrow when you, the descendants of the settlers of our lands, can say to the world, Look, we came and were welcomed, and then we wrought much despair; but we are also men of honour and integrity and we set to work in cooperation, we listened and we learned, we gave our support, and today we live in harmony with the first people of this land who now call us, brothers.

We hope that tomorrow will come.

—*1971*

Problems and Possible Solutions

It is indeed a pleasure for me to be given an opportunity to write an article in this year, the hundredth anniversary of the signing of Treaties number One and Two covering those lands held by Indians in what is now called the Province of Manitoba.

It may be of interest to note that in 1970 we all celebrated the centennial of the founding of Manitoba, a celebration that recognized that the Province of Manitoba was founded one year before the treaties were signed with the aboriginal owners of this land. One might take from that, that the treaties negotiated in 1871 were negotiated in an atmosphere of a *fait accompli* and that by virtue of the act of formation of the Province of Manitoba, white society had served notice upon Indians that they were determined to dispossess them of their land notwithstanding the agreements to be arrived at in 1871.

To fully appreciate the position of the Canadian Indian, one must consider the period prior to the white man's encroachment on the historic lands of the native people. For centuries, Indians lived in this country, mastered their environment, and learned to live with nature, without the necessity of dominating it. Indians were an independent, interdependent, communal people who harvested the natural resources of the land to provide the necessities of food, clothing and shelter without abusing that privilege. They were largely nomadic, migrating to some extent with the buffalo, relying on one another for their security and wellbeing.

The coming of the white man significantly changed the historic balance between man and nature. The Indian became a resource for the early white explorer to exploit and, with the development of the fur trade, the white man successfully altered the Indian's traditional way of life through the encouragement of the commercial harvesting of fur-bearing animals for which the Indian was to receive trinkets, fire-water, and arms and ammunition. The pursuit of the fur industry also created elements of commercial competitiveness between Indian tribes as, in their pursuit of fur-bearing animals, they increasingly encroached upon each other's territories. The result of this was to strain relationships between tribes and to upset the historic balance between the Indian nations.

The real tragedy of the treaties and the practices of public policy by succeeding governments over the past century has been to destroy that element essential to all people for their survival, man's individual initiative and self-reliance. At the point where the government designated reserves, it also suggested to people that if they stayed on such reserves, that government would in effect protect them and see that they did not suffer deprivation. A century of pursuit of such public policy finds Indian people now on the lowest rung of the social ladder not only suffering deprivation and poverty to a greater extent than any other Canadian, but also suffering from psychological intimidation brought about by their almost complete dependency upon the state for the necessities of life.

It is unconscionable not only in legal terms but in moral terms that white society has, wittingly or unwittingly, emasculated my people. You have not only denied us our traditional pursuits but you have also denied us our right to our identity and our pride in ourselves. It is impossible for any group of people to survive either economically or socially if they are compelled to live in both social and economic isolation from those who surround them. This deprivation of involvement and participation and the resulting effects of psychological depression and frustration can only be classified as the most subtle cultural genocide practiced by any people in the history of our times.

Government's lack of concern for Indian people can he clearly reflected in the past budgets of the government of Canada with respect to Indian programs. In 1946–47 the total Indian Affairs budget was 5.9 million dollars and as late as 1957–58 it was only 27 million dollars. When one considers that the generation of adult Indians presently in the work force is the product of that generation between 1946 and 1957, it is not hard to understand why many Indians of today are incapable of taking their place as contributing members of this society. It was not until the year 1966–67 that the budgets of the Department of Indian Affairs to provide for education, social services, housing and the other amenities of life reached 100 million dollars and even at that time this represented an expenditure of only some 400 dollars per Indian person in Canada. It must be kept in mind in considering these figures that a substantial portion of this money was eaten up in salaries and administration long before it was applied to the benefit of the people at the reserve level.

The end result of a century of indifference by white society finds the Indian today living in a situation of almost complete government dependence. His housing is not only disgraceful, it is intolerable. His academic achievement level is considerably below the level required to pursue almost any vocation, and his level of aspiration is considerably behind that of any of his fellow Canadians.

This, then, shows the bleak situation of the Indian people; a situation that is intolerable in a country that has the second highest standard of living in the world, and that is out of keeping with a country whose promise is unlimited.

While the picture is bleak, I do want to say that it is slowly but surely changing. The government of Canada is realizing more and more that there is a need for even greater investment in the human resources of the Indian people if they are to be able to achieve that level of participation that is the birthright of all Canadians. The government of Manitoba, for the first time in its history, has begun to recognize its obligations to Indians as citizens of the province. The public at large is becoming increasingly aware of and concerned about the general indifference and apathy that has existed with respect to the first Canadian, the Indian people…

We are hopeful for tomorrow if only because for the first time in the history of Indian people, Indians are united and organized and are demanding the right to self determination, to participation, to be contributing members of this society, and to express our self-identity.

Three things are required to successfully bring about a social and economic revolution for Indian people.

First, it requires commitment on the part of the Indian people. A commitment to a process of change, a process of advancement, a process of catching up with the rest of Canadians and sharing with them in contributing to and enjoying the benefits of a productive society.

Secondly, it requires the investment of considerable sums of money on the part of the population of Canada to redress the wrongs of the past and to give opportunity to those who have been denied, so that they can catch up.

Thirdly, it requires a conscious effort on the part of the generation of today and the generations of tomorrow to minimize conflict and frustration, to eliminate discrimination, to learn to understand one another, and to live in accordance with the precepts of the brotherhood of man.

To all white people I would say: dedicate yourselves to the development of an atmosphere of mutual understanding; commit yourselves to the process of redressing the ills of the past and to building for all of us a better tomorrow; open your minds as well as your hearts to the plight of your fellow man. We ask only that you approach the problem with objectivity and with an open mind; that you attempt to understand the difficulty of adjustment that is a burden the Indian must bear; that you attempt to recognize that there are no instant solutions to problems so long in the making.

If we appear to lack perception in our relationships with you it may be that you did not teach us to perceive. If we appear not to understand what you say, it may be because we were not taught to understand. If we appear slow to react, it may be because your acts have not always been creditable in our eyes and we are fearful and distrustful. If we make mistakes, it may be because our background lacks the experience of the mistakes that you have made and upon which, today, you base your judgements.

Having considered our position don't impose your solutions upon us for the experience we have endured for the last century. Don't seek solutions in isolation from those who must live with the problem but let's seek solutions together.

Don't apply corrective action. Let us apply that which we accept as being good and have defined for ourselves as a proper course of action.

Don't judge us harshly for our mistakes, for as it is said, let him who is without sin cast the first stone. Don't expect of us that which you would not expect of yourselves, and do recognize that we are, after all, human beings subject to all the human weaknesses and frailties that you are. In addition, we do not have generations of understanding in your way of life upon which to base our judgements.

Don't ask us to accept blindly and with the faith of religious fervor all that you tell us, but help us to learn to judge equitably the merits of a proposition. We ask not for your judgement but for your understanding, for we recognize the need for mutual understanding and mutual support.

—1973

Alice Masak French

Ninatakmuit Inuit (Mackenzie River Delta region) 1930–

Alice Masak French was born on Baillie Island, Beaufort Sea. After her mother's death from tuberculosis at the age of six, French and her younger brother Danny were left at All Saints' Anglican Residential School in Aklavik, because their father, a fur trapper and hunter, could no longer take care of them. French spent several summers with her father and his extended family but attended residential school the rest of the year until she finally left at fourteen to rejoin her father and his new family permanently. French struggled to relearn Inupiaq as well as to learn sewing, driving a dog team, skinning muskrats, and other skills expected from a young woman in a traditional Inuvialuit community. After moving to Manitoba, she wrote about the first fourteen years of her life in *My Name is Masak* (1977). Her second book *The Restless Nomad* (1992) continues this life story, recounting the loneliness she experienced and difficulties she faced reintegrating into her community. This second book also describes her two marriages, the deaths of two of her children, and travels with her RCMP husband. French's story documents the struggle of the Inuit as they attempted to preserve their seasonal trapping, traditional knowledge and familial bonds under the pressures of the outside world.

In the following excerpt from *My Name is Masak*, French recounts a powerful portrait of her resourceful, generous, and highly influential grandmother. Though Grandmother Susie is an exceptional figure in a number of ways, she is also representative of the very important place of women in Inuit culture. Her abilities as a *suptaki*, homemaker, and "head of the house" illustrate the centrality of Grandmother Susie to her family and community.

Grandmother Susie

My grandmother Susie was the head of our household. She was also a *suptakti*—an Eskimo doctor, and a very good one. She was a spry little woman with blue tattoo marks on her chin and black and gray hair that hung to her shoulders. She kept a close watch over her household, but she dropped everything if a sick person was brought to our house, or sent for her to come to them. Her services were always in demand in times of illness or when a baby was being born.

For a severe headache my grandmother would make a small cut on the crown of the head to bleed the patient. If the problem was internal she would rub the tummy with her small hands until she knew what was wrong and then she would put it right again. For snow-blindness she made a cut in the right temple or put boiled leaves in a cloth which she then laid on the eyes to soothe them. For a serious attack of pain in the area of the liver—which today we would call a gall-bladder attack—she would set coal oil on fire and allow it to burn until most of it had evaporated and turned brown. Then she would rub the tender area, gently massaging in the brown stuff until the gall stones were moved away from the bile duct. She used chewing tobacco for tooth-ache and she made us swallow tobacco juice for chest pains and coughing.

My grandmother helped many people. If I began to name all those whom she treated, I would be putting down half the people in the Delta.

We did not live in snow-houses in the Mackenzie Delta. We lived dur-ing the cold months in a house that had been built up from drift logs over a number of years. When the ice broke up in the spring it was the job of the children to watch for logs in the floating ice. When we saw one, the men would go out after it in a canoe.

The house was about twenty-six feet wide and twenty feet deep—all one room with an addition on it for a married aunt and her husband, and a porch where we stored harnesses and firewood and cooked food for the dogs. Inside, the beds were curtained off. My parents had their bed in one corner and my grandparents were in the opposite corner. In between were three beds for the girls, made of lumber and canvas, with mattresses and comforters stuffed with duck and goose feathers. The boys slept in eider-down sleeping-bags on caribou skins on the floor.

We had two stoves. One was a 45-gallon oil drum which we filled with green logs and lit just before bedtime. The other was our cook-stove. My grandmother always kept a can of Lysol steaming on the back of the stove. It made the house smell clean, she said, and it kept germs away.

My grandmother had a thing about cleanliness. On Saturdays we cleaned the house right through. The work began Friday night when we sorted the dirty clothes and filled all the boilers and tubs with ice that melted and heated while we were asleep. Then in the morning, right after breakfast, we girls got busy with wash-tubs and scrub-boards and lots of Sunlight soap. We put the bedding out on the line to air and in the afternoon we scrubbed the rough lumber floor with lye and water until my grandmother was satis-fied that it was white enough.

Every night before we went to bed we swept the house in case we had travellers come in during the night. We did not ordinarily use the table for eating because there were too many of us. Instead we spread an oilcloth on the floor and ate sitting around it. If a white trapper came by on his way to his trap-line he ate his breakfast on the table under the window.

In the summer we lived in tents. Each family had its own. In my day the tents were canvas, but long ago my great-grandparents made tents of cari-bou skins and willow branches. I saw them build these tents. The skins were scraped until there was no hair on them, and then they were sewn together. Quite a lot of light came in through the skins.

Not many Eskimo women held the position of head of the house as my grandmother Susie did. She administered the discipline, supervised the family, and ruled with an iron hand. During my sewing lessons she had me sit in front of her where she could look down on my sewing and see how I was doing. I am afraid I gave her a lot of problems. I did not know how to hold the needle or scraper properly or how to make thread from the sinew of caribou. In fact I was quite dumb, she thought. Any ten-year-old girl should have known how to do these things. So my lessons were longer than anyone else's. First I had to learn to scrape skins—they had to be soft enough for her to be able to scrunch up in her hand; that took days of scraping and rubbing. Then I had to learn to cut out mukluks and parkas, and to sew them. My stitches had to be so small that she could not see them from where she sat and that took some doing. If I made a mistake or took too big a stitch her finger, with a thimble attached, came down on top of my skull with a knock and I was told to take the whole thing apart and start over again, no matter how close the garment was to completion. It really was frustrating, but I soon learned to do things well the first time so that I would not have to do them over again and again.

When the sewing lessons were over I had to sit and pluck gray hairs from her head. This was to keep my fingers limbered up. I was not allowed to use tweezers for this job and she kept track of only the very short ones that I had managed to pull out. When she was satisfied that I had pulled enough out she released me from this chore. While I was doing this she would tell me Eskimo stories and so I really did not mind my job. I loved to listen to the folk tales. I wish that I had paid more attention to all these stories, now that she is gone—but at that time I was still going to boarding school and I thought I knew so much better. I did not think that life would ever change and thought that I had all the time in the world to learn about the things that belonged to my people, the Inuit.

My grandmother was most bull-headed when she wanted to be. No one dared oppose her when she decided on the course of action to take next. All of us, including her married sons and daughters who lived with her, had a healthy respect for her temper. She was a remarkable woman and kept the family together until her death.

My grandfather, on the other hand, was a quiet and soft-spoken gentleman. He did not need to scold us to make us do our work. He just made a suggestion and we did it gladly. When my grandmother was especially hard on me he quietly told her that I was doing fine for a girl who had no knowledge of the many things she expected of me. He was kind and considerate and acted as a buffer between her and the rest of the family. He never openly opposed her decisions, but sometimes he suggested doing things in a different way and made her believe that it was her idea in the first place.

Louis Bird (Pennishish)

Omushkego Cree (Winisk, Ontario) 1934–

Louis Bird (Pennishish) was born into an Omushkego (Swampy) Cree family near the now-abandoned village of Winisk, Ontario, on the west coast of Hudson Bay. He grew up on the land and received a traditional Omushkego Cree education from his parents and grandparents, except for four years when he was taken to St. Anne's Residential School at Fort Albany. When he returned home from the school, he resumed a traditional life and dedicated himself to hunting, trapping and learning his people's stories. For many years he memorized the stories of Omushkego Cree Elders, and he became an accomplished storyteller himself. In the early 1970s he was able to buy a tape recorder, and he began recording the Elders as well as recording his own versions of the stories. Many of these recordings are now available on the Internet at <ourvoices.ca> through the Centre for Rupert's Land Studies' Omushkego Oral History Project. Louis Bird is also the author of *Telling Our Stories: Omushkego Legends and Histories from Hudson Bay* and *The Spirit Lives in the Mind: Omushkego Stories, Lives, Dreams.* Many of the stories recorded in these volumes were performed in Winnipeg, where Bird worked with University of Winnipeg researchers for several years. He remains greatly sought after as a speaker, both for his storytelling abilities and for his extraordinary knowledge of Omushkego Cree culture.

Though Louis Bird was born in Ontario and still lives there in the community of Peawanuck, his people's traditional territory extends into Manitoba and he tells several stories relating to York Factory in particular such as those about John Sakaney and Bernard Gull, which indicate the effects of fur trading in the region and underlines the continuance of Omushkego Cree spiritual practices despite the arrival of different cultural values brought by non-Native fur traders. In "Our Grandmothers' Powers," Bird gives us a glimpse of the importance and the unique contribution of women in Omushkego Cree culture. These stories from *The Spirit Lives in the Mind* were told as oral stories and transcribed with minimal changes, in order to reflect the oral nature of the performance.

John Sakaney

Mitewiwin[33] was part of our spirituality and our culture a long time ago before the European came. A mitew is a person who exercises such a thing. Mitewiwin is a noun.

There was a man between, say, 1900 and 1920. When the first fur traders began to operate in the James Bay lowland, they used to build the York

---

33 Similar to the Anishinaabe Midewewin, Omushkego Cree Mitewewin is a set of spiritual practices, beliefs and powers. A Mitew is a medicine person who has special powers.

boats in York Factory. Sometimes they have two masts and they were open decked; they don't have no floor or anything. And the Native people were required to sail them around the west coast of James Bay, because there were only two depots where they unloaded the stuff from overseas. One of them was in York Factory in Hudson Bay, and the other one was within James Bay, on an island called Akimiski (Charlon Island).

And at the beginning they didn't have no compass! Open decked. Open decked, and the rudder had no wheel—it's just a plain rudder that you had to fight with. Dangerous material! Dangerous stuff.

So this particular man, his name was Kakitewish, his Christian name was John Sakaney—he was not a big man, but he was a great man. And he was a *mitew* at the same time. We were told that he sailed these open decked York Boats, two masts, from York Factory right into the tip of James Bay. I don't think he ever lost one boat in a wreck.

He was very courageous, using the stars as his navigating aid, using the waves, able to understand the waves and where he was, and how far he was. It was very fascinating how he navigated, and what he used. Omushkegowak[34] instinctively know their bearings, they have an inner compass. What was fascinating about this man was he didn't need the compass to go from one point to another. He knew exactly, he understood the salt water. When there were no stars at night, he knew how to use the waves to find out how far off-shore he was, or whether there's any obstacle ahead—a few miles ahead. So he knows about these things. That's what was so fascinating about this John Sakaney—his Christian name. So that's the blending of his culture with the other culture—using the white man's boat and his own Mitewiwin skill and knowledge to navigate storms in daytime or nighttimes, regardless. And he always found his way.

Bernard Gull

One small oral history that I want to recall is about a man who was impor-tant between 1890 and 1930, thereabouts. This was a man called Bernard Gull in his Christian name, or Kiyask in our language. In the Omushkego language we call him Penas Kiyask. He was one of the Hudson Bay key men—he was one of those guys who sailed the York boats on the south-west coast of Hudson Bay. Every summer he used to walk from Winisk into York Factory, which is about two hundred miles to the northwest from Winisk, to work for Hudson Bay Company—unload the steamship out in the Bay by York boat, put them into the York Factory warehouse, and then

---

34 The plural form of Omushkego, meaning Omushkego Cree people.

sail into a little community on the southeast coast for these goods to be sold to the Native people. And when he finished that, he was responsible, as a captain of this York boat, to beach the boat somewhere on dry land so it would be safe.

This man really did his best to get involved for the Hudson Bay Company, so he got good benefits—he had the materials that he wanted: process food, flour, sugar, tea, and all that stuff. And he has his own faults also.

So one story that's his: he had wrecked maybe three York boats and the last one he wrecked, or beached, he did it on purpose for his own benefit. He wanted to winter trap there around the coast, so he purposely beached the boat there without totally destroying the contents. And it happened! So he's an extraordinary man, he makes our recent oral history exciting. But I don't mean to be offensive—we do not tell the story about him because we want to offend him, we just want to show how Hudson Bay Company influenced people. It changed their style of thinking, increased the negativity in their character. We, all of us, have different inner faults. Some of us are so greedy. Some of us are wanting to be higher in the government and we'd do anything to get that.

Well this Bernard Gull was extreme about these things. He wanted to do what the white man do and he worshipped them almost. He wanted to be like them. And in that, he made a mistake—made himself so disgraceful—almost like a big laughing stock.

So two people: John Sakaney, who used his Mitewiwin expertise to be able to accomplish something which was new to him, where he didn't even require the compass to find his way in nearly five hundred miles of open water, regardless of any storm. That could not be possible for an ordinary man, so we learn something about Mitewiwin from him, an extraordinary person who was an accomplished shaman. He was gifted to navigate in the water. And the other—Bernard Gull—so extreme from one to the other! He was so greedy and took advantage of what he had. He made himself a shameful guy in the story, Bernard Gull. But we don't aim to degrade him or to make a laughing stock out of him. He did—he made himself a laughing stock at the time.

—*2007*

Our Grandmothers' Powers

There are extraordinary stories about women in the past—our women, our ancestors, our great-great-grandmothers. They were gifted with women's intuition. This intuition was very accurate and they could use it to tell the future.

I know that my grandmother had this women's intuition because she could feel when her son was about fifteen miles away, coming towards home. How did she know that? And she would tell us, "Watch the dogs, they are going to know it too." And then we would go out and, sure enough, the dogs started to make little movements—then they would sit up and stretch and start to bark the way they did when they knew someone was going by. And then we would tell our grandmother, "Yes, they got up." And about two hours later he would arrive.

This was what women could do. They could feel things ahead of time - they could see and have visions. They didn't go out on dream quests as men did because they already had it gifted to them. They were very accurate when they described what was going to happen.

I know an old lady who was able to predict something four months ahead, and it happened exactly as it she described it. Three times in our camp where we were hunting, she predicted something, and it happened. For example, she was just sitting with her eyes closed, but she was fully awake, and she sat up and said, "Why do I have this vision?" And we asked, "What did you see?" And she said, "I saw people traveling towards the community, and they carried a small coffin, a small, white coffin. I don't know who they are, but they were carrying that little, small, white coffin." This was in November. In April, sure enough, a family living up the river brought down a child that was dead, I think about two years old—they carried this little white coffin to the village to be buried. That's how this lady was accurate, and that's the gift of some of the women who lived here.

That's not shamanism, that's different—but there are those ladies who developed shamanism and who were just as powerful as men. Mostly the women were gifted to be healers. When they were young, and as they got older, they had this dream. One last story before I finish this. There was an old lady who died. Her son's face turned into a rash every April—his skin peeled off and he suffered. She had to just watch him suffer, because there were no hospitals in the bush. And one night, when she couldn't sleep, she sat by her son, trying to cool him off with a cold rag. She fell asleep and, towards dawn, all of sudden she heard a voice. The voice said, "Get up and go to the muskeg. In a little open space you will see some little tamaracks, they are about an inch in diameter. Cut two of those, bring them home, and cut them into blocks about an inch and half long. Take the inner skin, put it into a pan, and boil it. And then, with that water, wash the face of your son—wet every part of the skin that is broken." She did exactly as she was told by the mind, and the next day the boy's face healed—he never had that disease again. This is the truth—but this is not the Mitewiwin, it was not a shaman thing—this is a gift that women had and there's many more stories about these things.

—2007

Elders of Moose Lake

Cree (Moose Lake)

The following four stories emerge from a larger cultural and cooperative project by the Manitoba Native Education Branch, the Cree people of Moose Lake, and Cree teacher Dan Ehman. It features stories collected from Elders, written in Cree syllabics, translated into English. It is called *Cree Stories from Moose Lake* (1980). Individual storyteller's names are generally not attached to particular stories in the book, but some of the Elders who shared their stories for the project are Ben Sinclair, Robert Buck, Absolam Patchinose, and Andrew Sanderson. Collected over many years, this educational collection illustrates the vibrant culture at Moose Lake.

Moose Lake's history is rich with stories embodying many diverse experiences. These include close relationships with land and the beings who inhabit and visit this place, such as Jackfish and the bull moose in "The Story of East Arm Narrows" or the Americans in "The Story of Norris Lake." Some of the most interesting history of Moose Lake resides in stories about the powerful spiritual leaders who have met there, and the woman who became the Wetigo. All of these stories show how dynamic and vibrant life is in Manitoba's North.

The Story of East Arm Narrows

About 25 miles east of Moose Lake is a narrows connecting Moose Lake and Front Island Lake. People often go there to fish. There are many fish in that narrows, especially big Jackfish.

An American doctor has a cabin there and some other buildings. He has made himself a very nice spot there.

One thing you notice is that the water moves through the narrows in different directions. Some days it flows one way and on another day it might flow the opposite way. The people have a story to explain why this happens.

One time a big Jackfish lived in the narrows. He was the biggest fish in the lake. He considered himself the mightiest creature in the world. He was king over all the fish.

Living in that same area was a big bull moose. This bull moose was a grand animal and very proud. He considered himself king of all the animals. Often he used to go to the narrows to drink water.

One day as he went for a drink, he spoke to the other animals there. He told them that he was the greatest animal in the woods. He was king of all the beasts.

But the great Jackfish heard him. He became very angry at the words of the bull moose. So when the moose bent his head to drink water the Jackfish saw his chance. He rushed at the moose and seized him by the nose. He attempted to drag the moose into the water. But the moose put up a mighty effort and attempted to back out of the water. He almost dragged the mighty Jackfish out of the water but again the Jackfish pulled the moose into the water. Back and forth the struggle continued. Each time the Jackfish dragged the moose into the water, the water would rise on the shore. As the moose dragged the Jackfish out to the shore, the water would go down again. All day the mighty creatures struggled back and forth and the water continued to move up and down.

At long last, the two kings became tired. Neither one was a clear winner. They conceded that they were very nearly equal in strength. The Jackfish agreed to be king of the water and the bull moose would be king of the forest.

But to this day the water continues to move back and forth through the narrows, ever since it was set in motion by the battle of those two mighty animals. Can you believe it?

The Medicine Man, Two Claws

In the old days people considered Moose Lake the most frightening or mysterious place. This was because it was the headquarters where all the medicine men used to meet.

One medicine man was especially powerful. He was named "Two Claws" because the nails on his index fingers were much longer than the rest.

One time, this medicine man walked on the water to Shoulderblade Island. He went to see the monsters who had no noses. These monsters lived in a lake in the very center of Shoulderblade Island. They lived in the deepest part of the water in this lake. Occasionally, people have heard these creatures banging away on something under the water. It sounded like they were banging stones together.

Only men were able to see Two Claws walk on water. If women looked at him, he would sink right away.

He learned this secret in a dream. He was told the secret by the big spider that walks on top of the water. This spider told him that he could also walk on top of the water, just like him.

The Story of Norris Lake

There is a lake in our area here called Norris Lake, or Cow Lake in Cree. It is about 40 miles south east of Moose Lake Settlement on the other side of

Bracken Lake. For some reason, the water in this lake has a strange taste. Some say it is an oily taste. I know when fire fighters camped there the time of the big forest fire about 20 years ago, they had to get their water from another lake.

The reason it is called Cow Lake is because long ago, skulls of some kind of cows were found there. These skulls are most likely the skulls of wood buffalo.

People say that there is a lot of money to be found there some place. The story of this money is very interesting. The story was told to me by an old man and he was told the story by old people when he was young, so it must have happened very long ago.

One time, two men came from the United States, north through Grand Rapids to Norris Lake. They were fleeing a war in their country. That war might have been the American Civil War. They pulled all their belongings on a sleigh. There at Norris Lake, they built themselves a small cabin and attempted to live there.

These men were not too experienced with living off the land. They weren't too well equipped either. At times during the winter they would make their way over to Bracken's Lake. They would meet Moose Lake trappers over there. They told a little bit about themselves but mostly they wanted to buy fish.

One time they noticed a little pup at the camp of the Moose Lake trappers. They wanted to buy that pup for a pet, they said. The trappers agreed and sold them the pup. The men paid for the pup with money from a chest they had. The trappers say they had lots of money and gold bars in that chest.

The trappers suspected that the men really wanted that pup for food.

Anyway, those two men died there that winter, either by disease or starvation. But no one knows what happened to that chest of money that they had. Perhaps it is still there. Cow Lake is an isolated lake where hardly anyone ever goes.

Do you want to look for treasure? Maybe you or someone else will be lucky some day. At any rate, Norris or Cow Lake is a very interesting place to hike to.

The Origin of the Wetigo

Once there was a woman who used to trap way up north. She caught a great deal of fur. One day the dogs got at her furs and destroyed all of them. The woman was very upset. She was so depressed that she gradually became insane. Then she became a Wetigo.

She flew from the north and landed in Moose Lake. She followed a light to get there. She landed on a narrow road. In those days there was much bush in the settlement and nobody knew she was there.

One day, a medicine man happened to discover the Wetigo. He saw her peeking at him as he was looking in the mirror inside his log house. He went and asked her why she was sitting there. She told him her story about her pelts and the dogs. Then the medicine man said, "You have to leave here, because I don't want to kill you".

She answered, "I will leave, because I see where there is another light to follow". What she saw was Cedar Lake.

Where she sat has been seen by many people in Moose Lake. It is on the reserve side near the lake. To this day, the ground remains bare. Nothing grows there.

—*1980*

Tobasonakwut Kinew

Anishinaabe (Lake of the Woods) 1936–

Tobasonakwut Kinew, an Anishinaabe activist and teacher, has worked for over 40 years in the United States and Canada to strengthen indigenous treaty rights, languages, and cultures, and to improve the socioeconomic situation of First Nations' people and communities. He is a pipe carrier, member of the Midéwiwin, and a long-time Sundancer. Tobasonakwut has been a consultant to tribes and indigenous organizations, a lecturer in Anishinaabemowin and Anishinaabe philosophy, and a scholar-in-residence. A gifted orator, he is frequently asked to speak publicly on a variety of issues.

Kinew's words (below) were made at the Sacred Lands Conference held October 24–26, 1996, at the University of Manitoba. The conference focused on addressing the issues of sacred territories throughout the province of Manitoba and Canada, and, in particular, how Aboriginal cultures are embedded in their relationships with land. Kinew's words ask questions about who has control over the land and are a reminder of the intellectual values in Aboriginal traditions. The answers he finds provide reasons why he chooses to change his name (from Peter Kelly), work for his community, and continue traditional ceremonies. Kinew's words tightly wind and embed multiple ideas and stories surrounding the beauty and possibility evident in Anishinaabe knowledge.

"Let Them Burn The Sky": Overcoming Repression of the Sacred Use of Anishinaabe Lands

There are two streams of thought from elders. One group of elders says, "Don't be talking about these things because you're going to denigrate what you're talking about." Another group says, "Talk about these things because if you don't, how are the young people going to know these things?"

You'll know by what I'm going to say where I'm coming from. I belong to the Lynx Clan, the *pizhiw*. It's very important that I identify myself in this manner because that is who I am, who my family is. Another thing I find very important is that I have an Indian Affairs name, called Peter Kelly, but I'm not an Irishman so I'm back to Tobasonakwut. I totally rejected that other name. As I move forward in life, I find more people doing this. As recently as two days ago, I received a phone call from two people who wanted to change their names back to traditional names. This is something that is happening and it reinforces what I was told when I was growing up. It's called *ando pawachigen,* which means "seek your dream, live your dream, understand your dream, and move forward with your dream." That determines how I've lived all my life, and how my parents lived. It points to the fact that when I go into the forest, often I realize I have been here before, although I know full well that I have never before set foot in this particular piece of land. This particular piece of forest reminds me of a different time.

When I go to sleep at night, I may have a situation which I cannot comprehend. I make offerings, and invariably the choices I have to make to resolve the problem become clear. This is how I've always lived my life.

Since I was born I've thought I must understand the sacred landscape within me so that I can function in whatever society I live in. I have followed this thought throughout my life. I'm a product of residential schools. At school, I was forbidden to speak my language for fear of being beaten up. That beating I received made my resolve to speak my language even stronger, and I'm a very fluent speaker today. I don't agree that residential school wiped my language out. My determination to speak the language meant that I would always speak the language.

As life goes on, I was inducted into the Mite'iwin for the first time, and a second time. The third time, my son was supposed to go into the Mite'iwin but he died before he did. This meant that I had to go in his place, so I went in.

I talked to an elder whose name was Pikochiins. Pikochiins spent some time in jail because the authorities burnt his birchbark scrolls. There is no offence against burning birchbark scrolls as such, but what happened was that he resisted. The Indian Agent came with the priest one day, and with the RCMP the following day, and Pikochiins resisted. He spent some time for resisting arrest. This is how they were able to burn his birchbark scrolls.

When I went into the Mite'iwin, Pikochiins was my teacher, the one who initiated me. I asked him point blank, will there be a time when I can talk about these things in public. He said, "Certainly. If you can talk about these things in two hours, what you've learned here in two years, go ahead."

I talked to Pikochiins about the birchbark scrolls. "This is not the only way to learn," he said. Then he told me about *Niikaannan*. This is a word we hardly use in conversation any more. It refers to the spiritual brothers, four of them in one place. I asked, "Where are they?" And he replied, "You mean you don't see them?" I pointed out to him that there were a number of things taking place here that I did not understand. So he said, if you don't have the birchbark scrolls to teach with, then you use reed mats. If there are no reed mats, then you use the sacred tomahawks which are engraved. If there are no sacred tomahawks, then you use the sacred arrows. If there are no sacred arrows, then you use the sacred pipes. It became very clear to me why sacred items are carved or inlaid. That's what they're there for. I didn't realize that before.

I said, "What if you have no birchbark scrolls, no reed mats, no sacred arrows, and so on?" Pikochiins said, "Then you should use and get to understand who you are. To understand the rock carvings and rock paintings." "But they're coming back," I said, "and what they're doing is spray-painting these rock paintings and rock carvings." I asked him what do we do then. He said, "Well, if they're going to destroy the rock paintings and the rock carvings, then they should burn the sky." That's what he left me with. In traditional fashion, it was up to me to try to decipher what he said.

Eventually, I came to understand that what he was really talking about was this: Over here to the east, there is a constellation called *Pagonegiizhik,* the hole in the sky, hole in creation. So many of our teachings are attached to this particular constellation. One of our teachings is, when someone dies, they go to this constellation. They move from star to star, until someone makes that offering of tobacco. Then the spirit of the deceased rests on that star, waiting for the ceremony to take place.

As I went through life and experienced many tragic things in my life, I began to realize what he was talking about. What Pikochiins did say in fact was the four major stages of the journey that we have to take of the spirit world coincide with the four major stages of grieving. This is shock and confusion with denial, anger, making deals and bartering, and finally, acceptance. I didn't realize that. I used to think, as I was going through residential school, that what the elders were saying doesn't really make sense. Now it's my responsibility to make sense of it. When I went back to the elders, they made it very clear to me that it was my responsibility.

That is the way I see the Sacred Lands Conference: what this land is all about includes far more than the land that we see. There is also a teaching that the four layers of the sky, the four layers of creation refers to the four major stages of the thinking process. The Creator came through *pagonegiizhik,* the hole in the sky, and arrived on earth with such a tremendous impact, going down four layers. The bear carried the *miigis* [shell] four years till he brought it to the surface. That refers to the four major things that happen to us in our subconsciousness. So in dream interpretation, in the interpretation of the stories, of teachings that are given to us, then we must take into consideration eight levels of consciousness. At certain points, your dream fits into a certain category. If it's strictly a thinking process, if it's an intuitive process, then you have to figure out where it fits. I am essentially talking about the sacred landscape within us as Anishinaabeg.

There are many teachings associated with each category. In considering this, I've been able to put a lot of things into perspective as to what happens in the future direction. Invariably, when I'm in a problematic situation, as I've faced many times, I go to these teachings about our sacred landscape. When I go out to fast, as our people often do, then I find that having connected myself back to earth, back to the trees, back to the lake, then there is a peace that comes with it. There's a serenity that comes with it. Then it's so much easier to find direction. This is what the elders were talking about. Now I'm older, I think about it now. "Yea, that's what the elders were talking about *ando pawachigen.*" I hope that there's going to be more respect for the rock carvings and rock paintings.

Finally, in the rock paintings in Lake of the Woods, it's been said to us by learned scholars from universities all over the world, no one is able to interpret those ancient paintings. Why don't they ask me? I've been trained in the birchbark scrolls of the Mite'iwin. What I saw in the birchbark scrolls coincides with what is imprinted in the rock paintings and rock carvings. I don't think we've lost this knowledge. We still have it.

The essence of the language is the essence of what the land is all about. It is the essence of what the sky is all about and it is the essence of who we are as people. Our language relates the landscape, both in our spirit and in the land.

—*1998*

Elders of Grand Rapids

Cree (Mistipawistik/Grand Rapids)

Mistipawistik, or Grand Rapids is a Cree community located at the mouth of the Saskatchewan River where it enters Lake Manitoba. The community is named for the large rapids that once existed there, but this feature disappeared in 1965 when the Manitoba Hydro Grand Rapids Dam was built upstream of the community. This dam not only altered the landscape and animal habitat in the area, but also af-fected the social, economic, and cul-tural lives of the Mistipawistik Cree. Traditional ways of life were threat-ened by both this megaproject, and by the sudden arrival of many outside workers who brought different values into the community. In the 1990s, Frontier School Division sponsored an oral history project to record the sto-ries of Grand Rapids' Elders about what life was like before the dam and how the dam has affected the commu-nity. The result of this project is a two-volume publication, *Grand Rapids Stories* (1996, 1997), edited by Raymond M. Beaumont.

The three stories reproduced here give a personal perspective on what the Grand Rapids Dam has meant to the community. Bernadette Ballantyne's story tells of a garden and a graveyard that are now flooded, showing how the dam has affected the people's ability to connect with the land and, most impor-tant, with their ancestors. Fisherman Jo-seph Buck describes the effect of the dam on fish populations in the Saskatchewan River and in Lake Manitoba. Gladys Scott tells of the hard work and severe punishments she saw in a government industrial school, and she ends with a re-flection on how the dam has changed even the taste of the fish.

We Had a Good Life

When I was a child, when I was brought up in Pine Bluff, what I remember is we had a good life. We had big gardens, oh, I'd say, about the school to the arena. It was an island in the middle of the river. My dad had a garden out there. We had another garden close to the house. We used to have all kinds of things there, like vegetables, and stuff like that. My mom grew some straw-berries and rhubarbs in the other garden we had. And the vegetable seeds that we got, we got from The Pas. We used to have a cellar in our house underneath. That's where we used to keep our potatoes. They put hay around the pota-toes, cabbage, and all the other vegetables we didn't can. We canned in jars.

· · ·

It's just like a little hill now, just like a little island. It flooded all around. My uncle had a great big garden and that's all flooded. My mom and dad had a big garden plus they had another garden that was ... a long island, like, and it was good soil there, and my mom ended up making a garden there, and we used to have plenty of vegetables, rhubarb, strawberries. I think there's not trace of that island now. It's all under the water.

· · ·

I don't even know if they were even told. They were working on it but I don't know what. They were trying to get some kind of compensation 'cause we have a little graveyard there, too. It's kind of [flooded], like, it's not quite under the water. Like, we have two of our family members buried there, a brother and a sister, and my uncle has one, I think, one grave there. So the

Hydro, like, they got a monument made. Something like a big stone, and it says, "In the memory of the children of my mom and dad and the children of Alex and Florence." I didn't see that yet, and it's fenced in. I saw a picture of it, and it's fenced in. We're going to have some kind of a reunion down there, and we're going to get the priest to come and bless us.

Bernadette Ballantyne
—1996

No Fish Can Go Up There

You have to have help from the government now. The quota is determined per fishermen, per area. Yep, it's pretty basic. Once you fish your quota; that's it. You leave the lake.

I guess the first thing is to get more pickerel. Spawning beds. That's what we're aiming at. We're talking to Hydro.

The fish hatchery here is supposed to serve the community, but it's never ever done that.

Sidney Green, he was a Natural Resource minister. That's the time they shut down the lake because of mercury. The commercial fishermen couldn't even eat the fish, but Sidney Green allowed it, that the sport fishermen can go and kill the fish and eat it . What makes me mad was when I was with Hydro them days, I was on the operating staff, twenty-four hours, then some guys used to come from Winnipeg and use those scoops. The pickerel were sick right by the cable, and I used to go look at them, for God's sake. Scoop those fish, dump into their car, and we're not suppose to eat them. And they took them away to Winnipeg and fillet them. That's what they did, when Sidney Green was head of that stuff.

No such a thing as meeting. That's out. They just went ahead and built the bridge, road, and the dam.

There was quite a bit of work, but look at the fish…. Right away, they wrecked the fishing. Completely wrecked the fishing. The fish in them days was just loads … take them to Winnipeg and fillet them, and we are not sup-posed to eat them.

The fish, they're trapped in there now. Where else do they go? They have to stay there and spawn.

No fish can go up there. It's impossible. That much they told me. I was there [working for Hydro] for three years. In those propellers, no fish can go through there.

I had one sturgeon two years ago. One sturgeon. I caught it back here. I put it in the boat. My wife cooked it at 3:00 p.m., and we couldn't even eat it. It was tasteless. Nothing. No taste to it whatever. I had to throw it in the garbage.

As I told you before, they go through oil, filth, and dirt. I was there for three and a half years, and I was there emptying those things. I'm saying that, of course; I was there.

They only open the spillway a little bit, and it's not enough for the pickerel to spawn. We got some of their documents, and their materials. The spillway, there's a structural problem there. That's why they won't open it. I'm involved in negotiation with Hydro and the fishermen. I'm president of the fishing co-op here. So we're trying to get the pickerel spawning back again, but Hydro puts up a strong argument. Now we found there's a structural problem there. That's why they won't open the spillway. We just found that out about four weeks ago.

Joseph Buck
—1996

We Helped Each Other

When I went to school [I learned] how to clean up. We didn't have no teacher. We first go to school for four months, and then our teacher was very old and he left the school. And so, then we didn't have … no teacher, so they train us how to work. I was a big girl already.

I was a kitchen girl … the first three months.… I used to like it the best where I used to work in the kitchen.… And then … I would waitress and set the tables for the staff that lived in the school.… We dressed white, too, when we went there, you know… We take turns two of us at the time being a waitress because there were lots of staff there, around twelve or fourteen of them.… There was a nurse there … for the kids … and we had to iron these uniforms. That's the thing I didn't like. We have to do them perfect. We have to starch them. The uniforms, white uniforms. If you don't do it right, you have to do it over and over. The first time I used to do it two times, you know, but we come to know how to do it. You have to use a hot iron, and we didn't know that time.… Sometimes they send us the men clothes, because of these boys. They were rough and they're tearing their clothes and everything, and we have to mend them. There was a sewing room in the place. And our socks, we had to mend them. And pants.

They [the boys] were threshing … working … and they using those machines at the time, eh. Not like today.… But these ones you have to use horses … with those wheat. That's where they were working, those big boys, eh, gathering those … they stook those wheat … in the big field.… And those vegetables, enough to have in the winter, eh, potatoes and carrots and turnips…. We had a big farm to learn how to farm. The boys, too, same as us big girls. So we have to get up, kitchen girls, five o'clock in the morning, every morning, and we had everything ready by … eight-thirty. And then to school at nine o'clock…. It was rough…. If we do wrong, we get the strap.

They pick up big ones. Big ladies…. Like when we fight, eh, they have to come and broke us up, eh. And they used to get strap … I had a strap three times … Girls were fighting … in the night, especially in the night Oh, they used to fight a lot.

We didn't know this, they were going to strap that girl, those senior women, eh? They beat her up with a strap … oh, bruises around her [arms]…. So we all walked out. We didn't listen to them. We just about ganged up with them women [staff], cause of them big girls, they slap her. So they let her go … And we told them not to ever, ever do that to us again. We're going to gang up … if they ever do that to us…. And they told us not to ever do that to the staff. So that [one] staff left.

. . .

I remember when they started to build the bridge. They had the big cement [piers]. They built three or four of those to go across. And there was lumber…. It was scary. When we went across, they used to use barges. The first time we went across [the bridge], they didn't even fix it yet. It was scary when we went across. They wanted us to go and see it, so we did while they were building that bridge. After they fixed it, they started this highway, and everything. And the dam. Oh, there was lots of things going on.

There were Métis on that side [of the river] and this side Band, but we used to help each other…. When somebody killed a moose, they shared it. Everybody got it. There was lots of fish. They just had to fish down here by the mouth of the river. Nice, nice white fish. Not like these dark fish now. They were white, white. It was nice…. It doesn't taste right now when we eat [fish], just like moss. It tastes like that.

Gladys Scott
—1996

Bernelda Wheeler

Cree/Assiniboine/Saulteaux (George Gordon First Nation, SK) 1937–2005

Bernelda Wheeler was an author, journalist, radio host, actor and broadcaster. In 1946, her family left their farm on George Gordon First Nation to move to northern Manitoba. She suffered physical and emotional abuse while attending residential schools in Birtle and Brandon but continued schooling and graduated from high school in Churchill in 1955. Wheeler broke ground as one of the first native voices on CBC radio, bringing to the forefront First Nations people and their concerns and issues. From the early 1970s until the mid-1980s, she was most recognized for her work on CBC's radio newsmagazine "Our Native Land." Author of numerous short stories and poems, Wheeler was also an award-winning children's writer of books such as *I Can't Have Bannock but the Beaver Has a Dam* (1984) and *Where Did You Get Your Moccasins?* (1986). In recognition of her pioneering work in media and literary circles, she was awarded the Order of Canada in 1991 and a Lifetime Achievement Award in 2005 from the Anskohk Aboriginal Literacy Festival. Known for

her social activism, Bernelda Wheeler died of cancer in 2005.

In *I Can't Have Bannock but the Beaver Has a Dam,* Wheeler shows how Aboriginal people, even in today's world of modern technologies and industrialization, remain connected to animals in practical, everyday ways. Similarly, through lyricism and repetition, the poem "Our Beloved Land and You" explores the important role played by the land and our relationships to it, as generations of Aboriginal men and women attempt to teach and pass on traditional knowledge to their children. Wheeler's words convey remarkable and lasting teachings about the ethics, beauty, and complexity of life.

I Can't Have Bannock but the Beaver Has a Dam

"Mom, can I have some bannock?"

"I can't make bannock."

"Why not?"

"The oven won't get hot, so, I can't make bannock."

"Why won't the oven get hot?"

"Because the electricity is off. Without electricity, the oven won't get hot, so I can't make bannock."

"Why is the electricity off?"

"Because the power lines are down. Without the power lines, the electricity is off. Without the electricity, the oven won't get hot and I can't make bannock."

"Why did the power lines fall down?"

"A big tree fell and knocked the power lines down. Without the power lines, the electricity is off. Without the electricity, the oven won't get hot and I can't make bannock."

"Why did the big tree fall?"

"A beaver chewed the tree and the big tree fell and knocked the power lines down. Without the power lines, the electricity is off. Without the electricity, the oven won't get hot and I can't make bannock."

"Why did the beaver chew the tree?"

"The beaver needed the tree to make a dam, so, the beaver chewed the tree. The big tree fell and knocked the power lines down. Without the power

lines, the electricity is off. Without the electricity, the oven won't get hot.
And I can't make bannock."

"Where's Dad?"

"Dad's gone to put the power lines back up. When the power lines are up,
the electricity can go on. When the electricity goes on, the oven can get hot.
When the oven gets hot, I can make bannock. And the beaver still has a dam."

"After all that happens, can I have some bannock?"

"Yes, you may."

But what *is* bannock?

Bannock was, and still is, a staple quick bread much loved in northern
regions.

For individuals or families on hunting or fishing trips, the ingredients
were minimal and did not spoil. The bread could be cooked quickly in a frying pan over an open fire. In homes bannock is baked in the oven or on top
of the stove and is still a favorite food.

Bannock
3 cups (750 ml) flour
Dash of salt
1 teaspoon (5 ml) baking powder
2 tablespoons (30 ml) lard or bacon drippings
½–¾ cup water (125–175 ml) (enough to make a stiff dough)

1. Combine dry ingredients in a bowl.
2. Make a little well and pour the water in.
3. Mix into a dough and knead *well*.
4. Flatten it out, put in a frying pan, and poke holes in the top with a fork.
5. Cook over coals from an open fire, or oven medium heat on the stove top
   until brown. Turn and brown other side. Or, bake in the oven at 350°F
   (180°C) until well browned.

Bannock lends itself to experimentation and substitution: it can be enriched
by substituting whole wheat flour or by adding skim milk powder or one egg.
Raisins, other dried fruit, or a few fresh blueberries can be added. Bannock
can also be cooked over a campfire (just like marshmallows but healthier!)
After kneading the stiff dough, press it on the ends of a fresh stick in a hot-
dog shape and toast till good and brown.

—*1984*

Our Beloved Land and You

Great Grandfather
    In stories we learned of you and yours
        Stories of times long gone
            That travelled through them that came before
        And came to us and ours
    Of the great grandfather who journeyed the land
            Our beloved land
            And you

Small Boy
    Clever and fast, who questioned life
        Who ran and played and watched
            You they chose to leave and learn
        Then bring your teachings back to them
    To live, to change the ways of the folk of the land
            Our beloved land
            And you

Young Man
    Your wife and your small ones
        All at home learning a strange new way
            From a different world, a way
        Those strangers brought. A way they said
    Was the only way for you and yours, the prairie folk of
            Our beloved land
            And you

Church Man
    You followed that way your whole life through
        The half-remembered stories say
            And while you walked your eldest son
        Hunted the bison while others played
    He fished the rivers, the lakes of the land
            Our beloved land
            And you

His father
    You knew that food was scarce
        In those times that were then new
            Times when the others slaughtered all
        When bison were less, new shelters cold

Small spaces to shield those ones within, on the land
Our beloved land
And you

Wise One
You knew of the ways, of shelters shared
The ways of the ones without
The ones who knew a home no more
The ones who shivered and shook
The ones who starved, the ones in the valleys of the land
Our beloved land
And you

You cried
In a homeland losing its own
Losing its life, its lives, its strength
Grasping and gasping for love and soul
Turning to others for strength and food
Knowing full well that all was there, there on the land
Our beloved land
And you

Giver of all
You gave of yours, of shelter, of struggle and love
To the ones who had lost, to the ones without
You gave of your son and his will to work
You gave to the hungry and cold
These were the ways, the ways of old on the land
Our beloved land
And you

Teacher of old
Trudging those prairie trails, in snow, in heat and sleet,
Taking the teachings, the new but the old
Teachings you learned from them
You made them yours within your soul
Then shared with those of the hills and plains on the land
Our beloved land
And you

Of their faith
You they scorned, thought you simple, inept, those strangers
On our land. They paid you half a wage—they did

Then threatened to take the half away
You stole their time—their time! They said
To share, to give, to love, those heathens on our land
Our beloved land
And you

With your head held high
Take it, you said. Take the whole half pay
Abandon me if you dare
I'm here to do a job for God
My God of the prairie, of valley, berries and birds
I'll do my job, it's here with these, these of the plains on
Our beloved land
And you

At treaty time
Spoke the words of a foreign tongue
Spoke the words of your own
Signed the papers, the treaty was made
The lands were gone for the others to use
A small reserve was all you had on this land
Our beloved land
And you

With strength and tenacity
You did your job and journeyed the plains
You taught your folk and prayed to God
In your solitary way. You knew the trees
And streams and lakes as your journeys took you far
Far over valleys, forest and hills. Far over prairie land
Our beloved land
And you

In your stubborn way
Refused to yield when your old age came
Refused to rest though weary and worn
Still you trudged the trails to teach
The ways of strength for body and soul
The ways of a God who loved the folk, folk of the land
Our beloved land
And you

Your soaring soul
You left to those who still live on
Legacies that will not die
Of the stubborn strength
Of the one who broke the trails to another way
The one whose tenacity held to the ways of the land
Our beloved land
And you

—*2001*

The Prairie Call

The Prairie Call was a community newspaper founded in 1961 by members of the Indian and Métis Friendship Centre of Winnipeg. It was edited by Marion (Ironquills) Meadmore, and it featured writing by many Aboriginal activists, intellectuals, and artists. As Meadmore's editorial of February 1961 indicates, *The Prairie Call* was intended to bring news of the Friendship Centre's activities to people outside of Winnipeg, but it also had another important function: to create a sense of shared purpose among urban Aboriginal people who were dedicated to making a difference for their communities. Initiated at the beginning of the Native American Civil Rights movement (often called "Red Power".) *The Prairie Call* was very much a call to action for politically engaged Aboriginal people. Readers were encouraged to think about how to fight for Aboriginal rights and how to improve social, economic, and health conditions in Aboriginal communities. Many of the newspaper's contributors went on to make significant contributions as artists, politicians, and community activists. *The Prairie Call* contained important articles on human rights, traditional Aboriginal values, and the contemporary realities of urban Native life. The pieces reprinted here give a flavour of the excitement and the intellectual energy that coalesced in this important venue of Manitoba Aboriginal thought and expression. While many of the articles deal with the serious issues of racism, poverty, and social dysfunction that resulted from colonialism, the newspaper also provided an outlet for humour and personal-interest stories such as the final selection here, "The Damaged Goods."

Welcome to *The Prairie Call*

The first edition of our paper, *The Morris* last month, hit our readers rather as a surprise. No one but the few of us who worked on it knew that it was being born.

There are many things we realize that must have remained unclear in the minds of those who read our paper. So this time we will try to enlighten you on who are the people that put this thing together, why it was started, our purpose and last but certainly not least the title of the publication.

The title, *The Morris,* was simply an unimaginative name given for lack of anything else to call it. We would like to apologize to anyone taking offense at the name. *The Prairie Call* is the new name. We feel this will satisfy the majority....

The history leading up is very short. The Centre serves a transient group of people: those who train for a job in Winnipeg and find employment out of town. Many live in Winnipeg for the winter and take jobs elsewhere. These we feel, because they have used the Centre during their stay here, are indeed interested in the many activities that go on.

Others too *The Prairie Call* should reach: The parents or people on the reserves who have young people making use of the Centre, and generally interested white people who know the value of the Centre of this kind, but would like to see the progress we Indians are making. The service groups too are interested.

So it was not too difficult for a group of Indian people, who were having coffee at the Centre one day, to see the need of having papers published. And it was decided then to start this project and as a result *The Morris* came out on January 31st for the first time this year.

But while *The Prairie Call* will serve to bring news of the Centre, we feel the main purpose of the paper will be the voice of Manitoba Indians; thus the paper is not geared to any one man or woman.

We also find there is cost in putting out this paper so that we have to charge $1.00 yearly for a subscription or 10 cents a copy. If there is a profit, which we hope there will be, the money will be used to expand our paper. The address to write to is found on the back page.

We do encourage Indian people to express their ideas in letters to the editors.

Marion Meadmore
—*February 1961*

Unity

"In Union there is strength." This is a saying that applies to all forms of human endeavour. When a people unite for any purpose whatsoever be it good or bad, the force derived from this union is a hundredfold what it would be in scattered groups.

Our Indian people of Canada are composed of many and varied groups. At no time in history or pre-history were they ever united. This is quite understandable when one considers what a vast and varied country Canada is, and the great numbers of tribes that inhabited it.

Some of our people have been in constant contact with the white man for three hundred years and some in the northern reaches of Canada have never been in actual contact with white man except for the fur trader, Mounted Police, missionary and government officials. In actuality, they know nothing of the white man's way of life.

Therefore, we can see from this our people are diverse not only in geography, but in ways of living. Yet, we are all one people. At one time we never thought very much about this one way or another. An Indian from another tribe, or another part of Canada was as foreign as someone from Europe. His interests and problems were not our concern as he lived in a different part of the country.

There have been many native societies formed in Canada, but they mostly concern only one region or province. These societies are formed usually by a group of Indians who are proud of the background and traditions of their Indian people. They do not want to lose this, for by losing our identity as Indians, we are losing our most precious heritage. We may change our way of living, but as long as we do not forget or wish to forget we are Indians, we have lost nothing as a people.

There is a gradual realization amongst the Indians of Canada of the need for a national brotherhood. By uniting and considering our problems and their solutions as one people we will have accomplished something that is most necessary. This summer, on August 17, 18, and 19 in Regina, there is to be an all Indian Conference held for this very purpose. The formation of National Federation for Canadian Indians will be a great step forward for our people.

Joe Keeper
—*June 1961*

The Rain-Dance and the Car Lot

The Farmers, Dairymen, and Growers watched the skies very closely this spring for the rains which would come and win the race with that dreaded enemy… drought. They did not come in time.

Because the Canadian economy is still largely based on the farmers and growers, it is natural that people living in urban areas are concerned also. So it was that one used-car dealer took advantage of the anxiety of Winnipeggers to sell used cars. He announced through the press and TV that he was hiring "A Saulteaux Chief and his tribe to dance, until we are all rained out." We did not pay too much attention then, until later publicity said it was a Rain Dance "right on the car-lot."

The dancers came in and on a 10 plank platform, set on coke cases, began the dance on a hot Tuesday morning early in July. They were dressed in costumes often seen at a real dance, however the manager did not think them colorful enough so he went out and bought more feathers and junk to dangle on these people. Crowds of people did come down to his car-lot alright, but only to laugh and scorn these dancers. Some of our working Indian people felt the jeering and mocking at work where their fellow employees took up the whooping and hollering.

Because we felt this was using the Indian Rain-Dance for cheap publicity plus the fact that many of us still respect our Indian customs, prompted Tom Stevenson and myself to write a letter of protest to *The Winnipeg Free Press*, which read as follows:

> Dear Editor:
>
> The Whiteman is at it again! The Rain Dance has been held sacred in the minds and hearts of the Indian, a tie between the Great Spirit and man: in the past few days this ceremony has become an utter farce in the city of Winnipeg.
>
> The Rain Dance has been practised among our people for ages: it is a prayer in duration of three days, asking our God (probably the same God that the Whiteman worships) to favor us with rain. The ceremony was elaborate and sacred. The setting was important in that it required certain objects from nature (symbols), which entered parts of the ritual. These symbols, such as a tree chosen for perfection and used as an altar, were essential in their communion with the Great Spirit. The men and women who participated represented that group of people who upheld the highest moral standards of a tribe. These chosen few then proceeded to fast for three days and nights, during this time continuing their rituals of song and dance, and meditation. This ceremony was spent in deep reverence by the congregation of Indians. There was no laughing and mocking then as is taking place in the city today. This laughing and mocking is being done by supposed Christians who, showing disbelief in their own religion, find it convenient to laugh at one of the most unfortunate minority groups in our country.
>
> We, as Indians living here, still have great respect for our old people who practise their ancient rites and who have faith in what they do. While we realize the fact that our people are economically in a sad state of affairs, and will do almost anything (even at the sacrifice of pride) to earn a living, we can't quite forgive the ignorance of those responsible for this farce. Here too we feel that again the Whiteman is exploiting the Indian, this time for the benefit of selling used cars!

The following article came out as a result of our letter. There were no interviews with either Tom or myself, so we can see how a newspaper can twist things about to suit themselves. The article read as follows:

Winnipeg Indians have taken exception to a city car-lot company's sponsoring of a Rain Dance on its Main Street lot. Charging that again the Whiteman is exploiting the non-educated Indian, Mrs. Meadmore (Editor of a national newspaper—*The Prairie Call*) said Thursday that the city Indians are seriously considering picketing the dance which they label an "utter farce." Mrs. Meadmore said that she had been besieged by calls from fellow Indians asking action to stop the Sacrilege. "The dance cannot possibly be held on a downtown lot," Mrs. Meadmore said, "it is a sacred ritual and must take place in a certain setting, be attended with special set prayers and songs, and be executed by certain people chosen especially for high moral standards. I was down there yesterday and I was just ashamed of what I saw." She said, "This was travesty."

The setting and purpose of holding the Rain Dance—selling used cars—make it blasphemy, Mrs. Meadmore said. She criticized the laughing and mocking which was going on… "Which is being done by supposed Christians who, showing disbelief in their own religion, find it convenient to laugh at one of the most unfortunate minority groups in our country. The stunt is simply another example of exploitation of non-educated, economically hard-up Indians by Whitemen," she said.

The next day two more articles appeared in the newspapers, one in *The Free Press* and the other in *The Tribune*:

RAIN DANCERS LEAVE CITY UNDER CLOUD—*The Tribune* (July 6, 1961)
A group of Indians who have been performing a rain dance on a city car lot left the city Thursday night to continue in more natural surroundings. The Indians were brought into the city by the car firm on the agreement that they would dance until it rained.

Following cries of "sacrilege" from Mrs. Meadmore, the company decided to move the Indians out of town to a secret destination where they will continue the dance. Mrs. Meadmore complained that the dance must take place in certain settings and was never intended to be carried out on a hot city car lot with spectators laughing and mocking.

A company official said Thursday the Indians were prepared to continue the dance—but not in the scorching heat of the city—until their contract runs out or the rains come.

INDIANS FORCED TO STOP BY HEAT—*The Free Press* (July 6, 1961)
The Indian band which has been trying to dance up a squall at a Winnipeg car lot have returned home—but promised to continue their efforts on a proper, grassy surface. The heat of the sun, beating down on the pavement, was becoming too much for them.

Spokesmen for the firm, meanwhile, have said they were "hurt and disappointed" by Mrs. Meadmore's charges that the rain dance performed here was a "travesty… a sacrilege… a blasphemy… an utter farce." "These people were very, very happy here," said a spokesman. "They had excellent meals and very good accommodation out on North Main; they told is it was a holiday for them. We were hurt by the accusations because we felt they got exceptionally good treatment while they were here. But it's been very hot the last couple of days and they felt they'd like to go back to the reservation where they could continue the dance on a proper, grass surface. We drove them back at 11 last night. I understand it's not really proper to do this dance on pavement… But they certainly were not being exploited here."

The paternalistic attitude expressed by the sponsors of the Rain Dance, "These people were very happy here, they had excellent meals and very good accommodation out on North Main," cannot be accepted by intelligent people. The results of this recent Rain Dance proves how great is the need for a better understanding between the Indian and the Whiteman. While it is not in our hearts to hurt our own, as we were accused of doing, we simply cannot see the religion of our forefathers reduced to the level of a circus performance.

The Whiteman will continue to exploit us as long as we sit back and allow things like this Rain Dance to go on. We need to take more action as a group. Many of our White Brothers think that the Indian is devoid of all his pride; I think it is time that we lose some of our patience and show him that we still are a very proud group of Indian peoples.

Marion Meadmore
—*July 1961*

The Importance of Defending Our Culture

The young Indian student today is virtually ignorant of his own past culture; here I speak only of the Canadian Indian, though there are exceptions.

This fact cannot pass through my mind without instilling there a good deal of concern. Indeed the Indian often grows up with badly twisted ideas about himself, partly due to the educational system and to prejudice which has given him a complex. However, having associated with American Indians I can say with confidence that the exact opposite is the case among those Indians.

I have been very much impressed by and not a little envious of the knowledge of Indian-self which the American Indians exhibited in our relationships. For this reason, it seems to me that the American Indian reveals less puzzlement in his affairs with the Whiteman and much more confidence. It is true that he suffers also from prejudice and discrimination but since he understands himself it becomes less of a problem both in college and in business. It can be said that when a person knows himself he possesses a greater ability to orient himself and to relate himself to the world about him.

This, of course, is the influence of the Whiteman… and he is beginning to realize this; he has rather turned us upside down and has left us scrambling to get a hold of ourselves, and many of us haven't. True, ideas change. It used to be that ideas changed the times but here I am afraid it is the times which change the ideas. In a conformist society all have got to apply themselves to a certain accepted line of thought, and to depart from this usually results in outcasts from society. The Indian suffers here because the thinking of the two is vastly different. Though the Indian has come a long way in making this transition, he runs into difficulty because he fails to answer the question, "Why?" We often misinterpret the anthropologist and say, "There are no differences between the races," but let us be more cautious. There are differences, and it is these differences which add color, interest, and knowledge to humanity. It is these differences which determine a culture, whether it be German, Italian, American, or Indian.

Many of the Indian's ideas are vague, uncertain; they vary between the Whiteman's thinking and the old Indian thinking which has managed to survive. Many of us, for instance, find it difficult to cope with the impersonal attitude which is predominant in contemporary society. Who is sincere and who isn't? Who is genuine? Am I really accepted, or are they just tolerating me? Such questions typify this underlying uncertainty, this vagueness, this craving for that which was real.

It is fitting here to propose a challenge to the young Indian student to turn and study himself, and to ask himself just how much he knows about himself as an Indian…. Let him examine his attitude toward life, and compare his thinking with that of the Whiteman. Let him ask himself, of what did our religion consist, and how was it practiced? Why was it condemned? Was it because it was Paganism, or was it condemned by a group of people which knew next to nothing about it? What is our place in society and what can we contribute to society as a whole?

First he should take an interest (he must) in his history. Was he actually a brutal savage as he has been lead almost to believe? He can justify his denial of bestiality only if he can look for, and find, the facts. They are there, but who is interested! Why not study his legends and compare them with the mythology of other ancient cultures. The results are quite interesting as I have found. There is much to be found in the art of the legend. Look into his religion without any guilt of anti-religious leanings. In his ceremonies he communed with Spirits. Was this completely superstition, or was there more to it than meets the materialistic mind. I should like to write of this again in view of modern scientific research, even at the risk of appearing eccentric.

When a youth was initiated into manhood he was required to go into the forest to fast and meditate for approximately 2 to 3 days, at the end of which time he saw a vision. This vision determined the course of his later life. Silence is of great importance in the Indian character, and this is one characteristic which is often misunderstood by the Whiteman and now of the Indian himself. If he would find the answer as to why, it would become less of a problem. Is silence a sign of stupidity as the gabby intellectual would assume? Silence was respected, silence was wisdom, silence was the mark of a well-balanced personality. Silence is a part of our culture which has survived and come down with us. Preserve it. It is something which the Evangelist overlooks in his blantant sermons and his disturbing rambling prayers. The modern Whiteman is afraid of silence. He is afraid to be alone with himself; this is not a good sign. Indeed what he needs is occasional seclusion.

Yes, our standard of ethics has been shattered. Our honesty, loyalty, honor, respect, and bravery has gone down the drain. We steal, we bear little respect, and we hide when a Whiteman laughs. We run and hide because we are aware of the possibilities of his speaking the truth when he calls us stupid, lazy Indians. We run and hide because we have no knowledge of the past with which to justify ourselves. Many people talk of changing the Indian in order that he be successful in life. His attitude towards education, yes, but not his character. Nothing disturbs me more than to see the Indians sacrifice a rich heritage for the sake of being accepted in a rat-race. They want us to think like Whitemen. Great Zot!

Let us take an interest in ourselves and our integration into White society will be more certain, confident, and successful. Look into the early Indian's form of government, his manner of raising children, his ethics, his affinity with nature, his legends, his laughter and his silence. Our minds will be freed from doubt, shame, and contempt, and our hearts will open to the friendship of the Whiteman.

Tom Stevenson
—*July 1961*

Outlook in City—Bleak

If you have been thinking of coming to the city in the near future, please think twice. Unfortunately, many people think that the city is the land of "Milk and Honey"; that is jobs and education are here for the asking.

Well, what are the facts?

The job situation for unskilled, semi-skilled workers is at present very discouraging. Because of the cutbacks in government spending, high interest rates, the scarcity of money for business investments, high personal or corporate taxes; business and thus employment are very slow across the land. To add to all the confusion, the CPR and McGavin's Bakeries have steadily laid off many of their employees.

Anyone who nowadays lands a job, is very lucky.

Suppose *you* come to the city and land a job; what about finding yourself a place to stay. For a man and a family it generally costs one hundred dollars or more per month to find a decent place to stay, if you are lucky to find a place at all. Many unscrupulous landlords offer substandard housing to people in the slum area of the city and people are paying for dilapidated accommodation that isn't worth the price. Sometimes, it takes two or three weeks to find a good place to live because of the housing shortage, many people wind up on the streets.

Aware of the situation, the Centre is presently unable to find jobs for the people coming to the city. All we can do is refer people to the Canada Manpower Centre—where too, there are no jobs.

Jack Spence, of the Winnipeg Housing Authority, who is of Indian extraction, is having difficulty [providing] housing for welfare people let alone those who are not on welfare.

The general picture is not likely to change for quite sometime, so the next time someone tells you how great the city is, you will know he's not giving you the real story.

Graham Jones
—*March 1968*

The Damaged Goods

Don't let the title mislead you; we are not selling anything. It's the name of a newly formed rock n' roll group.

The Damaged Goods are regular guys who have been using the Centre space for practice. The band consists of three young Indian men.

Tom Jackson plays the rhythm guitar and is the lead singer of the group. He hails originally from Alberta but now resides in Winnipeg, where he has already lived for five years. Tom has been playing the guitar and singing for two years, beginning with folk music and switching to rock n' roll. He likes pizza, guitars, a sports enthusiast in football and basketball, short girls with green eyes; his favorite band is the "Strawberry Alarm Clock"; he dislikes

Country music, parents, spoiled kids, playing cards, batman, working, and extra long cigarettes.

Bernie Kihn plays bass guitar. He was born in Southern Manitoba and has lived in Winnipeg for nine years. He has played for one year. Bernie likes very fast cars and has made a hobby of overhauling them. He is now working on a '59 Ford with which he will attempt to win a national world record. He also likes music. According to Bernie, he has no dislikes.

The drummer, Roland Desjarlais, has been playing drums for six years. He is extremely good at it. Roland was born in St. Boniface and has lived in Winnipeg all his life. Roland is known around the Centre as Suzy. Suzy likes food, mainly pizza, pop, bananas and pears. He also likes beach parties, tackle football, swimming, fast cars, motorcycles, Thursdays, Fridays, Saturdays, long holidays and summer, girls wearing mini-skirts and long hair. Suzy dislikes winter, dentists, heights, getting up in the morning, getting a hair cut, Sundays, working, girls with too much make-up on, beans, pumpkin pie, ice cream and apples.

Author Unknown
—*March 1968*

Citizens of Camperville

Métis (Camperville)

On March 14, 1973, Métis high-school students from Camperville, Manitoba, held a sit-in at Winnipegosis Collegiate. They took this action to draw attention to the racism and discrimination they had been experiencing since they were integrated into the school system six years earlier. When the sit-in was over, 22 students were suspended and the alleged leader was expelled. The parents who supported their children chose a leader, Ferdinand Guiboche, to represent them. They requested a meeting with administrators and demanded an investigation from the Department of Education. During negotiations, two teachers were selected to continue teaching the suspended and expelled students until a resolution could be reached. Unfortunately, the students were lukewarm to these teachers, and many chose not to participate. The

incident divided the community of Camperville: some parents wanted to send their children back to the Winnipegosis school; other parents advocated for a separate Métis school where their children could obtain a culturally centred education.

The following passage is an excerpt from a collective statement made by the group advocating for a separate school. It was submitted to the Minister of Education for Manitoba, and describes the feelings of many Métis in the Camperville community. The passage captures the political awakening and new urgency of the Manitoba Métis communities in 1960s and 1970s as they began to organize and draw attention to the injustices long perpetrated against them. As Camperville students and many of their parents realized, the right to education in one's

cultural lifeways is of paramount importance, and negotiating integration and
autonomy while attempting to avoid
exploitation by a dominant culture is
something Aboriginal people will
continue to face as they work toward
achieving equality, self-governance,
and prosperity.

Statement by the Citizens of Camperville

The sequence of events can never represent the emotions and passions which
arise out of and surround the progression of events. Similarly, hindsight
allows us to see the various "ifs" which might have temporarily avoided
a confrontation.

The term *temporarily* is important because confrontation was inevitable.
Historically, since the invasion of Manitoba by Canadian troops in 1870, the
Metis people have held an inferior position both socially and economically.
Our flight to escape the persecution of white people and an effort to earn an
honest living led us to found communities such as Camperville and Duck
Bay. As we established small farms, developed the fisheries and operated
trap-lines, the white people followed. In the competition which followed,
too often the Metis lost out because they lacked capital to expand and uti-
lize the technology of society. Thus we were relegated to either living in ever
increasing poverty as independent fishermen and trappers (which resources
declined steadily) or became the poorly paid servants of white settlers and
did the jobs which they did not wish to do.

Such a situation has continued until the present day. With increased
awareness of our problems, needs, and the potential within ourselves, it has
become obvious to us that our greatest hope for equality was through having our children receive a good education. The Camperville people eagerly
accepted the opportunity to integrate their children from grades 7–12 with
the people of Winnipegosis. With the greatest of hopes we sent our children
35 miles away to a school. Integration of students from grades 7–12 was tried
for six years.

Over the years the disappointment and disillusionment has grown. There
follows just a few facts and feelings that brought this about:

1. The bussing of students to Winnipegosis meant that Camperville stu-
    dents had to leave the Collegiate at 3:30. Thus they were unable to join
    with other students in sports and social activities which would have made
    them feel that they were truly a part of the school.

2. Not all, but some of the white students in the collegiate treated the Metis
    with a disdain and arrogance that caused the Camperville students to
    lose their sense of confidence.

3. Not all, but some of the teachers considered our children as intellectually inferior. Such teacher attitudes developed an unhealthy state of mind in some of the Metis children.

4. Not all, but some of the adult residents in Winnipegosis held a double standard towards behaviour of people on the streets and in places of business. One standard for the whites and one for the Metis.

5. The Metis students, especially the girls, were subjected to taunts and obscenities by some men in the community.

6. It became obvious that the Duck Mountain School Division had a great pride in the "melting pot" role their schools played. But the people of Camperville did not wish their children to be "melted" into a homogeneous mass. We are Metis people who have a unique history, a unique culture and wish our children to gain a deeper knowledge of it through their studies.

7. The curriculum of the school denied the Metis students an opportunity to learn of content relevant to themselves. In the curriculum it was as though Metis and Indian people did not exist except in ancient times.

8. The parents became increasingly unhappy with a school system that seemed rigid, restrictive and appeared to force the children into moulds which stifled creativity and made the students less sure and confident as they progressed through the grades.

9. All of the above factors contributed to the fact that in all those years only six Metis students finished grade 12 and some of those did not pass all the grade twelve subjects.

Thus we say that if the teachers and School Board had involved parents in discussing the list of grievances a confrontation might have been "temporarily" avoided.

It would have come sooner or later for the situation was steadily growing more intolerable. Indeed one can predict that unless action is taken by government in co-operation with Metis people in many communities throughout the province there will be a series of such confrontations.

Historically, the Metis have retreated from the Manitoba province of 1870. Later they retreated in the face of advancing white settlement. Now the resources of our lands are being exploited in every part of the province by white people. The technology of print, sound, and pictures permeates every community and influences adults and children. Our horizons have expanded. We realize now that education is the key to our search for equality and that the only resource we fully own are our children.

They are our future. For their future we must fight for we have nowhere left to retreat.

—*1974*

George Morrissette

Métis (St. Boniface) 1938–

Métis poet and fiddler George Morrissette was adopted and raised in St. Boniface, Manitoba, by a Metis family. His grandfather, Jean-Baptiste Morrissette, had a strip farm along the Assiniboine River in the 19th century. The farm stayed in the family until 1950. Jean-Baptiste's father was Arson Morrissette, who came from Quebec to Manitoba in the early 1800s and married an Anishinaabe woman named Therese. George's foster mother was Aurore Lavallee, who came from a family that had a strip farm along the Red River in St. Norbert, Manitoba.

Characterized by musicality and the use of oral storytelling techniques, George Morrissette's poems resonate with Métis voices from the past and the present. His work arises from an abiding interest in the historical role of Métis people in Manitoba. "Michif Toune Buffalo" hearkens back to the centrality of the bison in Métis culture of the 19th. In "Le Pique-Nique des Purs," Morrissette seems to be comparing the post-World War II period to Homer's depiction of the classical world after the fall of Troy. However, the "Second Great War" mentioned in the poem may also be a reference to the Métis Resistance of 1885, which followed the first large-scale Métis Resistance in 1869–1870. The result of this double historical reference is a kaleidoscopic sense of history in the poem, which points out the similarities and the differences between moments of cultural crisis.

Michif Toune Buffalo

once chased by Winchesters and Gunships
the buffalo are back
increasing by a billion
every ten years
they swarm the prairies

      helplessly we watch

they chew, chomp, snort in our ears
paw our feet, shoulder us into the willows
swamps, rocky shield

      buffalo winter is a good paradise

yet they leave us the chokecheery bushes
bountiful this year by the La Salle River
rich red & purple, hanging clusters

our lips smeared with delight, we chew
the pits greedily

the buffalo pass by, snorting, chewing, rumbling
thunder herds sent by Jehovah and Jove
        and the Great Space Spirit

—2001

Le Pique-nique des Purs
(fragment after Homer's *The Iliad*)

After the Second Great War
the long war of the breaking of lives
people scattered like brief leaves
over our earth, groaning
when the war gods paused, spirit of men, women
and innocent children almost defeated,
the sun beamed hot on the prairies of waving wheat,
earth basking in the sun, fallow beneath the snows.

Our household in St. Boniface buzzed,
"Coming back! It's coming back, yes,
they say they're going to start it up again,
le pique-nique des purs
in St. Vital, where Louis Riel ran about as a boy."

Les Purs, horse breakers, were riding again
on the open prairie, beyond the baseball fields
racing for prizes, and the sheer joy of it,
their swift-footed horses shaking the horizon.

"It's true. There's going to be
a *pique-nique des purs* this summer."

Now that the Great War was over,
Alfred would hear again the galloping
that shook the horizon, recalling his team of horses
he once led, powerful memories,
the working hooves and neighing and snorting
his own fine team, life giving, pride of life,
ploughing the furrows, pulling the threshing machines
through waist high wheat, men stooping to stook.

People of the ironic smiles, *Les Purs*,
laughing, shouting across the prairies
by the Seine River, where Riel ran about as a boy,
struck by the great spaces, our natural church,
"*on est des purs Metchifs*"
of native blood commingled
with all blood come to the prairies.

The "Pure-Bloods" were gathering again in St. Vital
to play crown & anchor, bingo, and lasso prizes
by throwing wooden rings, the same
held by my mother "pour faire la dentelle"
the jigs & the fiddle, the red-river miracle,
horses beyond, not far yonder, beyond the bushes
(where the men sneaked away homemade drinking)
ride the horses, hooves thudding, earthly drumming,
at gallop to shake the horizon, whistle at the wind,
shout for the sun, once again breaker of horses.

All weekend, easy smiling faces,
to see one another again
under the sun playing on the prairies.
Great War and winter gone, chokecherries returning,
hooves thudding, earthly drumming,
dust rising, war and winter gone.
At gallop to shake the horizon, whistle at the wind,
shout for the sun, once again breakers of horses.

Memories of that Sunday afternoon
my mother trying her luck at bingo
my father playing crown & anchor
I throw the wooden rings
the grass trampled down with smiles and greetings
tonight the Red River Jig contest.

In late afternoon, the tug-o-war
my father would be anchor man, strength
for winters and wars, for mother and me,
in this world of wars and winters,
tying the rope about his torso, digging in his heels
the cheering for the tug-o-wars, each team surging
in opposite direction, the crowd urging

sun pouring down, earth basking, grasses trampled,
hooves pounding in the distance, my father's heels
digging in, slipping, holding fast again.

The male strength for winters and wars
horses to plough furrows, pull threshing machines
stoop for stooking, chokecherries red and blue,
hanging in thick clusters, wine and once pemmican,
the cheering for the tug-o-war, first one team
is dragging the other, now the other team of men
defeating the other.

Sun going down over the land, vast spaces to the horizon,
late sunlight on the grass, long walk on the gravel road
leading to the streetcar stop
away from the fiddle starting up
the dancing platform bright, waiting for the flying feet
the dancing will go on late into the night's mystery
We are leaving the special days, *pique-nique des purs*
his hand in mine, large, callused handler of horses.
Suddenly his rough palm pressing down hard on my shoulder
for steadiness, an alarming weight,
the man of strength unsteady,
about to stumble, my mother hurt and disappointed again.
Man of the team of horses, hand on my shoulder,
his weight pressing down to catch his balance,
for he has mingled with the other scarred men
in the bushes beyond, swapping stories on destiny,
beyond the bushes yonder, by the thudding hooves
men who had enlisted in the Canadian Army
to go overseas to bleed pure-blood

Now with jobs, working with other damaged men
having come here from the world over,
some from the gulags of eastern Russia,
others scattered here from elsewhere
after the long war of the breaking of lives
people scattered like brief leaves
over our earth, bleeding

—*2001*

Doris Young

Cree (Opaskwayak Cree Nation) 1940–

Doris Young is from Opaskwayak Cree Nation near The Pas, Manitoba. She is a residential school survivor who has travelled the world speaking and teaching about Aboriginal educational and justice issues. She speaks and writes Cree, was a senior researcher for the Manitoba Aboriginal Justice Inquiry, and is currently on the survivors national committee for the Truth and Reconciliation Commission of Canada. She holds a master's degree in public affairs and helped to build the Indigenous Women's Collective of Manitoba, of which she was the first president. A mother and Nokomis (grandmother), she works at the University College of the North in Aboriginal programming.

Young's piece is from a keynote speech she gave at a 1990 symposium, "The Conference on People and Land in Northern Manitoba." The symposium brought together many stakeholders with wide and divergent interests, including citizens of the north, political organizations, corporations, educators, academics, consultants, and government representatives. One of the criticisms that emerged at the conference—and a lingering one in today's world—is that the north is viewed all too often as a collection-site of resources for economic exploitation, not a place where people, cultures, and ecosystems thrive. Young's speech is a reminder of the richness of family, culture, and community in the north and of the responsibility all Manitobans have to the places we do not often see or hear about.

Northern Manitoba Hydro Electric Projects and Their Impact on Cree Culture

My earliest childhood memories are the lessons that my grandmother taught me. She took care to teach us the spiritual riches of my culture. She maintained that all life is sacred. She taught us that the earth, the fish, as well as plant and animal life, were as important as men, women, and children. In my culture there was no hierarchy system. We were all important.

I remember my grandmother's first and last function of each day was to pray. She was thankful for life. She would put her scarf on her head and bow her head to say her prayers. This spiritual outlook influenced me in a deep and meaningful way. I knew that my grandmother was sacred, just as the earth was sacred. I loved them both in a very special way. Today, I too am conscious of the sacredness of life.

My mother, on the other hand, taught us the practical things about life—how to work and how to relate to one another in a kind and respectful way. Her teachings were also centred around caring, sharing, kindness, and being respectful of one another.

This socializing process could be seen clearly during the gathering season. Every fall, the women and children of my community would go out to gather the abundant harvest of berries and moss in preparation for the winter season. Women and children were the gatherers and we worked side by side, in a co-operative way. Gathering season was also the time when we caught up on the summer's news. My mother and aunts enjoyed each other's company and during lunch break they would exchange stories about life in general. There was an order to the way in which the work was carried out. We all contributed to the berry pot. Each person, even the young children, was expected to put their berries into the pot. At the end of the day we would feel that we had made a substantial contribution to our food supply. When we were allowed to play, we did so knowing that our job had been done. We enjoyed ourselves.

Berry-picking season was always a time for working, learning and having fun. Prayers were said and tobacco was offered before we picked. My mother taught us discipline and diligence in our work, as well as giving back to Mother Earth. When we worked, we worked. We were not allowed to be noisy until our job was done. I learned that it was not good to carelessly grab a handful of berries and shove them into my pail. We learned to be clean pickers. When I pick berries now I think about how the plant feels if I were to pull its branches too harshly. We were taught at a very early age to be clean pickers and to be respectful to the plants.

We were also taught silence. My mother would tell us to sit down and just listen, be quiet for a while, listen to what is going on. Through silence, we learned the value of being attentive to our surroundings, to feel the interconnectedness of Mother Earth and to the universe. I learned how to look and see how much life the bush actually had. I learned to be respectful to the plants and to be kind.

The berry-picking season also gave us children a chance to climb trees and have lots and lots of fun. Swinging from the very top of the trees was great. Sometimes we weren't heavy enough to bring the tree all the way down to the ground, so an older sister or brother would have to rescue us and bring us safely to the ground. We learned to get along and to care for one another. This was a valuable teaching because the berry-picking area was also filled with danger. We were always mindful of bears, or of the fact that one of us might wander off in the wrong direction and get lost. I always remember being told to take care of one another and we did. If we were fighting and quarrelsome, someone always told us that this was not good behaviour. I remember the kindness with which we were told, and we listened. Today, I now tell my children to take care of one another.

Every fall we also gathered moss to keep the babies dry and warm, and to prevent diaper rash as well. Once the moss was picked, it was hung on the trees to dry. The children would then have time to play again. Moss picking was a very important job and everyone was expected to contribute to this activity. The moss was left on the shrubs for a few weeks and when we went back to pick up our moss, it would always be there. No one ever took it. We always seemed to know which was ours and which wasn't. We were respectful of others and did not touch their moss. My mother taught us to respect someone else's property. She always knew just how much moss to gather, as we had enough to last us till the next gathering season; no more, no less. She knew how to conserve and passed this knowledge down to us.

Water is a very important and sacred item to Aboriginal People and is a component of our spiritual ceremonies. Some significant reasons are these:
  · all living things are dependent on water;
  · human beings are mainly made up of water;
  · life begins by the breaking of the water, just before a baby is born;
  · women are life givers and are crucial to the survival and continuation of our culture.

It therefore follows that in my culture, women are the carriers and protectors of water. At our ceremonies, women bless the water and carry it around to each person to drink so that we are all blessed by this sacred gift.

I now understand why the women in my family carried the water from the streams and rivers for our cooking, drinking and washing. The pails were heavy and I would often complain about this. My mother would help me by taking some of the water out of the pail, but she didn't take away my responsibility. I still had to do my share and carry some water. Before we took the water, my mother would be silent in prayer. She gave thanks to the Creator for the gift of the water that we would be using. Today, I give thanks to the Creator whenever I see the river or the lakes.

WHEN I WAS YOUNG, my community was a safe and healthy place to live. We were relatively happy and confident people because we were able to sustain ourselves from the land. The land from which we received our food supplies was also the place where we learned our traditional values of caring, sharing and respecting. The socialization process in which we learned and accepted these wonderful values was so evident in everything that we did. We learned to use these tools in our work and in our play.

THE FLOODING OF OUR land altered our culture and changed our lives forever. Our economy, as well as our physical and spiritual health, has been drastically affected. The land where my mother gathered our berries and our moss was destroyed. The land where my father trapped was flooded. The lakes where my father fished are now contaminated. The hunting is less and less plentiful.

First of all, when my father lost his trapping area, a big part of our economy was gone. It's been about 30 years now since the flooding took place, and only recently has my reserve received some compensation for this loss. The lucrative summer fishing is all but a memory. Hunting has been affected in that the moose have moved further and further away. We find that it may now be dangerous to eat moose because they too appear to be contaminated. It is most distressing to read notices not to eat moose, particularly the liver because of mercury contamination. The liver was the delicacy that we all looked forward to eating. Gathering berries or moss as a vital economic activity of the community is a dim memory.

Our physical health has been affected because we no longer eat balanced meals. We have not been able to bridge the costs between the food we harvested from the land and store-bought food. The expense is too much for many community members who are now unemployed. People buy whatever they can afford and sometimes it's not always what's healthy. As well, we have not adequately learned to convert the nutrition of our former diets into the present way of shopping at convenient stores and shopping centres. Both my mother and grandmother had diabetes, and so have many, many others in my community. My mother and grandmother both died from diabetes complications.

Many people became welfare recipients. This position broke their pride and their generous spirits. My community suffered, as families became quarrelsome and agitated with one another. The welfare system does not encourage sharing; in fact I have seen people being chastised because they had shared their store-bought food with others. Besides, the welfare money can never be stretched adequately to share our groceries with other members of our community. Many people have not come to terms with this situation. Shopping from a grocery store also does not provide the same satisfaction to a hunter in providing a meal for the family. The hunter is, in fact, removed entirely from the process.

Our connectedness to the earth became less and less because it's hard to feel connected to the earth when one is picking up food from store shelving, or when one turns on the tap for water.

Our spirituality was also altered because we no longer practised the values we learned when we were out on the land. Going to the store for food doesn't teach us about the universe in which we live, or how to care for it

There's a gap in our generation with respect to our culture. My children don't know what living off the land means. Urban living prevents my children from knowing how to be connected to the earth. Picking berries is now a fun day, and is really no different from going to a city park for a picnic. It's not the same as knowing that our winter supply of food is dependent on that activity. The utility of picking berries is not the same today. The generation gap is, in fact, substantial when one considers the socialization process that is learned from living off the land. It's harder for my children to have a humanistic view of the land.

THERE IS A SAYING that when you destroy nature, you are destroying yourself. I believe that this is true. When our land was destroyed, my culture was immeasurably altered. The lessons that my family taught me about life, when I was young, were lessons that were related directly to Mother Earth: the plants, the animals, the fish, the water. Our socialization process was thus connected to our relationship with the universe. We learned to be respectful and to care for Mother Earth and one another. We learned to share the abundance that she provided. Yes, the flooding of our lands altered our culture and changed our lives forever.

In spite of all of our best efforts, there is a gap between myself and my children. The tragedy of this gap is that we will never share the same kind of understanding about life from the universe that my mother, grandmother and great-grandmother were able to share with their children. There is also a large gap in my own life knowing that that part of my culture has been destroyed. My generation appeared to be the last to know what living off the land really means.

—*1992*

Theodore Fontaine

Anishinaabe (Sagkeeng First Nation) 1941–

Theodore Fontaine has served Aboriginal people in many capacities. When he was seven, Fontaine was taken to the Fort Alexander Indian Residential School. He was incarcerated there for 10 years, from 1948 to 1958, and at the Assiniboia Indian Residential School from 1958 to 1960. He then worked in a multitude of jobs in labour, construction, and as crew chief in mineral exploration. By 1979 he had found his place working for his people. He served as chief of Sagkeeng First Nation, with the federal government in support of Aboriginal programs and First Nations lands administration, as executive director of the Assembly of Manitoba Chiefs

(formerly the Manitoba Indian Brotherhood), and now as chair of the national Indigenous Leadership Development Institute Inc. Fontaine is a director on the board of Peace Hills Trust, a member of the Board of Governors of The Manitoba Museum, and is a volunteer companion to clients of the Hospice and Palliative Care Association of Manitoba.

Fontaine's residential school experience profoundly affected his life and community, prompting him to write a memoir, *Broken Circle: The Dark Legacy of Indian Residential Schools* (2010). In the book, he examines the legacy of Indian residential schools on survivors, communities, and multiple generations. In the chapter "Killing the Indian in the Child," Fontaine explores the way in which Aboriginal children at the schools were quickly manipulated into blaming their parents for their abandonment, thereby building their trust in those who would often exploit them. Fontaine's bravery and unique storytelling ability is a shining example of the resilience of residential school survivors and illustrates the importance of storytelling in healing.

Since publication of *Broken Circle*, Theodore has been presenting his memoir and speaking about his healing journey with residential school survivors and with audiences in First Nations communities, universities, libraries, schools, and Aboriginal and non-Aboriginal organizations across Canada.

Killing the Indian in the Child

Mrs. B.,[35] the breadmaker, was one of a few of our loved ones who worked at the school. She also assisted the nuns and other workers in the kitchen, in the laundry and with such duties as knitting and sewing. Restricted from direct contact with us, these caring few acknowledged us from a distance, without fanfare, but such instances brightened our days and we craved even a glimpse of them.

Mrs. B. was well respected by children of all ages. In my era, two or three of her children were also at the school. That must have been a joy as well as a deep sorrow for them. Having their mother go home each day after work without them must have had devastating effects. I shudder to think what my attitude and feelings might have been if it had been my immediate family member who was there and he or she had been disallowed to show feelings and affection. I can't imagine a heavier burden than if my mother had worked at the school five days a week, yet been withheld from me.

Sometimes Mrs. B.'s children sought her out, hoping to catch a glimpse of her before she left. It was terrible for them if they missed even seeing her from a distance before she left. On the other hand, the anticipation of seeing her the next day must have been wonderful.

Years later, when a few survivors began to talk about their experiences, I remembered how I'd viewed relatives who worked for the school and the church: I'd slowly become indifferent to them. Eventually they were neither band members nor relatives. They were just workers at the school. Even children with mothers or fathers working at the school sometimes came to see them as "just workers" or servants. Some lost all understanding that the far-off woman in the kitchen was their mother. Some were ashamed that one or both parents worked there, and some saw them as a part of the residential school regime somehow. Yet, if you weren't immediate family, you could see

---

35 To protect the identities of those he writes about, Fontaine uses only first initials.

these people as a connection to home and the reserve, and as friends of your family, these servants of the church were a welcome distraction.

The last day of June was the beginning of our summer holidays, which lasted until the first week of September. Initially, that was our only release from the school. By our third or fourth year we were also given a week at Christmas.

For the first two or three years I distrusted Mom and Dad when I got home, and would stay away from them and my siblings, sometimes by myself, sometimes with my cousins. I'd spend a great deal of time at the river's edge and at its swimming areas, wandering along the bush trails with my slingshot and stopping to pick berries along the way. These excursions took me back to my younger days and my years of freedom before school. Mom and Dad always knew where I was; Kookum, Mishoom, my siblings or other relatives knew where to find me. By the end of the first two or three days, I'd have forgotten my mistrust and would greet Mom and Dad enthusiastically when they returned from work. Reflecting on these initial reactions, I see that I had learned to become aloof in my mistrust. This would be one of the typical behaviours that I and other survivors bestowed on people we love.

In our early years at school, we savoured the safety and freedom of our homes and became oblivious to having to return to school in September. After a few days back at home, we reverted to enjoying the closeness of family, the freedom to speak Ojibway and our relationship with the environment. We enjoyed these short holidays, not realizing they were meant to wean us off the way of life at home and on the reserve.

Our response to the holidays became more subdued the longer we were at school. The dull realization that in no time we'd have to come back to school lessened the joy of anticipated freedom in June. Even now, thinking about summer holidays and going home at the end of June makes me giddy, and then suddenly I remember that those times were short-lived and in some ways made our incarceration even worse.

This ambivalence ensured that we became more and more subdued as we got older. I began to see the unadulterated joy of young boys and wonder if they understood that they'd be back in September. As a young child free from school and at home for a while, I had resolved to do whatever I could to prolong the experience. But predictably, I became used to school life as time went on and related more with the priests and nuns who had become so familiar. I got so used to being in school that my closeness to and contact with my family became less and less important; the separation meant that our lives and interests had become disconnected.

Some residential school survivors still believe and vigorously defend their belief that nothing ever happened to them there. I disagree. The mind adjusts to any situation and attempts to attain a state of happiness and safety. When we refuse or are unable to achieve a sense of calm, our lives follow a path of turmoil and self-destruction. We suffer the consequences, manifested by our health and other physical realities. It's incredible how well our minds protect us to ensure our mental health and safety.

Survivors of Indian residential schools in Canada became victims of Stockholm Syndrome long before it was a familiar term around the world. The misguided sense that some of our keepers were kind and good was based on single and rare acts of kindness and support. In most cases, we came to see our keepers as saviours and protectors from hunger, isolation and abandonment. We watched parents and family leaving the school on that first day and blamed them for leaving us. We blamed ourselves for being left behind, abandoned because we weren't wanted or had been bad. We blamed ourselves for still being hungry, isolated and alone.

As young children, easily manipulated, we created new connections and rapidly bonded with some of our captors. Being malleable and wanting kindness and love, we slowly came to believe that there was kindness in those we were around every day and attached ourselves to those who looked after us.

Looking back on my years at school, I remember fondly some nuns, priests, and others who I think were truly there in the belief that they could help us adjust to a foreign way of life. I believed at the time that they didn't want to change us so much as teach us what we needed to succeed. I'd hate to think that those few priests and nuns who were kind were hoodwinked into practising a method of manipulation that resulted in the Stockholm Syndrome.

They emphasized that we wouldn't see our parents until the next Sunday, though we'd never before been away from home for even a night. They pounded into our little minds that our families couldn't look after us as well as the school could. This was the biggest hoax and tragedy bestowed on Indian people and their children in Canada by residential schools. The removal and separation of young children from their families and the manipulation of their minds to hate their Indianness was the biggest abuse and the most common method used to kill the Indian in us.

In some cases, the actual caring and benevolence by Church people was genuine. It was nevertheless very effective in manipulating the minds of young First Nations children. I remember the emotions and desperation of that first day of school incarceration in my first direct contact with the Church and priests. I still experience overwhelming feelings of horror, anger, hate and abandonment when I think of that day. Father R. allowed me to see my parents walk out the door and down the sidewalk and recruited my cousins to restrain me. Clem and Marcel used force to hold me. I blamed them then, and Mom and Dad. Although I eventually understood it was not their fault that I had to be left at school, the idea that it was their doing had been effectively planted in my mind. The blame had been shifted from the priest and the Church to my family members.

Over the years, I came to appreciate my cousins' genuine caring and concern. I remembered that they stayed with me through supper and the early evening. This gave rise to a brotherly love that remained with me until their deaths. I miss them still.

I also recalled later that Father R. approached me after supper that first evening as I sat in front of what was to be my locker for the coming year. Even though Clem and Marcel were there to console me and had hardly left me alone, I was deeply affected by the afternoon's activities and felt terribly alone and lost. I experienced strong panic when the priest sat down beside me. Although my knowledge of English was minimal and I only understood a word here and there, his voice and tone were very soft, and it sounded as if he cared about me. I thought he might protect me and make sure I was okay in this strange environment. Perhaps he'd help me get home somehow. After my forceful separation from Mom and Dad, his behaviour served as a first step to replace that abandonment by transferring my trust to him.

Father R. participated in a wide array of sports; his macho style endeared him to all the boys at the school. He was very competitive and this enthusiasm often pitted "his" boys against Indian boys and men on the reserve. Although we also often encountered his strap, head slaps, kicks and other physical attacks, most boys looked up to him.

Another man who had the support and following of a large number of boys was Brother M. He was somewhat like Father R. in that he sometimes appeared to have a deep disregard for the nuns and their rules. He sometimes changed those rules. For example, he ordered the nuns and kitchen personnel to allow a school hockey or baseball team to have supper while fully dressed for the upcoming evening competition in Pine Falls or Powerview. Such games were proud moments when we showed off to the other kids by parading into the refectory in our hockey gear. Brother M. would speak loudly to the nuns, who were either cooking or supervising, yelling that he wanted "his boys" ready to leave and not having to waste time getting ready after supper.

I remember him once grabbing a white lay farm worker by the scruff of his coveralls, shaking him and yelling at him because he hadn't finished cleaning and preparing a field so it was ready for "his boys'" baseball game. There were other such instances; his was an example of how children were conditioned to feel love and respect toward their captors.

One Saturday afternoon, after Brother M. had been transferred elsewhere, we were on our respective playgrounds, boys on one side and girls on the other. Various activities were under way, there was a baseball game on the boys' side. Suddenly a fielder lost focus as he stared at something down the road. He hollered, "Brother M.! Brother M.!" and pointed at a figure approaching the church. Immediately a group of boys, four or five at first, then more than a dozen, ran to meet him.

As they crossed the girls' playground and the rectory rose and thundered into the churchyard, there stood an awestruck lone figure contemplating taking flight up the road or refuge inside the church to get away from this scruffy crowd. Maude, an old friend to many on the reserve, was visibly taken aback and somewhat shaken by the unexpected crowd of young boys around him. Although he was well known and liked by almost everyone on the reserve, he wasn't Brother M.

Maude was obviously embarrassed and a disappointment to the boys, who immediately scampered back to the school grounds. For years, poor Maude endured jokes and laughter about this incident, and light-hearted comments like "you'll never be a brother" and "the priests have to save your soul first." The incident did provide some comic relief to the kids at school—even more to those who didn't run toward him that day.

Like Father R., Brother M. wasn't without a reputation for a quick temper and quick hands and fists, though most of us were fast enough to make sure his boots didn't connect with our most vulnerable parts. His violent and volatile temper was well known, and although he sometimes verbally belittled us as Indian people, our claim to being "real" Indians had been lessened by church sermons, classroom teaching and comments, the school environment, cowboy-and-Indian movies, condescending treatment of reserve residents, and the idea constantly instilled in us that we were now better than our reserve families and community. The job of getting rid of the Indian in us was being well done by the Church, government and teachers.

—2010

Marie Annharte (nee Baker)

Anishinaabe (Little Saskatchewan) 1942–

Marie Annharte (nee Baker) is a poet, storyteller, filmmaker, essayist, and educator. She was born and raised in Winnipeg, although her mother came from Little Saskatchewan First Nation, Manitoba.

Throughout the 1960s and 70s she lived in Minneapolis, a centre of Native American activism and political activity at the time. While there she worked as a community advocate, teaching Native

Studies at several colleges. She was one of the first people in North America to develop curriculum for a course about Native American women. In 1980, Annharte returned to Winnipeg and took a leadership role in changing the child welfare system. As a film and video maker, she has produced shorts such as *Too Tough* (1990), which celebrates the spiritual power and resilience of Native women, and *Moon Pause* (1995), a film that draws on a recurring childhood dream in which she brings spotted horses back to her people. Annharte has published three books of poetry: *Being on the Moon* (1990), *Coyote Columbus Café* (1994), and *Exercises in Lip Pointing* (2003). She is the co-founder of the Regina Aboriginal Writer's Group and a member of the Aboriginal Writers Collective of Manitoba.

Annharte's work challenges common stereotypes and concepts of orality and literacy, advancing new ways of understanding First Nations' aesthetics, art, and literature. The following selections of her poetry show radical honesty, irreverence, and complex senses of humour and irony. Her poems reveal how she has witnessed Indigenous resilience and challenges systemic inequality and a lack of respect for Aboriginal women by mainstream Canadian society. "Penumbra," in particular, calls for a critical awareness of the racial attitudes and misogyny that led to the murder of Helen Betty Osborne, a Cree woman from The Pas, Manitoba. These poems illuminate Annharte's wide range of voice and style—from sharp imagery, precise diction, exploratory humour, and performance.

Hudson Bay Bill

after so many years
Rupert wants me to pay
A bill   but he owes me

I am still for the most part
savage   my credit is no good
my fur is gone before I get it
I'm just a skin so bare

my story exploring history
is not told   I was not
in the way until somewhat old"

trappers liked my dark face
settlers did make a good party
their wives properly hid

dangerous touching trinkets
jumped   put in a jail claim
I stole those in my underwear

my way of being honest
is doubtful as heaven

I want a fair share not
what I end up begging

—*1990*

One Way to Keep Track of Who Is Talking

If I change one word, I change history. What did I
say today? Do I even remember one word? Writing is
oral tradition. You have to practice the words on
someone before writing it down.

I do not intend to become the world's greatest Indian
orator. Maybe I might by accident. I might speak my
mind even when running off my mouth like I'm doing.
Language finds a tongue. Maybe it will be an Indian
accent.

Counting hostile Indians is made easier because they
don't talk much or very little. They look the part
– the part in the middle with braids. You never do
know if you are talking to an Indian.

Frozen Indians and frozen conversations predominate.
We mourn the ones at Wounded Knee. Our traditions
buried in one grave. Our frozen circles of silence
do no honor to them. We talk to keep our
conversations from getting too dead.

—*1990*

Penumbra
for Betty

Temporary the shade my straw hat weaves
across my basket face of Caribe pleasure.
The bright sun makes me want to run and jump,
I had been told if I were smart, I'd stay hidden.
On my island, I keep to myself & lie around.
Turtles crawl past me to dig their nests.
Tortuga oil is outlawed and so am I.

Odd, this exposure of my not too recent killing.
Seventeen years it took getting to court
those who mashed my face because of dark skin.

Hating the contrast of each pinky penis
I left The Pas to be a turista and relax

They understand I stayed away to make sure
I'm not the only witness to their sorry act.
Not even good at it, I might add as insult.
The reserve is a huge donut around the town,
no place to go unless you're Indian like me.
Laughing at the other end of the beach
gets me wondering how it's my turn.

—*1990*

Pretty Tough Skin Woman

old dried out meat piece
preserved without a museum
missing a few big rips
her skin was guaranteed

her bloomers turned grey
outliving the city washing
not enough drinks to keep her
from getting home to the bush

tough she pushed bear fat down
squeezed into sally ann clothes
she covered up her horny places
they tried sticking her under

soft jelly spots remain in bone
holding up this pretty tough hide
useful as a decorated shield for baby
swinging in her sweet little stink

just smell her old memories, gutted fish
baked muskrat—she saw a lady
in a shopping mall with a fur coat
told her an Indian must eat such delicacies

her taste was good she just needed a gun
to find a room in the city to put down
her beat-up mattress where her insides fell out
visitors ate up the bannock drank her tea

they were good at hocking her radio or tv
everywhere she stopped she told her troubles
if I press my ear down on this trail I bet
I'll be able to hear her laughing and gabbing

—1990

Raced Out to Write This Up

I often race to write   I write about race   why do I write
about race   I must erase all trace of my race   I am an
eraser abrasive bracing myself embracing

it is classic to want to write about class   not low class but
up the nose class   I know I am classy   brassy   crass ass
of a clash comes when I move up a rung

we are different skins   different bins for brown rice and
white rice   not even a container of wild rice   you know
what they do when you are white and not rich   poverty
counts big when you count the cost of a caste a colorful
past

drunk as a skunk he danced at the Lebret Hotel   what for
no   not really   says he's not writing because they won't
publish his books   he does a number for a book   he
hugged me like I was his old Tibetan guru out on the
dance floor teleporting again

white racists notice color which they don't have   you
might be off-white   a bone white   a cream white
alabaster white   dingy white if you don't wash often
enough   nevermind a non-bleached white   white with
pinkish undertone   peaches and cream   white with
freckles   who is color blind   I write my black ink on
white paper   I white out write out my color lighten up

full of self I saw old whitey again but he wanted to be a
part of a pure religion not like ours   not that he was a
white racist but a pure racist in his heart which had no
color but our color   red   red   mind you a few white
corpuscles but compared to the red they were a minority
not invisible

so few of me yet I still write not for the white audience but
the color of their response to my underclassy class   the
flash of their fit to kill me why race away to the finish
when I cross the finish line will it be white   will I be red
from running   hot and cold touch me not less I am to be
divided against my self who is both red and white but not a
shade of pink maybe a beige pink blushed flushed off
white right I color my winning every time   I am still in the
red not the black   blackened red   reddened black   but
what about black n' blue   green at the gills   yellow belly
but what about the whitish frightish part I put it behind
behind me when I need to say my piece about togetherness
that we must breed not by ourselves but with everyone
out in the world who will listen   hey   I'm a half a half
breed   a mixed bag breed bread and butter bred my
whole grain bannock will taste as good to me even if I
smear on red jam sink my white teeth down into it down
the red hatch to the black hole   that is behind it all   the
whole black of me   the whore backing up behind me
the sore holy part of me which is the blackest darkest most
colored most non-Indian, non-white slice of me bred to
wonder

—1990

Jackson Beardy

Anishinaabe/Cree (Garden Hill Reserve) 1944–1984

Jackson Beardy was born on the Garden Hill Reserve on the shores of Island Lake, Manitoba and, like many, was removed to attend residential school at the age of seven. Later, he moved to Winnipeg and studied at Technical Vocational High School and the University of Manitoba. In the 1960s, Beardy focused more professionally on his art and created some of the most dynamic and expressive Aboriginal art existing today. He is known as a member of the famous "Indian Group of Seven." Even though he was famous, Beardy experienced profound racism during his career. In 1970, for example, an event was held at the National Arts Centre in Ottawa to commemorate Manitoba's centennial where Beardy's work was featured. Arriving at the gala, security guards would not let him enter. At the peak of his career, Beardy died suddenly of a heart attack. A special memorial service was held in the Manitoba Legislature Building to honour his life and contribution to Native art in Canada.

Beardy's work draws on the traditional knowledge he learned from his grandmother, as well as on his personal research into the myths and legends of his Oji-Cree heritage. In his written stories, he sometimes did not indicate which community or storyteller he received a version from, so it is difficult to tell the origins of these tales. Still, the distinctive drama and psychological complexity of these stories will be recognizable to anyone familiar with Cree oral traditions. "The Revenge" portrays elements of the harsh northern climate as malevolent beings that must be defeated through courage and intelligence. "The Story of the Giant Skunk" reveals an elaborate other-than-human world full of struggles and politics. "The Bachelor" is representative of Beardy's visual art, using imagery of transformation to describe the ties between humans and the natural world. These stories are deeply traditional, yet Beardy's retellings make them very relevant to the contemporary world.

The Revenge

Once there were two brothers living alone far out in the forest trapping for fur. The younger brother was a bachelor and the older brother sheltered him along with his wife and family.

One winter his younger brother was out checking his traps. On the way home, he walked into a storm and the Keewatin, the North Wind, engulfed him, freezing him to death. When his brother discovered his frozen body, he promised to himself he would avenge him.

In the spring when the ice started to melt with the warmer spring weather the older brother stood by the shoreline looking onto the melting ice.

"Ha! Serves you right for killing my brother," he sneered at the melting ice.

From out on the lake, the Ice replied, "You will regret next winter what you said to me."

The man laughed and howled as he watched the ice every day melting until it completely disappeared.

Then from that day on, and throughout the whole summer, the man and his family gathered and stored food. The woman dried as much fish and meat as the man could provide. And in the latter part of the summer, the whole family set about cutting dry wood for the long winter. In the early fall, they started to build a special lodge in preparation for the coming of the cold Keewatin. Firstly, he built a large round spherical lodge with split logs. In between he wedged the cracks with peat moss. Then after he completed it, he built a similar smaller lodge inside the first one. Where the outside door was located, he built the inner door on the opposite side of the first, creating a long hallway in between the two lodges. Hence, once one went in the outside door, one had to walk along the hallway to the opposite side in order to go in the second lodge. When he had completed his task, he carried all his food supplies and dry wood into the interior living quarters to store them. One half of the lodge was taken up by his winter supplies. When the last of the autumn leaves had fallen, he said to his wife, "Keewatin will come soon. It is time to prepare and move into our lodge."

When they had moved in, they could hear the cold breath of Keewatin crackling outside, freezing everything on earth little by little as Keewatin drew near. As the crisp crackling of the freezing grew louder, the man said to his wife, "Keewatin is drawing closer. The closer he gets the colder it will be. He will reach us by nightfall." Little by little, the huge fire began to die from the extreme cold and the lodge began to crackle and shake as the outer logs began to freeze solid. Still the man fed the fire with wood shavings to keep the dying fire going.

"He is here," the man said as he gathered tinder and fine birchbark beside him. Presently they heard footsteps outside, growing louder at each step toward their lodge. They listened quietly as they sat shivering beside the tiny fire. The sound of footsteps went around the lodge once and then stopped at the outer doorway. Then he entered the outer lodge. As soon as the nearly frozen man heard him enter, he quickly threw the tinder and birchbark on the tiny fire and it exploded into a huge, blazing bon-fire. Then he further added the finely chopped dry wood. The footsteps echoed in the hallway as he made his way to the inner door where they lived. Just as he finished feeding the fire, Keewatin, with his icy coat, emerged from the hallway into the lodge and stood there with his arms crossed. The man and his family still sat by the fire warming themselves as they watched Keewatin. In a few moments, Keewatin started to drip water all over his body and a pool of water formed by the fire. Soon, before he melted further, Keewatin turned and walked out the doorway into the night. As the footsteps reached the outer door, they heard a thunderous crash. However, the man kept adding wood to the fire all night as his family slept snugly.

In the morning when he went outside to track him down, he found the Keewatin had only made it to the outer doorway. As Keewatin took another step, he had fallen headlong out the doorway and smashed into a thousand pieces of ice. He had melted and crumpled from the intense heat the previous night.

From that winter on, the family enjoyed a warm winter, having defeated the cursed cold of the North Wind, Keewatin. The man had avenged the death of his brother.

—1970

The Story of the Giant Skunk

Once there lived a giant skunk who was feared above all by all the creatures in the land. And if anyone came upon his tracks in the snow, he would know by the arthritic pain in his bones. The creatures knew it was suicide if they tried to track him and also that if the giant skunk knew he would destroy anyone or anything tracking him by squirting them with his poisonous gas from his gland near his rectum.

One day a group of villagers espied a set of tracks in the distance. But they did not dare to investigate, fearing it might be the skunks. These people were winter people—animals who stayed behind to brave the winter instead of migrating south or hibernating. Finally, curiosity got the best of them and they approached the weasel, who was reputed to be the slinkiest of the creatures.

"Please, weasel, go over and see if it is the skunk's tracks or not. If it is, we are afraid to cross it to go hunting in that direction, where most plentiful game is found."

The weasel promptly bounded off, taking long leaps in the snow. A distance away, he began to burrow in the snow toward the tracks. Since the giant skunk was heavy, the weasel had to burrow very deep and came up from below to smell the tracks.

As once the skunk knew that someone was disturbing his tracks. He circled and followed his own tracks. When he had encircled his tracks, he found no other tracks leading from his. But he was sure someone had somehow disturbed his tracks. He retracked but only this time he dragged his hind feet deeper in the snow, propelling himself forward with his fore-paws. Soon he found a tunnel leading to his tracks. Then he followed the tunnel in the snow until the tunnel came up to the surface. From there he was able to follow a set of tracks of a weasel.

Before the skunk had discovered the tracks, the weasel had arrived at the camp of the winter people and delivered the warning that the tracks that they had seen in the distance was that of the terrible giant skunk. With that dire news, the whole camp moved away from the territory as fast as they could, taking the most difficult course along the high cliffs. They left an old woman who was too feeble and old to travel behind in the camp.

When the Giant Skunk arrived, he noticed that only one lodge remained but plenty of signs that plenty of people had lived here. Obviously, they had left in a hurry. Stomping into the lodge, he addressed the old woman, "Grandmother, where are the rest of your people?"

"Your pug-nose should tell you," the old woman answered snidely, knowing that this dreaded giant skunk was going to kill her anyway.

"Grandmother, what or whom are they afraid of?"

"An ugly pug-nosed smelly creature," she replied defiantly.

The skunk remained quiet for a moment. Finally, he broke the silence. "Grandmother, look over here," he said as he turned his rear end on her. The old woman turned but she did not have time to look as her head was blown off her body.

Soon the skunk was on his way tracking down his enemies. As he struggled up the treacherous cliffs, he grew furious at each step of the way because the more he struggled up the steep inclines he lost most of his poisonous gas at each breath involuntarily, which was why the winter people let him to the high rocky trails.

As the winter people struggled on, two young women in the group fell in the snow on their faces, too exhausted to go on further. When the skunk came upon them, the two women played dead. The skunk could see nothing that could have killed them. So he turned them both over and began examining them. When he saw their genital organs, the skunk thought to himself, "Yes, they must have cut themselves accidentally with a knife. But I don't see any blood."

Curious, he scratched one of the women around the "wound" for signs of blood. As he scratched, the woman suddenly began to giggle because she could not refrain from the tickling he apparently gave her. From that, he was so angry that he blew the women's head off in one mighty blow and started off the chase anew from his fit of anger.

By this time, the winter people were too exhausted to go on any further. "Let's devise something to rid of our adversary," they said when they stopped to rest.

"I'll volunteer to ambush him while you people go on ahead," the lynx said to the group. "I can bound away faster than most of this group."

"I think I am better suited to do the job," the wise wolverine interrupted. And so it was decided that the wolverine wait for the skunk. The lynx bounded away in disgust into the forest. The rest of the group again started out to a place not far away to hide and wait for the wolverine within hearing distance.

Before the skunk arrived on the trail, the wolverine dug a large pit in its path and waited for him opposite the pit. When the skunk arrived, he addressed the wolverine, "Who are you people so afraid of?"

"A pug-nosed smelly creature," wolverine answered.

"My friend, take a look over here and see what I've got," the angry skunk tried to control his voice as he turned around.

When the wolverine thought he was going to release his volley, he jumped into the pit and the deadly volley from the skunk's rear end passed over his head harmlessly. The instant the volley passed, he sprang up and bit the skunk's rectum close together. The wolverine closed his eyes as he was taken for the wildest ride of his life as the skunk leaped, twisted, bucked, and ran, trying to shake him off. But still he hung on for dear life, all the while hollering for his people for help.

When they came forward, they could not do anything because most of the winter people were small animals.

"Call the lynx!" the wolverine cried.

The winter people spread themselves into the forest to find the sulking lynx. The lynx heard their pleadings, but he let them holler.

"That'll teach them to under-rate me," he said to himself as he turned over to sleep.

"Hurry! My jaws are going to cramp," the wolverine pleaded.

After a long time, the lynx was seen coming out of the forest, taking his own time. He walked toward them as if he did not have a care in the world.

"Hurry! The wolverine is nearly exhausted!"

Still with ease the lynx climbed doggedly up a tall tree above the skunk. When he thought the wolverine was going to let go, he jumped on the skunk's neck and began biting and raking at his neck until the skunk fell dead to the ground. He climbed off and hissed his discontent at his own people for not looking up to his talents in the first place.

"Everyone go away far back from the skunk. I am going to let go my bite," the wolverine cautioned his people. As he let go his bite, a small volley of gas struck him full in the face, and into his eyes. The people were struck with grief as they saw that their liberator was struck blind with the poisonous gas. The wolverine assured them it was temporary and ordered them to go their ways. But before they did, they cut the giant skunk into little pieces whereupon small black and white skunks were created. "From this day on, the skunks will not pose a threat to anyone, and shall remain as tiny as they are now," the wolverine said.

The wolverine went his way, seeking a great lake to wash off the poisonous gas from his eyes. He bumped around the forest, asking the trees for directions. In this fashion he went from tree to tree toward the great lake until at last he came upon the poplar trees, who are plentiful along the shores.

"Oh poplar tree, am I near the great lake yet?" the blind wolverine asked.

"Yes, my friend, go straight ahead."

The wolverine headed toward the shore. Since it was winter, the great lake was frozen and it was necessary for him to walk many miles onto the lake until he came to span water. There he was able to wash off the poisonous gas from his eyes and was able to see again. From that day on, it is said that the great bodies of water were poisoned by the gas of the skunk, washed off the wolverine's eyes, and it is not drinkable for human or animal consumption.

—1971

The Bachelor

Two brothers came upon a spruce hut one day. Inside they discovered two young beautiful sisters living by themselves. By chance the elder of the two was looking for a wife. He at once claimed the elder of the sisters. The younger brother had vowed to himself that he was not, under no circumstances, going to have a wife. The younger sister, shedding her pride, outwardly asked him if he could be her husband because their older had done so. Still the young man clung to his vows. Even his brother's nagging proved to no avail. The younger sister slept by her sister and brother-in-law while the young man slept opposite the camp fire. He gave strict orders in the household that where he made a bed of spruce boughs, his place was not to be occupied by a woman. This custom between them existed as they lived day to day.

One day as the young man was gone for the day, the younger sister got up from her place and sat down in the young man's place opposite the fire.

"I wish we could sit like this all the time, us two facing you as two couples," she said to her brother-in-law.

"Please don't do that; my brother might see you in his place," her sister warned.

Just as she resumed her own place, they heard his footsteps approaching. He poked his head in and looked at his own place. Then his head disappeared outside.

"I cannot come in. A woman has been sitting in my place," he said as his footsteps faded away. He had disowned his relations, even his own brother.

The younger sister ran out and shouted after him, "I wonder what kind of female you want if you don't want me!"

As the young man wandered aimlessly in the forest, he came upon a home in a cave. There he met a Bear-woman and lived with her for a time. When he had gotten tired of her, he walked out on her.

"She is too lazy for me. She sleeps too much," he fumed as he walked away.

Not faraway, he came up on a Moose-woman. Again her fell for her and lived with her for a short time. Finally he got tired of her and walked out on her.

"Her nose is too big and crooked," he said as he walked away.

A little ways from the Moose-woman, he came upon a Deer-woman. This Deer-woman was the most graceful and beautiful woman the young man had ever seen. He asked her to be his wife and lived together a little while longer then the rest. The Deer-woman always had her white tail curled upward. Finally, one day, he walked out on her.

"You're always indecently exposing yourself with your tail pointed up like that," he said.

From the Deer-woman he went on to live with the Skunk-woman, where after a little while, he disowned her.

"She smells too bad," he said.

The next one he came upon was the Porcupine-woman. All the time he lived with her, the Porcupine-woman held her head low, so that he would not see her face. She did not want him to see her snub nose. When he thought it was high time to leave again, he tickled her ribs so that she would lift her head in laughter. As he saw her face, he walked out the door.

Not far from the Porcupine-woman, he stepped inside the lodge of the Whiskey Jack-woman. There he lived with her and helped her with all the chores. One day, as he carried a bundle of dried wood to camp on his back, the Whiskey Jack-woman ran to him and untied the wood on his back. As she dragged the wood inside one by one, a huge piece of wood became stuck on the doorway. She pulled and pulled with all her might. As it gave way, she fell backwards and broke her leg. Seeing her predicament, the young man said, "Now that you have a broken leg, you cannot make a good wife. I am leaving you after I bind your leg."

He took a dried nerve fiber of a fish and bound her broken leg up to her thighs. Then he left her sitting in her lodge.

Long ago, the main nerve fiber from the center of the vertebrae of a fish was pulled out like a rope. It was then dried over a rack above the fire. When it was thoroughly dry, it peeled into long strands of tough sinewy thread. This fiber was used for centuries for sewing together clothing or other useful leather utensils.

The Whiskey Jacks or Canada Jays today have long slender leather-like legs. But most curious of all, the black legs of a Canada Jay seem to be segmented. This is why Whiskey Jack's or Canada Jays' legs are like so, because of the bindings of its broken leg.

Meanwhile, his older brother had been troubled in mind over the loss of his brother.

"I love my brother, and if he feels what I feel for him, I shall find him again," he said to his wife as he left.

He tracked him all that year, asking each of the individual wives he had deserted. And finally one day, he came upon a great sea body of water. Near the shoreline came the familiar sound of wailing of his brother. Drawing near, he addressed his younger brother, "What are you crying for?"

The younger looked up with red tear-soaked eyes, "I want a wife so bad, but I cannot seem to keep her. I cannot seem to be happy."

"Why didn't you listen to me when I told you to keep the one woman that loved you in the first place? You have defied the laws of the Great Spirit in refusing the cycle of life on this earth. And it has become your doom. I have taken mine and I am happy."

The young man walked way from him sobbing along the sandy beach. He stood there listening to his fading voice. As the sobbing gradually faded little by little it began to change into the sound of a wolf. Looking up in the distance on the ledge of the shoreline, he saw a lone wolf howling at the sky.

—*1971*

Phil Fontaine

Anishinaabe (Sagkeeng First Nation) 1944–

Larry Philip (Phil) Fontaine attended Fort Alexander Indian Residential School where he learned first hand about racism, abuse, and powerlessness—experiences that led him to take an interest in politics. Elected Chief of his community at age 28, by 1991 he was elected Grand Chief of the Assembly of Manitoba Chiefs, where he helped engineer the defeat of the Meech Lake Accord and negotiate the first comprehensive self-government plan for Manitoba First Nations. In 1997 he was elected National Chief of the Assembly of First Nations, where he spearheaded initiatives combating poverty, settling land claims, and the successful resolution and settlement of claims arising out of the 150-year Indian residential school tragedy. The Final Settlement Agreement included over $5.2 billion in individual compensation, funding for a Truth and Reconciliation Commission, and other provisions.

On June 11, 2008, Prime Minister Stephen Harper apologized on behalf of all Canadians to Aboriginal leaders for the creation and delivery of residential schools. One year later, on April 29, 2009, Fontaine led a delegation of Aboriginal leaders to the Vatican for a meeting with Pope Benedict XVI, who also apologized in similar fashion. In response, Fontaine made the following statement. It acknowledges the ongoing role of Catholicism in First Nations communities as well as identifying the role churches have played in Aboriginal life positively and negatively. Following the meeting, the Vatican released an official communiqué which expressed the Pope's sorrow and hope for a new chapter in relations between the Church and Aboriginal people. Fontaine's speech is a model for how one can articulate past injustices while at the same time recognize the interdependent relationships two communities have with one another.

Statement to the Pope

Most Holy Father:

Today is a joyous day for the human spirit. It is a momentous day for our people and for our country, Canada. It is my highest honor as the National Chief of the Assembly of First Nations to represent our people in your presence in this awe-inspiring house of worship and grace. Most Holy Father, thank you for receiving us.

The Catholic Church has always played a significant role in the history of our peoples. Priests and nuns were some of the first Europeans to arrive on our shores.

Our ancestors taught the newcomers how to survive the cold, how to live off the land and how to navigate the vast continent. They taught them diverse and beautiful languages, including those of the Mik'maq, Anishinabe, Cree and Dene. In return, missionaries built schools, churches and hospitals—not just in cities but also in remote areas of the country where our people lived. They acted as intermediaries in treaty negotiations and interpretation and often expressed their serious reservations about the federal government's intentions in the implementation of the treaties.

Many embraced our languages with enthusiasm, wrote them down and created dictionaries, bibles, and books of prayers that we still use to this day. The Catholics recognized the deep spirituality of our peoples and introduced a faith to which many indigenous people devoutly adhere.

What brings us here today, however, was the failure those many years ago, by Canada and religious authorities, to recognize and respect those who did not wish to change—those who wished to be different. For reasons rooted in imperfections of the human condition, those at the highest levels of authority in Canada came to believe that our indigenous cultures, languages and our ways of worship were not worth keeping and should be eradicated.

To implement this belief, the Canadian government adopted the policy of forcibly removing indigenous children from their families and communities and placing them in Indian Residential Schools under the care and control of members of Catholic entities and other churches. The Catholic Church entities thus became part of a tragic plan of assimilation that was not only doomed to fail but destined to leave a disastrous legacy in its wake. Many children died in these schools, alone, confused and bereft. Countless others were physically, emotionally and sexually abused. The fabric of family life for thousands of our people, young and old, was shattered.

We suffered needlessly and tragically. So much was lost for no good reason.

The Catholic Church, too, was harmed by the residential school experience. Many good and decent men and women of faith were tainted and reviled because of the evil acts of some. The hundreds of years of good will and hard work by courageous and committed missionaries were undermined by the misguided policy Catholic priests and nuns found themselves enforcing. The reputation of the Catholic Church was impoverished. This, too, was tragic.

But today is a new day. We are here at the Vatican in your presence Most Holy Father, to change this sad history.

Our struggle has reached a decisive moment. While the past must never be forgotten, our destiny lies in building a future with enduring foundations, the cornerstone of which must be forgiveness.

Our elders teach us that we have choices in life. We can build up, or we can tear down. We can forgive with generosity of spirit and with the hand of friendship, or we can seek sustenance from bitterness and vengeance. We come here today Most Holy Father, with the spirit and lessons of our ancestors and elders in mind.

Reconciliation and friendship is what we seek. The time to re-build a better and brighter future together is upon us. The moment to bridge the gap has come. Healing the wounds of the residential school legacy will take years, perhaps even decades of work. But today marks an important milestone on the road out of darkness.

On June 11, 2008, I spoke to the Canadian Parliament in response to the apology of the Prime Minister and leaders of the Opposition. On that wonderful occasion I said, "This day testifies to nothing less than the achievement of the impossible."

Most Holy Father, I say the same to you today. The achievement of the impossible can only occur when there is hope. We are here because our people never lost hope. And today, together with you, we have merged hope with history.

We will never forget the visit of His Holiness, Pope John Paul II when he came to the Canadian North to visit our people, after bad weather prevented his first attempt. He celebrated mass in our house—a giant teepee—and he prayed with the scent of sweet grass and the sound of beating drums in the air. The reverence and respect he showed for our culture gave us the hope and strength we needed to pursue our goals, including those that have brought us here today. The co-existence of our unique spiritual values was evident on that day and set a hallmark for renewed respect.

We have learned over the many years of our struggle that none of us acting alone can achieve success like the events of today. So many have worked so very hard over the weeks, months, through many decades and generations to bring the residential school problem to a close. They deserve our deepest and most heartfelt thanks. Our endless gratitude is owed to those brave, fearless survivors who never lived to see this day, but whose contributions to its achievement will never be forgotten.

We offer you, Most Holy Father, our hand in friendship, reconciliation and yes, hope. Hope that we can work together to shape a new Canada for our people—a Canada where racism and discrimination will no longer exist, where the debilitating poverty that plagues us will be eradicated forever, and where our languages and cultures will once again flourish.

Much has been achieved in our struggle for equality and much remains to be done. But now we face the future with the confidence that never again should any Canadian, whoever they are and whoever their ancestors may have been, are treated with disrespect and disregard for their humanity.

Most Holy Father, you have reinforced our belief in justice. You have strengthened our confidence in the nobility of the human soul. You have added to the sum of dignity in the world.

Thank you, Merci, Meegwetch.

—2009

Joe McLellan and Matrine Therriault

Métis (Monterey, CA/Winnipeg) 1945– and Anishinaabe/Cree (Mishkeegogamang First Nation, ON) 1946–

Joe McLellan is an author, educator, and storyteller who was born in California but now lives in Winnipeg. Matrine Therriault spent her early years on the trapline in Northern Ontario and now resides in Winnipeg. They have collaborated on a number of children's books featuring Nanabosho, the spiritual teacher and protector of Anishinaabeg. Nanabosho stories are teaching stories, imparting morals, history, traditions, and other scientific and cultural knowledge. They have won several awards (including the 2009 McNally Robinson Book for Young People Award), and have introduced an entire generation of young people to Anishinaabe storytelling practices. All of their books, published by Pemmican Publishers, feature illuminating illustrations drawn by primarily Aboriginal artists.

In the story excerpted below, Nanabosho (a half-spirit always playing tricks and looking for something to eat) is introduced by Nokomis (grandmother) to a group of schoolchildren who are learning about light waves and reflection. Although written for children, this story could be used in senior subjects such as botany and philosophy, or to discuss notions of time, cause and effect, or education. As demonstrated in the story, Nanabosho must think about the world going on around him before he acts—a good message not only when searching for cranberries but along the path of life.

Nanabosho and the Cranberries

One day, long ago, Nanabosho walked through the woods by a lake. He was very hungry. He looked everywhere for something to eat.

All he could find were some cranberries growing high on a bush next to the lake.

Nanabosho was so hungry that he ran right to the bush and tried to pick the cranberries. Unfortunately, the cranberries were so high up that even when he stood on his tiptoes he couldn't reach them.

He tried jumping up to reach the cranberries.

He tried shaking the cranberry bush.

He tried knocking the cranberries off the bush with a big stick. Nothing worked. He just couldn't reach the cranberries.

Nanabosho sat down to think of a new way to get the cranberries off the bush.

While he was sitting, he looked into the lake. Right below the surface of the lake, he saw a big cranberry bush with hundreds of large red cranberries.

"I'll get my cranberries now," he said as he cupped his hands under a large clump of cranberries on the bush in the lake.

Poor Nanabosho. When he pulled his hands up out of the water the cranberries disappeared. He tried all day long, but the cranberries disappeared every time he tried to pick them out of the lake.

When night came, a strange thing happened. The bush disappeared completely. Nanabosho stared into the lake all night. He just couldn't believe that the bush had disappeared.

Finally the sun rose and the bush reappeared in the lake.

Nanabosho spent the rest of the morning trying to pick the cranberries off of the bush in the lake, but every time he took his hands out of the water, the cranberries disappeared.

He soon reached too far for the berries and fell in. He bumped his nose on the bottom of the lake.

When Nanabosho got out of the lake he cried because his nose hurt. Hundreds of birds heard him crying and came to see what was the matter.

They had a good laugh when Nanabosho told them what had happened. They sat in the cranberry bush and ate all of the cranberries while they listened to him.

After the birds flew away, poor Nanabosho sat on the shore as hungry as ever with a big, red swollen nose.

—*1998*

Ovide Mercredi

Cree (Misipawistik/Grand Rapids) 1946–

Ovide Mercredi is a longtime Aboriginal rights activist, politician, speaker, and mediator. A trained lawyer, Mercredi was a leader with the Assembly of Manitoba Chiefs and an advocate for Aboriginal rights across Canada. He advised Elijah Harper in opposing the 1990 Meech Lake Accord, and worked to diffuse the Oka Crisis at the Mohawk community of Kanehsatake. After his election as Grand Chief of the Assembly of First Nations in 1991, he helped steer the discussions of the 1992 Charlottetown Accord, which, had it been adopted, would have supported self-government and treaty review for Canada's Aboriginal populations.

Influenced by Mahatma Gandhi, Mercredi advocated for nonviolent civil disobedience in First Nations' activism and was nominated by the government of India for the Gandhi Peace Prize. Mercredi received the Order of Manitoba in 2006, and, in 2007, he became the first chancellor for the University College of the North. Mercredi serves as chief of Misipawistik First Nation.

Mercredi explains his position regarding Aboriginal self-government and Treaty rights and his vision for Aboriginal participation in Canada in his book *In the Rapids: Navigating the Future of First Nations*, co-written with Mary Ellen Turpel. In the following excerpt, we get a sense of Mercredi's clear and eloquent style and are introduced to his philosophy of nonviolent resistance for First Nations as influenced by the Mahatma Gandhi. It is a surprising story from a strong and brave voice in Manitowapow.

A Different Politics

Mahatma Gandhi had a profound influence on me as youngster growing up in a remote community in Manitoba. I encountered Gandhi when I was very young. Before anyone concludes that I have either a vivid imagination or no respect for the truth, let me provide more facts. I don't recall my age when I first learned of this man, Gandhi, but I do remember I had already started school and I was already able to read enough English to understand the written English in books and magazines. I am guessing that I was at least eight years old. A few of us Cree children were visiting a Catholic priest in my home village of Grand Rapids, Manitoba, when I came across a copy of Life magazine that carried the story of the life and death of the great spiritual leader Gandhi.

I still remember seeing the grief on the faces of thousands and thousands of people mourning his death. It occurred to me that burning the body was quite a different practice from the rite of death I knew. Cree people are buried, not burned, when they die, and I was surprised at how Gandhi was treated. More than this, I was surprised to see that Gandhi's people didn't dress like anybody else I had ever known. Since then, my village has expanded and I have seen many things that are different from Cree ways.

I was not a good reader in those days. I remember more from the pictures of that Life magazine than I do of the written stories that accompanied them. It occurred to me that this was no ordinary man—that he had been deeply spiritual, that the people loved him immensely, that he had been involved in some great deeds in the interests of peace, and that his death was in fact a loss to all of humanity. I felt that loss. I was sad. But at the priest's house in Grand Rapids, I was just as certain that he was in heaven.

Since my youth, I have become a reader of some of the writings and several of the books by or about Gandhi. Although far from being a scholar or even a serious student, I do know his teachings as they may be applied or adapted to our political resistance to end the injustice and oppression of the First Nations in Canada. The concepts of passive resistance, nonviolence, truth force and civil disobedience significantly shaped my approach to politics, although they have been overshadowed somewhat in recent years by the more spiritual teachings of this extraordinary human being. As one gets older, one's interests change. This is not to suggest that the political principles and practices of Mahatma Gandhi have no relevance to the First Nations or to Canada. We could certainly have benefited from Gandhi's moral authority, had he been around to apply his teachings and philosophy of conflict resolution inside the cabinet rooms in Quebec and on Parliament Hill as well as in the Councils of the Mohawk Warrior Society.

Gandhi's philosophy of nonviolent resistance as a means for changing society is not for the weak of mind, the greedy or the cowardly. Nonviolence and civil disobedience in the face of brute force, oppressive neglect and governmental tyranny require discipline, conviction, courage and sacrifice. It is far easier to succumb to anger and resentment and to resort to violence than it is to be generous and kind to your oppressor. Unlike violence, *ahimsa* or the way of nonviolence is a discipline. Violence is a negative force, while *ahimsa* is a positive force.

In Gandhi's own words we can see that his philosophy is a way of life, not just the means for carrying out political action:

> Nonviolence is a power which can be wielded equally by all children, young men and women or grown up people—provided they have a living faith in the God of love and have therefore equal love for all mankind. When nonviolence is accepted as the law of life, it must pervade the whole being and not be applied to isolated acts.[36]

Within our indigenous societies, we also have many teachers who show the superiority of the path of nonviolence. Our spiritual Elders teach us that love and compassion are the substance of human respect and understanding. We are taught the concept of non-cooperation with evil or with harm, whether active or potential. Non-cooperation is a response. It does not mean burying your head in the sand, hoping that the problem will go away by itself. Resistance can be passive or active but by not cooperating with negative forces you give them no opportunity to go anywhere but away from you. We learn to repel force not with less, equal or more force, but with non-cooperation.

In our traditional teachings we are told we have a choice. You can always walk away from conflict or you can walk into it. If you are so inclined, you can create conflict, but you can also defuse it. This means you can be a

---

36   From: *All Men Are Brothers, Words of Mahatma Gandhi*, compiled and edited by Krishna Kripalani, (UNESCO, 1958, 4th edition) p. 91.

troublemaker or a peacemaker. The choice is yours. In the end, what occurs is what you have decided to do or not to do.

Human problems exist to be solved. In most cases such solutions are within our immediate grasp or control. In certain situations, we need assistance. In all cases we need *shakeetowin*, which is Cree for love, and *keesaywatisseewin*, which is Cree for kindness or compassion. We have ceremonies, spiritual practices and prayers to help us resolve conflict by restoring balance and harmony.

—*1993*

Elijah Harper

Cree (Red Sucker Lake) 1949–

Born on a Red Sucker Lake trapline, Elijah Harper attended several residential and afterwards the University of Manitoba. In 1978, at the age of 29, Harper was elected chief of the Red Sucker Lake Indian Band, and, in 1981, he was elected as Member of the Legislative Assembly (MLA) for the Rupertsland constituency. He held that position for 11 years. Harper is best known for blocking the 1990 Meech Lake Accord in the Manitoba legislature because of the exclusion in the Canadian constitution of the Aboriginal people in the concept of the "two founding nations." Harper resigned as an MLA in 1992, and the next year was elected Member of Parliament (MP) for the Churchill constituency. One of his key successes was having June 21st named National Aboriginal Day in Canada. In 2010, he was awarded for his work in the province with an Order of Manitoba, and in 2011, he was honoured with a Doctor of Laws from the University of Winnipeg. Harper continues to work internationally advocating for indigenous rights and is an activist, lobbyist, consultant, advisor to Aboriginal organizations, and a popular public speaker.

The following piece, "What Canada Means to Me," was published in *Aboriginal Cultural Landscapes* (2004). For Harper, as for many Aboriginal Canadians, Canada is a land under contention, but no claims of home are more ingrained than for Aboriginal Canadians, whose very identities and ways of life are deeply embedded in these territories. Because of these spiritual connections with nature, Aboriginal people have much to teach mainstream Canadians about the land they are standing on and the sacredness of this privilege. Advocating for a spiritually based solution to address the systemic ills that are founded on colonialism, Harper supports an era of reconciliation between Aboriginal and non-Aboriginal Canadians and the complete restoration and restitution of Aboriginal communities and their institutions.

What Canada Means to Me

The land, the trees, the waters in the lakes and rivers, the wild birds and animals made up my primary consciousness as a very young child. They were a part of the territory around Red Sucker Lake where my parents, grandparents and I were actively involved in hunting, gathering, fishing and trapping. I did not think at all in terms of being a part of Canada, for this was an unknown to me; all I knew was that I belonged to the land in an integral and eternal way.

Recollections from My Youth

I had little contact with anyone outside my immediate family and the community; I would not go outside our territory until many years later. First contact with non-Aboriginal people came through Mennonite missionaries who taught school in the log cabin which also served as a church. I was about 6 or 7 years old. Then there was Treaty Days which came once a year and at which the RCMP came, dressed in full scarlet; I was frightened of them and hid my sling-shot when they were around. A medical party came in with them, too, and X-rayed everyone for TB. No one was given treaty money until the TB team was finished. Five dollars was a lot of money back then, and for me, it seemed like a fortune for us to have as a family.

I really did not know from where all these outside people came, except that it was from afar off. My parents called them *wempt-ikoosh-iwukk*. The older generation encouraged us youngsters to have respect for them because we had treaties with them, and because they represented a Queen from far, far away. The old people told us that the Queen would take care of us, and that the $5/year treaty money was an example of this. We were especially encouraged to have respect for other people who we did not know. But I was always afraid of the *wempt-ikoosh-iwitkk*, because I was shy and timid from being away hunting and fishing in the bush with my grandparents, for this had been my world for all my life so far.

My people shared everything—food in the form of fish, a big moose, or geese we caught in the spring and fall. As a family, we had a big single room in a log cabin; wintertime was so cold that when I'd awaken in the morning, the water pail was frozen over. I slept on the floor with my siblings, sharing a big blanket to keep warm. I did not realize until much later in my life that I had been living in substandard conditions, and that we were very poor. All I knew was the closeness within my family and to the land which always gave us everything we needed. I thought this was the life that everyone had, even those outside people who came into our community once or twice a year.

Then, I was taken away because I had TB and had a growth under my chin, which they took out. I was away for maybe 6 months but it seemed like forever to me. I remember seeing one of the old people from home— Jonah Harper—but I do not think he ever returned home, not alive, anyway. This was my first experience away from home, and a very lonely time for me.

Next came residential school where I learned about Manitoba, and Canada which was a big big country that was developed by the explorers. There was nothing at all positive about my people in the books. There were all kinds of written things about Canadian society, the English and French perspectives. Even then I recognized the misconceptions about who my people were, and I was taught to seek a different lifestyle from the only one I knew. I was told to leave behind my language and the old ways. It was to assimilate us, but I did not realize that then; I was not yet aware of the government policies until I was in University, after I finished high-school in Winnipeg. There, I indirectly challenged the views of the educational system because it seemed to me that it caused the way Canadian society viewed us.

I knew this was not the relationship that the old people talked about; they had talked about mutual respect and honour in our obligations to each other like in the treaties. We should live in peace and harmony, and not impose on each other, and share with each other. So we shared our land and its resources—that was the understanding of the old people, but the *wempt-ikoosh-iwukk* never seemed to reciprocate, and the Elders got tired of waiting, and some died waiting. It seemed to be always such a struggle to have government recognize these obligations and commitments that were made, those treaty pacts which we considered sacred.

Third World Conditions in Canada

Canada is a very prosperous country with one of the highest standards of living in the whole world. But many of my people's communities live in such poverty, in Third World conditions. We seem to be left out of enjoying the amenities that other Canadians enjoy. We seem to suffer from a lost identity, ungrounded in anything concrete, detached from both outer and back-home society, especially those of us who have had to seek city life for a better life. We seem to be like seeds caught in the wind, hoping to find fertile soil in which to plant new roots. My people are a whole nation in this quandary.

I am a man who was born among the spruce boughs in a trapper's cabin in far northern reaches. Now, years later, I have seen most parts of Canada, and many parts of the world, too. I am an Aboriginal leader, a chief in my home, the first treaty Member of Legislative Assembly to be elected in Manitoba and become a cabinet minister, an MP who sat in the House of Commons, and all these are extremely fulfilling occupations. Over the years, I have been seeing Canada become a mosaic of different peoples from all over the world.

Meech Lake Accord

Many Canadians supported my stance against the constitutional amendments known as the Meech Lake Accord in June 1990; they saw me hold an eagle feather, symbolic of my people's strength. Many Canadians did not feel like they were an active part of the constitutional process, especially the Aboriginal people. The proposed amendment was set to entrench into the Constitution the misconception that Canada was founded by only two nations; it ignored the First Peoples and all their contributions. It did not represent the truth. Our constitution should be built on the solid foundation of truth which will withstand all time and forevermore. The proposed constitution was like the story of the one who built his house on the sand, not on solid rock.

Our Vision

I have a vision for this country called Canada. It is not a new vision, nor is it only mine. It is a vision of my people, the First Nations, the vision of my forefathers. It lies in their hearts and souls, and inherent to our traditional values, beliefs, and philosophy. It is inherent to the land that sustains all life. Above all, it is a vision that acknowledges and embraces the supremacy of God our Creator.

It is the vision that is inherent in the Treaty relationships that were made with the Newcomers who brought along their governments with them. We agreed to respect and honour each other, to co-exist, to live side by side in harmony, to share the knowledge, land and resources. This vision is not very complicated, but it is strong. It embraces unity, care, love and sharing; it has been dormant, unappreciated and misunderstood by ordinary Canadians.

We know that God created different people and nations all over the world. We know that God has established "landmarks and boundaries." When the Creator so happened to place Aboriginal people in this part known as Canada, there were also responsibilities given to us towards this land. With this identity as Aboriginal people, God the Creator gave us our culture and language to maintain.

We also have a responsibility to ensure the unity of this land. We, as original people, have a greater responsibility than any other group to maintain the unity of Canada, because this is our home and our land. Land is very sacred to us. It is essential to our existence, our philosophy, our way of life. We live on the land, we belong to it, and we return to it when we die. Our forefathers had difficulty understanding the concept of owning land. It is alien, like the concept of owning air. But we understand the need to use the land for the benefit of everybody, not for greed. It is important for all Canadians to understand and appreciate this, that our relationship with this land is a responsibility that is not in our power to extinguish. This responsibility does not mean that we cannot share this land and its riches with the Newcomers who have built their governments here. But what it means is that we have a special relationship with each other, "for as long as the sun shines, the grass grows, and the rivers flow." The Treaty relationships reflect the need to live up to those responsibilities.

If justice is be done, if Canada is to have cultural and political harmony and peace, then it must first honour, respect, and complete the first order of business, which is the relationship with the First Nations, the Original People of the land. Canada must acknowledge the tremendous contributions and generosity that were extended to the Newcomers. Immigrants need to be aware of the history this country. All immigrants inherit this legacy. Just as they became responsible for the deficit that they did not create, they became responsible for this country's legacy of wrongs. These are good people, spiritual people, but they need to know about it so they can pray for justice, so wrong may not be perpetuated. This lack of recognition— this legacy of broken promises, dishonoured treaties, assimilation, and racist policies—has undermined our identity, our language and customs, our connection to the land.

Injustices were committed not only by individuals, but by institutions, by governments, and churches and schools. These institutions allowed individuals to deny responsibilities for what was done. We do not want to dwell on these injustices, but we must deal with them if healing is to take place. These injustices have led to a loss of dignity and pride, and chaos in our communities.

We continue to see escalating frustration because of these issues. Confrontations are developing, such as what happened in Oka and Ipperwash. It has become more apparent that these things need to be resolved, and that the political process has failed us. I believe something is missing, the spiritual element.

Conclusions

There needs to be a healing of the land and the people. There needs to be reconciliation, restoration, and restitution. Because of our relationship with the Creator and this land, this is a spiritual process, a sacred process. A nation without a vision has no hope. A nation without a vision has no future. We now embark on this journey together for the benefit of all people in Canada.

—*2004*

Charles Nelson (Mizhakwanigiizhik)

Anishinaabe (Bagwaaʼonishkoziibing/Roseau River First Nation) 1949–

Charles (Charlie) Nelson was raised in Bagwaaʼonishkoziibing (Roseau River First Nation, Manitoba) and is the second oldest in a family of nine children. He appears in the documentary, *Niigaanibatowaad: FrontRunners* (2007). Nelson was one of 10 residential school students selected to run a torch over 800 kilometres to Winnipeg for the 1967 Pan-American Games, only to have organizers refuse to let them carry the torch into Winnipeg Stadium. That privilege was given to a non-Aboriginal athlete. Nelson, a father to five children and grandfather of eight, has spent his career as an educator and band councillor. In 1988, he was raised up to be Ogimaw (chief) of the Western Doorway of the Three Fires Midewiwin Lodge, and in this capacity he works for his community as an activist and spiritual leader throughout North America.

A humble and soft-spoken speaker, Nelson's remarks here were made at the Sacred Lands Conference held October 24–26, 1996, at the University of Manitoba. The conference focused on sacred territories throughout the province of Manitoba and Canada, in general, and, in particular, on how Aboriginal cultures were embedded in relationships with land. Nelson's remarks illustrate many of the dynamic and interesting ways he and his community have ties to their traditional territories—in Manitoba and beyond. His plea is to understand that land is something held in sacred trust and with a sense of partnership, not ownership. Political movements toward land "protection"—while important—are about ownership. Nelson also points out that fellow Anishinaabe must inherit this responsibility and not forget the ancestral relationships of which they are part.

"Protection" Conflicting with Anishinabe Rights

I welcome the opportunity to share some facts with you today about my people. This morning, when I opened the session, we acknowledged the day and acknowledged the teachings with tobacco in our hands and sacred feathers, in order to begin addressing the topic of land.

When I come here, I represent my people, the Roseau River Anishinabe First Nation. We live on a plot of land that is very small in terms of what we once had. It's a plot of land like you have in the city. We have no other resources. Many live on welfare in houses that are probably paid by welfare. The economics have not been good for us.

We once derived strength from the land, from the medicine and animals that made us strong people. We are now weakened by the conditions that we live under. It needs to be understood that this cloud we live under has to be taken away. We have to get out from under the cloud that is this small parcel of land we live on. Even the animals have been taken away from the land they once roamed. At Roseau River, you look at the land around us and it is all farmland. There are no more deer and no more medicines. We must travel far to find either.

We still continue to work. For myself I came here to try and talk about my work for the last 20 years and more. We have sacred ceremonies at Roseau Rapids, the place of my grandfather's land, where he practiced *Mite'iwin*, and that practice continues today. I need to keep after it as much as I can. I need some acknowledgement that my children and grandchildren will continue to have the right to use that land. I need to share with my own people the thought that I would maintain those ceremonial rights because it is a long standing tradition in my family that the land be used in that manner.

We were once promised that there would be no encroachment on our lands—not only on lands set aside, not only on our Sacred Lands, but no encroachment on all our traditional lands. Encroachment still occurs.

Some of our knowledge is incorporated in the clothing and other items that we carry. We extract knowledge from certain articles like the sacred pipe and braid of sweetgrass. For example, the sweetgrass braid represents kindness—we are a kind people. There are other things that help us; like the deer who in spirit asked to be used, to feed the people. These are rights that have been taken away from us through "protection."

Even with the best intentions, "protection" sometimes takes away our right of access to these lands. Even myself, I observe sacred sites and think that I would like to establish a keeper of the sites. We had thought about that idea regarding Tie Creek, the petroforms in the Whiteshell Provincial Park of southeastern Manitoba. I talked to one of the elders and said I would like to establish a keeper of the site. He spoke to me in this way. He said, "As long as I don't have to ask you to use that which the Creator has given to us Anishinabeg." We did a study of the Tie Creek Petroforms in the Whiteshell. The government people doing the study asked us some questions, for our opinion. This often happens and they go ahead and do what they want anyway. So why should I give you an answer on what I think? I think people should listen to what we are trying to say.

We need to realize that those who institute policy or laws also limit us from access: and our right, as Anishinabe people, to take even a tree. We still want to have access to the tree and medicine to give us strength. Those are a few of the things I wish to share from my perspective.

The Native people who journeyed here to this conference have something to say. We need room. Once we roamed this place wherever the land could feed us and make us strong. But now, we are just in a house and we have no tools to make a living out of what has changed for us. Most of the land is now farmland.

Perhaps the Anishinabe people will attend other gatherings like this. Our communication continues in the lodges of our people, where we gather and share thoughts that we have in common, where we learn. I hope that someday our children, if they learn anything from us, will say that we always want to make room for ourselves. We want to make provision for ourselves. Those things we hold sacred will continue to be suppressed and will not grow unless we make provisions, unless we make those sacred places available for ourselves.

We must come first in those lands. We are going to save them and defend them and make it known that we are first in those Sacred Lands. Megwiich.

—*1998*

Emma LaRocque

Plains Cree Métis (Big Bay, AB) 1949–

Dr. Emma LaRocque is a scholar, human-rights advocate, literary critic, author, and poet. She was raised in a small Cree-speaking, land-based Métis community (Big Bay) in northeastern Alberta. Her parents were hard-working people who gardened, gathered, hunted, fished, and trapped, as well as worked for farmers, forestry, and the railroad to make a living, instilling in their children a strong work ethic and a lifelong reverence for the land. The women in her family were particularly gifted storytellers, and it is from them that LaRocque gained her love of words and expression, especially in Cree. LaRocque's poetry and academic work has appeared in numerous national and international journals and anthologies, and she has been a professor in the Department of Native Studies at the University of Manitoba for over 30 years. Her ground-breaking book, *Defeathering the Indian* (1975), is widely regarded as one of the most influential works in the discipline of Native Studies. Her most recent book, *When the Other Is Me: Native Resistance Discourse, 1850–1990* (2010), is a powerful interdisciplinary examination of Canadian historiography and literature, and situates Aboriginal writing as resistance response to the misrepresentation found in the colonial records. *When the Other Is Me* won the 2010 Alexander Kennedy Isbister Award for Nonfiction. In 2005 LaRocque also received the National Aboriginal Achievement Award and has been singled out a number of times as a "popular prof" in the annual *Maclean's Guide to Canadian Universities.*

LaRocque's poems are as sharp and layered as her essays and books. In these poems LaRocque resounds with her own resistance against racist and exploitative colonial systems that have assailed and dispossessed Indigenous peoples, including her own family. Her critique of western encroachment is based on both scholarship and personal experience. LaRocque not only stakes out her pride in her land-nurtured Métis heritage, she claims contemporary culture as her birthright through her rich poetry. Her footnotes and her words today are her home away from home.

Geese Over the City

In the city
one awakes to the sound
of man-made mobility:
    coughing motors,
    clanging truck boxes,
    wailing sirens,
    tire screeches.
There are treadmarks on my soul.

But this morning-day
Very early –
Even before the sun
made it through the October grey –
I heard the Geese,
    the Geese,
        the Geese –
           and in my half-sleep
                    I jumped up,
                ready to run out and see
              Their V-formation
        as was the tradition
        of the great northern Cree
But sounds of some shifting gears
made me stop,
and aware that
the obstinate elm leaves,
electric wires
and too tall buildings
would not let me see,
    let me see,
      let me see –
        so I fell back to sleep,
          no, to reverie
            I saw a little log-shack
              full of family faces
                    all embraced
                by a tangled tussle
            of green-gold laces
        And I smelled

        the racy fragrance
      of a widowed willow-leaf
    etched with the earth
  broken birch branch
and damp dew

ahh

Twice more
The Geese
went over the city
making me sad
that I could not see
making me happy
that I could see
there was much Cree in me
despite
town height.

—1995

Long Way From Home

I've walked these hallways
a long time now
hallways held up by
stale smoke
thoughts

I've walked these hallways
a long time now
hallways pallored by
ivory-coloured
thoughts

I've walked these hallways
for a long time now
hallways without windows
no way to feel the wind
no way to touch the earth
no way to see

I've walked these hallways
a long time now

every September closed doors
stand at attention
like soldiers
guarding fellow inmates
guarding footnotes
guarding biases

as I walk by

I do my footnotes so well
nobody knows where I come from
hallways without sun
the ologists can't see
they count mainstreet
bodies behind bars
they put Ama's moosebones
behind glass
they tell savage stories
in anthropology Cree

My fellow inmates
they paste us prehistoric
standing in front of us
as if I am not there too
as if I wouldn't know
what they think they show
showing what they don't know
they don't know what they show
they take my Cree for their PhD's
like Le Bank
as my Bapa would say
they take our money for their pay

When I first came to these hallways
I was young and dreaming
to make a difference
thinking truth

With footnotes pen paper
chalk blackboard
I tried to put faces
behind cigar store glazes
I tried to put names

behind the stats
of us brown people
us
us brown people
in jails
in offices
in graveyards
in livingrooms
but to them it was
just Native biases

I've walked these hallways
a long time now
hallways hallowed by
ivory-towered
bents

way too long now
hallways whitewashed with
committee meetings memos
promotion procedures
as fair as war
pitting brown against colonized brown
choosing pretend Indians

When I first came to these hallways
I was young and dreaming
to make a difference

but only time has passed
taking my Ama and Bapa
my Nhisis my Nokom
my blueberry hills

I've walked these hallways
a long time now
I wanna go home now
I'm tired of thinking for others
who don't wanna hear anyways

I wanna go home now
I want to see the evening stars
get together for a dance
the northern light way

like Ama's red river jig
I want to see the sun rise
hot orange pink
like Bapa's daybreak fire

no one could see the morning come
as my Bapa
no one could scurry in the stars
as my Ama

I wanna go home now
but where is home now?

I do my footnotes so well
nobody knows where I come from
my relatives think
I've made it
thev don't know
how long I've walked these hallways
my feet hurt
at 43
I wanna play hookey
but I can't
I have credit cards to pay
footnotes to colonize
My relatives think
I've made it
they don't know
who all owns me
they won't lend me money
from their UIC's
my relatives laugh.

Oh I did my footnotes so well
nobody knows where I come from

I've walked these hallways
with them a long time now
and still they don't see
the earth gives eyes
injustice gives rage
now I'm standing here
prehistoric and all

pulling out their fenceposts of civilization
one by one
calling names in Cree
bringing down their mooneow hills
in English too
this is home now.

—2001

My Hometown Northern Canada South Africa

How did they get so rich?
How did we get so poor?
My hometown Northern Canada South Africa
How did you get so rich?

We were not always poor

How did they get
our blueberry meadows
our spruce and willow groves
our sun clean streams
and blue sky lakes?
How did they get
Their mansions on the lake
Their cobbled circle drives
with marbled heads of lions on their iron gates?

How did they get so rich?
How did we get so poor?

One sad spring
when my mother my Cree-cultured Ama
was dying
Or was it
the sad summer
when my father my tall gentle Bapa
was dying
I stood on the edge
of that blue sky lake
to say goodbye
to something
so definitive
no words in Cree

no words in Metis
no words in that colonial language
no words
could ever say

I looked at my hometown
no longer a child afraid
of stares and stone-throwing words
no longer a child
made ashamed
of smoked northern pike
bannock on blueberry sauce
sprinkled with Cree

I looked at my hometown
Gripping my small brown hands
on the hard posts of those
white iron gates
looking at the lions
with an even glare

How did they get so rich?
How did we get so poor?

How did our blueberry meadows
Turn to pasture for "Mr" Syke's cows?
How did our spruce and willow groves
turn to "Mr" Therien's General Store?
How did our aspen covered hills
Turn to levelled sandpiles
for gas pipelines
just behind my Nokum's backyard?
How did our moss-green trails
down to the beaver creek
turn to cutlines
for power lines?
How did the dancing poplar leaves
Fall before their golden time?
How did my Nokum's sons and daughters
and their sons and daughters
and their sons and daughters
Fall before their seasons?
How did my auntie Julia die?

When she was 19 she was found dead
under a pile of sawdust
long after it happened
She was last seen with a whiteman
sometime in World War II they said
There was no investigation
Not even 16 years later

How did my Nokum lose her grandchildren
that she so carefully housed in her loghouse
made long by her widower sons?
Was it really about
a child stealing a chocolate bar from
Therien's Store?
Or was it about The Town
Stealing children to make us white

Taking Uncle Ezear's Lillian Linda Violet
Taking Uncle Alex's Lottie Robert
all they had left
after T.B. stole their mothers
in far away places of death

How did my uncles Alex and Ezear die?
Singing sad songs on the railroad tracks
on their way home from Town
2 a.m. in the morning
Was it really by the train as the RCMP said?

When did my mother and her sisters
Catherine, Agnes, Louisa and Mary
stop singing
those haunting songs in Cree
about lost loves and aching
to find their way home?
When did they lose the songs
those songs in their steps
Wasn't it when the Priests the Police
and all those Home and Town good boys doing bad things
came
No one talks about it
My Nokum and her daughters
Singing sad songs on the railroad tracks

on their way home from Town
2 a.m. in the morning

How did we put away Pehehsoo,
and Pahkak?
When did we stop laughing with Wesakehcha?
When did we cross ourselves
to pray to Joseph and the Virgin Mary?
How did we stop speaking Cree
How did we stop being free?

How did they get so rich?
How did we get so poor?

How did my Bapa and Ama's brothers
Alex, Ezear and Victor
and my aunties' husbands Stuart and Moise
lose their traplines?
Was it really for the Cold War planes
Or was it for one of those cold marbled lions?
And what war
takes my brothers' traplines today?
Some say to save the lions

My hometown Northern Canada South Africa
making marble out of lions
making headstones out of earth
turning the earth on
Nokum's sons and daughters
and their sons and daughters
and their sons and daughters
turning Nokum
into a bag lady
before she died in the Town ditch

How did they get all the stones?
Those stones in their fireplaces,
Those stones around their necks.
The boulders in the whites
of their eyes.
Those stony stares,
How did they get the marbled stones in their hearts?

I look at you
My hometown Northern Canada South Africa
I look at you
no longer a child afraid
of stony stares
and rockhard words
no longer a child
made ashamed
of my Cree
dipped in cranberry sauce
giggling with Wesakehcha
I look at the paper head-dresses
you got from Hollywood
for your Pow Wow Days
Trying to feel at home
in your postcard tourist ways
Giggling with Wesakehcha

I look at the turquoise
in your stones
I look at your lions
with an even glare
Even in my dreams I see

But still
I look
From the inside out
Gripping my still brown hands
on the hardposts
of White Iron Gates

My hometown coldstone Canada South Africa

—*2001*

Beatrice Mosionier

Métis (St. Boniface) 1949–

Beatrice Mosionier (formerly Culleton) was born in St. Boniface, Manitoba. The youngest of four children, she grew up in foster homes. Following the second suicide in her family, Beatrice decided to write *In Search of April Raintree* (1983), a novel that explores the lives of two Métis sisters as they try to make sense of their experiences of powerlessness, racism, and loss. The book has become a Canadian classic and has been reissued several times. In 2008, it was selected as the first recommended book for "On the Same Page: Manitoba Reads," a community literacy initiative. Mosionier worked for many years as publisher at Pemmican Publications, a publishing house featuring Aboriginal and Métis writers. She is also the author of several children's book, including *Spirit of the White Bison* (1985), *Christopher's Folly* (1996), and *Unusual Friendships: A Little Black Cat and a Little White Rat* (2002).

Mosionier's second novel is entitled *In the Shadow of Evil* (2000), and a re-edited version is forthcoming. The opening pages are excerpted here. A psychological thriller with many plot twists, it tells the story of an Aboriginal woman, Christine, and her experiences of prejudice, sexual abuse, and foster homes in Canada. This is juxtaposed by the life struggles of a family of wolves at the fictional Shadow Lake. The novel focuses on themes of self-forgiveness, power, healing, and how one must deal with the past. The second piece is from *Come Walk With Me: A Memoir* (2010). The book is about Mosionier's life and includes interviews with her mother, which give another perspective on her family's history. Mosionier recounts a life that parallels *In Search of April Raintree*—echoing themes of loss (of family/innocence/dignity) and self-realization—and diverges from it—exploring her journey into artistic, political, and personal fulfillment. These two texts illustrate the many challenges and triumphs, and the resilience from the imagination and the life of one of Manitoba's best-known Aboriginal writers.

From *In the Shadow of Evil*

Moonlight cast its silvery light across the quiet of the forest. High up in a black spruce a lynx lazily blinked, ever watchful for movement of prey. Its eyes widened, its head lifted, its nose quivered. In the distance, some of the surrealistic shadows created by the moonlight moved in and out, among the trees. Gentle air currents brought the low sounds of anxious whines and the soft falls of padded feet racing over fallen leaves to the twitching ears of the lynx. Its short tail switched back and forth nervously as the wolves came into view.

Neka, the black female and mother of two pups, was in the lead, followed closely by Okimaw, her mate and the leader of the nine-member wolf clan. Behind and off to the sides, were seven more wolves of various ages. Of the three adult males, only Otakosin came from a previous litter and had the same markings as his father, Okimaw. The other two males, Oskinikiw and Kanatan, were older but not quite as large or as formidable as Okimaw. Nimis now also an adult, was of charcoal colouring, not the deep black of her mother Neka, and she bore a white spot on her chest. Kisikaw and Wapan, the six-month-old female pups that had survived from a litter of five, were excitedly keeping up. Kehte-aya, the oldest of the wolves and once the matriarch, brought up the rear.

They were playing a game of tag. Oskinikiw shot by Okimaw to sideswipe Neka and bowl her over. She took it good-naturedly with a brief wag of her tail. Then she and the pack chased Oskinikiw. Okimaw brought the game to Shadow Lake. They lapped up water and, while five of the adults rested, Kanatan, the clown, and Kehte-aya, the old one, were drawn into more games with the exuberant youngsters.

Neka stood up and stretched, wagged her tail, and nuzzled Okimaw affectionately. He, too, stood up to stretch and then he looked around. Curious, Oskinikiw raised his head. Neka pointed her nose towards the sky and gave a few low tentative howls. Okimaw immediately raised his head and blended his lower-pitched voice with hers. This duet brought the rest of the wolves racing back in delight. With tails wagging, they greeted each other as if they had been apart for weeks. The pups threw their higher-pitched, almost squeaky voices into the symphony. By then the rest of the adults joined in, all seeming to give the moon a disjointed serenade.

As abruptly as it started, it ended. In the intervening silence the wolves listened intently. They heard answering calls that carried over the mist of the night air from perhaps twenty kilometres to the west. Wapan whined impatiently and approached her father to nip at his muzzle. Kisikaw followed suit by nipping at Kehte-aya's mouth. Tails wagging, they were all soon nipping and licking at Okimaw, and the rest of the pack joined in, all looking like pups begging for food to be regurgitated. In fact, the young ones did want to be fed. It was time for the hunt.

Okimaw pointed his nose in different directions, sorting out the many scents drifting by on the placid air currents. Then he set out with a deliberate wolf trot, followed by Neka. All playfulness was now gone. The wolves were on full alert. They had an oblong summer route that they had marked out as their territory. But now they were able to leave the den and the rendezvous area; they could expand into their winter territory, an area that covered roughly 200 square kilometres. In some areas their runway overlapped the territories of neighbouring wolf packs. Elk, deer, moose, and caribou were their main large prey. From denning season to autumn, the wolf pack would spend much of its time in the valley containing Shadow Lake.

In the past, they had been a pack deep in the wilderness with little contact with humans, and they had remained healthy as traditional teachings had passed from generation to generation. Among the most important teachings was the warning to avoid humans, "*Awasis*, watch them if you like, but do not be seen."

Now it was the season for the hunters from the south, the ones with the telescopic, high-powered, automatic rifles. In the foothills of the Rockies, reports of rifle shots cracked like thunderclaps, reverberating back and forth across mountainsides. In the lower forested regions, the sounds were more like muffled snaps. The smell of gunpowder in the air meant the days were dangerous times, and most of the wildlife took deeper cover.

That night, Okimaw led the pack away from the south shores of Shadow Lake towards the north. He soon scented an elk nearby and stopped to sniff the air. He circled, trying to get a visual fix on the prey. When he saw the young animal casually browsing on the sweet sapwood of a black spruce, then turning its head to scan its surroundings, the wolf froze. The others behind froze likewise. Lowering himself close to the ground, the wolf stalked forward to close the distance to the prey. Whenever the elk raised its head, Okimaw would freeze. Neka was just to his rear. When they saw the elk twitch its ears and look in their direction more alertly, the whole pack sprang forward.

The elk merely turned its body so it was facing them, stopping the wolves in their tracks. Oskinikiw circled to the elk's right side. Without moving his head, the elk eyed Oskinikiw, Okimaw, and Kanata as they moved up one by one. So far he still had some lead time. Escape to the left seemed like the best choice. With a sideways leap he was off and running. The chase had begun. The elk was young and strong. The distance between predators and prey began to increase. When the elk sensed that the pursuers were giving up the chase, he turned and watched the wolves trot off, then browsed on the vegetation around him. It was useful for both prey and predator to conserve their energy. The elk would live to see his first rutting season, if a hunter's bullet didn't get him first.

The wolves rested after the fruitless chase, then, one by one, the adults left in different directions. The youngsters with Neka and Kehte-aya made up a smaller unit. It was another way of hunting. The wolves could cover more ground by spreading out. At this time of the year, when the smell of gunpowder was released into the air, chances of finding wounded prey were possible. More than once, the wolves had seen and heard the two-legged predators stumbling through the woods.

The next day, when the wolves regrouped, it was Nimis who returned carrying the scent that she had been successful. She had found and fed on the fresh carcass of a mule deer. Whenever they met, the wolves greeted each other by nuzzling and sniffing. The wolves backtracked over her trail, Okimaw in the lead, and soon they joined the ravens already feeding on the carcass.

Ravens, crows, and jays, all members of the crow family, kept company with the wolves, sometimes leading the wolves to carcasses and sometimes following the pack on their hunts. Crows were quite daring around the wolves, settling down in their midst, regardless of whether the wolves were feeding or resting. Only the young inexperienced wolves would try to pounce on the birds, but they soon learned it was an exercise in futility.

One afternoon, after gorging on a moose carcass, the wolves with their bloated stomachs were napping. With his muzzle resting on his front paws, Kanatan was sleepily watching one of the crows hop among the other wolves. The crow approached Otakosin's head, deliberately pecking at the ground in front. Sensing some fun, Kanatan raised his head to watch more closely. Now the crow was pecking closer and closer to Otakosin. With one swift movement it pecked the sleeping wolf right on the nose. Otakosin jumped straight up in the air, yelping, but the crow easily managed to avoid Otakosin's pounce. Otakosin spotted the amused Kanatan and, since he couldn't vent his indignation on the agile crow, he went after Kanatan. Kanatan took his licking and showed his subordination to Otakosin by rolling onto his back with his tail tucked between his legs, pleading for mercy. When Otakosin had satisfied himself, he returned to his resting spot, circled to settle down, and gave Kanatan an icy stare. Kanatan immediately turned his eyes away from Otakosin's. Some wolves have no sense of humour.

Until the mating season, when a change in leadership might occur, Okimaw was the alpha male. He was also a breeding male. Later, he might still retain the leadership, but the breeding male might be one of the lower-ranking males. He was from Kehte-aya's second litter and was now in his eighth year. Okimaw decided when, where, and how a hunt would proceed. He always ate from the kills. All the members of the pack were submissive to him. Neka was the alpha female and was submissive only to Okimaw, but, as his mate, she could be more persuasive than submissive, and sometimes Okimaw allowed her to lead the pack. They were affectionate with each other all year round. If a female wolf were the largest, strongest wolf of a pack, it was possible for her to be the alpha wolf. But Neka was a docile, gentle wolf for most of the year.

Oskinikiw was the beta male. If Okimaw were killed or seriously incapacitated, Oskinikiw would assume the leadership and could take Neka as his mate, or he might choose Nimis or even a wandering female. He had been adopted by Neka and Okimaw when his mother was killed by a grizzly.

Four years earlier, Oskinikiw's mother had detected the presence of a marauding grizzly bear. She had already moved two pups to a new den a kilometre away and was on her third trip. There was one pup still in the den when the grizzly located the entrance. Panicked at being alone, the pup had disobeyed his mother and wandered out of the den to look for his littermates. His whimpering immediately attracted the bear. The mother wolf tried in vain to save her pup, but the grizzly turned on her and, with one swipe of his large paw, caught her across her head and broke her neck. When the rest of the wolves returned at the end of a long hunt and discovered the remains, they moved out of the area.

Neka and Okimaw had been on a romp while Kehte-aya remained with Neka's litter. The romp became a hunt and the hunt took them into the overlap of their runway, where markings had already become aged and where the new den was. Neka heard the cries of the pups and began sniffing the area until she found the den. Deep inside, she found the two three-week-old pups still alive, but barely. She nursed them both and then, picking one up by its belly, she brought it out and Okimaw followed her back to her own den. For some reason she did not go back for the other pup. Perhaps it was too sick or weak, or perhaps she didn't have enough milk, or perhaps she simply forgot about it.

Otakosin was a year younger than Oskinikiw and had begun to challenge Oskinikiw for beta position. This past summer, Otakosin had left the pack for a few weeks and, on his return, he reassumed his standing in the pack hierarchy. Any of the subordinates could leave to start their own families or join another pack. Occasionally, a wolf from another pack stayed for a few days before re-joining its own pack. It was a way of overcoming inbreeding and, possibly, it was also a way of exchanging information from distant places. However, a pack of wolves could just as easily turn an intruder away or even kill it.

One cool sunny afternoon in the late fall, as the wolves were sleeping after eating their fill of a bull moose, the sound of a rifle shot snapped. They were immediately up, scattering in different directions into the surrounding stands of black spruce and jack pine. One wolf did not get up. Oskinikiw had flipped to his side with his legs splayed in a sudden tense spasm. He shuddered a few times, then his body went limp and he died. That evening, back near the south end of Shadow Lake, Okimaw raised his voice to call his wolves to him. They all eventually returned, except for Oskinikiw. When they howled the next time, it was a mournful song. Afterwards, Okimaw led the wolves further to the northwest. It was time to travel deeper into their winter territory.

In December the wolf pack was again marking its winter range and they were hunting more often during the day. In their hunts, they attempted to get as close to the quarry as possible, hoping for a quick rush and a kill, their strong jaws ripping and slashing. Today they would split up and some of them would feed on hare. Many times they made their rushes and chased elk, deer, and moose, and many times they settled for beaver, hare, and marmot. For some of them, long periods without food were not unusual. Their stomachs were made for the feast-and-famine way of the wild.

Between September and January the days and nights in the lives of wolves were spent hunting, resting, playing, and marking out their expanded territory. By January the pups, Kisikaw and Wapan, born in the previous March or April, could take part in kills of larger game. Only a discerning human eye could pick them out as youngsters. They would be fully mature at about twenty-two months, after which they might wander off to form new packs or join others, or they would establish a place for themselves in this pack.

The mating season began in January, and the normally tolerant dispositions of Neka and Okimaw changed dramatically. Okimaw became testy, mostly towards his son, Otakosin, taking every opportunity to show his brute strength. And Neka enforced her dominance over Nimis, over every real or imagined transgression. This show of dominance passed down the line, and the wolves went around avoiding eye contact and keeping their tails well tucked between their legs. Only the alpha pair went around with their tails raised high.

Neka and Okimaw finally left the pack after three weeks to carry out the remainder of their courtship in private. After they had successfully completed their mating ritual, life among the wolves returned to normal.

In March the pack returned to Shadow Lake, where they had their denning area. Shadow Lake was seven kilometres long and, in some places, three kilometres wide. If seen from the air, it was shaped like a tight S, and it supported a family of common loons. The lake at the southeast end became marshland, an attraction to moose and fowl. On the opposite side where the lake was indented by land, the wolves had their den.

Neka prepared the den, making some slight renovations. It was located about one hundred yards from the water, and high banks provided views of the surrounding clearings and of the entrance. Stands of trembling aspen, black spruce, jack pine and hemlock protected three sides, and thickets of willow shrubs along the lake hid the den's entrance. The interior was a narrow twenty-foot tunnel, winding through the root system of the trees above, and it widened slightly at the end, where Neka would give birth to the pups.

At the beginning of spring, about two months after conception, Neka crawled in to give birth to a new generation. Six pups were born. Of these, two might survive to adulthood. The wilderness can be a harsh environment. For now, the whole pack celebrated the birth of the pups. With tails wagging, they danced around outside, whining and licking each other. Then, remembering that Neka might be hungry, they performed their prehunting ritual, nipping and licking at Okimaw's jaws, and he led them off to the hunt. He and other members brought food back, either swallowing it so they could regurgitate it on their return or, if portable, bringing back chunks of meat.

By the third week, all the puppies' eyes had opened and most of them were no longer deaf. Some of them were already crawling towards the entrance. Neka decided it was time to introduce them to the rest of the family. On that day, all the wolves gathered at the entrance, watching with anticipation. Each pup was greeted with much fuss. Neka, proud mother, watched her grunting, squealing pups.

Wapan, now thirteen months, was especially intrigued with the pups. Kehte-aya, Nimis, and Kanatan often took turns staying at the den while the others were away hunting. When Wapan was allowed to stay with the pups, she was quite pleased. She would settle down and allow the pups to climb all over her. If she went on the hunt, she made sure she brought back partially digested food to be regurgitated for the pups. But she preferred to be the one to stay with the little ones, although, more and more, it was Kehte-aya who remained at the den.

Kehta-aya was still agile, but she had become slower and stiffer with age. One day, she joined the hunt while Wapan remained behind. The pack came upon a mule deer, chased it, cornered it, and closed in on it. Kehte-aya was at the front while Okimaw and the others were tearing at its flanks. One of its sharp front hoofs caught Kehte-aya in the shoulder. It wasn't unusual for wolves to be struck. They healed well, and quickly, from such injuries. When the deer was down and the feeding frenzy began, Kehte-aya limped up to the carcass, but Okimaw chased her away and would not allow her to feed. She limped off to a thicket of willows to watch the feeding wolves and lick at her wound. She would not heal from this wound.

. . .

The pack could afford to raise a healthy new litter to continue a generation of wolves. But when food was hard to come by, when each adult member had to carry its own weight to stay strong and sustain the pack, the pack could not carry the injured and the weak. Kehte-aya would not recover, and instinct dictated that she be excluded from the pack. Even if she had not been wounded, her age and condition would have guaranteed her exile sometime in the coming year.

That night, the howls of the wolves seemed to have an intensely lonely sound, almost as if they were in mourning once again. Kehte-aya, now feeding on what was left, raised her head to listen, knew her fate, and accepted it. She sighed and lowered her head to resume her meagre feeding. From now on, when Neka was away, it would be Wapan who watched over the pups.

—2000/2011

From *Come Walk With Me, A Memoir*

Me, Sonny—that's my older brother—Vivian, Kathy, Mommy, and Daddy, we live on Jarvis Street across from the train tracks. In the summertime, me, Sonny, Vivian, and Kathy, and all their friends play on the trains when it gets dark. We play tag and run up and down the aisles of the trains. We make lots of noise, yelling and laughing, and our feet bang on the floors as we run. I am the baby of my family, so everyone looks after me. I am never scared, not even the times when the big man comes and chases us home. I think he is playing too.

One nighttime I have a dream. Me and Daddy are in a big parking lot. A whole bunch of black and white birds with long mouths are coming closer and closer. They can stand up and are not afraid of us. They are taller than me but not my daddy. Daddy is holding my hand and we are backing away from them. I look up at Daddy to see if we should be afraid, but he is just staring at them coming closer. Then we are at a wall and we can't back up any more. I wake up. I never forget the dream. It is the first time I'm scared for real. And I'm scared because Daddy seems scared too.

Daddy tells us a story about the boogeyman. The boogeyman comes out at night and he looks for little girls and boys. And if he can catch them, he takes them home and eats them up. That's a scary story, but Daddy's not scared, so I like it.

Sometimes me and Sonny wake up early. We have to play quietly so we don't wake anyone else up. One morning he spots two breads up on the counter and decides we'll clean them for Mommy. He pushes two kitchen chairs over to the sink. He gives one bread to me. As we wash them, they turn into white sticky stuff. We try to get it off our hands with the dishcloth and, after, we wipe that on our clothes. Pretty soon it's on our faces and in our hair and on the chairs. When everyone else gets up, they're not happy with us. I am the baby of the family so just Sonny gets heck.

Only me, Daddy, and Mommy are at home when a strange lady comes to visit. The lady is mad at Mommy. I don't know why. She is yelling and Mommy yells back. I am sitting on Daddy's lap at the kitchen table. He is watching them and laughing. I don't know why he doesn't make that lady go away. The lady is big and she pushes Mommy. Mommy pushes her back. Then that lady pushes so hard Mommy bangs into the washing machine and falls down. She stands up again and they are yelling and slapping. First I am scared. Then I get mad at that mean lady. I slide down from Daddy's lap and kick that lady as hard as I can. Pretty soon after that, she goes away. I don't know why Daddy didn't help Mommy, but it makes me sad.

MAYBE WE STILL LIVE on Jarvis Street. We are all in a dark room. All the places we live in are dark. I don't know why. The door on the wood stove is open 'cause I can see the fire. I sit on Kathy's lap. Across the table, Vivian turns the handle of a meat grinder. I watch the squished meat come out of the holes. I reach over to clean some meat out of one of the holes with my middle finger. I feel a sharp pain and I scream. Something inside the hole bites my finger and I pull it out fast. My finger looks like the squished meat and it is bleeding, bleeding, bleeding and I am screaming, screaming. Mommy and Daddy take me to a hospital. When I wake up a doctor tells me he took some skin from my arm and covered the tip of my finger. Now a big bandage covers my finger and another one is on my arm. I want him to show me what my finger looks like but he says I have to wait.

ONE DAY WE ARE at home, and then Sonny and me are in a big building looking at Daddy on the other side of a big see-through fence. We are so excited to see him but we can't get outside to talk to him. After he leaves, me and Sonny have to stay there.

THE HANLEYS' IS MY first foster home. I don't know where they took Sonny and I don't know where my big sisters are. Maybe they are at home with Mommy and Daddy. I want to go home.

The Hanleys are rich. They buy me all new clothes. The dresses feel crispy and smell new, and the underwear and socks are so white and soft. They have an upstairs and, in the bathroom, they have a toilet that flushes, not a pail in a closet like at home, and they have a big bathtub. Sometimes they fill it with water and bubbles, and Mrs. Hanley or an older girl gives me a bath with soap that smells so, so good. They have a little spaniel dog that pees on the carpet every morning even though it gets heck.

I am three years old but I have to sleep in a baby crib. Two older girls sleep in the room too. One's got light brown hair and the other one has dark hair. From the way Mr. and Mrs. Hanley talk, the one with the dark hair is a "bad" girl. I think the Hanleys have an older son. He takes me for car rides. I sit on the front seat and I am too little to see outside so I watch his foot push the pedals. Sometimes we wait for a train to come, and he tells me to wave to the man on the train. I kneel on the seat and wave and I am so happy when the man waves back to me. The big boy ends the rides by telling me that I'm too heavy and his foot is getting sore from pressing on the pedals, and he takes me back home.

AN OLD, OLD MAN lives there too. His bedroom is upstairs, next to our big bedroom.

MR. HANLEY TAKES ME down to the basement and sits me on a high chair. Then he cuts off my hair.

MY BEST FRIEND IS NANCY. She lives one, two, three houses from us. She is older and she takes me to bible school, down the block and across the street. I like bible school 'cause they let us cut and paste paper and they have colouring books. They show movies on the wall, about Jesus and God. Jesus and God have really nice voices.

ONE DAY, I'M IN the front yard. I look all around me. Everything is brand new. I don't feel too hot and I don't feel too cold. I feel just right. Someone mows a lawn and I like the sound. I breathe in all the way and smell the grass that's getting cut. Someone is painting a fence and I like the smell of that too. I lie down on the grass and look up at the grey, grey sky. I smell something else. It's the earth. I roll over and pick some up. I breathe in all the way again, and the earth smells so good. I put some on my tongue. I know I'm not supposed to eat it but I got to taste it. And I am so happy—happy to be alive!

I know about dying 'cause I already asked Mrs. Hanley about it. I asked 'cause of bible school and the prayer I have to say every night: "Now I lay me down to sleep. I pray the Lord, my soul to keep. If I should die before I wake, I pray the Lord my soul to take." Mrs. Hanley says that means if I die while I'm sleeping, I'll go to heaven. Only good people go to heaven.

THAT OLD MAN UPSTAIRS, at first he reads me books and sometimes he tickles me and makes me laugh. Then later he tells to me to visit him in his room. I look at things on his dresser and shelves. There's a funny smell in his room. I don't like it but I don't say anything. He wants to show me something special. He tells to me to climb up on his bed where he is lying down. His bed is way high up and he has to help me climb up. He tells me to lie down beside him. Then he pushes back the cover and he shows to me the special thing. I know what it is and I know what it's for. it's to put in a woman. He takes my hand and puts it on his thing. I know this is bad. I am bad. So I never tell anybody about it.

I AM SICK AND I have to go to a hospital. I have to always obey grownups. Vivian told me so. A nurse puts a bedpan in my crib. Then she tells me to pee in the bed. I don't know what to do. If she wants me to pee in the bed, why did she bring me a bedpan? I have to obey her, so I pee in the bed. When she comes back, she seems kind of mad and she changes the sheets.

The next time she brings the bedpan, she tells to me to pee in the bed again. I don't want her to be mad at me but I have to obey. Again she is mad at me. When she brings the bedpan one more time, she just puts it in my bed and walks away. So I use the bedpan. I know how to use a toilet, but she never asked me that. Back at the Hanleys', I pee in my crib so the old man won't touch me when he comes in at night.

ONE DAY MRS. GIRWELL comes to pick me up in a car. She's a social worker. She is the lady who drove me to the Hanleys' place to live. I love car rides and we go for a long one. She tells me I am going to see my parents. Inside me I am so excited but I don't let her see that. I don't know if Mrs. Girwell likes me or not. She doesn't talk to me very much. If she doesn't like me, and she knows I am excited to see Mommy and Daddy, she might not let me see them. So I just be very quiet.

We come to a Children's Aid building and she leaves me in a small room. Later a woman opens the door and says, "Eddie's coming up the stairs."

Eddie? Who's Eddie? I think she should be telling someone else. But then, Sonny walks in. That's how I find out Sonny's real name is Eddie. Eddie has thick, curly hair like Mommy. Mine is straight. And short. Vivian and Kathy and Mommy and Daddy come too. They bring us donuts and candies. Kathy and Vivian are almost grown up.

Everybody talks and laughs. I mostly listen. I tell them only a good thing about the Hanleys: they have a piano that makes music so I danced a jig for them. I don't tell them about the old man.

When this visit is finished, I think we will all go home together. I wait and wait. When Mrs. Girwell opens the door and tells to us it's time to leave, I'm so happy. We all put our coats on to go home, but Mommy bends down to hug me goodbye. I can feel her wet cheek on my face.

Another time I'm in the back seat of Mrs. Girwell's car and I have to go back to the Hanleys' place. I see Mommy and Daddy walking down the sidewalk, holding hands. They don't see me but I'm so excited. This is like having an extra visit. Maybe Mrs. Girwell sees them but she doesn't say nothing. I watch out the back window and they get smaller and smaller. Mrs. Girwell makes the car go on another road and I can't see them anymore. I'm happy they are together but I wish I could be with them too.

At another family visit I find out that Sonny lives with an old lady in a place called King's Park. Vivian lives with a family in St. Norbert. Mommy and Daddy give me a panda bear and he is black and white, and I call him Andy Pandy. I sit on the floor and play with him and I hear Mommy and Daddy talk to Vivian about Kathy. Kathy doesn't come to family visits anymore. Children's Aid says she is a bad girl and they make her live with other bad girls. The social worker said Kathy runs away to go back home to Mommy and Daddy. To me, she is good for doing that. When I get older, I think I'll do that too.

When Kathy was at the family visits, me and her are quiet. Vivian and Sonny, they talk a lot and make us laugh. Vivian is my favourite sister 'cause she teases me and makes me laugh so much. Mrs. Girwell told me I can't go live with Mommy and Daddy. Maybe they are bad. I don't want anyone to know I think that so I can't ask anybody about it.

I ASK MRS. GIRWELL and I keep asking Mrs. Hanley if I can go live with Vivian. If I live with her it will be a little bit like to be at home. I will be so happy. And one day, it happens!

—2010

Patricia Ningewance

Anishinaabe (Obizhigokaang/Lac Seul First Nation) 1951–

Patricia Ningewance is an Anishinaabe artist, writer, and publisher who lives in Winnipeg. She is of the Bear clan and has written seven Anishinaabe language books: *Survival Ojibwe* (1993), *Anishinaabemodaa: Becoming a Successful Ojibwe Eavesdropper* (1995), *Talking Gookom's Language: Learning Ojibwe* (2004); its workbook and CD; *Pocket Ojibwe* (2006); and *Word Racing, Games to Play in Language Camps* (2010). She has over 30 years experience teaching language, working as a translator, and doing media work.

Many Aboriginal authors continue to write stories in their ancestral languages. In this nonfiction story, written in Anishinaabemowin, Ningewance recounts an evening she arrived in Pittsburgh, Pennsylvania, to attend a Lakota-Sioux Yuwipi healing ceremony. She describes how all of the participants were non-Aboriginal, while the ceremony leaders of Mexican-Aboriginal descent. In a narrative that recalls her own fears, prejudices, and anxieties, Ningewance explains how this interesting scenario teaches her many things.

Aabiding E-niibing Gichi-mookomaanakiing

Aabiding nin-gii-ganoonig bezhig ni-wiijiiwaagan Gichi-mookomaanakiing bi-onji-giigido. Michi-zhaaganaashiimo awe, wemitigoozhi aaniish. "Gi-daabi-wiiji' ina?" ndinig. "Nin-gii-gimoodimigoo ningitochigan."

"Ishe," indinaa. "Aaniish niin ge-gii-doodamaambaan?"

"Nin-gii-ganoonaa bezhig awiya omaa," ikido. "Nin-ga-wiiji'ig ji-mikamaan iwe. Yoowiipii izhinikaade iwe gaa-gikendang ji-doodang. Daabishkoo anishinaabeg gii-gozaabanjigewaad, amii wiinawaa ezhinikaadamowaad bwaanag iwe izhichigewin. "Nin-ga-diba'aan ji-izhaayin wedi Pittsburgh ge-danakamigak. Nishiime Dave gewiin da-biizhaa. Aapiji nin-daa-gichi-minwendam biizhaayin," nindig ni-wiijiiwaagan." John izhinikaazo.

"Haaw," nindinaa. "Nin-ga-biizhaa."

Wedi ishkoniganing gii-biizhaabaniig wiin zhigo odinawemaagana'. Oklahoma dash onjiiwag. Aapiji nin-gii-minowiijiiwaag gakina igi. Aapiji minwaadiziwag.

Niizhodwaate e-izhiseg nin-gii-bagamaash wedi Pittsburgh. Bezhig wemitigoozhi nin-gii-nagishkaag bimisewigamigong. Gaamashi wiin imaa ayaasii iinzan John. Aapiji gichi-waawaanadinaa iwe aki Pennsylvania. Ozaami-onizhishin. Wedi dash noopimiing inake nin-gii-izhi-dagoshinomin. Awakaanigamig badakide. Niibiwa waakaa'iganan imaa ayaawan. Gaye bebakaan dino gitigaanan. Nin-gabaa. Nim-biindige imaa gichi-waakaa'iganing. Bizhishig igo wemitigoozhiwag imaa ayaawag, wemitigoozhiikweg gaye. Gaawiin awiya anishinaabe ni-waabamaasii. Baamaa maawiin da-dagoshinoog nindinenendam. Gaawiin awiya nin-ganoonigosii. Asemaan odazhi-dakobinaawaan igi ikwewag. Gigagoodewag gakina igi ikwewag, daabishkoo sago gaa-izhi'owaad anishinaabekweg owe gii-inakamigak. Nin-gwenawi-izhichige. Gaawiin aaniish awiya nin-gikenimaasii. Gaawiin gaye awiya nin-baabiziskenimigosii. Ndawaa nin-gii-gawishim ajina. E-zhiingendamaan gaa-gii-onji-gawishimoyaan. Daabishkoo e-nagadamaan iwe gaa-gii-onji-nibaayaan. Goshkoziyaan anishinaabeg da-dagoshinoog nindinenendam. Gaa-izhi-nibaayaan. Maagizhaa ango-diba'igan nin-gii-nibaa. Gii-goshkoziyaan, nin-gii-niisaandawe. Gaawiin awiya anishinaabe. Gaawiin mashi gaye ni-wiijiiwaagan, gaye oshiimeyan. Ndawaa miinawaa nin-giiwe-nibaa. Ango-diba'igan geyaabi nin-gii-nibaa. Gii-goshkoziyaan nin-gii-niisaandawe. Amii sa gaawiin anishinaabeg ni-waabamaasiig. Nin-gotaaj gaye ji-izhi-gagwedweyaan. Nin-gotaaj igo gaye. Aaniin ge-izhichigeyaan giishpin wemitigoozhiwag eta owe izhichigewaad? Wenji-waabamag ni-wiijiiwaagan. Gii-dagoshin iinzan, oshiimeyan gaye. Ni-minwendam e-waabamagwaa.

Aazha ani-onaagoshin. "Aazha gegaa gi-ga-madoodoomin," nindig ni-wiijiiwaagan. Nin-gii-awi-bisikaan ningoodaas. Amii gaawiin awiyag anishinaabeg. Ni-maajii'adoomin wedi gaa-wii-dazhi-madoodoong. Wiinge sa ninzegiz. Amii ji-baataa'agwaa nindinawemaganag nindinendam. Wegonen naa gaa-onji-biizhaayaan? Wiinge ninzegiz. Gaawiin dash gegoon nindikidosii.

Gii-dagoshinaang imaa madoodoswaaning, ni-waabamaa imaa Mexican dinookaan anishinaabe. Gichi-zhawiingweni e-waabamid. "Ooh, nishiime," nindig, "aapiji ni-minwendam e-waabaminaan!" Wiinge jiisinaawizi. Nin-zagininjiinaa. Ni-minwendam geniin e-waabamag awiya gaa-izhinaagoziyaan e-izhinaagozid. Amii gaa-izhi-nayendamaan bangii. Amii dash gaa-izhi-wiindamawid ni-wiijiiwaagan, bwaanan iinzan e-gii-gikino'amaagod awedi Mexican ji-doodang owe dinookaan izhichigewin.

Nin-gii-biindigemin imaa madoodoswaaning. Waakaanabiwag imaa wemitigoozhiwag, wemitigoozhiikweg. Weweni gii-waawiindamaage awe Mexican anishinaabe, weweni izhichigenid ini gaa-biindigenid imaa. Geyaabi dash ninzegiz. Wiinge nin-gii-gichi-anami'aa imaa gii-namadabiyaan, epiitaanimiziyaan. Aapiji nin-gii-gichi-inendam gaa-gii-izhinamaan imaa.

Gaa-ishkwaa-maadoodooyaan, apane miinawaa nim-biindigemin waakaa'iganing ge-danakamigak. Aasamisag nin-gii-onab. Gabe-dibik ngwana imaa nin-ga-ayaamin. Wiinge gashkiidibikichigaade iwe ge-danakamigak. Ngojigo gii-ishkwaa-aabitaa-dibikag gii-maadakamigan. Wiinge miinawaa ninzegiz. Ningotaaj ji-onjine'agwaa nindinawemaaganag. Wiinge miinawaa nin-gii-gichi-anami'aa gabe-dibik. Amii wenji-ayaayaan omaa e-bi-wiiji'ag niwiijiiwaagan e-gii-andomid ji-biizhaayaan. Gii-maadakamigizi awedi inini. Amii miinawaa gaa-gichi-izhinamaan. Amii dash iwe e-dibikag gii-gikendamaan wegonen gaa-onji-gotaajiyaan. Nin-gosaag ngwana wemitigoozhiwag ji-odaapinamowaad anishinaabe-izhitwaawin. Giishpin gewiinawaa maajii-dagwiiwaad owe gii-izhichigeying gii-anishinaabewiying, amii ge-izhi-gagwe-niigaanishkamowaad. Amii aaniish enaadiziwaad ogo wemitigoozhiwag, e-wii-gagwe-dibendamowaad gakina gegoon, nindinendam. Amii owe ge-gagwe-makaminangwaa. Amii dash miinawaa ni-naanaagadawendam. Daa-maanzhise na dash gewiinawaa wemitigoozhiwag biminizha'amowaad anishinaabe izhichigewin? Nawach na maanzhise e-ani-waniseg anishinaabe izhitwaawin? Aazha misawaach giinawind gidani-wanitoomin owe. Amii bangii gaa-izhi-na'endamaan.

Amii dash naanaage gaye gaa-inendamaan, naasaab achaak gakina awiya odayaawaan. Aana-bakaan-inazhageying, amii naasaab ezhinaagozigwen achaak. Gakina bezhigwan gididzhinaagozimin wiiyaw ayaasiwang. Amii iwe gaa-izhi-gikendamaan iwe gii-izhaayaan imaa.

Gii-waabang gii-giizhakamigan. Gii-wiikwandim e-gizhebaawagak. Wiinge sa mino-giizhigan. Gaa-ishkwaakamigak nin-gii-ando-babaamose, niin eta. Wedi ogidadin nin-gii-izhaa. Ozaami-onizhishin. Ni-niibaw dash imaa ogidadin. Migizi gii-biidaashi imaa gaa-izhi-niibawiyaan. Apane miinawaa animaashi. Aazha miinawaa bezhig bakaan migizi wenji-biidaashid. Miinawaa imaa gaa-izhi-niibawiyaan gii-bimaashi. Gii-aazhideshkodaadiwag imaa gaa-izhi-niibawiyaan. Amii gaa-izhi-gichi-na'endamaan. Onizhishin iinzan owe gaa-gii-inakamigak nin-gii-inendam. Gwayak gii-inakamigan. Nin-gii-apizo'igoog dash bimisewigamigong ni-wiijiiwaaganag. Nin-gii-nagajibiz dash. Wiinge enigok nin-daana-gii-bimibatoo e-gagwe-oditamaa ge-izhi-booziyaan. Amii gaawiin. Wiinge aanjigo nin-gichi-baapi'igoog ni-wiijiiwaaganag. "Amii izhi-aanishiitan!" nindigoog. "Aanjitoon miinawaa naanaage ji-booziyin," nindigoog. Amii dash gaa-izhichigeyaan. Anishaa nindoojaanimiz. Nin-gii-ando-wiisinimin dash, e-gii-mawadisidiyaang weweni.

Moozhag ni-waawiindamaage owe dibaajimowin. Nin-gii-gikino'amaagoo iwe nindinendam, ji-dibaajimoyaan. Amii ko ningoding gaa-onji- izhiseying gegoon, ji-onji-ondinamang gikendaasowin. Amii dash miinawaa wenji-aanike-dibaajimowaan owe.

—2011

Once on a Summer in the United States
English translation

One time an American friend called me, out of the blue. He spoke only English, that's because he is non-native. "Would you come and help me?" he asked. "My musical instrument has been stolen from me."

"Ishe!" I said to him. "And what could I do about it?"

"I called someone here," he said. "He said he'd help me find it. He knows how to perform a *yuwipi* ceremony." This is just like the Anishinaabe shake tent ceremony; this is what the Dakota people call this ceremony. "I will pay for your expenses to fly to Pittsburgh where it will happen. My younger brother Dave will come too. I would be so happy if you could come too to be a support for me," said my friend. His name is John.

"Okay," I said to him. "I will come there."

He and his relatives had come to my home community one time. They are from Oklahoma. I became good friends with them. They are very kind people.

Two weeks later, I arrived by plane at Pittsburgh. One white man met me at the airport. John apparently had not arrived yet. Pennsylvania is very hilly country. It is very beautiful. We arrived somewhere in the forested area. A barn stood there. There were many other buildings there. There were also other kinds of gardens. I got out of the car. I entered the large house. I just saw all white people in there, white women too. I didn't see one native person. Maybe they'll arrive later, I thought to myself. No one spoke to me. Those women were making tobacco ties. All those women were wearing longish skirts just like native women do at these occasions. I didn't know what to do. I didn't know anybody here. And I was being ignored. I decided to take a nap for awhile. I figured that when I awoke, the native people will have arrived. So I went to sleep. Maybe I slept for an hour. When I woke up, I went downstairs. No native people. And my friend and his brother had not arrived either. I decided to go back upstairs to go to sleep again. I hated this situation. I slept to escape being there. I slept for another hour. I went downstairs again when I woke up. There still weren't any native people there.

I was also afraid to ask about this. I was just afraid. What shall I do if it's just white people doing this ceremony? I saw my friend then. He and his brother had arrived. I was happy to see them.

It was starting to be evening. "We're going to have a sweat soon," my friend said to me. I went to put on my long skirt. There were no native people around. We started walking towards the sweat lodge. I was scared. I was afraid that I might bring bad luck to my relatives by doing this. Why had I agreed to come? I was very scared. But I didn't say anything.

When we got to the sweat lodge, I saw a Mexican native man there. He smiled broadly when he saw me. "Hey, my little sister," he said to me, "I'm happy to see you." He was very friendly. I shook his hand. I was happy to see someone who looked like me. So I felt a little bit better. So then my friend told me that a Dakota man had taught this Mexican man how to conduct this *yuwipi* ceremony.

We entered that sweat lodge. The white women and men sat in a circle inside. That Mexican then instructed the people on how to behave inside the sweat lodge. I was still scared. I prayed really hard as I sat there; that's how scared I was. I was very impressed with what I saw in there that night.

When we finished with the sweat, we went inside the big house again where the ceremony would take place. I sat against a wall. We would be there all night long. The room where it would take place was completely darkened. It began some time around midnight. I was getting nervous again. I was afraid to bring sickness and death to my family. I prayed hard all night. Whatever happens, I thought, I'm here out of love for my friend who asked me to come and help him. That's my reason for being here. That man began his ceremony. I saw many unusual things that night. That's when I realized what I had been afraid of. I was afraid of white people taking over native ceremonies. If they begin taking part in these ceremonies that were ours, they will start dominating them. That's because that is their nature, to try to own everything, I thought. This is what they'll try to take away from us. And then I thought some more. So would it be so bad if white people began following the native traditions? Is it worse that native traditions are being lost? We native people are beginning to lose this aspect of our culture. I felt a little settled with this thought.

Then later the idea occurred to me that we are all the same colour of the spirit. The soul has no skin colour. Only our surface skins are of different hues. This is what I learned from this night.

In the morning, the ceremony ended. There was a morning feast. The day was beautiful. When it was all over, I went for a walk just by myself. I went to the top of a hill. I stood on top of the hill. A bald eagle came flying towards me and flew right above me. And then it flew away. Then another flew from a straight angle, right over me. So those two eagles had criss-crossed right over me. So then, I felt right about where I had been. This ceremony had been done properly. It had been right.

My friends drove me to the airport. I missed my plane. I ran really hard to try to catch the plane but no. My friends were laughing at the desperate way I tried to catch that plane. "Give up," they said. "We'll change your flight and have a proper visit." So that's what we did. I was stressed for nothing. We went to have a meal and a good visit.

Many times I tell this story. I feel that I was given this teaching so that I will pass it on. I think that's why we go through these different experiences so that we will gain some important knowledge and that we will pass it on to others.

—*2011*

Murray Sinclair

Anishinaabe (St. Peter's Indian Reserve/Peguis First Nation) 1951–

His Honour Justice Murray Sinclair was born and raised north of Winnipeg, on the original grounds of the St. Peter's Indian Reserve. After serving as Special Assistant to the Attorney General of Manitoba, he graduated from the Faculty of Law at the University of Manitoba. As a lawyer, he was known for his passionate representation of Aboriginal people and his knowledge of Aboriginal legal issues, which led to his appointment to the Provincial Court of Manitoba in 1988 as the first Aboriginal judge in Manitoba's history. Soon after, he was appointed Co-Commissioner of the Aboriginal Justice Inquiry, which examined the shooting death of J.J. Harper by Winnipeg police officer Robert Cross and the murder of Helen Betty Osborne and the experiences of Aboriginal people with the justice system in Manitoba. In 2001, he was appointed to the Court of Queen's Bench and, in 2009, as Chair of the Truth and Reconciliation Commission of Canada., This non-governmental commission was formed to examine the legacies of Canadian residential schools and to inform all Canadians of what happened there. Justice Sinclair has been awarded a National Aboriginal Achievement Award and several honourary degrees from universities across Canada.

Justice Sinclair's "Suicide in First Nations People" is a speech he gave in 1992 at the national conference of the Canadian Association for Suicide Prevention. Aboriginal people, Sinclair points out, suffer from suicide rates six to ten times the national average, and the reasons for this are primarily due to a history of colonialism in Canada. Illustrating his dynamic speaking style, Sinclair's speech is a combination of many topics and issues, consisting of personal reflections, history lessons, and a statement of hope through a plea for change. Of particular interest is the way Sinclair weaves cultural lifeways, political contexts, and events in Aboriginal history together. It is a remarkable piece of educational storytelling that explores the past, present, and future of Aboriginal life in Manitoba.

Suicide in First Nations People

How We Got Here

Growing up Aboriginal in Canada is, and has been, a difficult and sometimes traumatic experience. Our lives as Aboriginal youth are filled with images and expectations that sometimes have little basis in, or are at odds with, our individual realities. We have to reconcile all of the pulls and pushes acting upon us within the confines of our own sense of identity. Yet the development of our sense of identity often comes about only after a long period of being or feeling lost…. All youth, I suppose, have to struggle with that sort of conflict, but for Aboriginal youth it is particularly more difficult.

People have described the manner in which Aboriginal people have been treated by Canadian governments and Canadian society as cultural genocide. It is a rather dramatic phrase, but it does convey a certain concept—which is that past government policies and efforts were aimed at 'killing' the cultures of Aboriginal people. That is what genocide means—the killing of a people—and cultural genocide is the killing of a culture. Other writers have coined the term 'ethnocide' to better capture the flavour of what went on, but the two phrases mean the same thing: that the cultures of Aboriginal people were to be annihilated. Genocidists believe that a people must be destroyed. The ethnocidist believed that the people could be saved, but that the inferior cultures to which Aboriginal people belonged had to be destroyed in order to save them from a life of barbarism, paganism, and backwardness.

It is hard to envision the possibility that the genocidist could be motivated by anything other than malice or evil, or at the very least cold-heartedness. With cultural genocide, however, the motivation was not an evil one. Almost always, it involved a belief that what the practitioner was in fact doing was in the best interests of the people. Acts of cultural genocide were perceived by both the practitioner and others as being acts of kindness. It was, we are told, unfortunately, a case of having to take strong medicine to overcome a terrible condition. The legal and political efforts and policies of the institutions of government—including those of justice—insofar as Indian people are concerned, in the past and to a certain extent even today, were motivated by a belief that what needed to be and was being done, in the long run, was the best thing for Indians: their gradual civilization.

Cultural genocide has largely been eliminated from our thinking in modern times, but its strong role in historical times has given rise to policies, programs, and laws over the years and generations that are still with us. The result is that much of what we think and do today concerning Aboriginal people and Aboriginal issues is permeated with inherent biases. Cultural bias is the problem that we must begin to address. It is important to recognize and come to understand how the phenomenon of ethnocide or cultural genocide has been implemented if we are to protect our present and future decisions from it. We must, however, begin with one very important thought. There is no cure within the assertion of the superiority of one culture's beliefs and values over another. The sad truth is, as we are now discovering—and as Indian people have known all along—that the intended cures of the past have only worsened the condition.

While I was growing up in the community I come from, I was always struck by the fact that as Aboriginal people we appeared not to have a history. The beginning of our history as Canadians started with European explorers such as Christopher Columbus, Jacques Cartier, John Cabot, Henry Hudson, La Verendrye, and Samuel de Champlain. It continued with colonizing figures such as Talbot, Montcalm, Wolfe, and Lord Selkirk, and with the growth of European settlements at Montreal, Ottawa, and Toronto, and at the forks of the Red and the Assiniboine Rivers.

As Aboriginal people, however, we apparently never had a history worth discussing. We were, literally and figuratively, irrelevant. That can and does have a dramatic effect upon one's sense of identity and self-worth. Yet the absence of such history in the public schools I attended was the result of many deliberate acts over the years, a few of which I would like to discuss. In doing so, however, I wish to make it clear that I am not trying to make anyone feel guilty. Rather, I want to show you how history has fashioned the problems that we face and, in turn, how history can teach us how to develop better solutions that respect Aboriginal aspirations and needs.

Where We've Travelled

It is a wise person who said that if you do not know your history, then you are doomed to repeat it. It is time to stop repeating the historical mistakes of this country. The *Indian Act* was a remarkable tool of assimilation designed not to protect the Indian people in their lands and rights, but to facilitate the government's plans to abolish their special rights and to integrate them fully into Canadian society. The premise and promise of the Act was to assist in the eventual extinguishment and extinction of Indians as Indians, and to overcome whatever legal obstacles might lie in the way of that goal. Thus, the initial provisions of the Act granted powers to the minister of Indian affairs to "enfranchise" Indians and entire bands, to remove traditional chiefs from office, and to prevent Indians from engaging in economic activities on their lands that could compete successfully with local white businesses.

Indian farmers were prohibited from selling their grain and farm produce; by official government policy they were prevented from establishing anything more than subsistence farms. Indians could not sell or lease any of their natural resources from their lands. Businesses could not locate on an Indian reserve unless the minister's permission was given. It rarely was.

When Indian people of the prairies signed treaties with the Queen's representative, they did so knowing that they were being asked to surrender their rights to exclusive use of large parcels of land. However, it was also clear that they wanted lands for their exclusive use as tribal homelands—a concept the government understood but that it took advantage of and perverted into a policy to corral and control Indian movement and growth. In the 1880s, the government of Canada enacted special amendments to the *Indian Act* of Canada at the request of missionary societies who had been mandated by the government to educate Indians. These amendments became known as the Potlatch and Sundance laws. They made it an offence for any Indian person to participate in any traditional Indian ceremony or to wear traditional Indian costume or dress. The intent was to remove tribal traditions from their positions of importance in the lives of Aboriginal people. Many of those who were prosecuted under these laws were the traditional leaders of the tribe, and upon conviction they were invariably sentenced to hard labour. The statistical evidence (such as it is) available for Stony Mountain Penitentiary in Manitoba at the turn of the century shows that many of the Indian people incarcerated at that time were sentenced under these laws. In this way as well, the influence of those leaders within the tribe was reduced both by their removal from the community and by the fact that the government could show Indians that it had the power to lock up their most influential people.

There is ample evidence from Canadian and provincial archives of ministerial and departmental directives issued both before and for some time after the turn of the century to prosecutors, judges, and magistrates in western Canada exhorting and, in some cases, demanding that they sentence Indian offenders harshly so as to make it clear to their fellow tribesmen that they must abide by the laws of Canada. It was easy for the government to get its way on this point. At that time magistrates did not enjoy any type of judicial independence, holding office "at pleasure" of the government. In addition, most of the magistrates in the Northwest Territories (before the western provinces were created) were employees of the federal government, foremost among them being Indian agents and RCMP (NWMP) officers.

In the 1880s, the federal government enacted amendments to the *Indian Act* by which Indian children were legally required to attend schools established or arranged by the minister of Indian affairs. This was, interestingly, some time before compulsory education existed for the rest of Canada. The only schools established by the minister at that time were residential schools patterned on the industrial-school model then popular in the United States for Indian children and juvenile delinquents. Pursuant to these policies, Indian children were taken from their parents (and from their influence), the minister was appointed their legal guardian, and they were educated in schools run sometimes by the department but generally by missionary societies. This policy coincidentally facilitated the Christianization of the Indians—and fit neatly into government policy that Indian people needed to be saved from their pagan existence through Christianity.

At the same time, the Department of Indian Affairs inaugurated what came to be called the "pass system," whereby Indian people were not allowed to leave their reserves without the written permission of the local Indian agent. The system was designed and requested by the Canadian military following the Saskatchewan Rebellion of 1885 in order to control Indian movement in western Canada (then the Northwest Territories) and prevent another Aboriginal insurgency. Though never legally mandated or sanctioned, the system was primarily used to prevent Indian parents from traveling to where their children were attending schools and 'interfering' with them, or attempting to remove them. Not only could Indians not leave their reserves to see their children, but the pass system was also sometimes invoked to prevent Indians from seeking employment outside of their reserves. There is considerable evidence that it was abused in many other ways to enhance the power of the local Indian agents over the lives of the band members.

In the 1890s the minister was empowered by further amendment to the *Indian Act* to declare that traditional leaders and chiefs of the band no longer held any authority in the tribe and that only chiefs elected under the supervision of the local Indian agent were allowed to represent the tribe. Only men could run for chief and only men could vote for them. This rule greatly interfered with the traditional role of women in such strongly matriarchal societies as the Ojibway and the Mohawk. The amendment also required that any time the newly elected chief wished to hold a council meeting he had to notify the Indian agent. The Indian agent was, automatically and by law, the presiding officer of the council meeting. Any legislation enacted by the tribe could also be disallowed by the minister of Indian affairs. These amendments were, ironically, entitled "The Indian Advancement Act."

Amendments to the *Indian Act* at around the same time made it an offence for a lawyer to represent an Indian or a band in action against the government unless the consent of the minister of Indian affairs was first obtained. Needless to say, many perfectly valid legal claims against the government languished for decades—nobody ever got the minister's permission. As an example, the famous case of St. Catherines Milling, which decided the nature of Aboriginal title in Canada, was decided not only without Aboriginal representation in the form of counsel, but also without any evidence from Aboriginal people about how they understood their rights.[37] Finally, the *Indian Act* was amended at around this time to include a definition: "person" was defined to mean "anyone other than an Indian"—the ultimate reflection of government thinking.

For the most part, the children who were removed from their families and sent to residential schools suffered emotional and psychological harm that had differing degrees of impact upon their own coping and parenting skills. Often, the result was a belief on their part that what was "Indian" was bad—their languages, their ceremonies, their beliefs, their rituals, their religion, and their Elders. When these children became adults, they sometimes carried on the culturally destructive attitudes and attacks of the missionary people with whom they had grown up. In addition, children returning from residential schools generally lacked the skills necessary to cope with life on the reservation. Hunting, fishing, trapping, hide tanning, food preparation, beadwork, and other traditional pursuits that had formed an integral part of Aboriginal lifestyle, not simply for economic but also for social reasons, were activities that many did not know how to perform and were not inclined to learn. Despite the promise of the residential school system, most who were sent there did not receive any training in an employment-related field beyond physical labour. Reliance upon government handouts or social assistance subsequently became commonplace. None had received instruction in how to raise children, so that when they had families they experienced coping problems.

Because of the legal ban on Indian ceremonies and rituals, traditional Indian men and women were harassed and persecuted. The public display that had always accompanied such practices became dangerous, and so the practices went underground. They were never effectively wiped out—many Indian people still practised their traditional ways and customs but they had to do so clandestinely. This secrecy reduced the effectiveness of those customs as tools of societal bonding, for the numbers of those who could

---

37 The 1888 case *St. Catherine's Milling and Lumber Co. v. The Queen* was a leading case on Aboriginal title in Canada for more than 80 years. It ruled that Aboriginal title over land was allowed only at the needs and desire of the federal government and could be taken away at any time.

attend such ceremonial gatherings and teaching sessions—for that is what they are—were necessarily limited. In addition, with the advent of new religions among many of the tribes, some tribal members became agents for the "white man's churches" and for the Indian agents who were bent on destroying Aboriginal practices. Such Indians actively assisted in the discovery and destruction of ceremonial gathering places and symbols, which occasioned considerable distrust between the older traditional people and the younger ones returning from the missionary schools. It further prevented the public transmission of the cultural values inherent to the tribes that the traditions and ceremonies were designed to promote.

Although traditional ceremonies and rituals continued to be practised by a number of tribal members, the utility of the tribe's beliefs and practices as a social tool was limited to older people and to those who were outside the influence of the missionary societies. In addition, the churches could not replace what was lost, for in losing the right to publicly and regularly engage in their traditional practices and customs large numbers of Indian people lost contact not only with their religious rituals but with an entire lifestyle.

The enforcement of the kinds of laws I have mentioned created distrust of the white man's laws and legal systems on the part of Indians, as one can well understand. During the course of the hearings of the Aboriginal Justice Inquiry we heard considerable evidence of that distrust, which has clearly contributed to the fact that Aboriginal people are up to five times more likely to plead guilty than non-Aboriginal accused persons. There is considerable evidence to show that they often plead guilty to offences of which they are in fact not guilty...

It is fair to say that Aboriginal people have generally regarded the schools and courts of our country as tools of oppression. They do not see our courts as vehicles of dispute resolution or as a positive influence. The vast majority of Aboriginal contacts with the justice system even today involve appearances in our criminal courts as accused, as parents of a young person charged with an offence, or as parents in our family courts fighting some child-welfare agency that wishes to remove their children from the home. Aboriginal people do not go to our court system for relief of their civil and domestic problems. We are not providing the same type of service to them that other members of society receive. Civil and family disputes are resolved informally or not at all. Interestingly, geography has nothing to do with it; Aboriginal people in urban areas are just as unlikely to make claims for relief in our civil and family courts as are Aboriginal people in remote isolated communities.

Interestingly, despite the early belief on the part of those involved in the administration of justice as to its educational utility, there was generally little

effort outside of larger remote communities to establish courts on Indian reserves until the 1960s and 1970s. Indian people charged with offences were
generally transported, or were required to travel on their own, to larger urban centres for court appearances. Though this practice was perhaps cost
effective, the absence of a connection between the community and the process of dispute resolution undoubtedly led to further misunderstanding and
perhaps even mystery. We encountered several elderly people in our hearings in remote communities in Manitoba who asked us to find out what happened to their children who had been arrested and taken away years ago.
They had not seen them again.

The absence of traditional leadership, the removal of tribal institutions,
and the lack of appropriate replacement with Canadian models or institutions led almost invariably in some places to situations bordering on social
chaos. To list the kinds of things that can go on in communities in which
there are few effective social controls would be too depressing, but I am
sure that you can well imagine what I am alluding to. In a strange sort of
way, this state of affairs—an almost direct result of the ethnocidal policies
mentioned—reinforced the unspoken belief that Indian people were inher-
ently inferior. The result of the practice confirmed its premise—a true self-
fulfilling prophecy.

Finally, there is one other effect I want to mention, which I would call a
collective social depression. Many Aboriginal people came to believe what
society was telling them, that there was no hope in being an Indian. The fact
that the government of Canada was officially opposed to aspects of Indian
culture so basic to their continued survival as a unique people was the cat-
alyst for a pervasive belief among the rest of Canadian society that it was
best for all Aboriginal people to assimilate and surrender their 'Indianness.'
Any attempt on the part of Indian people to resist doing so was dealt with
harshly. All Aboriginal people were affected by this belief—Métis, Indian,
and Inuit—for Canadian society could not distinguish between the variety
of Aboriginal groups in society. Some Aboriginal people who were the object of such policies actually came to believe the propaganda. Others, even
if they did not believe it, would have at least sensed the futility of resistance
and thereby sought passivity. Resistance very quickly led to punishment, and
any person who felt inclined to speak out would have very quickly found
out that discretion was the better part of valour.

There was silence for the most part from Indian people to the oppression they were under, at least until very recently. From the perspective of
Aboriginal people, for the past few generations governments have essentially
'had their way' with us. If one were to try to describe the Indian attitude to

what was going on, one could easily describe it as individual passive resistance—a dropping out resulting from an unwillingness to be co-opted as part of the system. The impact upon us as Aboriginal people has been devastating. Our people have been terribly, horribly, and sometimes brutally oppressed. It is very hard to articulate in a meaningful and accurate manner what that has done to us—to our grandmothers and grandfathers, to our parents, to our aunties and uncles, to our brothers and sisters, to our very souls. I hope you can sense even a small flavour of what I am talking about.

There was historically, and still exists, a generally unspoken belief that Aboriginal people, because of their cultures, their beliefs, and their customs, are just not capable of dealing with the complicated and complex social problems of the day. Aboriginal values, beliefs, traditions, and practices have for too long been rejected as a means of resolving serious social and community problems for Aboriginal and Canadian societies. The perception and belief that Western civilization, with its basic tenets and roots firmly founded in Christianity and its fixation on education, training, and specialization, held the answers and is a better road to travel on than the Aboriginal one is now being challenged not only by Aboriginal people but by governments as well.

The Aboriginal Road

The problem is that many people do not know what the Aboriginal road is all about. There is still a great deal of misunderstanding and even ignorance about Aboriginal people, their cultures, and beliefs prevalent within Canadian society, and to a certain extent among Aboriginal people themselves. This latter problem is one that must be addressed quickly. From my own experience as an Aboriginal person, this experience was strongly reinforced during my work as co-commissioner of Manitoba's Aboriginal Justice Inquiry. One thing remains abundantly clear to me. So long as Canadian society and governments lack the willingness to look to Aboriginal societies for some answers, the problems that Canadian and Aboriginal people face not only with the administration of justice, but in society generally, will be perpetuated. The violence we see today among and between Aboriginal people will evolve. There is a great deal to be concerned about.

Equality has not always been the hallmark of Indian life in this country. The result of this reality has been the social and spiritual desperation that we now observe in the lives of too many Indian people. As Beverly Slapin and Doris Seale state in their 1988 book *Books without Bias: Through Indian Eyes*: "Educated people are likely to have acquired most of their attitudes towards Indians from the writings of anthropologists, for whom Native societies are considered worthy of study insofar as they have preserved aspects of pre-conquest cultures. For them, contemporary Indians are, by and large, degenerate survivors of a more glorious past. The idea that such people may have meaningful contributions to make is one that is received with scorn. At the same time, to be educated is to somehow become less 'Indian'; to be successful is to find oneself dismissed as no longer 'authentic.'"

That is part of the very real dilemma that Aboriginal people, particularly Aboriginal youth, face. I can remember, as an Aboriginal student, and as an, adult I have observed, that Aboriginal youth are burdened with anxieties and vulnerabilities in addition to those that burden the average white youth. The accusation that Aboriginal young people have always had to live with, from early childhood and throughout the course of growing up, is that they are inferior. Inferior simply because they are Aboriginal. This accusation has been so uniform that it has become ingrained in the cultural imagery of this country. It has been enforced by law, by custom, and by every form of power at play in Canadian society. As a result, it has left its mark.

Aboriginal inferiority was a precept not merely accepted, but encouraged by the European settlers of this nation. It was a principle of social organization that relegated Aboriginal people to the sidelines of Canadian life and regarded them as irrelevant. When young Aboriginal students move from their home communities, or reserves to schools and universities in urban environments, they find themselves surrounded by people who historically have claimed to be superior. They are surrounded by the myth of their own inferiority because they are surrounded by people who believe in the myth of their own superiority. This is so both inside and outside of educational institutions, but for Indian students within educational institutions the stress and pressures can have particularly devastating consequences. Not only are our educational institutions the shapers and moulders of the thinking of our youth, but it is in those institutions that future leaders of our societies make their most fundamental career choices. That is why it is important for all people to understand what has happened to Aboriginal people and why.

The irony is that, because of our history, of fewer opportunities made available to us, and of racism, we as Aboriginal people are in a sense inferior, but our inferiority has to do with the inferiority of the position to which we have legally, politically, and socially been relegated and with the limited opportunities to overcome that status made available to us. What has been done to our parents is the problem, not any inherent inferiority. The problems we face in achieving our rightful place within society must therefore be seen as a challenge rather than a mark of shame. To a certain extent, for

Aboriginal people there is some truth to what Martin Luther King Jr. once said: "When you are behind in a foot race the only way to get ahead is to run faster than the guy in front of you."

The Road Ahead

There is much that needs to be done. To begin with, it must be seen that the problems Aboriginal peoples face arise from their unique histories. As well, it should be apparent that solutions to the problems faced by Aboriginal youth will arise partially at least in their ability to approach those problems with a stronger sense of self-determination and identity. In many places, medical and other professionals are beginning to recognize that there is merit in the utilization of traditional Aboriginal methods of healing. The use of the sweat lodge, the naming ceremony, the clan dances, the sundances, lodge gatherings, and so forth are some methods of addressing the despair of those who contemplate surrendering their lives. It is an issue that needs to be given greater acceptance. Those Elders with whom I am associated tell me that the spirit of the people needs to be healed. From a medical perspective, I have encountered some professionals who ask, "What can we do about that?" The answer is, "Whatever you can." If you give a man a fish you feed him for a day, but if you teach him how to fish you feed him for a lifetime.

Aboriginal people, individually and collectively, must—if they are to come to terms with the tremendous problems they face—take control of who they are to be, and they will have to feel and to believe that they are in control of their destiny. If the Serenity Prayer is to have any meaning for us as Aboriginal people— "God grant me the serenity to accept things I cannot change, the courage to change the things I can, and the wisdom to know the difference"—then Aboriginal people will first have to believe that they have the power to change or to accept. They will have to have faith that whatever they do, right or wrong, is part of this great mystery we call life. We do not have that faith now. The people of Shamattawa and other communities have not felt they had it. Their despair and frustration over that feeling of powerlessness and hopelessness is evident.

It is clear that ideas shape the course of history. This is true of the future more so than of the past or the present, and this notion has particular implications for Aboriginal people in this country. If their future is to include controlling their Aboriginal destiny, then that future requires an Aboriginal academia. We need to begin to speak and write about some of the issues facing us in the future. No culture or society of people has ever evolved without debate and the discussion of ideas. We need some of our own people to begin to present some of their ideas about the future direction we should be following as Aboriginal people. We can no longer restrict ourselves to writings intended only to educate white people about who we are. We need that type of writing, but we need more. We need Aboriginal people to write about twentieth-century Aboriginality; about what it means and where it is going and, most important, about where it should be going. As Aboriginal people we need to begin to think about issues that we would have been thinking about if we had had control of our lives to this point.

This is the role and the challenge that I see for the future Aboriginal leaders of this country. The temptation to train our children to be only technicians and tradespeople must be resisted. Those are worthy professions, but no society has ever existed which did not recognize and develop its dreamers and thinkers. We need to develop our philosophers, thinkers, and writers —our people of wisdom and foresight. Our educators must look for those abilities in all our children and, when discovered, nurture and feed them. We have those people now. I've met many of them. They are the ones who still have the spark of life within their eyes, who have not yet had the ability to think or dream or believe in their dreams taken from them.

In my father's generation, those abilities were snuffed out when Aboriginal children crossed the thresholds of the residential schools to which they had been sentenced. In my generation those abilities were denied to us from the time we were born because our parents tried to live an artificial life constructed for them. But some of our parents and grandparents never did lose those abilities, and some of my generation has learned to think and dream once again. We need those thinkers and we need those dreamers, for we are a people in need of ideas and dreams.

—1992/1998

Inmates at Stony Mountain Institution

Anonymous

Stony Mountain Institution, located outside the town of Stony Mountain, Manitoba, is a medium-security federal penitentiary with a capacity for over 550 inmates. The institution opened in 1877, with some its first inmates being the Plains Cree chiefs Big Bear, One Arrow, and Poundmaker, who were arrested after skirmishes with Canadian authorities during the Métis Resistance of 1885. The imprisonments of these chiefs foreshadowed a trend of statistically high incarceration rates at Stony Mountain for Aboriginal offenders. The Aboriginal Justice Inquiry of Manitoba observed that prior to World War II Aboriginal prison populations were no greater than Aboriginal representation in the general population. By 1965, 22 percent of the inmates in Stony Mountain were Aboriginal, and, by 1989, this number had risen to 41 percent. By 1995, 47 percent of inmates at Stony Mountain were Aboriginal, whereas Aboriginal people made up only

10.6 percent of the population of Manitoba. Today, the percentage of Aboriginal inmates is approaching 60 percent (or higher). Considered by many to be another form of Aboriginal reserve communities, thousands of Aboriginal persons "live" in Manitoba prisons every year. The Aboriginal Justice Inquiry found that this stark, unjust, and increasing overrepresentation of Aboriginal people in prison populations was the result of systemic discrimination affecting all parts of the criminal justice system. Much research has also revealed the abusive conditions within prisons, leading to the formation of Aboriginal gangs and high recidivism.

The following are some of the Aboriginal voices at Stony Mountain. The first piece is a collective letter that appeared in the May 1961 issue of *The Prairie Call*, written by an organization called "The Native Brotherhood of Stony Mountain Penitentiary." In the letter, the authors refer to the issues they face when leaving prison in 1960s Canada. The second piece, written for the classroom and published in the 1990s in *Inside the Walls: Writings from Stony Mountain Inmates*, relates an inmate's frustration with the lack of learning programs for Aboriginal prisoners to enroll in. Those programs that are offered, he says, are not respectful of Aboriginal traditional ways or their ceremonial practices. The third piece, also from *Inside the Walls*, is a traditional story of the battle between a Thunderbird and a serpent, which, interestingly, suggests that sometimes to save a relationship it needs to be destroyed first. All of these pieces remind us of the important Aboriginal voices behind the walls at Stony Mountain Institution and other prisons, voices that cannot be forgotten or ignored.

Unemployment & Indians

It may sound strange to some people that an editorial of this type is written behind bars. Society in some measure may disagree with some of our statements and convictions. It is commonly said, there are many reasons why an Indian is considered a problem, individually or as a group. A number of examples can be found in all institutions throughout Canada. This is a serious problem. Today crime involving Indians is on the increase and employment is decreasing. Many Indians are uneducated and unskilled and if no action is taken on the reservation in bettering and providing trades training for our Indians, they will continue to return to prison.

Heaps of big talk is continually heard around the country about bettering the Indians but very little action is taken. If a poll or a survey were taken of Indians serving time behind prison bars, it would be found that seventy to seventy-five percent of them have virgin minds. It is quite evident that these minds have an aching desire to be fully developed. They are taking full advantage of the various trades and shop training provided in this institution; but why must they learn all skills in institutions?

We feel that the federal government should set up a commission, not merely to talk about it, or just to investigate, but to take some definite action.

We in our present predicament do not want to go back to the way of life that has placed us behind bars. Something must be done to rehabilitate those who have come out of some institution, by giving them gainful employment and providing the means for trades training.

We are deeply concerned about what is going to happen with the hundreds of men and women of Indian origin being released from our institutions across Canada. At present no provisions are being made for these people to obtain suitable employment to help in their rehabilitation and in turn make it that much easier for them to mix with their white brothers. Those released from prison will have no other choice, if for no other reason than self-survival or preservation, but to return to crime or resort to some illegal means of obtaining money enough to feed and clothe their bodies and to take care of their families. What choice have we got? If we are honest we are immediately rejected. When asked in applying for a job, "Were you ever arrested?" if we deny we were ever investigated and the company investigates and discovers we were not telling the truth we are fired. *What choice have we got?*

If we expect an Indian under present conditions to compete on the same economic level as the white wage-earner, then we need the same educational and social opportunities.

Signed, The Native Brotherhood of Stony Mountain Penitentiary
—*1961*

When the Aboriginal Justice Inquiry Came to Stony Mountain

When the Justice Inquiry came into the institution, I listened to how we Native people have been treated.

Some Native people spoke. I really liked what they had to say about us Aboriginal People not having enough programs about our tradition in the Institution; for we are losing the footsteps of our Ancestors.

Some people may not know too much, and this is why I believe we should have more programs about our way of life. I certainly hope this will be successful in the near future. So that we can be taught, not only to the people that are already here, but for others that may someday end up in the Institution, I also heard when the searches are taking place they should respect the feathers and the pipes, instead of throwing them around, again I hope this will be successful, because I feel in my own opinion that it isn't right to throw around what we Aboriginal People respect.

—*1990*

The Great Snake and the Boy

Once upon a time, there was a boy who wandered off from the village. He was told not to go too far into the woods, but he did. In the woods he was abducted and taken far away by the bush man. He was brought to a small point of rock, sticking out in the middle of a large lake and left to sit there for days. The bush man left the boy there and paddled his canoe away.

Many days and nights the boy sat there without any sleep. He was very hungry. The boy shouted for help and cried for his mother. Suddenly, the Great Snake with horns on its head appeared in the waters. The Great Snake asked the boy what the matter was. The boy said that he wanted to go home. The Great Snake had pity on the boy.

He made a deal with the boy to take him home. The Great Snake was afraid to cross the lake because of the Great Thunder. He could be killed by the Great Thunder's lightning. So the Great Snake agreed to take the chance of crossing the lake if the boy would make sure to warn him when he heard the Great Thunder coming. That way the Great Snake would have enough time to turn back and hide underwater where the tunnel was.

The Great Snake told the boy to climb on his neck and hold on to his mysterious horns. The Great Snake moved with tremendous speed across the large lake, the boy holding tightly onto his horns. He did not know that the Great Thunder saw him swimming.

The boy heard the Great Thunder coming behind them, but he did not warn the Great Snake. He was too anxious to go home. The Great Snake reached the shore of the large lake and let the boy off safely. The boy was very happy and very sad. After saving the boy's life, the Great Snake hurried back across the lake as fast as he could, but it was not fast enough. The Great Thunder had seen him and with his lightning he blew him into thousands of pieces. These pieces fell all over the earth and a small portion of the Great Snake's blood fell in front of the boy. That small portion of blood asked the boy why he never told him that the Great Thunder was coming. The blood then crawled away like a snake. They boy went home, happy to see his mother again.

Today, the Ojibway Indians tell this legend to their children as a bedtime story to make them sleep. The legend of the Great Snake and the boy is also told by the elders of the New Osnaburgh Reserve. The large lake is Lake St. Joseph and the village is probably the Osnaburgh Reserve. The rock which stuck out in the middle of the large lake cannot be seen today because it is under water.

It is believed by the Ojibway Indians that the snake grows and becomes a giant size like the Great Snake with the mysterious horns. It is destroyed by the Great Thunder for protection. The Great Thunder is doing two special things. It is destroying the large snake but it is restoring the snake through many small snakes which multiply in numbers all over the earth. This legend of the Great Snake and the boy is a valuable lesson to know.

If the world was a better place, with equal opportunity, maybe we would all have a chance to go places in life as a whole people.

Why must all the people be scared of each other? Or why must we be rich and others be poor? Tell me.

Why can't we all live as one people? Why can't the poor get back on their feet again? We should all as a caring people lend a helping hand.

—*1990*

Tomson Highway

Cree (Brochet) 1951–

Tomson Highway is a playwright, novelist, and pianist who was born on a trapline in the far northwestern part of Manitoba. When he was six years old, he was removed from his family and placed in a residential school in The Pas. He later studied at Churchill High School in Winnipeg, then trained as a concert pianist at the University of Manitoba and the University of Western Ontario. Later, he became involved with the Native Earth Performing Arts Company in Toronto, where he was the artistic director. During this time, his first plays were produced and received immediate acclaim. He won the Dora Mavor Moore Award for *The Rez Sisters* (1988), as well as for its follow-up, *Dry Lips Oughtta Move to Kapuskasing* (1989), the second installment of the fictional Wasaychigan Hill "rez" series of plays. Both plays have recently been made available in Highway's northern dialect of Cree, the language in which they were first conceived. All of Tomson Highway's drama explores the humour and resilience of Aboriginal communities, but the plays are also passionate critiques of systemic community violence as a result of colonialism, and particularly of violence toward women. Highway's loosely autobiographical novel, *Kiss of the Fur Queen* (1998), is a long-time bestseller. A recipient of several honourary doctorates, Highway lectures and teaches at various universities. Highway received the National Aboriginal Achievement Award in 2001.

The following selection from *Kiss of the Fur Queen* displays the humour of Cree culture, the transformational and fantastical power of story, and, maybe, even some elements from reality (Highway's own birth in a tent in northern Manitoba). The passage also demonstrates Highway's dazzling prose style, which mirrors the wondrous events being described. The excerpt from *The Rez Sisters* portrays three of the main characters fantasizing about what they will do when they win "the big bingo," which is the main structuring element of the play. These ecstatic speeches are almost like arias in an opera; they tell us what these women most fervently hope for, and show us a great deal about the realities of their lives in Wasaychigan Hill. The section from *Iskooniguni Iskweewuk* gives us the same three speeches from the Cree version of the play, which Highway published in 2010 along with *Paasteewitoon*

Kaapooskaysing Tageespichit, the Cree edition of *Dry Lips Oughta Move to Kapuskasing.* At the book launch for these new texts, Highway said, "the Cree versions … are actually the original versions. As it turns out, the original ones that came out 20 years ago were the translation."

From *Kiss of the Fur Queen*

One trillion miles above the aboriginal jamboree, the ghostly foetus continued its airy descent towards Earth. And only medicine women, shamans, artists, and visionaries were aware that a star-born child would soon be joining their dance.

MARIESIS OKIMASIS HAD ONCE won a contest for which the prize had been to have her picture taken by an itinerant British anthropologist who had claimed that never in all his travels had he seen cheekbones such as hers.

"That guy never did send us a copy of the picture," moaned Mariesis into her husband's tingling ear as she slipped under him, he over her, their mountainous, goose-down-filled sleeping robe shifting like an earthquake in slow motion. Mariesis could see the left side of her husband's face, and for this she was glad, for nothing in life gave her more pleasure than the sight of his thick, sensuous lips.

The moonlight drifting in the little window over their bed made them look like large ripe fruit.

"That's all right," the large ripe fruit breathed into her ear as she struggled with her white flannel slip. "I don't need a picture when I have the real thing." He slid out of his underwear.

The moonlight led Mariesis's eyes to the floor beside the bed where her sleeping children lay, those four still at home; she listened to their delicate snores wheeze their way in and out of her husband's heavy breathing, a sweet kitten's purr floating up to her. Then the light took them to the dresser top, where sat the trophy her champion of the world had brought for her from the distant south. Beside it stood a photograph: Abraham cradling in his arms the silver bowl, his cheek being kissed by the young woman radiant in her white fur cape and her silver-beaded fur tiara: "The Fur Queen," he had explained, "the most beautiful woman in the world. Except for Mariesis Okimasis," of course.

Suddenly, the light was coming from the Fur Queen's eyes. Mariesis half-closed hers and let this moment take her, out the little window above the bed, out past the branch of the young spruce tree bending under its weight of snow, out to millions of stars, to the northern lights: the ancestors of her people, ten thousand generations, to the beginning of time. Dancing.

And somewhere within the folds of this dance, Mariesis saw, through tears of an intense joy—or did ecstasy inflict hallucinations on its victims?—a sleeping child, not yet born but fully formed, naked, curled up inside the womb of night, tumbling down towards her and her husband.

The ancestors—the women—moaned and whispered. Mariesis could hear among them her mother, who had left this Earth mere months after Mariesis had become a bride, one among many to have succumbed to tuberculosis. And though barely audible where she lay in her pool of perspiration, the women's voices said to her: "And *K'si mantou,* the Great Spirit, held the baby boy by his big toe and dropped him from the stars…"

And that was all she remembered.

POOF! HE WENT ON his bum, smack into the most exquisite mound of snow in the entire forest, making crystals of silver spray shoot up to join the stars. He disappeared into the mound and would have stayed down there indefinitely if it hadn't been for his bouncy baby flesh and his supple newborn bones.

"If you throw them on the floor," one-toothed Annie Moostoos would brag about her nine brown babies to all who cared to listen, "they'll bounce right back into your arms—it's true. Why would I lie to you?"

And the baby boy came shooting out of the mound of snow in two seconds flat and landed on his feet, right beside a small spruce tree that happened to be sleeping there. The little spruce tree opened one drowsy eye to see who could have made the whispering bump in the night and just managed to catch the tail-end of a spirit baby sprinting off into the darkness. There being nothing left to see but the little whirlwind in the baby's wake, the spruce tree went back to sleep.

The spirit baby ran through the forest, and ran and ran and ran. Hunch led him on, guided him, something having to do with warmth, he knew, something to do with hunger, with appeasing that hunger, something to do with love hunger, with appeasing that hunger, something to do with the length of string that led from the middle of his belly, a string almost invisible, so refined it could have been a strand of spiders web. This string and a hunch. That was all.

Bang! The baby tripped, falling flat on his face, with a shriek more of surprise than of pain, in front of a cave. Growling like an ill-tempered bitch, a large, hairy animal lumbered out of the cave, admonished the prostrate child for having roused him from his winter sleep, and gave him a swift kick in the bum. The baby yelped, jumped up, and dashed away from the cave and its cantankerous occupant through the forest towards a tent standing on the shore of a lake.

Then the child bumped into a rabbit, who took pity on him, for, by this time, the naked child was shivering. The rabbit slipped off his coat and wrapped it around the child's shivering, plump midsection. The as-yet-unborn infant made his gratitude clear to the rabbit, who turned out to be a writer of lyric rabbit poetry, and the travelling baby and the now naked, shivering animal would be friends for life.

Finally emerging from the forest, glinting with crystals of snow and frost, the child ran around the tent by the lake, across the pile of woodchips strewn at the entrance, just missing getting sliced in half by a man flailing away with an axe, and burst through the tent flap like a comet.

The tent interior glowed golden warm from the kerosene lamp. Moaning and whimpering and crying softly, Mariesis Okimasis lay on a bed of spruce boughs, a minuscule and very ancient woman hovering over her like the branch of an old pine tree: Misty Marie Gazandlaree, Chipewyan, ninety-three years of age and one of the most respected midwives in the north at that time. The silver baby scooted under the old woman's left arm, took a little hop, two small skips, one dive and half a pirouette, and landed square on top of Mariesis Okimasiss firm round belly: 5:00 A.M., Saturday, December 1, 1951.

He lay puffing and panting, when die man with the flailing weapon entered the tent, his arms piled high with firewood, his eyes aglow at the sight of the child. And the last thing the child remembered, until he was to read about it years later, was shutting his eyes and seeing up in the dome of his miniature skull a sky filled with a million stars, the northern lights pulsating, and somewhere in the web of galaxies, a queen waving a magic wand.

THE BABY BOY WAS floating in the air, his skin no longer silver blue but pinkish brown. As he floated, he turned and turned and laughed and laughed. Until, lighter than a tuft of goose-down, he fell to Earth, his plump posterior landing neatly in a bowl of silver.

"*Ho-ho!* My victory boy!" the fun-loving caribou hunter trumpeted to whatever audience he could get, which, at the moment, was his wife. "*Ho-ho!* My champion boy!"

"Down! Put him down, or his little bum will freeze!" cried Mariesis Okimasis, though she couldn't help but laugh and, with her laughing, love this man for all his unpredictable bouts of clownishness. Jumping up and down, the short Mariesis was trying to get the tall Abraham to put his World Championship Dog Derby trophy down so she could put their baby back into the warmth and safety of his cradle-board. This was, after all, a tent, not a palace, not even a house, and this was, after all, mid-December and not July, in a region so remote that the North Pole was rumoured to be just over that next hill. In fact, if it hadn't been for the curl of smoke from its tin chimney, the little canvas shelter would have been invisible, that's how much snow there was when Champion Okimasis was born.

≡≡≤

Atop a low, moss-covered rock that overlooked Nameegoos Lake, Champion Okimasis stood singing a concert to his father and the caribou. The three-year-old stretched and pumped the miniature accordion strapped to his chest with such abandon that its squawk was frightful. Somewhere out on that lake, Abraham Okimasis and his team of eight grey huskies were giving chase, and if Champion performed with sufficient conviction, the Okimasis family would be feasting on fresh hindquarter of young caribou before the sun touched the prong of that first pine tree.

"*Ateek, ateeh, astum, astum, yoah, ho-ho!*" Champion's robin-like soprano rang out, his lungs small balloons. By the time he got to the tenth repetition of the phrase, a herd of caribou would come bursting out the other side of that first island, his father not twenty yards behind them.

"Caribou, caribou, come to me, come to me, *yoah, ho-ho!*"

Down the rise of land, Champions mother was squatting on bare ground, clearing used dishes from a lunch table of spruce boughs three feet from the smouldering remains of their campfire. The early afternoon sun, amiable enough for early January, wasn't making much headway on the top layer of snow, but its golden light made Champion Okimasis and his family feel warm and at ease with life.

Covered in earth-toned cotton dress and winter parka, midriff ripe as a full moon, Mariesis Okimasis looked, to the singing Champion, like a boulder, a part of the earth. She was nine months into her twelfth pregnancy and the fateful event could pounce upon her any minute now, so Champion had been informed by his older sister, the pouty and bossy Chugweesees Okimasis.

"*Ateek, ateek, astum...*"

So proud was he of his first original composition that Champion wanted it to be appreciated, not just by his father and the caribou, not just by the two other hunting families on the other side of the island, but by the world. Her face glowing with an inner light, Mariesis smiled at the impassioned, swaying, rocking musical wonder and said, "Champion. My boy. You will soon have a brother who can dance to that little caribou song of yours."

Champion would have had ten older siblings but for TB, pneumonia, and childhood ailments, Mariesis had explained to an uncomprehending Champion; but here at least were Josephine, five, and Chugweesees, seven, playing with sticks and stones, and Chichilia, eleven, repacking the grub box for her mother. William William, nineteen, was up in Kasimir Lake, just south of the Northwest Territories border, helping one-eyed Uncle Wilpaletch trap mink and otter and arctic fox; and Marie-Adele, twenty-one, was married with children of her own and moved to her husband's home community of Ootasneema, Saskatchewan, so far away that Marie-Adele Weechawagasnee-Okimasis barely existed for Champion.

Sure enough, before he could launch into his forty-third verse, a herd of caribou came charging out from behind that first small island on a lake so white that it was difficult to look at for any length of time. Umpteen-umpteen caribou, Champion estimated their number as he squinted and banged his accordion with even greater vigour, the song kicking into a tempo he would later come to know as allegro con brio. When he saw his father zoom out behind the stampeding animals, hunting rifle in the air, his huskies racing as though demons were nipping at their tails, he yelped his father's famous *"Weekschiloowew!"* Two other rifle-waving hunters came dashing out behind Abraham.

At this distance, Champion, his mother, and his three sisters couldn't see the details, much less hear the sounds; but the thunder of caribou hooves was so familiar they would hear the rumble in their dreams of any ordinary night. They also knew that Abraham was expressing his joy by yodelling the only word in his yodelling repertoire, the word Champion loved with all his heart.

Josephine and Chugweesees and their puppies Cha-La-La and Ginger went tumbling, screaming, yelling, and barking down to the lake and would have run clean across the ice to join their father if the wise-beyond-her-years Chichilia Okimasis hadn't grabbed them and dragged them back to shore. "You wanna be stomped to death by wild caribou?" she screamed. "You wanna leave this Earth looking like two ugly little meat patties?"

Champion knew that the most effective way to help his father was to keep singing, and this he did, the song now more a furious jig than the anthem of hope it had been. Champion was so surprised by the new effect that he slipped into the key of D, although C was the only key he knew.

"Champion! Champion, call your father!" Alarmed by the sudden sharpness in Mariesis's voice, Champion saw that her face was contorted, her arms wrapped around her belly, her body rocking back and forth. The little musician stopped in mid-vibrato. Accordion still strapped to his little torso, he scampered down to the shore.

"Chichilia! Chichilia!" cried Champion, the accordion bouncing up and down on his little belly, squeaking and sputtering out random clusters of semitones. "There's something wrong with Mama! There's something—"

Splat. He had tripped on the root of a dying tree and lay on his accordion with the breath knocked out of both of them.

When he looked up, his face covered with dirt and dirty snow, all he could see was Chichilia's feet striding up to his face. Her dog, the remarkably intelligent Suitcase Okimasis, sniffed around his neck for a trace of broken vertebrae.

"Mama's belly is hurting! Mama's belly…"

Chichilia wasted not a word; the young woman strode across the ice towards her father and the stampeding herd.

Though he couldn't hear it from such a distance—at least a mile was his estimation—Abraham knew that his son was singing for him. For wasn't it his greatest pride to have finally sired a child with a gift for the making of music, one to whom he could pass on his father's, his grandfather's, and his great-grandfather's legacy? The assurance that this ancient treasure of the Okimasis clan could rest intact for at least another generation inspired him to glide across the ice with even greater skill, greater precision, greater speed.

"*Mush*, Tiger-Tiger, *mush!*"

The caribou now loomed a mere fifty yards in front of him; his soul began to sing.

Then a yearling veered to the left. The hunter's heart jumped three half beats. Separated from the herd, this yearling would give Abraham the perfect opportunity to display to the other hunters trailing him what was admired throughout northern Manitoba as caribou-hunting prowess without equal.

"*U*, Tiger-Tiger, *u!*" Abraham yelled to his lead dog, and Tiger-Tiger swerved, his seven team-mates following; the sled made an elegant turn to the left.

"Such a prince, my Tiger-Tiger, such a prince," Abraham whispered, for he and his part-wolf, part-husky had learned, over the seven years of Tiger-Tiger's eventful life, to communicate both with and without words. This was fortunate because Tiger-Tiger's Cree vocabulary was limited, though he had learned how to ask for "black coffee" on blizzardy Tuesday mornings. Keeping his left hand firmly hooked around the handlebar of the sled, Abraham took aim at the frightened caribou with his right. The sled's sudden encounter with patches of unevenly packed snow, however—and the fact that the fleeing animal, knowing death was imminent, was running erratically—was making his aim unsteady. His finger was about to press the trigger when a human figure beyond and to the right of his quarry drew his focus. He shot and missed.

"Damn," he cursed the ill-timed appearance of this human, who was waving frantically. He would have taken a second shot but recognized his intrepid daughter, Chichilia. She may not be able to sing a note, much less play one, try as Abraham might to teach her, but she could shoot a sling-shot with such accuracy that, at eight years old, she killed an entire warren of rabbits, whose ears she made into a stunningly succulent stew. For a girl who astonished audiences with highly polished displays of level-headedness and self-possession, Chichilia's current agitation was downright alarming.

"*Cha*, Tiger-tiger, *cha!*" the hunter yelled into the wind. The leader of the team swerved to the right so suddenly that the left side of the sled came off the ground. Abraham was now heading straight for Chichilia.

"Whoa, Tiger-Tiger, whoa!" he shouted, and the dogs began to slow down, though not fast enough for Abraham's comfort.

"Whoa!" he screamed, dropping his rifle into the sled as Chichilia's legs took great strides through snow that, in places, hadn't hardened quite enough to bear her weight. But all the hunter had to hear was "*nimama!*" to under-stand her message.

He pulled his sled to a halt beside the girl, sending fountains of pow-der snow everywhere. With well-practised motion, Chichilia leapt into the canvas-sided conveyance with the intention of sitting at the bottom. But Abraham had already slashed the air with one grand sweep of his moose-hide whip, shouted "*mush!*" and the dogs were off like bullets, making a beeline for the campsite. Chichilia went flying and slammed headfirst into the handlebar.

The caribou hunter was in such a rush that he forgot his normally fine-tuned manners. It was a few days before he remembered to apologize to his daughter for causing the rather spectacular bump on her head that would remain with her for the rest of her long and passionate life—a bump that would become the subject of many hours' quality conversation.

It couldn't have taken more than four minutes for father and daugh-ter to reach the spot where they had stopped for lunch on their way to Eemanapiteepitat one hundred miles south for the birth.

Mariesis was not, however, bent over in pain or crying for help. She was unpacking their tent with the intention of erecting it, help or no help from her three small children. Josephine and Chugweesees were gathering sticks for tent pegs, and handling the hatchet with a less than admirable skill. Champion sat perched on the grub box, singing and playing his only song, "to make her feel better," he would explain to his father later, "so she wouldn't hurt so much."

Not waiting for his sled to come to a full stop, the caribou hunter leapt out and ordered his wife to lie down on a blanket.

"Won't stop jumping up and down" were all the words she could muster.

"*Ho-ho!*" the caribou hunter exclaimed. "Gonna be a dancer, this one." And in no time, the tent was standing.

THAT NIGHT, MARIESIS lay half-covered by her enormous goose-down sleeping robe, the light of a kerosene lamp dancing on her perspiring face. To Abraham, hanging a white flannel bed-sheet across the middle of the small room to give his wife a measure of privacy, she looked beatific, the darkness of her deep-set eyes bottomless wells of love. From a carpet of newly cut spruce boughs, a fresh, moist, minty aroma filled the room to overflowing.

He tested the twine that held the sheet, then bent to put more wood into the stove he had fashioned out of a once-red oil drum, black from years of use. Abraham had to keep the hardy little appliance going, for if it stopped, they froze to death, it was as simple as that. Having refilled the stove, the hunter went outside to chop more wood.

Champion lay on the other side of the hanging sheet, his head next to the accordion he loved so much that he refused to be parted from it, day or night. Josephine and Chugweesees wiggled like worms beside him. Covered by a puffy down-filled sleeping robe, they whispered furiously.

"The Great Spirit must be holding our little sister up by her big toe by now," said the bossy Chugweesees. "Getting ready to drop her, right from the centre of the sky." She left no room for anyone to argue that the new arrival might be a boy; Chugweesees Okimasis simply assumed she could predict the future.

Across the lake, a lone wolf raised its howl, the string of notes arcing in a seamless, infinitely slow, infinitely sad glissando, then fading into silence, leaving the hearts of its listeners motionless with awe. Then two wolves joined the first in song. One of Abraham's dogs, tethered to trees behind the tent, answered, then a second dog, and a third, until a chorus of weeping souls, as if in mourning for one irretrievably lost, filled the night air, numbing the pain of the woman now deep in her labour in this snow-covered tent on this remote island.

Stifling a yawn, Champion looked up at the hanging bed-sheet and made up his mind that he was not going to miss a second of whatever shadows played on it. He made the mistake of blinking, however, just once, which was enough to send him slipping across a river to the world of dreams, where he had long ago learned how to fly, where he might fly up to meet the falling baby halfway and tell him to go back. For was not this brazen new arrival about to depose the unique Champion Okimasis from his status as not only baby but star of this illustrious caribou-hunting family?

—*1998*

From *The Rez Sisters*

ANNIE: When I go to the BIGGEST BINGO IN THE WORLD, in Toronto, I will win. For sure, I will win. If they shout the B 14 at the end, for sure I will win. The B 14 is my lucky number after all. Then I will take all my money and I will go to every record store in Toronto. I will buy every single one of Patsy Cline's records, especially the one that goes (*Sings.*) "I go a-walking, after midnight," oh I go crazy every time I hear that one. Then I will buy a huge record player, the biggest one in the whole world. And then I will go to all the taverns and all the night clubs in Toronto and listen to the live bands while I drink beer quietly—not noisy and crazy like here—I will bring my daughter Ellen and her white guy from Sudbury and we will sit together. Maybe I will call Fritz the Katz and he will take me out. Maybe he will hire me as one of his singers and I can (*Sings.*) "Oooh," in the background while my feet go (*Shuffles her feet from side to side).* while Fritz the Katz is singing and the lights are flashing and the people are drinking beer and smoking cigarettes and dancing. Ohhh, I could dance all night with that Fritz the Katz. When I win, when I win THE BIGGEST BINGO IN THE WORLD!

MARIE-ADELE: When I win THE BIGGEST BINGO IN THE WORLD, I'm gonna buy me an island. In the North Channel, right smack-dab in the middle—eem-shak min-stik *—the most beautiful island in the world. And my island will have lots of trees—great big bushy ones—and lots and lots and lots of sweetgrass. MMMMM! And there's gonna be pine trees and oak trees and maple trees and big stones and little stonelets—neee—and, oh yeah, this real neat picket fence, real high, long and very, very, very white. No bird shit. Eugene will live there and me and all my Starblanket kids. Yup, no more smelly, stinky old pulp and paper mill in Espanola for my Eugene—pooh!—my 12 Starblanket boys and my two Starblanket girls and me and my Eugene all living real nice and comfy right there on Starblanket Island, the most beautiful incredible goddamn island in the whole goddamn world. Eem-shak min-stik! When I win THE BIGGEST BINGO IN THE WORLD!

VERONIQUE: Well, when I win the BIGGEST BINGO IN THE WORLD. No! After I win THE BIGGEST BINGO IN THE WORLD, I will go shopping for a brand-new stove. In Toronto. At the Eaton Centre. A great big stove. The kind Madame Benoit has. The kind that has the three different compartments in the oven alone. I'll have the biggest stove on the reserve. I'll cook for all the children on the reserve. I'll adopt all of Marie-Adele Starblanket's 14 children and I will cook for them. I'll even cook for Gazelle Nataways' poor starving babies while she's lolling around like a pig in Big Joey's smelly, sweaty bed. And Pierre St. Pierre can drink himself to death for all I care. Because I'll be the best cook on all of Manitoulin Island! I'll enter competitions. I'll go to Paris and meet what's-his-name Cordon Bleu! I'll write a cookbook called "The Joy of Veronique St. Pierre's Cooking" and it will sell in the millions! And I will become rich and famous! Zhaboonigan Peterson will wear a mink while she eats steak tartare-de-frou-frou! Madame Benoit will be so jealous she'll suicide herself. Oh, when I win THE BIGGEST BINGO IN THE WORLD!

—*1992*

From *Iskooniguni Iskweewuk: The Rez Sisters in Cree*

ANNIE: Ispeek ANIMA MAAWACHI KAANPAYMISHAAK MISTI-BINGO OOTA WAASKEETUSKAMIK itooti-aani ootee Toronto-eek, n'gowtow'waan keetnaach n'gowtow'waan. Keespin B 14 teepweewuk, m'tooni keetnaach n'gowtow-waan. Athis ee-agoo ageetaasoowin mawachi maana eemithoopathee-eegooyaan. Igweespeek kaagithow n'sooniyaam n'ga-oot'now igwa kaagithow ata-igumigwa ita nagamoona kaataawaachi-gaateegwow n'ga-itootaan. Kaagithow Patsy Cline oonag-amoona n'gaataawaan, waawees anima (*kaanagamoot*) "I go a-walking, after midnight," ka-iteetaagwuk, hey, eemithoota-maan eeyagwaanima nagamoon, m'tooni maana keegaach eemooskoomigooyaan. Igweespeek misti-kitoochigun n'gaataawaan, ana kitoochigun mawachi kaamshigitit oota waaskeeetuskamik. Igweespeek kaagithow mineegwee-igu-migwa nantaypeetigwaateen igoota Toronto-eek tantayn-tootawagwow kaagithow oogitoochigeewuk eegitoochigeechik igwa eenagamoochik meegwaach beer eemineegweeyaan nun-seegaach—mootha itha kithipee igwa poogweethigook taksee-weeyaan taaskooch oota - n'chaanis, Eclen, igwa ootayms'chigooseema Sudbureek oochi n'gapeesoowaawuk igwa mamawee igoota n'gaapinaan. Apweetigwee apoochiga Fritz the Katz n'gateepwaatow ayami-iguneek igwa naanta-itee n'gaytootaa-ik. Apweetigwee apoochiga n'gaatooskaa-ik oonag-amoo taytaapachee-igawiyaan igwa nageenagamoon (*kaanagamoot*) "Oooooh," ootaanaak meegwaach Fritz the Katz weetha tipithow eenagamoot neegaaneek igwa waskooteenigana soogi eewaawaasteepathigi igwa itinoowuk eemineegweechik igwa eepeetawchik igwa eeneemee-itoochik, hey, kapeetipisk nugee-weechineemeetoomow ana Fritz the Katz ispeek ootow'wi-aani, ispeek ootow'wi-aani ANIMA MAAWACHI KAAN-PAYMISHAAK MISTI-BINGO OOTA WAASKEETUSKAMIK.

MARIE-ADELE: Ispeek ANIMA MAAWACHI KAANPAYMISHAAK MISTI-BINGO OOTA WAASKEETUSKAMIK ootow'wi-aani, minstik n'gaataaweestamaasoon, oota Keeweet'noo-wapaak ka-ichigaa-teek, m'tooni aapeetow, anima mawachi een'paymithoonaagwuk minstik oota waaskeetuskamik. Hey, kwayus tameecheetoowuk seetuk igoota niminstigoomeek—eemshigitichik seetuk, eegi-nawskoosichik, eeweegimaagoosichik—igwa meecheet meena eyemee-i-maskoosiya ta-itagwanaw igoota, mmmm! Igwa kwayus tameecheetoowuk ooskaatigwuk meena seetukwu-naatigwuk meena waskwiatigwuk meena meetoosuk meena muskeegoowaatigwuk meena seeseepaskwataatigwuk meena mistasini-uk meena eeyup'sees'sichik asineesuk—neeee—igwa meena, eehee, igwa meena meenigun ee-ispaak igwa eeginawk igwa poogweethigook eewaapskaak. Maw keegway keeyaaskoomay m'tanawgaach igoota taastao. Eezen igoota n'gaweechaa-amik asichi n'chawsimsinaanuk Starblanket ka-isitheegaasoochik kaagithow eetusichik. Eehee, mawch awusimee een'payweecheeguk m'si-atooski-igumik Eezen kichi—pooh!—m'tat neesoosaap ka-itusichik nigoosisinaanuk igwa neesoo ka-itasichik n'chaansinaanuk igwa neetha igwa nee-Zenim kaagithow igoota n'gaweeginaan igoota tipithow Star-blanket Minstigook, anima mawachi kaan'paymithoonaagwuk minstik oota waaskeetuskamik ka-ichigaateek ooma aski. Ispeek ANIMA MAAWACHI KAANPAYMISHAAK MISTI-BINGO OOTA WAASKEETUSKAMIK ootow'wi-aani.

VERONIQUE: Igwa neetha ispeek ANIMA MAAWACHI KAANPAYMISHAAK MISTI-BINGO OOTA WAASKEETUSKAMIK ootow'wi-aani. Mawch! Ispeek ANIMA MAAWACHI KAANPAYMISHAAK MISTI-BINGO OOTA WAASKEETUSKAMIK kee-ootow'wi-aani, n'gantayn'toonawow ooskaa-i kootawnapisk igwa n'gaataawaan. Igoota Toronto-eek tipithow. Neeta anima misti-ata-igumik Eaton Centre ka-ichigaateek. Eemshigitit kootaw-naapisk, itooweek Madame Benoit kaayaawaat, itooweek n'stoo ataameek keegwaaya kayaagi - ita isa paagweesigun maana kagees'soot? igwatooweek. Neetha mawachi eemshigitit kootaw-naapisk oota iskooniguneek n'gaayaawow. Kaagithow awaas'suk oota iskooniguneek n'gap'minawataawuk. Kaagithow Marie-Adele Starblanket oochawsimsa m'tat neeyoosaap kaa-itusithit n'gowtinaawuk igwa n'gap'minawataawuk. Apoochiga Gazelle Nataways oochawsim'sa kaagithow kanunpaagatsoothit anooch kaageesigaak n'gap'minawataawuk meegwaach ana k'saanagoos eemaamaasi-aat Misty-Joeywa igoota oon'peewineek ithigook kaan'payweecheeganthik, taaskooch meesee-igumik ka-isimagwuk mana anima n'peewin ithigook een'payweeguk. Igwa Pierre St. Pierre tageen'pay-mineegwaatsoo igwa maw m'tanawgaach naantow n'gayteetheeteen. Athis neetha mawachi oota Manitoulin Minstigook n'ganeetaap'minawasoon! N'gantaym'waynee-igaan n'p'minawasoowin oochi. Paris n'gaytootaan tantay-nak'skawuk ana oop'minawasoo Cordon Bleu ka-isithee-gaasoot! P'minawasoowini-masina-igun n'gamasina-een, "Veronique St. Pierre Een'payweegasinthik Oop'minawa-soowin," ta-iseethigaatao anima masina-igun igwa meecheet n'gaataawaagaan, apweetigwee apoochiga m'ta-at m'ta-at m'ta-at m'ta-at m'ta-at m'ta-at m'ta-atoo m'tanow igwatooweek masina-iguna n'gaataawaagaan igwa kwayus n'gaweethootsin igwa kwayus nak'skeethimigawin poogweetee apoochiga New York! Saapoonigan Peterson saagweesoo-asaagay tugik'skum meegwaach manchoosa keechigamaak oochi eemoowaat igwa champagne eemineegweet. Madame Benoit ithigook ta-ooteetheetum m'tooni tataagamisoo ooti-eek misti-moogoomaan asichi. Hey, is-peek ANIMA MAAWACHI KAANPAYMISHAAK MISTI-BINGO OOTA WAASKEETUSKAMIK kee-ootow'wi-aani.

—*2010*

Duncan Mercredi

Cree/Métis (Misipawistik/Grand Rapids) 1951–

Duncan Mercredi is a poet, writer, storyteller, and fan of the blues, originally from Misipawistik (Grand Rapids), Manitoba. He was raised by his grandmother as a storyteller and, like many from his community, has been profoundly affected by Manitoba Hydro and the introduction of dam projects (which since the 1960s have impacted life there). He now resides in Winnipeg, where he has been a longstanding member of the Aboriginal Writers Collective of Manitoba. He has performed countless writing workshops for youth, and his work has been featured in anthologies and periodicals such as *Prairie Fire* and *CV2*. Mercredi has published four books of poetry: *Spirit of the Wolf: Raise Your Voice* (1991), *Dreams of the wolf in the city* (1992), *Wolf and Shadows* (1995), and *The Duke of Windsor: Wolf Sings the Blues* (1997). He is also a screenwriter and is working on a film script entitled *Oomsikakispanik*.

Mercredi's work embodies a pride in traditional lifeways and reflects upon the radical—and often discomforting—impacts of transforming community and land-based cultures into Manitoba's urban environments. With brilliant detail and a sharp eye for the ironic, Mercredi's work includes political and social advocacy with rhythm and metaphor, forming a unique and complex aesthetic that resembles the improvisation and dynamism found in his beloved blues music. For Mercredi, the complex struggles of Aboriginal people take place everywhere; in the screaming silence echoing from the murder of Helen Betty Osborne, in smoke-filled blues clubs, and in the bush. Change presents a challenge for us all, and Mercredi refuses to give easy answers to tough questions, as illustrated in "Wachea." Nostalgic, loving, and transformative, Mercredi's poems are critical vessels, surrounded by a strong belief in resilience and cultural continuance.

Betty

Betty, who heard your screams that night
a gentle man, a family man, a silent man
a respected man

walking home, no cares in the world
glad to be alive
a car pulls up full of young men
four looking for an easy time

Young men who'd heard stories
about easy dark-haired girls
they force you into their car
but you fight

Betty who heard your screams that night
a gentle man, a family man. a silent man,
a respected man

Bruised, battered, you struggled on
out of town they drove
in a well-known car
but you fought because to give in
would be giving in to ignorance
what was yours was to be saved not used
by ignorant men
who'd heard stories of dark-haired girls

Betty who heard your screams that night
a gentle man, a family man, a silent man
a respected man

Clothes ripped you fought on
only with will and pride you fought
these men who thought that by virtue of their color
you were theirs to use

—1991

Blues Singer

I always wanted to sing
the blues
in a smoke filled room
with empty tables except one
a table under a red colored lamp
hearing the roar
from the single table holding
friends laughing and singing
the blues

i always wanted to play the blues
to feel the music in my hands
to breathe my spirit into the harp and hear
my soul escape into the night

i always wanted to play the blues
to feel the heartbeat of the drums
and escape to a pine scented cabin
to dance to the beat of my heart

i always wanted to play the blues
to calm the rage of silver strings
as they vent their anger at a black moon
feeling the fury in my hands

I always wanted to sing
the blues
to soothe my spirit's restlessness
and calm an angry heart
from the single table holding
friends laughing and singing
the blues

—1991

born again indian

long black hair braided hanging down his back
he don't walk he glide
he winks as he talks trying to win with his smile
he disagrees without seeming to
can't be seen as difficult

know what i mean, wink wink nudge nudge
shaking his head pointing at the whites
as if they cannot hear
talking about phil and ovide like they were old friends
we're no different
yeah yeah he says but we're one with mother earth
we feel her pain
that's what i was trying to say in my dance
i thought it was a grass dance
and what you were shaking was for the white ladies
he laughs
flavor of the month man
let them have a taste
loosen up bro you take this traditional thing too seriously
just another church without walls
bottles loosen lips
smoke clouds the brain
and secrets are blurted out
silencing a bewildered audience
not knowing who to believe
i'm not ashamed of being an indian
said in the same breath as i want to use someone
for a change
he/she what does it matter
the night is dark
it's how you dance in front of the camera
you've sold your soul
born again indian laughs
we're savages remember we have no soul
then he talks about secret societies
rituals performed
all the while drowning his sorrow in smoke and drink
and his pain reaches out and grabs me
forcing me to look inside his hurt and confusion
who am i he asks
i pray to a creator and he looks like jesus
with attendants in black robes
that haunt my dreams born again indian cries
it's not fair what you have done
making me a side show with pretty colors

dancing to a discordant drum
surrounded by tourists with cameras
born again beings to droop clutching a bottle
his only hold to what keeps him in chains
he finds it slipping away
and the priest in his dreams mocks him
dancing drunkenly at the foot of his bed at night

—1995

yesterday's song

i wish i could slip into muskeg and spruce
encircling myself with northern lights
wolf songs and night hawks rustling the underbrush
catching the smells of the past still on me
even though my feet are concrete hardened
and my spirit tells stories of neon and blues
i am the son of muskeg and spruce
i still dance to the music of yesterday

—1997

Wachea

Tansi, aneen, boozoo, sago, words of greeting or are they, strange coming from the same voice, whispered across the land with no one listening, *tansi,* how are you, *aneen,* how are things, *boozoo,* good day, *sago,* a greeting of well-being coming from the eastern door, and travelled along the rivers and the trails now covered in gravel and asphalt, making its home on the flatlands of the prairies, riding the waves of the lake, mingling with all those other greetings of well-being and safe travels, old words, older than the land, greetings carried from the stars, mixed in with other words and phrases I don't know, yet I have heard whispered on the streets and paths of today and yesterday, slipping in and out of places like the back alleys of main street, carried into the northend and now some are even found in the suburbs, old words, planting their seeds into new memories. Unable to shake free of these words, older than this land, we glance into the shadows looking for their origin, but the picture is shrouded in mist and the voice is but a whisper, still weak, *tansi, aneen, boozoo, sago*, ah but much stronger now than yesterday or even the year before that; the voice is old, the body weak, the mind forgetful, and the trail is faint, but the footsteps are straight and do not waver from the path though the sharp stones rip and tear soles of the feet—somehow it is comforting, to feel the pain and smell the blood: it means life these words, *tansi, aneen, boozoo, sago.*

We cover it over with concrete and asphalt, we lay manicured lawns over the scars, we tend to the soil as though it is unspoiled, we erect buildings to hide the sky and the stars, we lock the doors and turn down the lights giving the impression that only ghosts walk the streets after dark, we never venture to places where the drums haven't stopped, we know like you know that one time at that place where the rivers meet were burial mounds, ones that did not hide the sky or the stars, and the soil was nurtured by our flesh and our bones and the mounds, beautiful mounds that children climb, and as they lay down to count the stars, the dead, not dead would whisper stories of dance and song, and the children did not fear the dark but walked among the ghosts, but times change and so did we and we had no time for ghosts or old songs, so we removed the mounds to build roads into the future. We built roads, a parking garage, boutiques and restaurants to attract tourists to this once sacred meeting place. Then we forgot, for a time, but ghosts they never leave, they stay and wait, knowing we can't hide behind the concrete and the asphalt and the darkened houses forever, they wait, downtown, maybe, where the rivers meet, yes, beneath your manicured lawn, I am told that there were many burial mounds here, so when you close your eyes tonight, just before sleep, listen closely.

In spite of it all, what we have been through, the heartaches, the deaths, the births, the river becoming silent, so silent but we were so busy riding the wave, chasing a new dream, not knowing its nature or the pitfalls that lay ahead, we never saw that our lives were changing so drastically and in such a short period of time, our skins, our eyes, our hair had become a lighter shade of brown, almost indistinguishable from the strangers that had invaded our village; our language, too, was now the second voice, our past guardian, no longer recognizable after years of abuse, was spoken in whispers, eyes downcast; we became angrier, our anger directed against ourselves and those around us; through all this, we never realized that the river's voice had been silenced, not until the roar of the machines, that had been brought in to stem the flow of our lifeline, ceased, only then did we begin to comprehend all that we had lost: instead of heralding the arrival of spring with its awakening, the river sat silent, barely alive, its flow dictated by that monstrosity that sat above all, the silver wires hummed and lifted the hair on our heads when we passed beneath them, sang a different song, one we could not dance to, nor could we remember the words—the old people were the first to go, then the children, then us, our world had become a stranger, we no longer recognized the lake and the river, once full of life, was lifeless, and yet at times it seemed menacing, we could feel the anger just below its surface. As time went on, so did we, moving on, going away then back again, but all that had been familiar was now strange, the river barely alive, had gotten old, sluggish, the lake, though, had been reborn and the fish returned but from where I sit a new danger has risen and the blue/green sludge that covers its surface is sucking up its life force and with it another way of life that teeters between life and death.

When I was a child, the voices of the village would echo from house to house and across the river, the laughter would last well past sundown, and if you listened hard enough you could hear the whispers of the old ones, saying this is the way it should be, but now it seems we need to hear these stories more than ever, before they go the way of the river and the lake, fading.

—*2010*

Lorraine Mayer

Métis (The Pas/Brandon) 1953–

Lorraine Mayer is a Métis scholar with a Ph.D. in philosophy from the University of Oregon, where she completed a dissertation about Cree philosophy. She is an associate professor in Native Studies at Brandon University and is a member of the Manitoba Métis Federation. Her research interests are in the area of cross-cultural relationships and how they affect perceptions of the world around us. Included in her research are the experiences of Aboriginal women as they pertain to colonization, familial abuse, and contemporary social and political issues. She is the author of many articles and poems and of the acclaimed book, *Cries From a Métis Heart* (2007).

Mayer is a teacher who uses her poetry to instruct as well as inspire critical thought. In "Scrip" one can see her vibrant use of language to illustrate how a single word carries tremendous power, ideology, and can affect the lives of everyday people. "À la façon du pays" describes in great detail many of the historical and physical struggles Aboriginal women have experienced during the colonization of Canada and how men have played a subjugating and oppressive role. In particular, she draws upon the experiences of Métis women and their relations with fur traders. With keen detail, Mayer uses imagery and symbol to discuss some of the dual roles and representations women were subjected to by men and how these women asserted resilience and inner strength in the face of such treatment.

Scrip[38]

A tiny piece of paper
forged by government
to seduce the land
from me

hesitate, prevaricate
the process
till homeless Métis
left confused

those marketers
so newly come
swooped in like pirates
lusting after gold

for love of wealth
these swindlers
offered rotten bait
to steal our land

from helpless children
their legacy,
their identity
denied

by government officials
bureaucrats and law
and now we sing O Canada
our home and native land

but I remember scrip
I remember
Manitoba
and I remember 1870

—*2007*

---

38   FROM THE AUTHOR: A popular method the Canadian government used for distrib-
uting land in the 1800s was through issuing scrip, either land or money scrip. Scrip
looked like money and often came in dollar amounts, but neither money scrip nor
land scrip was really money in the strict sense of the word. The only real value it had
was that it could be exchanged or redeemed for a certain amount of Dominion land
from the government. Money scrip was seen as personal property and could be sold
easily. Land scrip, however, was seen as real estate and could be redeemed only by
the person named on the scrip, though it would not be too difficult to find someone
willing to pretend to be the person named in the scrip and to forge a signature.

À la façon du pays

You need her
That brown skinned
Squaw
The winter freeze
Will steal your mind
Without her
To comfort
Your terrors away
whetiko waits
In silent
anticipation   .
knowing you'll
run the gauntlet
Of Canadian snow
Then pounce
Your flesh will be his
You need her
that brown skinned
stranger
she warms your furs
she knows the land
swells
the dog sun
she knows the stories
that breathe strength
to foreign fears.
You need her that
Spawn of this
new land
She knows the skill
To track the
Snowshoes that
will give meat
to your bones
she knows the knots
To mend your soul
And make your soup
From berries

Never seen before
Listen…
Can you hear the
Wind whistling
Through poplars?
Its calling her
Speaking to the heart of
Her land, her people
She'll comfort you, feed you
Bear your sons
And you
You will give her back
To the land
Bereft of dignity
When you cast her aside
You know the land now
You no longer need
Her brown skinned
Comfort
Her survival skills
Her personhood
You've taken her
Value, like furs
And cast aside
When petticoats,
Fancy lace
with gentle sway
in proper wedding
dress
remind you who
you are

The being of her soul
Poor brown skinned
Lady
a pawn in the
custom of the country.

—*2011*

Marvin Francis

Cree (Heart Lake First Nation, AB) 1955–2005

Marvin Francis was a Cree poet, playwright, actor, and a visual artist born on the Heart Lake First Nation in Alberta. After quitting high school, he travelled across Canada, working at a succession of odd industrial jobs on oil rigs and the railroad. In the late 1970s, Francis arrived in Winnipeg and made it his home. He attended the University of Winnipeg, where he first began to write and perform his work, initially focusing on writing plays, such as "The Sniffer" and "Punching Out Judy." His poem, *city treaty* (2002), which was adapted from his University of Manitoba M.A. thesis, was published to considerable acclaim, earning him the John Hirsch Award as Manitoba's most promising writer. He was pursuing a Ph.D. in English at the University of Manitoba when he passed away from cancer in 2005. His second book of poetry, *bush camp*

(2008), was published posthumously. Francis was proficient in a wide array of art forms, including virtual Internet exhibits and visual arts. During his life, he surrounded himself with other artists in the community—through his tireless work with the Manitoba's Aboriginal Writers Collective, Urban Shaman Art Gallery, and the Manitoba Writers' Guild.

Francis's work offers a unique perspective, showing the rewards as well as the struggles Aboriginal people have faced in an urban landscape. Francis was a keen observer of human interactions and human nature, and his critiques of colonization and capitalism are personal, full of humour, and include popular cultural references. Playfulness with language, awareness of how text looks on page (typography), and theatricality are all evident in many of his most experimental poems.

mcPemmican™

first you get the grease from canola buffalo
then you find mystery meat
you must package this in
bright colours   just like beads

let the poor intake their money take their health
sound familiar
chase fast food off the cliff
speed beef
deer on a bun
bury in the ground

special this day
mcPemmican™
cash those icons in

how about a
mcTreaty™

would you like some lies with that?

—2002

PULLING FACES

Pull off your face
Underneath lies a Pirandello mask

And under that   Death mask, lurks loudly

Colour shifty shapes edges blur   Slippery pictures delight

Pull your face in a little   Red red wagon   That you show to the world
One face for your friends   One for trevor   One for that job application

Now that is one helluva mask   Go paint your face hollow

Certain colours scream bright   Stripes   divide   definite
Region synthetic cool   Paint   the thinnest mask

Could be hooker red   Warrior green trickster blue
Paint the oldest disguise   Belladonna delight
blinding   Fools nobody's god only Your
selves know how many layers   Pile upon skin
brown back Drop eyes light this human Stage
So pull your mind face to the Thoughts of
others Pull faces from history Into today
carny images Pull family faces   into
museum fodder   Art   gallery
features Acrylic dream   masks
for those to follow keep pulling
that face   Down the street
Down down town Down
most roads   And
Down most

coughing

roads

—2002

Soup for the Hood

Time for a food bank poem
               Brother   Can you spare me a potato?
Slice those carrots thin
                  Feed me   feed me   feed me
                    Join bellies first
               Before minds canned meat
                Mr. Grocery man
                Sets on potato hill
             Yukon Gold looking down
                  Pile gets fat

Shrinks within

Core so rotten
So do not try to hide the hungry   Because potatoes got
eyes.

—*2008*

Air Miles Poem

NO! I don't have a freaking air miles card
I'm living on Furby Street, you think I got someplace to go?
Disgusting blue hatred plastic card telling me to fly
Airport to hotel to airport
Sightseeing-assed dazed
Back to the airport
Never seen nothing
Never leave bleach hotel
Club med hell   prairie scale
Tick tick goes the card
Tick tick goes the life
You gotta live there
Live there
To live, baby.

—*2011*

Duncan Donut Cig Poem

Have U really ever seen anyone, including yourself, actually dunk a donut?
Is this weird, or just plain american?
I'm scared to try it?
What if I waste my coffee?
My donut?
There goes my furby supper
Or breakfast
Depends what time I wake up
Either way it is kinda tragic
Kinda street
I watch all of the good donut customers
Thru my shades so they cannot see my curious eyes
Not one of them
Not even those who talk to themselves
Dunk a donut!
This is freaking false advertising!
I oughta sue
U cannot go thru life without suing somebody
Maybe I will ask a poet
A wolf poet
I'll ask Duncan
He can dunk donuts
He knows all.

—2011

Ila Bussidor

Dene (Tadoule Lake) 1955–

Ila Bussidor (nee Cheekie) was born in Fort Churchill in the spring of 1955. The Cheekie family, like most Sayisi Dene, were caribou-hunting people whose traditional territory covered northeastern Manitoba and what is now southern Nunavut. In the fall of 1956, and due to a poor decision by government officials, Ila's community was forcibly relocated to Churchill from their seasonal encampments around Duck Lake. The Sayisi Dene, who had always lived healthy and proud lives, suffered as their life ways were radically altered and ruptured, replaced by life in the slums of Churchill where they suffered local prejudice and derision. In their substandard "suburbs" of Camp-10 and Dene Village, life for Ila and her community became one of poverty, despair, alcohol, abuse, and death. From 1956 until the community's return to the land on the reserve at Tadoule Lake in 1973, one-third of the community died from alcohol, violence, and neglect. Ila and her husband began their own family at Tadoule Lake and have been positive leaders, with Ila serving as chief of the Fort Churchill Sayisi Dene Band from 1987 to 1990. Bussidor enlisted CBC journalist Ustun Bilgen-Reinart to co-author her 1997 book, *Night Spirits: The Story of the Relocation of the Sayisi Dene,* to honour those who died, as well as those who managed to survive.

In the following excerpt from the introduction to *Night Spirits*, Ila prepares us for the story of the Sayisi Dene, which is a journey full of hardships and challenges, but also of strength, pride, and resilience. It is a remarkable story of the Sayisi Dene and the struggles they have overcome to survive, thrive, and continue.

From *Night Spirits: The Story of the Relocation of the Sayisi Dene*

One spring day, when I was ten or eleven years old, I went to the town dump in Churchill with some neighbours and carried home food scraps in a little box tied on my back. There was nothing unusual about this. All of us went to the dump to look for food. But that day, when I came home and put the box on the table, my father stood near the window of our house. He was crying. As he stood there, he turned towards my mother and said, "I was once a leader for my people and my children. I stood tall and walked with pride and dignity. My people and my children never went hungry. When my family needed food, all I had to do was to go out on our land and hunt. I never came home empty-handed. The clothes I wore were the best—beaded caribou-hide jackets, beaded mukluks, and gloves. I would never wear anything that was torn or even a little ripped. This is how proud I was. I had the confidence and respect of my people. Now, look at my baby daughter, bringing food thrown away by other people, so that I can eat." When he said this, I couldn't understand what he meant. I was too young. All I knew was that I loved my father, and it made me sad to see him cry.

I will never forget how my father lifted me in his arms and sobbed that day. That memory came back to me with a great force twenty years later, when I was chief and was standing at a microphone to make a presentation to the minister of Indian Affairs at a national chiefs' conference. Suddenly, I understood what my father had meant on that spring day in Churchill. I understood how it must have broken him as a man, as a leader, and above all as a father. I understood his burden and his shame. It was as if he were there and I was speaking for him. I broke down and cried when I thought about Holly, my daughter. I would rather die than see her scrounge for food in the dump.

There was a time when the Sayisi Dene men made their annual trip from Duck Lake to Churchill with their furs just before Christmas. They were dressed so well in traditional clothes, in beaded jackets trimmed with wolf or fox fur, with beaded gloves and mukluks. Their sleds were so well-made, and decorated so beautifully with ribbons and with bells, that they were the envy of outsiders. Those men had hope for their people and their children. My father was one of them. In ten short years, that hope was crushed out of them.

During the 1960s and the 1970s, most of the people in Churchill despised the Dene. We were thought of as drunks. We were in and out of jails. Our children and youths would run around all hours of the night, breaking into stores and stealing whatever they could. There was violence and neglect everywhere. How ignorant were those people? Didn't they realize that the Sayisi Dene had been competent enough to live in one of the harshest environments in the world, that at a moment's notice, the whole community could move to follow a caribou herd in the dead of winter? Did no one see how tragic it was that men like my father—in the prime of their lives, men who had once stood on top of the world—had now sunk so low? Didn't anyone in that town see that these people hadn't been drunk all their lives?

They said we were useless, drunken, lazy Indians. That there was no hope for us. That's what made me so ashamed to be Dene when I was a child. I did not know the history of my people as I do today. I want my daughter, Holly, to know that history and to never be ashamed that she is a Sayisi Dene.

Today, as we approach the twenty-first century, we face contradictions and challenges. We have a lot of catching up to do. At a time when my people should have been negotiating with the federal government, we were living in a slum. No one consulted us before sectioning off a big part of our territory for the Nunavut land-claim settlement between the Inuit and the federal government. This was another injustice done to the Sayisi Dene.

After leaving Churchill, my people slowly drifted together at Tadoule Lake, and, from the fragments, in 1973 we came to be a community of people again. We are now connected to the outside world through a computer system and satellite TV, but we live without running water or sanitation. No roads lead into our community. Tadoule Lake is now over twenty years old, but there is still a feeling of emptiness in our hearts. Many of the generation of people that we needed to teach us the Dene way died in Churchill. The older people who are alive today have never fully recovered from the ordeal of the relocation. Without them, we are alone to rediscover our traditions and to rebuild our culture.

But today we slowly are reviving our traditional drum songs, drum dances, and feasts. We are teaching our language at our school. As we gradually take control of our own health, education, and social programs, we turn to our traditional culture for strength and for pride.

In this story, I want to tell you some beautiful memories that live in me, and also the many sad ones of physical and sexual abuse that took place in what was called "Dene Village," probably one of the worst slums in Manitoba's history. As a young girl growing up to become a woman, I also abused the poison fire-water. I sank to depths of misery and shame, close to death, many, many times. Today, the generations of Sayisi Dene that survived the relocation still struggle with alcohol and drug addiction, and I am no exception.

As a survivor of the Churchill years, by telling the true story of my people and my family, I am beginning a journey that's very important for my life and for my children. This is a good day to begin to travel the road towards healing. My spirit is allowing me to be free and not to be afraid to stand in my truth.

Maybe today my story will help some young Native person experiencing hardship, someone the same age as I was when my people lived in Churchill, to reach deep within herself and realize that, no matter how hard life can be, there is courage and strength that lies within each and every one of us. It's just a matter of looking within; everything we need is there. Listen to what your spirit tells you. You must believe in yourself. Perhaps it will strengthen children like my own.

May this story be a living monument to our relatives who lost their lives to the Churchill relocation. Every story is a tool we can use if we want to. That is what our elders say. Ma See Cho.

—*1997*

Douglas Nepinak

Saulteaux (Pine Creek First Nation) 1960–2005

Douglas Nepinak was a second-generation residential school survivor. He spent six years in the Navy, travelling the world (stationed in Germany for three years), before coming back to Winnipeg and earning his B.A. Honours degree in English from the University of Winnipeg. A journalist, poet, playwright, and self-proclaimed "propagandist," he was a founding member of the Aboriginal Writers Collective of Manitoba and a prolific writer who wrote critically acclaimed plays such as *The Crisis in Oka, Manitoba*. Nepinak died of cancer in August 2005, and continues to be sorely missed by the many writers he mentored and supported throughout his life.

Nepinak's poems and brief narratives are alive with streetwise humour and brilliant social critique. His work focuses on urban settings, giving particular attention to Winnipeg, as we see in "Main Street." His writing is attuned to place, giving tactile details to help readers imagine themselves in a particular location, even if it is not a pleasant locale. By connecting this gritty realism with a wildly imaginative sense of humour, Doug Nepinak creates boundary-crossing satire that makes us think deeply about Aboriginal identity.

Main Street

Main Street you are ugly. Plastered, psychotic, acting like some fuckin' sniffer. You laugh, sitting in your own puke. Crazy, cold, hard and the only mother some of us have ever known. All your FAS kids adore you.

The rubbies along the river pay homage to your great wasting body. They know the subterranean refuge you provide. You nurture. You sustain. They have thrived in the city beneath the city. Sub-existence sublime. They have passed amongst us unknown. Many times we have asked them why they do not die. Why they go on and on, on nothing at all.

JESUS SAVES. And they have sung hymns with no conviction of a bowl of soup, a sandwich, stale donuts. Prayers to a Jesus who should have given up long ago. But rubbies have more stamina than Jesus.

Main Street. I can still smell your secret places. You are pungent, POWER, beautiful. And some nights the moon shines, the stars align, and anything is possible. MAGIC. Five star whiskey. Sniffers huffing, puffing. Main Street you are the dream that never ends. The addiction that promises, promises. Main Street you are a big rip-off.

And a parade of cars down Martha Street on a Saturday Night, or any night. Stream of light. Teenaged boys gawking. Shouting insults at drunken indians. Laughing. Middle-aged men from the better side of town looking to get sucked off.

And Rachel on the corner is the most beautiful child. Rachel, who's been used as a cunt for as long as she can remember. She sings love songs of Main Street. She sings about the whore that welcomed the Deutschers, the Poles, the Italians, the Ukrainians, the Jews. With arms, legs, mouth wide open, she has been there, historic.

Rooms to rent. By the month. By the day. By the hour. Sanctuary for the down and outers. Lonely old men, killing time. Going nowhere. The end of the line. The Salvation Army. The Lighthouse Mission. Main Street Project. Jack's Place.

Main Street. The blood is never dried. The angry young men that screamed in rush-hour traffic. Slugging at the past. Raging at the air about them. Smashing themselves against the world, again and again. Becoming broken old men, broken knuckles, broken noses, broken hearted, laughing toothless in between swallows of beer.

Old men out in the sun, smoking rollies, chewing snuff.

Drinking openly on the street. They were warriors once, they will tell you. In ww2, Korea. And this world is a shittier place than the one they fought for, they tell you that much for nothing.

Main Street. I sold some empties as a boy to watch three cheap movies at the Regent Theatre, or the Colonial. And sometimes when I was busted, I'd just watch the drunks fight. SMUCK. A fat man crashes to the pavement. His tremendous stomach heaves. An old woman laughing, takes a gulp of rubble.

Blood on the sidewalk.

Dangerous. Exciting. Main Street. You have been all the hell most people will ever need.

—2004

Bone Memory

I remember you in my bones
Once you were marrow
And pure liquid spirit singing
Banging substance into ecstasy
Flesh into the sacred
But they injected me with the poisonous lie
That you never existed
And I nodded in compliance
Because I was weak
And I was tired of fighting
And crying
And being afraid
And them being strong
And me being alone and weak

But I resisted in my way
And in the depths of my core being
I kept you alive
I remembered your hot sex
And told nobody
That on the many dark nights
I was never alone

—2004

indians

I think my penis is shrinking. Or at least it seems to be. I think it used to be bigger at one time, when I was younger. Or maybe my expectations and my dreams were bigger then. Or maybe my body just got bigger around it. Or maybe I had a healthier imagination back then. I don't know. After a shower, I stand in front of the mirror simply confounded.

This is more or less how I feel about being "Aboriginal." It just all seemed like so much more at one time. I always thought I was Indian enough, big nose, brown face, black hair, attitude problem. But now all of a sudden I have to be "Aboriginal."

Remember when we were all just Indians, and people would try to beat us up about it? And white people were scared of "Indians." Indians are made of pure gristle and nerve. Nobody is afraid of Aboriginals, bearing sweet-grass, sharing, caring, handing out dreamcatchers. What's the good of culture if you can't scare somebody with it.

Gone are the good old days. You either got beat up, or you didn't, and you didn't have this legally ambiguous term hanging over your head.

These days you're Aboriginal, and white people say that you have to count yourself in. White people are still scared to sit beside you on the bus, but they say they're not.

I just don't get it. Did things just get better?

It just seems that we went from a time when we had no rights at all, to a time when white people were telling us that we had too many rights. There was probably a split second there somewhere when we had enough rights. I must have been out taking a piss or something cause I missed that.

Also, did you ever notice that there are no penises in Indian artwork? Have we learned our lessons so well that we don't even dare look at our own penises, much less paint them in our artwork? Shrinking domain or not.

And why is it all so "spiritual" in the sweat lodge? With all that heat and brown skin around, it seems a shame that all people would do is sit there and sweat. And our people of old were practical people. I'm quite sure they didn't waste the heat.

Did it ever occur to anyone that sex might be spiritual?

I just happen to think that our penises are hanging off a rear-view mirror somewhere, right beside a crucifix. Souvenirs.

Maybe we ought to petition the Pope to send them back. I mean, we did repatriate the Constitution, did we not? I think we should get our penises back. They might not be the biggest around, but damn it, they're ours. Maybe then we can be men again. And then maybe we'll quit fucking up our women, running away from our children, and be true respecters. Truly be the caretakers of Mother Earth.

Truly be Aboriginal.

—*2006*

Darrell Racine

Métis (Turtle Mountain) 1960–

Darrell Racine was born and raised in southwestern Manitoba. After studying at Harvard, Cambridge, and Oxford universities, he returned to the area to teach Native Studies at the University of Brandon. In addition to his scholarly writing, he has written two acclaimed plays with his collaborator, professor and dramatist Dale Lakevold. Although Lakevold is not Aboriginal, their collaborations have focused on Aboriginal communities and the ways in which colonization has affected family identity and individual freedom.

Racine and Lakevold's first play, *Misty Lake* (2000), tells the story of a Métis journalist who travels to interview a Dene woman from northern Manitoba about her difficult and tragic life. Their second play, *Stretching Hide* (2007), is about a Métis lawyer, Frank Ducharme, who returns to his home community after living in the city and becomes embroiled in a mystery involving game wardens, a poached deer, and lingering family resentments.

In the excerpt from scene six of *Stretching Hide*, reproduced here, the main character, Frank, is talking with his father, Alfred, a Métis patriarch in the community of Willows. Frank has been accused of killing a deer out of season, and he is now warning his father that the game wardens will be searching everyone in the area. The scene reveals the tensions between father and son, symbolizing the conflict between two very different notions of Métis masculinity.

From *Stretching Hide* (with Dale Lakevold)

The fur shack. A knock. Lights up as ALFRED *sets his bottle on the table.* FRANKY *is looking out the window.*

ALFRED: I don't need to burn my meat.

FRANK: Yes, you do. They're checking everybody's.

ALFRED: They know my meat's all got tags from last season. Now, come on over and have a drink.

FRANK: Maybe you got nothing to worry about, but me? That damn deer was shot on my land.

ALFRED: You already told me that.

FRANK: Look, Dad. I don't know if you realize, but if I'm charged for this—

ALFRED: Yes, I know you'll lose your licence—

FRANK: And how do you think that's gonna look in the community? The only lawyer these Metis got and he's in goddamn jail. And on top of that, I won't be building any house. And without that house, I'll have no wife. And without my wife, I'll have nothing.

ALFRED: I wouldn't worry about her too much.

FRANK: Now what's that supposed to mean?

ALFRED: Well—the women up here know this place—

FRANK: And Clara will get to know it too—

ALFRED: Just like that goddamn Sandy.

FRANK: That goddamn Sandy?—

ALFRED: Yes, that goddamn Sandy. She's from the same place as that girl of yours. She belongs to the same people who wouldn't buy my wood when I was starting out. If you remember, and I suppose you wouldn't cause you were too young, I had to go all the way—

FRANK: You had to go all the way to Prince Albert—

ALFRED: That's right. To sell my timber.

FRANK: Clara doesn't even come from the city. She's from Invermere.

ALFRED: Where those Scotch come from? Those pure blood Scotch are all the same. Look at Sandy. Once they move in, they think they own it all.

FRANK: Sandy doesn't own a thing.

ALFRED: They took your grandfather's land when he couldn't pay his taxes. And you watch—that girl of yours will be digging in your wallet—

FRANK: You don't even know her.

ALFRED: No, but I do know you'd be happier with one of the local girls. What's wrong with them?

FRANK: The local girls?

ALFRED: Like that Marie. You two had something going one time. Whatever happened to that?

FRANK: You sent me away to school in Saskatoon—

ALFRED: Well, after your mother passed away—

FRANK: For five years.

ALFRED: Yeah, but you coulda come back and married that Marie.

FRANK: Dad, I was at university and then I went to law school. Besides she ended up with Eugene.

ALFRED: Yes, I know she went for that sonuvabitch. And if there's anyone that shot that deer, I'm telling you it'd be him.

FRANK: Who?—Eugene?

ALFRED: Someone should pick up the phone and turn that black bastard in.

FRANK: You can't be serious. Eugene wouldn't just take the horns. You know that better than anybody. No one does that down here.

ALFRED: Just hold on there. I remember last year when he shot that moose down at Dry Lake. I was coming back from the trapline. And there was Eugene cutting off the horns with a hack saw. I thought he was gonna take that meat home. But it wasn't two days later he was at my door looking for a bit of meat. And I saw that carcass out there—maybe not all of it—but most of it was still there—wasted.

FRANK: He couldn't have done that.

ALFRED: You don't know Eugene any more. Why, he's at my door every other week looking for a handout. You watch, he'll be at your door the same way. If it's not a case of beer, he wants me to write him a cheque—so he can pay his fucken Hydro.

FRANK: I know he's like that with money, but I've never known him to waste an animal.

ALFRED: If you knew what you were doing, you'd phone them game wardens and tell em to check him out. I know he's got them horns stashed somewhere.

FRANK: I don't care if he did or not, I couldn't turn in one of my own friends.

ALFRED: Do you want to be a lawyer or not? Someone's gonna have to do it. Otherwise—you're gonna get charged.

Slight pause.

FRANK: I know.

Troubled, Frank goes to leave.

ALFRED: That's right. You just do what you gotta do.

FRANK *turns and looks at him.*

If you don't have the guts to make that call…

FRANK *exits.*

After a moment, ALFRED *looks up at the antlers. He takes them down as the music comes up and fades.*

—*2007*

Joanne Arnott

Métis (Winnipeg) 1960–

Joanne Arnott was born in Winnipeg and has been living on the West Coast of Canada since 1982. Her book, *Wiles of Girlhood* (1991), won the Gerald Lampert Award for best first book of poetry, and she has published three other poetry collections: *My Grass Cradle* (1992), *Steepy Mountain: love poetry* (2004), and *Mother Time: new & selected poetry* (2007). She has also published the nonfiction book, *Breasting the Waves: On Writing & Healing* (1995), and a children's book, *Ma MacDonald* (1993). Arnott is a founding member of the Aboriginal Writers Collective West Coast and the Aunties Collective. She served on the National Council of The Writers' Union of Canada, and with the author's committee for the Writers Trust of Canada. She is a mother of six, five sons and one daughter, all born at home.

Influenced by her years as an Unlearning Racism facilitator, Arnott incorporates social justice perspectives and peer counselling approaches in her work. In the poem "Manitoba Pastoral," Arnott subverts the idea of pastoral genre that usually describes rural life in an idealized way. The poem vividly portrays a rural setting where amid poverty the violence directed at mixed-race girls and women comes not only from the outside but also from inside their community and families. While still speaking to the challenges women face, the poem "Migration" plays with the ideas of mobility, roots, and interconnectedness with the physical world that can be overwhelming but may also provide personal strength and understanding.

Manitoba Pastoral

In a peculiar way, he favoured her,
She got to hold the chickens
while he cut off their heads
While I cooked and washed dishes,
she dragged the honey bucket to the bush;
it was heavy as she was.
When he worked at the mushroom farm,
she had to wash his clothes out by hand, night
after night, getting the shit out.

One summer we went to a barbecue
held by a neighbour, to honour his mother.
She arrived before we did, in tears
and bruises because her boyfriend
couldn't tolerate her being honoured
in any way. Her son was enraged.
A little guy, he started drinking right away
singing "Hit the Road, Jack" over and over;
Jack was the boyfriend's name.

After we had arrived and once
the guys were sufficiently tanked up
he said Okay, let's go, we're gonna kill
the motherfucker. The men
piled into trucks and started driving
away. My father grabbed my sister
said, They're going to kill a man. You have to
come with me. We have to stop them. Off she went,
and they all ended up at our farm,
gang-raping my sister The rest of us
women and children
passing time
watching the sun go down
waiting
for the men.

—*1992*

Migration

The most recent thing

simply tugs on a rope a long
chain of similar
things that
were we trees and cut in half
you could read by the rings

these things

incident upon incident linked
by the essence
the message
or by an image
sensation

because you are female
because you are Indian
because you are smaller than me
because you inconvenience me
because you're handy

you are in danger
I am your danger

roots

the fingers we plunge into the soil
of our worlds

everytime that I cried and was safe
everytime I was endangered and saved
each and every gentle human contact
that is made

one of my roots is the moon

another is the taste of cold weather
the feeling of a warm sun
the sound of rain
and of thunder
the feeling of a strong wind

big sky
snow

earth
the colours of plants and trees
the quiet crackle of autumn
the feeling of me
the sound or scent or sight
of favourite people

and these are the chains

the curve of a white shoulder
white breasts
a man's round belly
something approaching fast from above
or before or behind
not believing me
looking disgusted by me
no one looking at me
everyone looking at me

the forest
should stand
many lifetimes

but sometimes I just can't

in preparing to go

for the first time I am pulling
my roots up gently

rattling my chains on purpose
not ripping up and tearing off

only to be brought up short
in a stunning cessation

—1994

Brenda Isabel Wastasecoot

Cree (Churchill) 1963–

Brenda Isabel Wastasecoot comes from a family of 16 children just outside of Churchill, Manitoba. She is the only child in her family who did not attend residential school. Having taught at Brandon University and now pursuing her Ph.D. in education at the University of Toronto, Wastasecoot is a writer of children's books, including *Granny's Giant Bannock* (2008). Her academic work was first published in *Voice of the Drum: Indigenous Education and Culture* (2000).

Wastasecoot is also a poet. "Down the Flats" is a poem that was published in *Ecclectica*, an e-magazine of Brandon University. It honours the home where she grew up and her memories of the many children who would return from residential school, taking a long and winding train ride home. It rings with the sound of voices and echoes from her community, of parents calling for children while checking their nets along the river, and of mosquitoes, animals, and the land. It is a poem that yearns for youth, and an honour song for home.

Down the Flats

Far north of prairie skies and high above Eagle hovers,
peering down at all the movement of life below.
Down the flats by the rivers edge,
with dusk approaching and colors fading,
dogs are heard howling in the nights beginning.
Their howls echo the far away curfew siren in town,
Every night they call back from down here, from down the flats.

Their howls soften and fade into the soft tundra floor
into dusty pink and yellow and white flowers blooming;
into the graying tarpaper exteriors of houses,
faded and softened from rain and sun and snow;
into old outhouses standing wooden, unpainted,
into the hand scrubbed clothes hanging on lines,
dresses with fading floral patterns
shirts, pants, and white long-johns now gleaming,
as daylight dims,
in the soft, warm breath of earth
misting and rising into the cool evening air.

Mosquitoes rise up from their hiding places,
from the tall sweet grass, gold and
swaying slowly in the gentle breeze,
from out of shadows growing and stretching
as the red sun lowers itself
into the lilac and pink and crimson dance of the northerly flowing river;
from under wild flowers that release their scents
into the dusty haze of the wheat trains being emptied and poured
into the waiting empty bellies of ships.

The fragrance of river mud and dying fish lingers and wafts its way up
mixing in with the reek of whale carcass farther down,
just outside the village of houses exposed by the sinking tide,
the shore line is dotted with families checking their hand made nets
that hold some flapping, some lightly twitching, swimmers.
Netting, tied down by carefully placed piles of rocks
are outlined with empty plastic containers, their labels removed.
Eagle hovers for a while longer, for her share of those fish,
unwanted and tossed back
as if in a way of thanks for the plentiful harvest.

Later, as night begins to fall
the windows are illuminated by
oil lamps glowing brighter and brighter,
with each new flicker from distant stars above,
as the deepening, thickening blue of the northwest sky approaches.
Flying northward, leaving the sweet warm perfume of fish frying and
bannock baking and tea brewing,
she makes out what appears to be a long shiny snake
slowly bending and winding as it inches back down the railway

south toward the trees.
Eagle recognizes the salty sea air of the Hudson Bay,
as she glides northward and westward to her nest of eaglets,
gripping her catch from down the flats.

—2005

Jordan Wheeler

Cree/Anishinaabe/Assiniboine (George Gordon First Nation, SK) 1964–

Jordan Wheeler was born in Victoria, British Columbia, and is a member of the Gordon First Nation in Saskatchewan. He has called Winnipeg home since 1972. He began his career as a writer at the age of 18 and later worked in the film and television industry. By 1989 he combined those interests by co-writing his first television script, a drama entitled *Welcome Home Hero*. Since then, he has written and story edited many TV dramas, including *Tipi Tales, Just a Walk, The Rez,* and *North of 60*. In 2006, he won a Gemini Award for Best Writing in a Children's or Youth Program. All the while, he continued his fiction writing, publishing the collection, *Brothers in Arms* (1989) and several children's books: *Adventure on Thunder Island* (1991), *Just a Walk* (1998, 2009),

Chuck in the City (2000), and *Christmas at Wapos Bay* (2005).

"Sap" explores a modern-day Aboriginal tradition throughout the north—hockey tournaments. It is the story of Gilles, a for-hire goalie who spends more time on the road and in arenas than he can remember, and his struggles with his own temper, rival hockey players, and how to impress a city girl he meets. Wheeler paints Gilles with frank honesty and deft humour, and his hockey scenes are dynamic and multi-layered. As we read, Gilles must keep moving and be aware at all times, using his skills and abilities to persevere. "Sap" is about learning to defend and protect yourself from forces trying to defeat you while continuing to battle until the final whistle.

Sap

Rising from the ice in soupy layers, fog obscured the far end of the rink. Like a cloud it moved through the neutral zone, forcing Gilles to concentrate on the play. At its thickest it was a wall of white, broken only by the occasional opposition forward lurking for a breakaway pass.

Gilles' team, the Swan Bay Muskrats, had control of the game and kept the puck in the opposing end. It was the third period, and the Muskrats were up by two. Three minutes separated Gilles and a shutout, but it had been ten minutes since the McNabb Construction Bulldogs managed a shot on goal. For the goaltender, inactivity is deadly. Gilles' mind began to wander.

Stacey? Lacey? Names rattled his head like crushing bodies rattled the boards. Tracy, that was it. A night that began when a look became a stare and in the lingering moment, they succumbed to the destiny of a bump in the night. Alcohol had that effect. Gilles marvelled at his stamina. Valentino would have been proud, his mother would have been appalled, and in the morning, she was gone. It was just as well. Only now was he able to remember her name, and experience told him that was important. He fantasized what it would be like, what he would try, how far she would let him go.

At the far blue line a McNabb Construction Bulldog shot the puck with a crisp smack. Slicing through the fog the solid rubber disc rose through the air like shrapnel and struck Gilles square in the forehead, shattering his JOFA helmet into three pieces. The force of the shot knocked him back against the cross bar and to the ice.

Fluttering, Gilles' eyes attempted to focus as his head rung with a thousand bells of the Catholic Church. The girders that held the roof seemed a million miles away and at the same time, right on top of him. Gilles tried to get out of their way as his trusted defenceman, Barry Bignose, suddenly filled his vision. With his head throbbing, Gilles heard his brain implode, then realized it was the buzzer signaling the game's end. "Nice save," Barry blurted. Gilles groaned and rolled onto his side.

It was oven-hot, the mercury pushed to an oppressive 39 degrees. It dried the earth and sucked the elm trees (still laden with the spring rain) of their protective sap. Mixed with the feces of the aphid, sap fell like rain, covering the road, cars, and small children with a fine, glue-like sheen. Everything stuck.

Listening to the Stones and sucking on a beer supplied by the tournament sponsor, Gilles Flamond watched the sap fall. It became a grimy layer between living things that made walking messy and turned tree leaves shiny. It was like a person's past, a residue that allowed crap to stick after contact, sometimes welcome, sometimes not. Gilles felt laden with it. It melted and mixed with sweat wrung from his body by the heat as it rose from the parking lot asphalt. "Going to the social?" Barry Bignose asked. Gilles pondered it.

"Likely," he spat.

Gilles Flamond, a name courtesy of a courier de bois, was twenty-five. He'd been playing hockey since he was five and had gone as far as Junior A with the old Winnipeg Warriors of the WHL. He played one season, then became a mainstay of Native hockey tournaments. He was a steady goaltender with a quick glove hand, but he had a penchant for taking stupid penalties and initiating the occasional fight. His style earned him the nickname "Hextall," after the NHL goaltender known for using his stick more as a machete than a puckstopper. He played for anybody who would pay him, and this summer it was the Muskrats.

Never married, there had been rumours and one accusation that Gilles had fathered a son during a tournament in Gitchi River. Once in a while he wondered, but he never dwelled on it. "I'm doing what I want to do," he once defended himself.

"You're a selfish prick," his sister once told him after he'd slept with Veronica Monkman. The meeting produced a genital itch and both blamed the other. On the ice he was Hextall. To the women who had broken the cycle of abuse, he was the "selfish prick." The names stuck like aphid shit and sap.

"I have sinned," Gilles said in confessional.

"You are forgiven," said the Catholic priest.

When the third National Aboriginal Summer Hockey Championships started, Gilles spotted Tracy in the crowd behind his net. He would see her that night at the social. She was with a Muskeg Laker, but the burly winger was in the can when Gilles caught her eye. Then came the smile, the commitment, and back at his hotel room (paid for by the Swan Lake Band) came the bump.

"How was she?" Barry Bignose asked in the dressing room.

"She was good."

Socials and tournaments went one with the other—like hockey players and fans, labour and management, politicians and voters, crime and punishment, Abbott and Costello. A veteran of them all, Gilles learned the art of the snag from his cousins on the pow-wow trail. Eye contact, smile, snag—and it worked, provided you didn't look half bad and you didn't smell.

Sitting with his Muskrat teammates, Gilles sucked his beer and looked around. To his right, Rodney Flett and Alex Bone had built a pyramid seven plastic beer cups high. Finishing another beer, Barry Bignose tossed his cup over and it was added to the pile. Oblivious, Gilles glanced across the hall seeking eye contact. He found it with Melissa Starr, an ex-teammate's cousin from Pickerel Lake. He also noticed a young guy, almost a kid, sitting beside her. He tapped Barry. "Who's the kid with Melissa Starr?" Barry squinted, then pulled Rodney Flett's attention away from the beer cups.

"Who's the kid with Melissa Starr?"

"Billy Gordon," Rodney said, turning back to the pyramid. Gilles took a second look at the kid. Billy Gordon. He knew the name. He had tried out for the Detroit Red Wings and played two seasons with Adirondack before giving it up. He was from Pickerel Lake, too.

"Hot shot," Barry mumbled. "Heard he's got an attitude."

"Everyone's got an attitude," Gilles answered. Seeing Melissa Starr sent a pang through his gut. Suddenly, he couldn't wait to meet Billy Gordon on the ice.

"Word is, Pickerel Lake will make the finals with him playing," Rodney said. Someone threw a beer cap at the pyramid, knocking out a cup on the bottom, and the structure collapsed. Cursing, Rodney and Alex sat down. Gilles downed his beer and stood up.

"Anyone else?" he asked, holding up his empty cup. Five beer tickets shuffled forth. Barry went with him, and they slowly made their way to the bar.

"Got your bell rung today," commented the Sandy Bay coach.

"Just woke me up," Gilles replied. Ordering seven Blue, Gilles felt a tap on his shoulder. Turning, he found Tracy staring at him.

"See you later," said Barry, grabbing all seven beer. Relieved, Gilles saw that the alcohol hadn't done him in.

Tracy was cute. She looked at him coolly, then turned when the burly winger from Muskeg Lake walked up beside her holding two beer and a vodka and seven. The winger glared at Gilles, obviously knowing that Gilles was the one his girlfriend had disappeared with the night before. Gilles glared back. His name was Henry something, thirty-three or thirty-four. He'd been a good winger once, really good, but too much beer had settled around his waist and he'd lost it, along with some teeth. The sad thing was, he didn't know it, or wouldn't admit it.

Gilles continued to glare, challenging him. Henry looked at Tracy, who was oblivious, then he turned and walked away. Surprised, Gilles watched Henry-something-or-other leave, his shoulders struggling not to sag. For a moment, Gilles wondered why he had given up so easily. He had lost it, but he could still have some dignity. He turned to Tracy. Tracy smiled.

GILLES ROLLED ONTO his back. Panting heavily, he stared at the stucco ceiling as she cuddled up and wrapped herself around him. Her flesh was warm and soft, but she wasn't Tracy, and Tracy was who Gilles was thinking about—her taste, her smell, and he wanted her. Not for more sex, though he wouldn't decline a forward advance, but he found himself wanting to hold her. It was unfamiliar, disconcerting, yet as he wrapped his arm firmly around Melissa, he felt warmed by his thoughts. Gilles buried his face in her hair, squeezed himself closer, and slept. In the morning, Melissa was gone.

The arena fog hadn't lifted, but Gilles was able to concentrate through the Muskrats' semi-final victory over the Muskeg Lakers. Henry-something-or-other, the toothless has-been, wasn't around. Gilles wondered at his absence. Did a player call it quits when time beckoned or when humiliation demanded? For Henry it must have been humiliation, and Gilles felt uneasy about his role in it. The incident the night before made him think. Henry turned away without a fight.

Apathy, Gilles thought. Resting on the bench waiting for the final game, Gilles wondered at his own fate. Would it be humility or humiliation? Staring at the aging, jaded players around him sitting against the cold brick walls, he wondered if it would be a good idea to go out now, before it hurt, before there was a chance he might only be remembered as an aging, battered, toothless goalie too slow to play and too proud to admit it. First would come the hints, then the antagonism of the younger players, then the ridicule. He couldn't live through that.

And he wondered why Tracy walked away the night before and left him standing at the bar.

Doubting her attraction, he began examining himself. Hockey, it seemed sad to say, was his life. An endless procession of tournaments, of long drives from reserve to reserve, of cases of beer in dressing rooms and the social trap of beer tickets and one-night stands. For the first time in his life he could see the end of the road, and it led right into the same footsteps as toothless Henry who had been dumped by the beautiful Tracy. Is that all there is? Respect your elders. Gilles heard his grandmother, but he'd never listen to Henry.

He shivered under his cooling sweat and he wiped it with a towel stolen from a hotel room somewhere up north during some tournament some time ago. Grabbing his chest protector and pads, he scrutinized the purple patches inside his thighs caused by slap shots and the cold rubber disc. Pulling up his garter belt, he noticed a red line over his hip. At first he thought it was the line of his belt dug into his skin, but under closer scrutiny, he saw a stretch mark.

"One more win," Alex Bone yelled, trying to inject life into the weary crew. No one caught the enthusiasm. In the corner, Barry silently filled out the game sheet. Gilles sipped from his beer and contemplated real employment, not the season-to-season work fabricated by the bands solely interested in his goaltending ability, but a real job, a trade, a profession. Was it too late for university? Was it too late to start over? He threw on his equipment and donned a borrowed CCM helmet and cage. A Muskrat rookie, barely out of junior B, walked past and smacked Gilles in the pads.

"Screw off!" Gilles muttered. No one commented. Goalies were expected to be moody.

The ref stuck his head in the room and announced that the ice was ready. No one flinched. It was Muskrat tradition to let the other team go on the ice first. Let them argue with the Zamboni driver who had to dodge errant pucks before he could get the cumbersome machine off the ice. Gilles added tape to the butt end of his stick as the hungover hockey team slowly rose and made its way from the dressing room to the ice, dodging patches of cement along the way. Gilles would be that last one out, purposely skipping the pre-game shooting gallery, where most of the purple patches on his thighs were born. Like the sap falling outside, the bruises would remain for days, turning from purple to jaundice yellow as they slowly faded away—like the memory of Tracy's warm body and soft skin cuddled against his. He'd settle down, they'd have kids, marry, get a house on the reserve, and spend the rest of their lives together.

He frowned. A week ago that thought would have struck like a bad dream. Yet today it was palatable, plausible, desirable. He had to have her, and only her. It was time, while he still had all his teeth.

The final game was played before a boisterous, capacity crowd who had picked the Muskrats as their favourite. Gilles saw Tracy in the crowd behind the Pickerel Lake bench and rehearsed words he might say to her. Something more meaningful than "Come back to my hotel room." Something that voiced his honourable intentions. "I care for you," he pondered, "Move in with me."

Pickerel Lake scored one minute into the game. Distracted from his Tracy watch, Gilles concentrated on the play. The Muskrats tied it on Barry's slapshot from the point, but Pickerel Lake battered three more home by the end of the first period. As the buzzer sounded, Gilles spun around and checked the scoreboard. PICKEREL LAKE 4 – MUSKRATS 1. Gilles scuffled to the bench.

"You're going down too early," he was told. "Protect the five hole. Watch the rebounds." Hints, Gilles thought, and he told them all to shut up. Goalies were supposed to be moody. Barry sidled up beside him against the boards.

"Billy Gordon got three goals." Gilles looked up. Billy Gordon the hot-shot, Billy Gordon with the attitude. He slapped his stick against the ice. Billy Gordon with the bruised ankles.

In the second, the Muskrats stormed back to tie it, then the two teams traded three more goals. For every crack Gilles gave Billy Gordon on the ankle, the kid got a goal. Pretty goals, dekes that left Gilles flat on his butt. Skates are too dull, he told himself, but he knew that wasn't it. He was over-extending, over-reacting, hesitating, guessing, unsure.

Twice he mishandled the puck and both times it landed right on a Pickerel's stick. Bang! Bang! Two goals. When the buzzer sounded, the score was seven all.

"Last shot wins," Alex Bone joked. Gilles wanted to ring his neck, but guzzling from his water bottle, he headed for the bench instead. Humility, Gilles brooded. He looked behind the Pickerel Lake bench. Tracy was still there. Waddling back to his net for the start of the third, he watched the face-off. Don't think, he told himself, react.

The play came into his end. BANG! Billy Gordon picked up his seventh goal before Barry flattened him. The crowd, dazzled by Billy Gordon's play, turned in Pickerel Lake's favour. Gilles didn't give a damn. The next time Billy Gordon got near his net he wound up and with a high arc, crushed his stick into the hack of Billy's left leg. The kid went down, and Gilles casually brushed snow into his net. He was called on a five-minute slashing penalty. The crowd booed. Billy Gordon was out of the game.

The Muskrats came back with a short-handed goal, and Rodney Flett scored another halfway through the period. For the first time in the game, the Muskrats were ahead, and they were in control. The one-goal margin remained into the last two minutes, then the crowd suddenly roared. Billy Gordon had hopped the boards. The Muskrats bore down and hemmed Pickerel Lake in their own end. Alex Bone covered Billy Gordon like sap.

Gilles could taste the victory. Thirty seconds left. Pickerel Lake tried again to break out, but Barry intercepted the pass and fired the puck back into the corner. Fifteen seconds—Rodney Flett tried to stuff it in the net, but the Pickerel Lake goalie was there. He'd faced more shots than Gilles, made brilliant saves to keep his team in the game. Eight seconds left. Billy Gordon grabbed the puck, deked out Barry at the blue line, and raced into the clear. A breakaway.

"Shit," Gilles muttered, moving out to challenge. The kid skated in, ripe with the benefit of professional coaching. Gilles tensed up. Don't think, he told himself. The kid swerved right, then left. Gilles stayed with him. At the hash marks, he deked left, right, faked left, and went to his backhand. Off balance, Gilles left him the entire left side of the net. Out of the corner of his eye, he saw the kid release the puck. Gilles shifted his weight and desperately lunged. His left pad and glove hand sprang out, but the puck was by him. For a fleeting moment, he felt his heart collapse.

BANG! The puck bounced off the post and into the corner. The buzzer sounded. Game over. Muskrats 9–Pickerel Lake 8.

Gilles lay on the ice, thanking the girders above. The Muskrats piled onto the ice in jubilant celebration. The fans, jumping sides once more, cheered. Gilles sat up and looked behind the Pickerel Lake bench. Tracy was gone.

The quiet social made him think, but the loud music saved him. There were enough people, but not too many: the Muskrat team, Pickerel Lake, a few Bulldogs, but many left when their teams were knocked out. An exodus that spanned as far away as Six Nations and Prince George. It was the end of July—hot nights and red skies. But in the air-conditioned Greater Core Area Centennial Sport and Recreation Complex, now filled with tables, chairs, people without hockey equipment, cigarettes and beer, Gilles was isolated from the heat—he was searching for Tracy.

"Gilles," Barry began, tossing another two tickets on the table. "You played like shit today, but you came through in the clutch, and that's a mark of a great goaltender."

"It hit the post," Gilles admitted. Barry looked at the tickets for a moment.

"What the hell," he said. "Everyone thinks you made a great save." He pointed at the beer tickets. "Get us another round, then find Tracy."

"Where is she?" Gilles blurted.

Barry shrugged. "I thought you knew."

The faces were familiar, but distant—broken bridges and separate alliances. As he walked to the bar some waved, others watched—most didn't notice. Walking to the dance floor from a corner table, Tracy was one of those who didn't.

Seeing her, Gilles walked across the dance floor to follow. Suspiciously, he watched for Henry as Tracy stepped from the rink and walked to the women's washroom. Trying to be inconspicuous, Gilles drank from the water fountain between the washroom doors, hoping he could stay there until she came out. Bending down, he felt his bladder under pressure, then stood up again. People were beginning to line up behind him. Shutting the water off, he walked to the Plexiglas.

There hadn't been a fight tonight, he reflected. Scanning the thinned-out crowd he felt an amiable wind of chatter, buzz, and Tom Petty. Faces were smiling, some serious in discussion, others jubilant in recognition of a long ago friend or relative. Gilles stuck his hands in his pockets. Downright jovial, he thought.

"About time for the jig, don't you think?"

It was Tracy. Gilles hadn't heard or seen her walk up.

"Did you see the game?" he asked.

"Yeah, too bad it hit the post."

They were silent as the Tom Petty song ended. Then they heard the fiddle, and parts of the crowd howled in delight. It was the jig. Slowly, individuals left the crowd for the bare dance floor—three, four, five. Among them, Gilles was surprised to see, was Henry-something-or-other jigging up a storm. His teeth were shot, but he still had his knees. The crowd responded and clapped. When the fiddle ended the dancers, huffing and wiping foreheads, sauntered to their seats.

"What are you doing later?" Gilles asked.

Tracy stared straight ahead. "I'm going home."

"Pickerel Lake?"

"I live in the city."

Gilles was silent as the options rolled through his brain. He turned to her and smiled. Tracy turned to him, but she wasn't smiling. "Are you going to ask me to dance?" Gilles thought about it for a second. It hadn't crossed his mind. "I don't jig, but when they play a decent Stones' tune, we'll dance."

Tracy smiled curtly. "They probably won't play one."

Gilles thought of the probability with some relief. He didn't dance.

"I've been thinking about you," he told her.

Tracy looked at him, that same patronizing look as when his sister called him a prick—light smile, raised eyebrow, narrowed eyes. She turned and walked into the echo of "The Devil Went Down to Georgia." Listening to the bass riff, Gilles replayed the short conversation in his mind and asked himself, "What happened?" He looked back at the crowd and felt isolated from their joviality. In a shadow of humility, he turned and walked outside, passing teenagers and children as he went. They didn't notice him either.

The night was hot, but no longer red. The moon had that brown look of pollution, but Gilles mistook it for the coming autumn. The tournament was over, and so was the summer. Hands in his pockets, he felt for his keys, then found two chunks of cardboard. "BEER," they read. Crumpling them up, he put them back in his pocket and headed for his car. The wind ruffled his hair and whisked through his back window, shattered when he locked himself out in Peguis. Opening his door, he wondered who could fix it for him before winter. Somebody at home.

He cranked the motor and turned on the radio. Putting it into gear, he pulled out of the parking lot and headed for the Embassy. Finding it difficult to see, he turned on the windshield wiper, but he was out of fluid. The rubber blades struggled over the sap and spread a fine, glue-like sheen over the windshield. Small bits of debris, blowing in the wind, stuck to it. It reminded Gilles of school; then he wondered if he should go. He had his grade twelve. Peering through the aphid crap, he turned on the radio; 1470 was playing "Stairway to Heaven." Gilles hummed the tune and imagined himself on the Fort Garry campus playing inter-mural hockey.

—*1992*

Cheryl Smoke

Dakota Sioux (Sioux Valley) 1964–

Cheryl Smoke grew up in Brandon and attended Brandon University, studying Native literature, creative writing, and journalism. Previously, she worked as a TV reporter and radio announcer in northern Manitoba, focusing on Indigenous issues. In addition to writing prose, she writes novels and screenplays.

Her work appeared in the Aboriginal creative writing anthology *Who Put Custer's Bloomers on the Pony?* (1998).

The short story "The Hills" is a fascinating account of the power of land, history, and the people within. Told through the eyes of a young girl (and her grown-up memories), it is about an encounter in the hills near her home and the beings who live there. Questions of what might be the train "with no tracks," who might be the faceless "passengers," and what the role of "hills that watched her as she grew up," are sure to provoke interesting discussions and thoughts regarding the relationships gestured to in this story.

The Hills

The little girl ran as fast as she could, desperately clutching her brother's and sister's hands. Her black braids swung wildly as they tried to catch up to the rest of her. Her heart pounded painfully in her waif-like chest as panic and terror gripped her small body. The instinct of self-preservation burned strongly in the ten year-old girl.

The girl and her seven siblings tore down the newly blackened hills. The girl's white socks and sneakers were stained with charred grass and bush; the hills were regularly burnt in the fall ensuring a healthy growth for the next summer season. The hills and valleys of the Reserve served as a playground for the little girl and her numerous relations. They could spend the whole day in the hills, a natural playground, exploring and playing various games of pretend. Their parents never worried about them, as long as the children could be seen or heard. The parents had a perfect view of the hills from the house; the children were well observed, unbeknownst to them.

THE LITTLE GIRL, now grown up, smiled as she stood at the same window and viewed those same hills through her adult eyes. She recalled the exhilaration of sliding down the hills during the winter. How the snow used to sting as it pelted her face when they glided down the hills on pieces of cardboard or, if they were really lucky, on the hoods of derelict cars. There were lots of those in one part of their playground, the old shells half-buried under the bush in one of the valleys. She remembered walking among the crocuses carpeting the hills in the springtime, sometimes picking a few for her *kunsi*. The children used to converge on the hills to play in the summer, while the teenagers converged on those same hills for another reason.

The hills that watched her as she grew up, and the secrets that they held, had fascinated her all her life. This was especially true since that long ago day when something happened, something which to this day cannot be explained.

THE LITTLE GIRL didn't dare look back; she couldn't bear to see it again. The children ran and ran until they reached the gravel road and their home was in sight. Collapsing in the ditch, she felt the hotness of her face and tried to catch her breath. They all stared at each other, not knowing what else to do. After calming down, they agreed that they had better not say anything to the adults; they just wouldn't believe it anyways. Clutching each other's hands, they made their way home. Later, much later, when she was an adult, she told her father about what they had seen. He couldn't explain it either.

The eight of them used to play hide and seek in the "valley of the cars." It was fun playing there with so many places to hide. The little girl and one of her sisters hid between two old car shells. They giggled and watched as their brother proceeded to catch the others one by one. The little girl and her sister were the last ones. She grew excited and almost gave away their hiding spot, until her sister covered her mouth with her hand. As she tried to dislodge her sister's hand, she suddenly heard her brothers and sisters yelling frantically.

Run, run, run, they yelled. Hurry, it's coming, hurry! Suddenly she realized they were all standing and looking in her direction. She heard a loud clattering sound and turned around. Heading straight towards them was an old steam train. That's weird, her ten-year old mind thought, there's no tracks around here.

The girl and her sister ran to the others. The children turned and stood dumbfounded as the locomotive raced towards them. The girl's eyes bulged at the terrifying image. As the train torpedoed by, a passenger car came into view with what appeared to be human figures in the windows. The children stared at the passengers; simultaneously the ghostly figures turned to face them. The little girl and all her siblings screamed in terror. The older children took off running, but the little girl was transfixed. The faces of the passengers were missing! Instead, grinning skulls sat atop the richly dressed bodies. Suddenly the little girl was yanked, almost brutally, by her sister and brother, as they fled with the others. That night, only their parents slept soundly.

—*1998*

Trevor Greyeyes

Anishinaabe (Peguis First Nation) 1964–

Trevor Greyeyes has been a freelance writer/journalist in Winnipeg for over 15 years. He has also worked as a pizza delivery driver, steel grinder, carnival worker, and at a host of other jobs. He has been published in *Prairie Fire* and is a member of the Aboriginal Writers Collective in Winnipeg. He has workshopped stories with Thomas King, Armin Wiebe, and David Bergen. He explores the contemporary urban Aboriginal experience. With a wry sense of humour, he explores themes of Aboriginal identity and the changing roles of Aboriginal people in society.

Greyeyes's short story "Jupiter and Mars" is a satirical examination of perceptions—particularly racial ones. In it, the author skillfully illustrates how perspective informs our claims of truth, God, and love. As Greyeyes shows, truth is not owned by any particular race or point of view—for all viewpoints are faulty, ironic, and, ultimately, funny.

Jupiter and Mars

My God, here I was at another millennium party. That's where I saw her. A crowd of people surrounded her as she told everyone that in a previous life she had been an Ojibway woman. There had been an early morning raid, and her husband was killed by a Dakota warrior.

I had heard enough.

I went off to bug my friend Harold about holding a millennium party in the year 2001 to which he said, "The new millennium doesn't start until the year 2001."

I fired back, "What the hell is the year 2000 then?" Harold just waved his hands over his head. "You should've put this much work into your solstice celebration," I yelled as he exited the room.

Harold was one of those guys who was a nouveau Aboriginal. The equivalent in the Aboriginal world of a born-again Christian. I've learned you should never argue with anyone who is a true believer in whatever their spirituality represents to them.

I remember finishing a shower and getting ready to go to a psych class or some other bullshit class when the doorbell rang. I peeped through the little hole and saw two guys, one with a briefcase, and a teenage girl. What the hell, I thought to myself and opened the door.

The guy without the case shoved a pamphlet in my face while the other guy asked me if I had heard the Lord's word lately. Or something to that effect. The teenage girl just stood there smiling prettily. Her face still tried to smile as they realized I had answered the door naked but I just had my head and shoulders showing from behind the door. The guy with the case apologized for coming at a bad moment and they started to move along. I yelled after them, "God doesn't exist!"

The guy with the case just smiled, and the girl looked uneasy. The guy with the pamphlet turned around holding his pamphlet up like a shield. He looked angry. "Why do you people have a hard time accepting the word of Jesus Christ, our Lord and Savior? His words lifted me up, and I am like Lazarus," he said amazingly in one breath.

I was stunned or, rather, just standing there in my dripping silence, noticing the draft coming from the hallway.

"The Lord is all around us," he said, gesturing like some bad Sunday morning television preacher. "Can't you see his work? The divine is in everything."

That was all I needed to forget the draft shrinking my penis. I should tear down his obvious teleological argument, I thought. Or perhaps I should use the logic in William James's *The Will to Believe* crap and turn it around.

No. Too practical. Too philosophical. Too argumentative. Instead, I let the door open up some more.

Oddly enough, I was never charged with anything. Then again, maybe there wasn't enough there to press charges. As I've grown older, I've learned the uselessness of engaging any believer in the rightness of what they practice. Let God sort them out. It's not just Christians who need sorting out.

I had brought a good old case of beer. Domestic. Around me were all these goddamn yuppie Indians who really piss me off sometimes but they never know it. "Here," one of them said, "try this Chianti. It's from California." "No thanks, man. I already have a brew happening." To which he looked at me kind of puzzled.

A woman stood behind him with a long fluted glass and raised it to me as the music blared. I was sitting there with a domestic beer while people filled glasses and cooed to each other about how hard it was to score that bottle from Portugal. "Uh, dude. I've just about drank everything there is and then drank it again to justify to myself why I didn't like it." "Well, aren't you just a working class hero. As educated people it's up to us to define new tastes for our people." I got myself, my working class beer, and my ass out of there.

I joined a small group in the kitchen smoking a joint. The abbreviated conversations marked by occasional "here, man" with a thin puffy whiff of smoke escaping the lips as you held out your offering to the next person. After we finishing puffing, a buxom blonde woman with blue eyes grabbed my hand before I could turn away. I recognized her as the woman who was Ojibway in a previous life.

"I hope you don't mind?" she purred. "I couldn't help but notice your hands. Take this line. It's your life line." She traced the line from the edge of my hand to my wrist, sending little volts of electricity to the more primitive parts of my brain.

"As an Aboriginal person," she said while looking into my eyes, "you are more in touch with the spiritual world than a white person."

"I often try to touch myself nightly."

"I love Ojibway humor," she said with a big smile, and I swear to God her eyes were twinkling underneath the fluorescent kitchen light.

"How do you know I'm Ojibway?"

"I can sense these sort of things." She grabbed my hand as she slowly swayed to the beat that pounded from the living room. I just stood there with my limp arm going back and forth.

The night passed by in a haze of swirling beats, alcohol, trite party conversation, and purple smoke. Harold was dancing by his CD player when he asked everybody if they wanted to go "Indian."

I was sitting there with the blonde beside me, and she would tease me by giving me a playful squeeze every now and then. I can't believe some Indians' manners, because while I was entranced by this woman another partier tried talking to me.

"Man. Don't you just love the ancient rhythms?"

"Hmm. Oh, yeah. Whatever you say." While the blonde looked me in the eyes and licked her lips, I had to focus on the crap the guy was saying instead of on her.

"Do you know what those guys are screaming about?" I asked.

"Who needs to? I can almost see myself painting my body. Getting ready for battle. The medicine man blessing me and my horse before we go into battle."

Before I could tell this lame ass, who was a Mohawk, that his people never rode horses into battle, the music ended. Everyone looked in the direction of the stereo to see a small woman in braids wearing a buckskin vest over her pink blouse. She approached Harold. "It's bad enough you have drinking at your party but this is just way too outrageous. Don't you know it's bad medicine to be playing this kind of music here? This music is your people's hymns."

For a small person she could sure make a big sound. The more she screamed at everybody, the more howls of laughter came from the party. Personally, if I were Harold I would've puked all over her neat moccasins.

I remember at one youth gathering this same woman had harassed a couple who was selling moccasins, dream catchers, and wood-stained images of Elvis Presley. They had the nerve to sell sweetgrass, sage, and tobacco with everything else. I can still remember the looks on their faces as they were packing everything into an old blue van. The woman in the van screamed "bitch" and gave the believer the finger as the van bobbed along the grass.

Being the good Aboriginal person and role model that I am, I sat there waiting for the cab company to phone and tell me the driver was waiting downstairs. The blonde from earlier grabbed me by my love handles as I was stooped over putting on my winter runners.

"Where are you going, my brown-skinned knight?"

"Does that make me a dark knight?"

"Sometimes your Ojibway humor can be quite annoying," she said. I thought my humor had always been mine. "Do you want to come to my place for a nightcap?"

"I must tell you the honest truth, ma'am. I never wear a cap to bed."

She laughed that polite laughter when you don't really mean it.

In my town at this time of year, it's cold enough to force a polar bear to build a fire. This year minor lakes formed as the snow melted. I knew the cab driver must have stopped over one of those sloughs when my foot went ankle-deep into water as I stepped off the curb. Goddamn global warming, I said to myself.

As the cab slushed along, she put her arm in mine and would occasionally put her head on my shoulder. Still. It's hard to be truly romantic as you walk down the hallway to her place with shoes making that plop plop sound.

"Isn't my place fabulous? Take them off. We'll have you going right away."

"You know, that's what I love about free spirits. Ready to do anything at a moment's notice."

I was trying to sound cool as I removed my belt. "No, I meant give me your socks, silly." She disappeared into the kitchen, and I heard the familiar binking of a microwave being programmed. She came out with a bottle and two glasses. "I love to warm my socks up in the winter time. It makes them so toasty."

I walked into the living room, and it was decorated with all these ebony carvings. "These are African aren't they?"

"You have a good eye for indigenous art."

"Are you a collector?"

"I am of all things indigenous."

We sat there and talked. I found out she was a third-year sociology student. Funny. I would've though she would have been an anthropology major. She was in her last year looking to getting her master's. I gazed down the front of her sweater while she went on. Spiritualism had entered into her life when science couldn't explain what she felt. For some odd reason, her naked ankles below her pant line were turning me on. She told me white people had lost their spiritual selves with bureaucratic institutions called churches. I could smell the faint hint of her body through a thin veil of perfume and nodded as she kept talking. In previous lives she had lived as an Aboriginal woman many times on Turtle Island.

"Do you want to see my bedroom?"

"I was getting worried you were never going to ask."

"Oh, believe me. I think you'll be very surprised."

To say I was surprised was like telling Custer there were a few Indians over the hill. The walls were painted with a clichéd prairie scene. Some wild-looking Indian armed with a lance on a horse chasing a buffalo. On the other wall there were women gathering something. Children were playing in the background. There was also cloth hanging from the ceiling. It looked like the lower half of a teepee. Inside the folds, there was a genuine imitation rug and some sort of large bowl blackened from something burning inside it.

"What the hell is this?" I asked as I crawled further into her fake teepee.

"My spiritualist helped reconstruct this from a previous life. Don't you think it's great?"

I was looking for the right words to say. However, I had enough liquor inside me that only an angry husband or boyfriend would have made me run.

"I knew you in a previous life, you know," she said, moving closer.

"Wait, don't tell me. We were married in a previous life."

"Not quite. You were the Dakota who shot my husband."

—*2001*

David McLeod

Anishinaabe/Métis (Pine Creek/Camperville) 1964–

David McLeod has had a long career in broadcasting, writing, and the recording arts. After completing the broadcasting program at the Southern Alberta Institute of Technology in Calgary, Alberta, McLeod studied television production at Ryerson Polytechnical Institute in Toronto. He is the general manager for Native Communications Incorporated (NCI), and sits on the Manitoba Audio Recording Industry Association board. McLeod has written and directed three series of children's television programs for NCI, which were broadcast on CBC Manitoba North. McLeod has also hosted television and radio talk shows, and he worked for several years as a reporter covering stories in northern Manitoba. He received a Canadian Aboriginal Music Award in 2002 for his efforts in promoting Aboriginal music. McLeod is a member of Winnipeg's Aboriginal Writers Collective.

His poem "I write" interrogates the self as Aboriginal artist caught in a world of contradictions—selling pain for profit, dealing with stereotypes, and searching for a "validated voice." "Statement of Account #346" is a freewheeling, kaleidoscopic dream poem that is also a critical look at a world in which creativity is defined as almost criminal. The narrator's wonderful response to this situation is to continue transforming that world through his brilliant metaphoric vision. In "Boy I Can't Wait to Get My Cheque," McLeod makes insightful, tongue-in-cheek commentary about Aboriginal poverty in Canada.

I write

I write about foster homes poverty street
gangs and the vanishing
Indian that Custer and John Wayne prayed for
Because this is what I know

I write about making red willow dream
catchers in the penitentiary healing journeys
powerful visions vision quests and peyote
(metaphysical exotica erotica not known to the outside world)
Because this is what I know

I write about legends the oral tradition
stories passed down relatives who have passed out
Because this is what I know

I write about alcoholism diabetes residential
school abuse and more abuse slot machines and bingo dreams
I am lost in true confessions
lost within Native identity
Because this is what I know

I write about the Aboriginal world view (i.e., positive images)
circle eagle coyote raven number four faceless trickster mother
earth medicine wheel four directions heartbeat of drum
smell of sage tobacco braids of sweet grass and cheap marijuana
Because this is what I know

I write about the urban apple Indian experience internalized
colonialism being lost without a Native identity
Because this is
all I know

I write to prove that Indians are still real still sweating
outside of museums listening to the elders spiritually
connected to all things I am all things
Because this is what I know

I write because all these things are so seductive so marketable
authentic so ultimately oppressive because this is what I know
Because this is my validated voice

Awiya na omaa ninisidotaag?
Amii eta owe gekenda maan.

—*2001*

Statement of account #346

I was arrested today for pissing on the flowers. I didn't want to but it was hot and I felt sorry for those dandelions. Some snitch called the cops. They showed up to take me to jail. You see I had no money for the ticket. The officer told me I was crazy for doing it in the first place. I told him that the flowers didn't think so and that the sheer beauty of it all had gifted me. I had received a concept of openness and an expanded awareness, simply put, we were one! Unfortunately for me the officer was not won over by my absolute sincerity. In a derogatory tone he said that I "had extended my artistic boundaries" and that I would in fact "be taken to the prison for poets." Prison for poets? I paused then quickly replied that I was not scared at all, I was, on the contrary, exhilarated by the opportunity. Smiling and thinking all the while that my poetry would never be the same.

Riding in the police vehicle we made our way to the prison grounds, hours down a winding road. Suddenly there, in the middle of a lost prairie, stood the prison building! Obviously it was a coy attempt at copying the Chelsea Hotel in New York City. I recognized it from the photos I'd seen in Life magazine. I boldly asked the cops, "How can anyone really prepare themselves mentally, when you're about to enter the quandaries and complexities of a defining moment?" What was I to expect? They said nothing. Who cares, this was my creative jackpot. I would finally become a part of the underground's consciousness.

I was quickly taken by the cops into a small grey room and stripped of all clothes except my jockey shorts. A man who strangely resembled Lenny Bruce then entered. He wore a blue silk suit and cheap Yugoslavian shoes. Loudly he said, "Get hip to this, kid, you've been schlepped in here because you're a schmuck! And I will tell you, the standards are going down the toilet. Paranoia was used as a ignorant excuse to let you in here! There's a stadium full of poets who are nothing but cheap hustlers filling their pockets with someone else's juice, until they are on a sinking ship. Sinking right into a pile of books that nobody wants to read. You know what kills? ...Jim Morrison's poems do not sink. They're fished after by pimply faced black-haired girls who can only read between the lines. Poetry is an excuse for a scam artist who is too damn lazy to write a book! Are you listening to me? Because right now I'm writing a Broadway play to expose the whole damn thing!"

He then threw some unfashionable prison clothes at me and left the room. Two men dressed as snake charmers entered and assisted me in changing. I was then escorted down a long hallway and rudely pushed into a cell. Before being left all alone, I was given a pencil without an eraser and one-ply toilet paper. Here I would write my prison poems and learn to become, at last ... my own PR man. The afternoon started out quiet. But as the evening approached, typewriters took flight like a flock of birds. Sounding the season! The prisoner in the next cell began yelling, "Who is the establishment if we are not? Who is the establishment if we are not?" Those words sounded strangely familiar; his presentation was politically irresistible. He was a very effective poet. I believed him to be a saint who wished to be a mother. I too began to shout, "Publishers are evil kings who only print words that suffer upon their crowns!" I didn't know what it meant, but damn it, this was revolution! Here in this place I was finally living an outsider's life, completely free of laxative encouragement. Let my epitaph read "to be a poet is a virtue, not a sin."

This place, among a thousand poets, Catholics, Protestants, Jews, Muslims, and probably a few aging Marxists, and other men who had no names for their philosophy, I could call home. I felt the magic in all things again. That possibility was far larger than even death itself. My pencil would surely give birth today, maybe to a minimal style … a sort of post-literature. A language with real guts. Then, suddenly, before the water broke, the Lenny lookalike entered my cell with the snake charmers and said, "You're free to go, there has been a mistake. You are not in fact an artistic outlaw but a wanna-be phony!" He began to laugh and said that there was only room in this prison for persons with clamorous belief systems, in other words, real poets.

Upon my knees I dropped, tearfully pleading with him, that my words were hungry, that my poems could be read in the rain. I only wrote of bosoms because everyone else did. Could he not understand that my bladder passed faith upon thirsty flowers? Surely I was delivered into this world to climb stars and distant moons, to become a poet with clamorous belief systems. Suddenly, I became a dying sea, thirsting for a distant shore…
(FADE TO BLACK)

The next thing I remember is awakening on a Greyhound bus with a terrible headache and a fortune cookie sitting on my lap. I immediately opened the cookie and it read, "Praise be to all poets, the true few who remain witness. That to shun any heaven is to accept any hell."

What was this? Poetic justice? This forsaken note offered me no liberties or graces. I yelled, "Driver, let me off." There in silence, I saw my shadow touch the earth. I realized that I, myself, am a dandelion. A weed moving in the wind, searching for roots in order to be close to something.

—*2001*

boy I can't wait to get my cheque

boy I can't wait to get my cheque
things are gonna be better around here,
we'll get outta the bush for a while.
go see the other side of the world…really!
I'll get him, tommy-ish to drive us to town.
when I get that cheque I'll bring back KFC for all the kids
two barrels. never mind, three full barrels.
we'll have left overs…imagine that left over KFC!

boy I can't wait to get my cheque
I'll tell those store workers, I'm not poor.
I can make my own damn decisions!
I'm here to stock-up I'll say.
get off your ass I'll say.
get me 5 cans of rothman's tobacco, that buck owens record,
new needles for aunt doreen's sewing machine, and work pants too!
bag it up! this is history in the making!

boy I can't wait to get my cheque
I'll buy a new cowboy shirt…red and white, just like the square dancers in
duck bay.
come laundry day that shirt will be waving on the clothes line like a flag.
people will say, who's shirt is that anyway? That's dave's shirt they'll
say…
I guess he got his cheque
I'm not going to be cheap either!
in my community if you're cheap, you're sober
and if you're sober you got no friends (except the ones in church)
even if you go to church you need money, one time I had nothing for that
plate and I got a dirty look. I bet if jesus himself was in there
with no money he'd get that same look.
that's why I'll call my party a service…
I'll bring home a few cases and we'll have one hell of a good time!
it'll take a week to clean up after my party
ahhh, I love the smell of pine sol in the morning.

boy I can't wait to get my cheque
the bootlegger will be crying when he sees me going to town.
ah, I'll give him the empties after the party, see…see I'll say…
I'm a better man than you.
no charge I'll say!

boy I can't wait to get my cheque
things are going to be better around here,
my uncle norman said, "live each cheque like it's your last."
those are wise words from a guy who hasn't got a cheque in two years
might as well be dead!

boy I can't wait to get my cheque
what time is it anyway? the post office opens at nine.
but those kids are never there til nine thirty.
if my cheque comes in, I'll buy you breakfast at the cafe, anything you
want.

hey you gonna come with me to town? I'll show you a good time.
the kind of good time you'll wanna forget about but never can.
ya, but right now I gotta wait for my cheque…
I gotta wait…wait for my cheque..

—*2004*

Paul DePasquale

Haudenosaunee (Six Nations of the Grand River, ON) 1965–

Paul DePasquale is an Upper Mohawk member of the Six Nations of the Grand River Territory in Ontario. Raised in nearby Brantford, he has Mohawk and European backgrounds. Paul is an associate professor of English at the University of Winnipeg, where he teaches courses on Aboriginal literatures and cultures. DePasquale is co-editor of Louis Bird's *Telling Our Stories: Omushkego Legends and Histories from Hudson Bay* (2005), editor of *Natives and Settlers Now & Then: Historical Issues and Current Perspectives on Treaties and Land Claims in Canada* (2007), and co-editor of *Across Cultures/Across Borders: Canadian Aboriginal and Native American Literatures* (2010). He is currently editing a collection of Iroquois historical and contemporary texts for University of Nebraska Press. Paul also writes fiction and poetry.

DePasquale's poetry is lively and inviting, blending traditional aesthetics with sharp political wit. As a writer teaching in a university, he is often faced with contradictions in the ways Aboriginal people speak and are understood, and this theme comes out in his work. These previously unpublished works are historically rich pieces that offer a window into his life and experiences as both creative and critical artist. The poems also offer the experience of an Aboriginal person far from his home territory—showing how one looks at one's family from far away and through the media of text and story.

At the Edge of the Woods Is a Fire

Father was a clergyman,
ai ya, ai-ya, ai-ya, o,
praised women long and beaver hats,
ai-ya, ai-ya, ai-ya, o,
wrote a fine prayer for Duncan Scott,
but those people, they cut the kids' hair all off.

Father was a shopkeeper,
ai-ya, ai-ya, ai-ya, o,
bartered model cars, trains, and stained glass,
ai-ya, ai-ya, ai-ya, o,
hid some money from Trudeau's men,
so those stooges, they run him straight out of town.

Father was a diplomat,
ai-ya, ai-ya, ai-ya, o,
wore a white suit and travelled across the sea,
ai-ya, ai-ya, ai-ya, o,
offered the queen a silver cup of strawberries,
but that lady, she took our water and magic away.

Father was a highwayman,
ai-ya, ai-ya, ai-ya, o,
moved whiskey and smoke across the line,
said he was a lawyer from Orchard Park,
ai-ya, ai-ya, ai-ya, o,
a gun hidden under his seat.

—*2011*

School of Hard Knocks

Inside these squares in this rectangle attached to rectangles and squares, I often need to slip outdoors. "Why would we necessarily assume that a Native person is better qualified to teach on a Native subject?" A short run up Main, the Perimeter, the 59 north of Brokenhead, where Nelson's ghost reminds me that I am a visitor, fish jump, sun and trees. "Exactly how does literature by *those* writers help *our* students understand how Natives were colonized in the past? Haven't we made enough progress so that everybody can just be themselves and race doesn't factor in?" The balsam firs my children and I transplanted, the pileated woodpecker standing next to the dead crow on the old wood shed. "If you had only told me that you're Aboriginal, then I would have understood your position." Pike and white bass all around Grand Beach, pickerel at Traverse Bay, bullhead, carp. "You look about as Native as our recent hire. I guess we have to start somewhere." Beyond Lester Beach, Hillside, Victoria Beach, up, up. "Oh, you'd love this guy. He's Native, a film-maker. He's just like us—he loves to laugh!—I was so surprised!" You could paddle all day and witness only lake, outcroppings of rock, poplar, birch, fir. "An Indian, eh? How'd you get to be so lucky?" You call a relative far away. "You sound surprised," she says. "You been a university student half your life and now you work in one. You should be an expert on that system by now." "But," I want to say. "That's why I wanted to become a teacher. To encourage other views, to critique, to create." Inside the staff washroom someone before me has left another gigantic turd for me to look at while I pee. I can hear my father, the most conscientious toilet bowl cleaner on or off the Six Nations, saying, "Those guys are the worst. They always leave their crap for others to clean." I never wanted to believe him, never wanted to think bad things about so many people, some of them related. I tell myself that perhaps a Black man or Native man forgot to flush the toilet, though I'm aware that the odds are slim. Maybe a woman used the wrong stall or it's a simple matter of poor plumbing. "With so much opportunity today, why do the same problems continue to exist for Aboriginal people? I mean, anybody can achieve whatever he puts his mind to. You must know all about that." I call my father far away. He tells me to keep my head up, my eye on the ball. "I give you credit, though," he says. "That's why I quit school as soon as I could. I figured the school of hard knocks was enough for me. But at least things are different now and you can do something." My talk with my father reminds me again of all that has been, and is, possible for us.

—2011

Shayla Elizabeth

Cree (Pimicikamak/Cross Lake First Nation) 1965–

Shayla Elizabeth is a Cree storyteller, poet, writer, spoke word artist, and an emerging playwright who has been a long-standing member of the Aboriginal Writers Collective of Manitoba. Her work has been featured in books such as *Bone Memory* (2004) and *xxx ndn* (2011) and journals such as *CV2*. As a speaker and writer, she explores her experiences as an adoptee from the 1960s scoop to advocate for Aboriginal women and how to use the power of tradition to overcome oppression and poverty.

Her poem "chief miska muskwa" is a tender narrative of a conversation between a mother and child. It illustrates the beauty of teaching ancestry and tradition through the media of story and song, as well as how history and politics are embedded in cultural and spiritual traditions.

chief miska muskwa
(on the occasion of the chief big bear monument unveiling)

mama, am I Cree?
  yes   baby girl   you are of the People
  to be Cree/Iniwe is a good thing
why mama
  I will tell you

the stories tell of how Mother Earth was alone
    when Great Spirit called her into being
  which is how the sun and moon and stars then came to be

followed by the four-legged brothers and sisters
   the winged ones the ones that swim
 the plant people   the tree people
    grandfather   grandmother stone
but Mother Earth was still lonely

so she created the People   her children
   (your ancestors   baby girl)
and all were happy

but then the Great Flood happened
   where all the waters rose higher and higher
 and it looked like all would be lost
   even the People

so Giant Turtle was sent out
   for the People to climb on his back
   not to be swept away by the waters
 that's how our ancestors were saved
    and came to live   here on Turtle Island   (baby girl)

the way of the people is a good way to live
   kayusk ooma kapmachisik Ininowak

   baby girl

like eating blueberries while you gather them
   medicine picking with kookum in the warm sun
   mopping up moose stew with just-baked bannock
hearing the drum   heartbeat of Mother Earth
        call out at powwow
  dancing   jingle   grass   fancy   traditional
expressing your joy to Mother Earth
   for the Gift of being alive
this is living a balanced life   a good life   (baby girl)

but then the visitors came
   they had forgotten what living a sacred life meant
 all four quadrants of the medicine wheel
   the physical   feeling   thinking
    as well as the spiritual

because they had forgotten Mother Earth's gift
   they were scared of the People's way
   and tried to stop it   make it go away

but some of the People said no
   this isn't right   long before you were born   baby girl
  like Chief Miska Muskwa   Chief Big Bear
    whom we are honouring today   baby girl

he was put in jail for saying
   the People's way is good
and when he got out   he soon went on to
               the spirit world
   but his message isn't forgotten
  'cuz that's why we are here today   baby girl

I'm Iniwe and you're Iniwe
   the way of the People
  is a good way to live
kayusk ooma kapmachisik Ininowak

    baby girl

—*2004*

Gregory Scofield

Cree/Métis (Kinosota/Portage La Prairie) 1966–

Gregory Scofield is one of Canada's leading Aboriginal writers—his many collections of poetry have earned him both a national and international audience. He is known for his unique and dynamic reading style that blends oral storytelling, song, spoken word, and the Cree language. His maternal ancestry can be traced back to the Métis community of Kinosota, Manitoba, established in 1828 by the Hudson's Bay Company. He has served as writer-in-residence at the University of Manitoba and Memorial University of Newfoundland. His book of poetry and memoir, *Thunder Through My Veins* (1999), is taught at several universities and colleges in Canada and the United States, and his work has appeared in many anthologies. Other published collections include *Kipocihkan: Poems New & Selected* (2010), *Singing Home the Bones* (2005), and *I Knew Two Métis Women* (2000, republished 2010 along with a CD). His most recent collection of poetry is *Louis: The Heretic Poems* (2011). Scofield lives in Maple Ridge, British Columbia.

In much of his work, and particularly in these two poems from *Singing Home the Bones*, Scofield examines the lives of his own family and his ancestors in Manitoba, particularly those "Cree women whose Indian names have long since been forgotten." In "Women Who Forgot the Taste of Limes," he writes a letter to Mary Mathilde Henderson, his great-great grandmother who was born in the Red River settlement. The poem conjures up the time in which she lived and the hardships that she endured. At the same time, the poem is very much a meditation about the hardships and dangers that contemporary Aboriginal women continue to experience; a legacy that Scofield suggests is connected to the treatment of these women in the past.

Similarly, Scofield's "The Repatriation of Ida M. Scofield" connects with his great-grandmother by imagining her life through the medium of a photograph. Haunting and beautifully written, these poems are songs honouring ancestors and devastating assessments of politics and history in Manitoba and Canada.

"Prayer Song for the Returning of Names and Sons" looks toward the fur-trading post of York Factory and follows Scofield's genealogy further into the past, making a powerful connection with the spirits of his *ni-châpanak* or ancestral grandmothers.

Women Who Forgot the Taste of Limes
Letter to ni-châpan Mary

ni-châpan, if I take ki-cihcânikan,   *my ancestor, your fingerbone*
press it to their lips,
will they remember the taste of limes,
sea-salt bled into their grandfathers' skin?

If I pull from this bag of rattling bones
the fiddle, the bow bone,
if I go down to the lazy Red,
lay singing in the grass

will the faces of our ancestors
take shape in clouds
and will the clouds name themselves,
each river-lot stolen?

If I take ki-tôkanikan, ni-châpan,   *your hipbone*
place on them a pack to bear
will they know the weight of furs,
kawâpahtamiwuk chî   *will they see?*

the city is made of blood, wîni   *bone marrow*
stains their grandmothers' aprons,
swims deep in the flesh, a grave of history,
a dry bone song.

ni-châpan, if I take ki-kiskatikan,   *your shinbone*
will they offer up the streets,
lay open their doors and say I'm welcome?
Or if I take ki-tâpiskanikan,   *your jawbone*

place it scolding on Portage and Main
will all the dead Indians
rise up from the cracks, spit bullets
that made silent our talk?

If I take ki-mâwikan, ni-châpan   *your backbone*
I could say to them
I'm not afraid of gunshots, stones
or the table I sit at—

this table where I drink tea with ghosts
who share my house and the words
to keep it clean.
ni-châpan, if I take ki-cihcânikan,   *my great-great grandmother,*
                                               your fingerbone

press it to their lips
will they remember the taste of limes,
hold silent their sour tongues
for once?

—*2005*

The Repatriation of Mrs. Ida M. Scofield

I. The Family Portrait: Portage la Prairie, Manitoba, c. 1904–1905

It is all here   unravelling
in black and white
the meaning of salvage, the last
sepia-toned remnant

of your gleaming white life,
the stiff likeness of yourself
appearing more the photographer's prop,
the settee

holding the seized woman
whose hair is neatly piled,
pinned into place   you waiting
to tear off the thick brocade dress

and throat pin, this presentation
of perfect ordinance
caught in tatters   fraying apart
all in good black order.

It is all here, Ida:
you, the portrait in the portrait.
Knotted and carefully stitched,
nothing visible, nothing misplaced

except for the soft-shaping bones
inside, my grandfather's
small body of exile, the bastard bones
of freedom   freedom

from the tit-tat talk of town,
the man to your right
who is raging beneath his collar,
who is not my blood—

my blood name
that is not my grandfather's name,
the name
given to our history.

And it is all here
in the eyes of the woman beside you,
grey and death-marching
her lips pocked with crucifixion

that I can see   in black and white
the meaning of salvage,
this careful unbolting
of your life's fabric,

although the drop behind you
is silk, such lovely silk
your eyes have cut past
the photographer's vision

already gone   away dear Ida,
from his composition.

—*2005*

Prayer Song for the Returning of Names and Sons

YA-HEY-YA-HO
YA-HEY-YA-HEY
YA-HEYA
YA-HEY-HEY-YO

HIYA-HEY
HEY-HI-YA-HEY
YA-HEYA
YA-HEY-HEY-YO

HIYA-HEY
YA-HEY-YA-HEYA
YA-HEY-HEY-YO

HEY-HI-YA-HEY
HEY-HI-YA-HO
—prayer song taught to me by my adopted brother
       Dale Awasis from Thunderchild First Nation, Saskatchewan

â-haw, ni-châpanak Charlotte,   *an invocation, my ancestral grandmothers*
Sarah, Mary ekwa Christiana.

â-haw,

kâyas ochi nikâwîmahk   *my mothers of long ago*
natohta   *listen*
my song, nikamowin   *the song*

âw,
this song I am singing

to give you back the
polished swan bones,

the sewing awl, the birchbark bundle
holding the whetstone,

the drawing stone, the pounding
chokecherry stone, âw

the spirit of your iskwew   *woman*
names, the ones

not birthed from the belly
of their ships, not taken

from their manitowimasinahikan,   *bible*
âw, their great naming book

ni-châpanak Charlotte,   *my ancestral grandmothers*
Sarah, Mary

ekwa Christ-i-ana,   *and*
these are the names

I've thrown back across the water,
I've given back

to their God
who has two hearts, two tongues

to speak with.
âw, natohta   *listen*

my song, nikamowin   *the song*
the renaming song

I am singing
five generations later,

natohta   *listen*
my prayer song

so you will be called,
sung as:

Tattooed From the Lip to the Chin Woman,
êy-hey! Sung as:

She Paints Her Face With Red Ochre,
êy-hey! Sung as:

Charm Woman Who Is Good to Make a Nation
Woman, êy-hey!

I give you back
ni-châpanak

the names to name
the names of bones, oskana   *the bones*

you laid down
to build them a house, âw

the blood, mihko   *blood*
and warm skin

earth, askîy   *earth*
that built them an empire.

natohta   *listen*
my song, nikamowin   *the song*

the prayer song
I am singing

to bring back
your stolen sons

whose sons and sons
and their missing bones

are unsung geese
lost in a country

across the water
ni-châpanak   *my ancestral grandmothers*

I've thrown back
your names;

nâmoya kîyawaw   *you are not*
Charlotte, Sarah, Mary

ekwa Christiana.   *and*
nâmoya kîyawaw môniyaskwewak.   *you are not white women*

â-haw, ni-châpanak   *an invocation, my ancestral grandmothers*
kayâs ochi nikâwîmahk   *my mothers of long ago*

natohta   *listen*
my song, nikamowin   *the song*

this prayer song
I am singing.

êy-hey!

—*2005*

AUTHOR'S NOTE: My châpanak of five generations past and my mothers of long ago came to find me while I was researching my maternal genealogy. The meticulous records that the Hudson's Bay Company kept on their employees serve as an invaluable source of information. My grandfathers of that era, many of whom came from the Orkneys and London, arrived in Canada in the mid-to-late 1700s. Some of them, such as James Peter Whitford, landed at York Factory, one of the Company's principal posts. Records state his full name, the parish he belonged to in London, the date he entered service, his various appointments and positions, the dates of his postings and his death on May 5, 1818 at Red River settlement. Below this information, it simply states: *Wife: Sarah, an Indian woman. Married pre-1795 at Severn(?) Buried 27 Apr. 1845, 70 years old, at Upper Church.* I am certain my châpan Sarah, my kayâs ochi nîkâwi— who eventually gave birth to eight children—came to my ancestor/grandfather carrying a name too sacred for him to pronounce. During my research I began to talk to her in a language that caused her bones to shift beneath the earth. I asked her to help me, her little ni-châpanis, to find and sing the proper names, even though the old names are forever lost. The women of my blood, my other châpanak, came to listen. I was grateful to have made this connection, to be a part of a ceremony that cannot be recorded.

Warren Cariou

Métis (Meadow Lake, SK) 1966–

Warren Cariou was born in Meadow Lake, Saskatchewan, into a family of mixed Métis and European heritage. He has written many articles about Canadian Aboriginal literature, especially on Métis culture and storytelling, and he has published two books: a collection of novellas, *The Exalted Company of Roadside Martyrs* (1999) and a memoir/cultural history, *Lake of the Prairies: A Story of Belonging* (2002). He has also co-directed and co-produced two films about Aboriginal people in western Canada's oil sands region: *Overburden* and *Land of Oil and Water* (2009). Cariou has won and been nominated for numerous awards. His most acclaimed work to date, *Lake of the Prairies* (2002), won the Drainie-Taylor Biography Prize in 2002 and was shortlisted for the Charles Taylor Prize for literary nonfiction in 2004. His films have screened at many national and international film festivals, including Hot Docs, ImagineNative, and the San Francisco American Indian Film Festival. Cariou has also served as editor for several books, including an anthology of Aboriginal literature, *W'daub Awae: Speaking True* (2010), and he is the fiction co-editor of *Prairie Fire*. Cariou is a Canada Research Chair in Narrative, Community and Indigenous Cultures at the University of Manitoba, where he also directs the Centre for Creative Writing and Oral Culture.

In "Going to Canada," Cariou focuses on a terrifying moment of misrecognition in order to make his readers reconsider the common idea of Canada as a nation of peace and generosity. Instead, he wants us to think about the violent history of colonization—violence that is still visible today in the lives of Canada's Aboriginal people. By seeing the name "Canada" at the centre of the 20th century's most infamous horror, he is forced to reconsider the meaning of his home country. At the same time, the essay finds hope in the resilience of Aboriginal Canadians who have managed to thrive in spite of colonial history that has attempted to transform their land into "a warehouse of stolen goods."

Going to Canada

We didn't know we were going to Canada that sun-blasted afternoon. We thought we were going to Auschwitz. From Krakow we took the train, a lumbering Soviet-built tram with brick-like seats and windows that lolled up and down to the rhythm of the clanking wheels. It moved at the speed of a bicycle, which gave us more time to think. We rode past broken towns, Polish graffiti on barns and fences, red laundry whacking the breeze. Wild irises populated the ditches, their yellow scarves half-hidden in the grass. In a farmyard, two goat kids galloped into a flock of pigeons—a confusion of wings. Farther along, hawks hung in the air like drab flags.

At one desolate stop, about thirty school kids got on, shuffling and pushing and gazing at themselves in the spectral reflections of the windows. They were about fifteen. The girls all chose our car, but they sat four to a seat to avoid sitting across from us. As the train began to move, a homely girl in a dingy white sweater was pushed from her seat and forced to stand in the aisle. She seemed accustomed to this treatment. Eventually she slid in across from us and sat with her hands on her knees, staring at the luggage rack above my head. I could tell from her face that she was going to Auschwitz too. It must have been a school trip. She had that look of wanting and not wanting to see, that nervous ambivalence that accompanies the tourism of dread. I knew it intimately.

We got out at Oświeçim, walked the three kilometers past mundane yards and dilapidated bungalows, and then through the enormous parking lot with its hundreds of gleaming tour buses. By then we could already see the guard towers, the barbed wire. But it took a long time to get inside Auschwitz because of the crowds. Before we even entered those horrible gates, we realized that Auschwitz had become a meeting place of the world. As we pressed into the Information Centre, a multitude of languages swirled around us. Faces of all tones and shapes, tour guides holding aloft different-coloured ribbons. "Watch for Pickpockets," a sign said in at least a dozen languages. Even here, even now, thieves.

I carry that day inside myself now like an incredibly heavy seed, something I swallowed because I knew I should, because I believed it was important, though at the time I didn't understand how it would weigh there, or what might sprout from it. Many things have, nightmares included. But before I even saw the worst of it, before the mountains of shoes, before the hair and the soot and the nearly endless rows of barracks, before the man collapsed on the ground in front of us and wailed for the lost generations, I saw something else that has fixed itself in my memory, something not nearly so visceral as those other experiences, but nonetheless impossible to forget. There were two maps on the wall of the Information Centre, maps of Auschwitz itself and the nearby "twin" death camp of Birkenau, also known as Auschwitz II. And as I pored over these maps I noticed a small rectangle in the northwestern corner of Birkenau that was labeled with the name of my country. "Canada" was all it said. Other nearby buildings were labeled "Crematorium II" and "Laundry" and "Barracks 43." It was a disorienting moment in a day of huge disorientations. What was the name of my home doing there, in such a place? I was sure that Canada had absolutely nothing to do with what had happened in Auschwitz, so why was it marked there on the map? Thinking back on it now, this discovery was like something from a W.G. Sebald novel: a tiny quirk of history that grabbed onto me in that moment and wouldn't let go. It would become something of an obsession in the following months. At that point, all I was able to learn about this place called Canada was what I found in one of the guidebooks in the Information Centre. It said, " 'Canada' was the name of a warehouse used to store valuables taken from newly arrived prisoners." But there was nothing more. No explanation of how the place had gotten its name, or whether it was a nickname or an official one. How strange.

For most of that afternoon, these questions about Canada fell away from my mind, because I was so overwhelmed by everything else we saw at Auschwitz. But eventually we decided to walk the two kilometers to Birkenau, and during that time I began to think again about Canada, and I resolved to go there and see it so that I could learn more about what it was. What could it possibly mean that a warehouse of stolen goods had been named Canada? Who had named it? In the absence of any explanation, I imagined that Canada must have been named by the prisoners of Birkenau, that it was a place of hope for them, a symbol of plenty, maybe even a byword for freedom and human rights and justice—everything that they didn't have access to. I thought maybe Canada was a place where some of the prisoners had escaped from the hell of Birkenau, or where they planned to escape. The building was close to the railway terminal, after all, and maybe some of the prisoners had been able to stow away in the stolen valuables and find their way to freedom. I thought of the stories of the Underground Railroad in America, in which Canada was named Freedomland, the fugitive slaves' place of escape. It seemed to me that for the Birkenau prisoners, Canada must have meant a place of solace, of fundamental goodness, of decency.

I was wrong in my theory of the naming. But it's instructive for me to look back on how I imagined my nation at that moment, and how I assumed that others must also imagine it. I see things differently now.

Holding my own crumpled version of the map, walking toward that northwest quadrant of Birkenau, I could tell from a distance that there was not going to be much to see. Like so many other buildings in that part of the camp, Canada had been burned to the ground. The Nazis had set it on fire as the allied army approached, probably to cover the evidence, but perhaps also because they resented the idea of valuables falling into enemy hands. As we approached I saw dozens of concrete foundations where the buildings had once been, and endless rows of concrete posts that had once held multiple strands of razor wire.

I counted down the rows and walked over to Canada, despite the fact of its absence, wanting to see what, if anything, was left. It was almost indistinguishable from the other vanished buildings: a rectangle of foundation, a few fragments of red brick strewn in the middle. But Canada also contained several low mounds of ash and assorted rubble. I stepped up to the edge of the foundation to look more closely, unwilling to move inside the perimeter of Canada itself. In the nearest windrow of detritus I made out a couple of twisted, half-melted spoons. A few buttons. A nearly toothless comb. Flecks of unidentifiable metal and brightly coloured paint chips mixed into the dark grey of the ash. All of it had been lying there for more than sixty years.

If I had been inspired by W.G. Sebald, I would likely have taken a photograph of these remains of Canada, but I had purposely left the camera back in our hotel room. It didn't seem right to bring a camera to such a place, to turn it into more of a tourist experience than it already was. In any case, sometimes the distortion and bleariness of unaided memory is more powerful than the hard-edged factuality of a photograph could be. My blurred recollection of those twisted spoons, those dull and distorted buttons, that gaping comb, has lodged in my consciousness. Who once owned those items? What terrible story do they have to tell? I thought of them long after I returned home, when I started doing my research into the history of Birkenau's Canada.

There is very little written about Canada in all the voluminous literature about Auschwitz and Birkenau, but I was able to find enough information to put together a sketchy version of its story. As I had read in the Auschwitz guidebook, Canada was a warehouse that held the valuables stripped from the prisoners who arrived at the nearby train terminal. It was the hoarding-place of their silver, their best clothes, their jewelry, their finest blankets—anything that was valuable enough to be shipped directly to Germany and sold.

But as far as I can tell, Canada was not a place of refuge or hope for the inmates of Birkenau. It was not their Freedomland. It did however symbolize wealth to some of them, and in some cases it was known as a place where inmates were treated more leniently. In Eva Wiseman's novel *Kanada*, for example, the main character Jutka is chosen to work at Canada, where she is forced to search through mountains of stolen clothing to find hidden coins and jewelry. She is given better food at Canada than in the rest of Birkenau, and she realizes that "in Kanada I had a chance to survive" (115). Nonetheless, she turns down the chance to continue working there, because she can't ignore the fact that she is helping the Nazis to steal from her own people. The putative benefits of working in Kanada are more than offset by the fact that she is being made complicit in one small part of the atrocities of Birkenau.

I now know that Canada was named not by the prisoners of Birkenau but by the Nazi commanders who built it. Their reasons for doing this remain somewhat mysterious. What perversity could have inspired them to name this storehouse of stolen goods after a country they were at war with? What does this act of naming say about the meaning of Canada in the global symbology of the mid-twentieth century? Were the camp commanders gesturing toward the legendary wealth of Canada when they coined the name? Did they think that such a name might make the prisoners feel well disposed toward the camp, feel that it was a good place, a safe place? Or did they offer this name with the same sense of vicious irony that we see in the sign over the gate to Auschwitz, which reads "Arbeit Macht Frei," or "Work Sets You Free"?

It's probably impossible to be certain, now, what the Nazi commanders were thinking when they gave the name "Canada," and I suppose it might not matter much in terms of the history of Birkenau itself. But for me, my visit to that strange version of Canada has become indelibly connected to my thinking about the other Canada, my home. It hovers there in the background, haunting my idea of the nation, making the multiplicitous story of Canada one level more complex than it had been before. This is not because Canada the nation had any real connection to the horrific events that occurred at Birkenau, but because the juxtaposition of the two Canadas in my mind brings up a disturbing metaphor, a different lens for picturing my home. Think of the nation, Canada, as a storehouse of vast wealth. But it's stolen wealth. And think of Canada also as a place of ashes, a place that has been burned—as if to obliterate the traces of what has happened there.

I'm not interested in arguing for equivalencies among the various atrocities the world has known. I don't want to make any claims that anything that has happened in Canada is equal to what happened in the holocaust, or that arithmetic or any other quantifiable method can be used to calculate the degree of any crime against humanity. Each group of victims deserves the dignity of not having their suffering measured against anyone else's. But I am interested in parallels, in contiguities, between these events in world history, these injustices, because holding them beside one another can help us move toward some tentative answers to the most difficult questions that the twentieth century left us with: Why do these terrible things happen again and again? How can they occur in supposedly civil societies, in communities that think of themselves as generous and enlightened?

A partial answer to those questions may be that the stories we tell each other about who we are and where we belong can have powerful effects on what we are capable of. Stories have the power to occlude certain things as well as to reveal. It seems likely that the stories that are told, and believed, within communities can lead to particular actions by those communities. Maybe those narratives also provide alibis or cover for acts of violence against particular groups and individuals. Certainly, we know that this happened during the holocaust and its aftermath. But if stories can incite, and if they can cover up, they can also be the agents of remembering and restitution. This is one reason why the stories and poems and songs of Canada's Aboriginal writers are so important. They provide an alternate way of understanding what has happened here, and what is still happening. They expose the legacy of theft and dehumanization that indigenous people in this country have had to live with for many generations.

So much of the literature by Canada's Aboriginal writers is written against forgetting, against the obliterating narratives of conquest and progress and profit that have made the nation possible. These writers give us stories of dispossession, of the loss of land and language and identity, but they also, crucially, give us narratives of persistence and survival and even celebration. They remind us of what has been lost, but they also remind us that not everything is lost. After a fire, something always remains: something that must be accounted for and honoured if we are to have any idea where we are and where we are going. I am reminded of the beginning of Joseph Boyden's novel *Three Day Road,* in which two young Cree men paddle their canoe through an enormous forest fire that threatens to engulf their entire homeland, a fire that symbolizes the ideological violence that is already raging in the outside world. In their context, the name of this fire might be imperialism or modernity or manifest destiny. It represents a new and unsought reality for these young men and their people, a reality that they will have to deal with whether they travel the world or remain at home. And that fire-blasted landscape is what Xavier must ultimately negotiate when he returns to his homeland, devastated by his experience of war. It is the place in which he must somehow find healing, despite the fact that it too has been terribly changed.

Today, Canadians often think of themselves as peacekeepers, as people of justice and civility and freedom and generosity. That was why I assumed that the prisoners of Birkenau must have named the building "Canada"— because I thought they must see my nation in the way I had been taught to see it. But of course that version of Canada is simply a product of those cover-up stories that almost always come after violence. They are the stories we prefer to tell ourselves, because they sound so much more attractive than the older narratives that attended the rise of colonialism. The Canadian government has apologized, repeatedly and publicly, for the excesses of the colonial record, as if we can put it behind ourselves so easily. Our leaders have even sponsored the creation of a Canadian Museum for Human Rights, which its promoters describe as "a powerful symbol of Canada's unwavering commitment to recognizing, promoting and celebrating human rights" (CMHR website). While the museum may yet go on to do important and nuanced work in the field, it must be said that that this characterization of Canada bespeaks either a breathtaking naiveté or a willful ignorance. Anyone familiar with our colonial history knows that Canada has "wavered" a great deal on questions of human rights over the generations—and it still wavers, much more often than most Canadians like to admit.

In a time of bland apologies and celebratory smugness about Canada's record of human rights, I believe it is all the more important for our writers and artists to critically investigate the national consciousness, to point out what is happening in such a way that it might have a real impact on people's lives now. As part of that role, I think all of us need to learn to listen as closely as we can to the stories that are already out there, the stories being told by the people in our communities. We need to "go to Canada" again and again, rather than taking for granted our ideas of what the place is. And going to Canada is something like Fred Wah's "Waiting for Saskatchewan": you never quite arrive, even when you are already there. This is because it is too big and contradictory, and because it's constantly shifting, evolving, and also because it is a symbol that has been constructed in such a manner that we are conditioned to look away from certain aspects of it, and to focus instead on the wholesome, the self-congratulatory, sides of it.

About two years after going to the "Canada" of Birkenau, I made a journey to another Canada that I knew very little about. This time it was within the nation's borders, and in fact it was very close to my home, Meadow Lake, in northern Saskatchewan. I went with a camera crew to make a film called *Land of Oil and Water*, a documentary about Aboriginal communities in the oil sands region, which begins only a few kilometers from Meadow Lake and stretches far into northern Alberta. The oil companies were expanding their operations into Saskatchewan, and for the first time my homeland was going to be affected. I wanted to find out what the people there thought about this new development, and I wanted to learn what the Native communities in northeastern Alberta have already experienced in their decades of living near the oil sands operations.

I had never visited the Alberta communities, even though they are not very far from my home. I had heard about the magnitude of the development there, and the boomtown economy of Fort McMurray, and the growing importance of the oil sands in Canada's relationship to the rest of the world, but I'd never had a reason to see it for myself. Now when I finally witnessed it and spoke to the people there, I kept asking myself one question: how could I not have known about this before?

What I saw was a landscape very much like the one of my childhood—the aspen forests, the wetlands, the lakes and rivers—except now it was completely obliterated, sometimes for as far as I could see. I saw pits the size of townships, and vast tailings ponds with oil slicks floating on them, and smokestacks trailing kilometer-long plumes. I smelled the bitter petroleum stench of the refineries even before they came into view. I saw enormous machines cutting away the forests, draining the swamps, chewing up the earth itself. And in the middle of all this apocalyptic activity, I saw the reserve community of Fort Mackay, which some of the locals described as the wealthiest First Nation in Canada. That claim was certainly believable, given the rows of beautiful new houses there, and the full employment, and the band's considerable investments in local oil sands businesses. But many of the people I interviewed were very concerned about the future of the community. They worried about the air pollution that seemed to come at them from all directions, and about the toxins in their water, and about the effects of all this pollution on the wildlife and plants of the area. They worried about cancer, mercury poisoning, ammonia. They expressed dismay that the companies were denying them the ability to access their own land for hunting, trapping, and berry picking. Almost all of them voiced alarm that the Athabasca River, the source of their livelihood for generations, had fallen dramatically in recent years, quite possibly because of the huge volumes of water the oil sands companies extract from the river.

Further north on the Athabasca, downstream from the oil sands plants, I visited the community of Fort Chipewyan, which at first appears to be simply a quiet town on a gorgeous and pristine lakeshore. But devastation is hiding beneath the appearances. For years the people in Fort Chipewyan have been trying to find an explanation for what they see as an abnormally high rate of cancer in the community. No one knows for certain what is causing these terrible health problems, but many point toward the toxins released into the Athabasca River by oil sands operations. One community member, Lionel Lepine, told me about his friend Steve who had recently died of cancer. Lionel worried that he and his family and everyone else in Fort Chipewyan might be at risk too, from something that they couldn't see or measure, something that the oil companies and the government seemed unwilling to investigate thoroughly. Lionel also commented on the broader impact of oil sands development in the area when he mentioned the people who chose to work for the oil companies. "They don't realize what's happening to the land," he said. "They don't realize that they're assisting with the destruction of our way of life."

There is no substitute for seeing the situation first hand, or at least viewing film footage of it like we reproduced in *Land of Oil and Water*, but I hope this brief description of the oil sands region helps to explain why it reminded me of that obliterated warehouse in Birkenau. It is a place of almost unbelievable wealth, but at the same time a place of ashes, a place in which the land itself is literally being stolen from the people who have depended upon it for generations—stolen and processed and eventually sold, to be burned up in the engines that power our daily commutes as well as our national economy. In the Canadian national imaginary, the profits of the oil sands, and the convenience that our domestic oil supply affords us, and the strategic clout that this oil gives us in the rest of the world, can very often cover up the devastation, or at least offer an excuse for it. The money makes it so easy to overlook the horrific effects, especially when all of this is happening in a remote place, to people who don't have the ear of the media.

I believe there are many more "Canadas" out there: suppressed histories, silenced people, uncomfortable juxtapositions. Once you've discovered one, the others start to become more visible. We can find them through reading, or by listening carefully to the stories we hear around us, or simply by looking again at what we think we already understand.

Go ahead. I bet the next Canada is closer than you think.

—*2010*

Gilbert James Fredette

Cree/Innu (Norway House) 1966–

Gilbert James Fredette, an emerging writer, is a proud Cree/Innu Indian living in Norway House, Manitoba. He is the father of six children. Fredette has a B.A., and is interested in traditional lifeways. He also likes to challenge the political obstacles and stereotypes that stand in the way of Aboriginal people. He is currently a Masters of Arts student at the University of Manitoba.

Fredette's "Visions or Screams" describes the anxiety of newness and the fears one has when entering the unknown.

Importantly, these fears also illustrate the importance of familiarity and home through tradition and language. His poem "A Lifetime Ago" is a rhythmic journey from past to future through song, and the assistance one gives a friend on his path from this life to the next.

Visions or Screams

the first Indian what was he thinking
when he arrived in this new wonderland known as the City
did he wander aimlessly like the vanishing buffalo
was he mesmerized by the lights like a moth to the flame

at last! another Indian, he says and he runs to meet him
what he sees is an Asian man who turns him away
confused and alone with nowhere to turn
he wanders to a place where few dare to go

Main Street is where he shall drink and where he shall die
a lost vision swallowed whole by the City
under the northern lights he will dance no more
the first Indian dead beneath the bright neon lights

Winnipeg an Indian word
Winnipeg where no Indian shall be heard

—2008/09

A Lifetime Ago

there was an old Indian poet that I used to know
he would tell me about the wind and how the grass would grow
he would tell me about the clouds and the rain
and with a tear in his eye tell me about the pain
from all those years ago and this is what he said

the sun will always shine, the moon will always glow
some people will come and some people will go
but an Indian's life is one you have to know
this used to be a free land where we would roam
we would grow our crops and hunt buffalo

and we would play our drums… a lifetime ago

an old Indian poet now lives on the street
searches for change for a meal to eat
why do some Elders have to live this way
finish their lives on the streets of the PEG
you know this isn't right, things will have to change

it was a cold and lonely November day
when an old Indian poet passed away
now he's going home to the land we used to roam
he will grow his crops and hunt buffalo
the sun will always shine, the moon will always glow

today I play the drum for his journey home

I sing heyya, hey ya, hey ya, hey ya, hey ya, ho
hey ya, hey ya, hey ya, hey ya, you're finally home

he would tell me about the clouds and the rain
and with a tear in his eye tell me about the pain

and we would play our drums... a lifetime ago.

—2010

Randy Lundy

Cree (Barren Lands First Nation) 1967–

Born in Thompson, Manitoba, Randy Lundy began to write poetry as a teenager in Hudson Bay, Saskatchewan, where his family moved when he was nine years old. Lundy completed an Honours B.A. and M.A. in Native Canadian literature at the University of Saskatchewan. He also studied religion and philosophy. He has worked as a graduate teaching fellow at the University of Saskatchewan and as a professor in the English Department at the First Nations University of Canada. His books of poetry include *Under the Night Sun* (1999) and *The Gift of the Hawk* (2004). He is working on a third book of poems, tentatively titled *A Backyarder's Guide Toward a Vocabulary of Faith.*

Randy Lundy's poetry explores the interconnectedness of humans with the natural world and reminds us of myriad ways all forces of creation form a dynamic system of beauty, pain, and power. The passion of love and the memory of some of Native people's worst tragedies (such as Sand Creek and Wounded Knee) coalesce in Lundy's work. His poetry expresses a yearning to listen to and communicate with everything that surrounds us and reminds us of the crucial importance in ancestral memory, our bodies, and teachings of the land.

deer-sleep

this place does not require your presence
and beneath the staring stars
you have discovered
your offerings are meaningless

you are left with nothing
but silence

you have forgotten why you came here
you were looking for something

the wind wanders among willows
muttering forgotten stories
it has been everywhere
and cannot
keep quiet
you must learn
to listen, to be alone

only then
will you bed down with the deer
to sleep in the long, deep grass
wrapped in the warmth
of slender bodies
of slow-moving breath

each time you awaken with the dawn
stars and moon fading memories
the deer will be gone

all day you carry with you
the sound of their sleeping

the howling song of coyotes
the common dream
that binds you

—1999

ghost dance

I

at sand creek, at wounded knee creek
the valleys are filled with bones

after the first green shoots of spring
when the wind stirs
the leaves and knee-high grasses
they will come, a gathering of many tongues

to hear of new soil coming like a tide
to greet the return of the buffalo
the herds of wild horses
the sound of thunder on the plains

they will dance and chant
from dawn until dawn
they will dance and chant
until they feel the earth move

II
the wind whistles a dry song
the sun touches the valley floor
the hills breathe a dusty breath

there is a shaking and rattling
tired bones coming together
each scattered part finding a place

brittle fingers gather
flesh of roots and moss
eyes of rounded stone

the laughter of the coming storm
shakes the world with its voice

—*1999*

ritual

this is a ritual, this uncovering of flesh
we shed cloths like tired skins
frost presses its face against the window

what are the words we should recite
the words this ceremony demands?

our tongues stir
deep roots reaching into earth
with no memory of sky

our hands move
new light on a landscape
coaxing a sound from silence

three thousand miles away
birds are beginning to flock

—*1999*

the trees are spirits

the trees are spirits
answering the call

wind and moonrise
conjuring from absence

these slow-swaying figures

and you too hear the call
come wandering

your belly-roots embracing
stone-heavy words

your throat
a slender flute carved from bone

clogged with river silt
and sleeping seeds

you came to this place
to unburden yourself

to raise your voice
into silence

you find only other voices
speaking words you have never heard

as you listen you forget
your half-remembered stories

how to begin and where to end

your heart a small drum beating
a bird's dreams of flight

the moon, your mind
gliding through trees   singing

—*1999*

Ian Ross

Anishinaabe (McCreary) 1968–

Ian Ross was born in McCreary, Manitoba. He studied at the University of Manitoba, where he earned a B.A. in film and theatre. He has delivered newspapers, pumped gas, sold men's clothes at The Bay, and worked in various capacities at different arts organizations. Mostly, though, he has been a writer. An award-winning playwright, Ian works mainly in dramatic genres such as theatre, film, television, and radio. His thought-provoking and hilarious "Joe from Winnipeg" commentaries penned for CBC radio and television have been published as *The Book of Joe* (2000) and *Joe From Winnipeg* (2004). His first play, *FareWel* (1997), was hugely successful and won the Governor General's Award in 1997. He received further acclaim for his subsequent plays, *The Gap* (2001) and *Asamikawin* (2003).

The texts reproduced here are from Ross's "Joe from Winnipeg" series, and they capture his sense of the absurd in Manitoba life. By writing in a dialect form of English, Ross draws his readers (and listeners) into the stories at the same time as he is playing with stereotypes of Aboriginal people and challenging us to think beyond superficial impressions. The character of "Joe" is an everyman philosopher who breaks down boundaries between people by asking the kinds of questions that most people overlook.

NSF

Hey you guys, this is me, Joe from Winnipeg. Today I'm gonna be talkin' to you 'bout the NSF. Or maybe I should jus say NSF, if I say "the" NSF den you might tink I'm talkin' 'bout an organization der. An what's up with dat anyways eh? How come we got to make the names of stuff into letters. Like da NHL. Or da AMC. CFS. IBM. CBC. Does dat mean we're lazy? Or is it kine of like a nickname? I doan know. Maybe it's to make it soun more intimidatin' eh. I know if I'm dealin' with a place known by its letters it's either really big or else it can do scary tings. Like the CSIS eh? I doan even know what dat las one stans for it's so secret. So anyways, NSF. I got a bill back 'cause the cheque I wrote had the NSF eh. Not sufficient funs. I was waitin' for like a refun from the goverment. Well actually it was my frien's cheque, but I always like to be da one who has da good news an han dem der cheque like dey jus won da lottery eh. I tink dat would be a good job too. Hanin' out the lottery cheques to da winners. 'Cept I tink you'd get jealous after a while. Pretty soon you'd be, "How come dey get to be millionaires an not me?" Boy, dat's crazy. Anyways, instead of my frien's cheque. I get a bill. An the bill tells me my cheque was no good. Da NSF eh. So dey was informin' me dat dey wanted der money an dat dey were chargin' me for da bad cheque. An da bank was chargin' me for da bad cheque too eh. Boy, I jus felt like a criminal. Mad at myself. An mad at dese guys for chargin' me for my mistake. I didn't write dat cheque bad on purpose eh. Boy did I feel stupid eh. An embarass. An how come dey get to charge us for da mistake? What's up with dat? How come we doan get to charge dem money if dey make a mistake or fail to provide a service eh? We could jus walk in da bank der an say it's the kine of bank where der open but der's no teller service, an we could say, "Hey. You guys owe me 20 bucks. Plus I wan dis cheque cashed." Oh well, I guess it serves me right for not bein' more fiscally responsible eh. I should use our governments as da example. Dey never write bad cheques. So after I tole my frien da bad news dat der cheque didn't arrive, she said, "Oh dat's OK. You know what happened to me?" "No," I says. An den she tells me the story of how a 'Nishnawbe on da street asked her for money 'cause he was NSF in his life eh. An she gave him some. An he said, "Tank you." An she said, "Meegwetch." An I guess dis guy never heard somebody who wasn't 'Nishnawbe talkin' his own language to him before eh. An she said his eyes lit up an she even taught he was gonna give her back da money he was so happy. Dat's a funny ting what can happen when we say what we mean in a way we unerstan eh? Maybe we call tings by letters like say, CFS or NSF, 'cause we're not too happy with what dey are eh? Sometimes I wish da places dat sent us money was more like our relatives. Instead of NSF dey could put a note in der, "Hey. Where's our money? An don't sen cheques. Cash or money order only." But den if dey was more like my famly I guess I'd take my time to pay dem back more. I keep getting' surprised dat whenever I get in a bad mood 'cause of money or not havin' sufficien funs I get taught da same lesson over an over again. It's not dat importan eh. Money comes an goes, but stuff like the 'Nishnawbe guy on the street, you never forget dat. I can't re-member none of all da money I've had. I'm Joe from Winnipeg. Meegwetch.

—1999

Moose on the Road

Hey you guys, this is me, Joe from Winnipeg. Today I'm gonna be talkin' to you 'bout moose on the road. I had dat dessert all prepared too, eh, an den I went an dropped it. "Oh no" I says out loud, "my mousse is on da road." Jus kiddin'. Das not da kine of mooses I mean. You know one ting I love about talkin' words out loud? You doan have to be too literate eh? Moose souns the same if it's da dessert or da animal or even da guy in da Archie comics. Moose. I tink da politicians like dat too, eh? 'Cause den if dey say someting like, say, "I need more time," an we say we waited long enough already, den dey could say, I'm talkin' bout the spices der. Or no could become k-no with a double o on der. Jus never stops eh. Even when day say "I doan lie," dey could mean dey sleep standin' up. It's a good ting promise means da same no matter how you say it. Anyways, boy I missed you guys. I fell asleep on the bus an ended up in Thompson eh. I woked up an I looked aroun an I said, "Where is dis beautiful place?" An den I saw some of dose Thompson turkeys eh. Big black birds. I'm not sure why dey're called turkeys, maybe 'cause dat's da Tanksgivin' bird up der. I doan know. So anyways, I figured I came dis far why doan I go a little bit further. So I did. An den I ended up in

Gillam. More beauty up der, too. I even foun a shirt der with my name on it. So I put dat on. An den I went even further up north to Tadoule Lake. Wow. Das all I could say eh. 'Cause it was beautiful an dey still have der language an culture. I was jus jealous. An den I was all ready to go on further adventures up in da north eh, even past da North of 60, but I figured I should come home. So I did. I ended up drivin' for my new frien Conway. I got to drive an he got to sleep. What's up with dat eh? How come da passengers always get to sleep, not the driver? Anyways, I was tinkin': Man, dis place we live in is BIG. Really big. An den I saw someone walkin' on da road. Way far away. An I got all excited 'cause I was gonna pick dem up. Even if dey weren't hitchhikin' I was gonna make dem a hitchhiker. An dat road from Gillam is hilly eh. Imagine dat. Hills in Manitoba. I get so prairie-centric sometimes eh. Anyways, as I get closer I see dat dis person on da road turns sideways an has four legs. In my head I was sayin, "Is dat what I tink it is?" An my passenger said it out loud eh. Dat kine of scared me for a minute 'cause dat's all he said on da whole trip. An sure enough. Der it was. A moose on da road. I wasn't even disappointed dat I wouldn't have a hitchhiker now eh. I was jus happy to see dat ole moose. So I drove all da way home. All fourteen hours eh. Dat ole Conway jus kep sleepin'. I kep havin' to stick my head out da window to stay awake for a bit. You guys doan do dat eh. Drive sleepy. I'm not doin' dat never again. Anyways, I get home an I go for a hamburger. I hate to say it but dat moose made me hungry eh. I tank when some peoples who aren't 'Nishnawbe see a moose dey tink, "Ahhh Canada. I love dis country." Me. I look at mooses an tink, "Mmmm, supper." So anyways, I order dis burger an talk to my friens John an Roger an dis guy's starin' at me. An he says, "Are you Joe?" "Yeah" I says to him. An I was scared eh? 'Cause dis guy was big. An he had a beard. An I asked him how he knew my name an he said. "It's on yer shirt." "Oh," I says to him. An den he shakes my han an says, "I'm Trior." Boy I got scared again eh. Den I see dat Trior's like the moose. He's not what I'm tinkin' he is. An den we talk an he even says "Meegwetch" to me. An boy, dat warmed my heart. Someone who ain't 'Nishnawbe usin' dat language. So doan be like me an tink a person's a moose when really dey're somebody nice. I'm Joe from Winnipeg. Meegwetch.

—1999

A Little Dog Wearin' Nail Polish

Hey you guys, this is me, Joe from Winnipeg. Today I'm gonna be talkin' to you 'bout a little dog wearin' nail polish. Get to that in a sec. You guys hear dey're talkin' 'bout floods again. All over da place, in the north an south an in our basements. Boy, I'm glad I doan live in a basement no more. It was bad enough tryin' to get some sleep with people thumpin' aroun on top of you without havin' to worry 'bout flooding. An I know lots of you is worryin' right now. I'm sure der's better tings to do dan dat, but I know if I was in yer place I'd do da same ting. So, little dog wearin' nail polish. What's up with that? I was usin' a payphone the other day eh. An I was listenin' to the computer or whoever dat was. You know how dey trick us into tinkin' we're gonna get to talk to somebody. I really miss talkin' to people when I use da phone now. Anyways, da phone's sayin' to me, "If you know da name of da person you wish to speak to, please enter dat. Followed by number sign." So then I start spellin' with numbers I guess TOM what's his name, but it says "No such person." Oh, I was getting' so frustrated eh. 'Cause I couldn't remember Tom's last name. So I started guessin'. I was typin' all kines of numbers an names in there, sometimes even talkin' to people, some of dem even sayin' "How'd you get dis number? You're not s'posed to be actually talkin' to anybody." So jus as I'm about to give up dis woman stands beside me an ties up her little dog to the payphone beside me eh. An she talks to him an says "Now you be good an don't go nowhere." I like how people assume dogs speak English eh. Maybe dey speak German. Or Chinese, who knows. Anyways, da dog looks real scared, so I figure I better not touch it. An I look at its little nails eh, well actually they were kine of big for a little dog. An I got bad flashback eh, of little dogs nails on linoleum. You know how that souns? Tsk tsk tsk tsk tsk. Ho. Anyways, I look closer an I see dis little dog's got nail polish on. Kine of bubblegum coloured. What's up with that? I'm tinkin'. An right away I start judgin' dat little dog, tinkin' dat's not right. You shouldn't be wearin' dat. Other dogs won't be carin' 'bout what shade nail polish you got. Or even dat you got nail polish. Boy, I was so shocked I even forgot to hang up the payphone. I just walked away. Den I was tinkin', why is dis botherin' me. Dat little dog wasn't doin' nothin' to me. It didn't even know itself dat somebody put nail polish on it. Or snipped its tail. Or put dose funny tings on its ears to make dem stick up straight. Here I was judgin' it just 'cause I wouldn't do dat. Or it offended my idea of how dog's is s'posed to be treated. Den I get a little scared and sad eh. 'Cause I realize dat I'm not alone. Dere's lots of people who judge each others. An say you shouldn't be doin' dat. Or dis. Or you're livin' wrong. Or I'm livin' right. I tink maybe dat little dog with the nail polish's doin' a good ting eh. Mindin' his own business. Livin' for nice walks. An crunchy food, occasional steak bone in der. Jus bein' hisself. Livin' an let live eh. I'm Joe from Winnipeg. Meegwetch.

—*1999*

Nichola Tookoome Batzel

Inuk (Haningajumiut and Tikerarjuaq/Whale Cove) 1970–

Nichola Tookoome Batzel is an Inuk educator in Winnipeg and an advocate for Inuit issues throughout the province. She is a board member for the Manitoba Urban Inuit Association. Founded in 2008, the organization promotes individual and community quality of life for Inuit living in Manitoba by assisting with issues related to health, environment, and economy. She identifies with her spirit name of Wabishki Mahkwa Equay, given to her by an Anishinaabe elder, and her Inuit name of Tookoome. Along with her English name, these play a role in how she views her role as an educator, a mother, a family member, and member of Manitoba's community. She is also a writer whose work has appeared in *Strength and Struggle: Perspectives From* *First Nations, Inuit, and Métis Peoples in Canada* (2011).

In the following piece, Batzel explains the presence of one of Manitoba's often neglected Aboriginal communities—the Inuit. As she explains, Inuit stories belong here too and make critical contributions to Indigenous intellectual expression in Manitoba. Her narrative also illustrates how weaving one's personal story with that of a community is an innately personal and brave act that both illuminates the complexity of culture and reflects individual experience. As Batzel's rich stories remind us, the beauty of family, land, and community live in the stories we tell and in the world around us; they are found by listening, learning, and remembering, or simply by looking at the stars in the sky.

Our Stories Belong Here Too: Manitoba Inuk

I have a story I would like to share with you. We all know Inuit live in the Arctic. But Manitoba is our home too. As an ever changing and globalizing society, we are constantly reminded that boundaries and people change—and what we remember often changes too. Many forget that Inuit do have traditional territory in Manitoba; lands where (I am told) they can continue to hunt without a license today.

Inuit continue to have a strong relationship with Manitoba, even as their "official" land claim boundaries lie outside the province's boundaries. Many Inuit, for example, were born and went to school in Churchill, others come to Manitoba for medical reasons, post-secondary school, or simply to shop for items at a fraction of the cost found in the North. Inuit not only call Manitoba home, but contribute millions of dollars to our shared economy every year.

Why do I mention this? Because Inuit are a part of this place. Our stories belong here too.

I am an Inuk who grew up here in Manitoba. I was born in 1970 in Churchill and my ancestors are from North West of Baker Lake. My birth mother and grandparents lived and survived on the land for many years; if they were not able to endure and adapt to the rapid changes and challenges they faced, I would not be here today.

My birth mother went to residential school and, like many, endured hardship, an assimilative curriculum, and isolation from her identity. Later, in Churchill, my mother met my birth father in the late 1960s and I was conceived. For many reasons, I was given up for adoption—but the many struggles my birth parents endured continue to reside in me.

I commend my birth family for living through adversity and so many rapid changes. I am happy they kept smiling and laughing through tough times. It is a wonderful way to live. It is also a good reminder to me as I rush through life to slow down and appreciate what I have and all the life and opportunities around me.

It is true that I walk and talk very much like a *Qalunaaq*,[39] and I don't have a problem with that. Still, even as I grew up I always knew that my identity was important to me, and this is due in large part to my adopted parents, who encouraged me to search for it and express myself openly. This allowed me the freedom to search for my birth family, who I eventually found. I was taught by all the members of my family to believe in myself and to make this world a better place for us and for our children. Today, I live a rich life. I am very lucky.

I am very attached to Manitoba and my family and friends here, but I carry a deep connection and yearning to visit the North and the land there. Sometimes, I wonder if I am missing out on many great opportunities there and wish I could just drive to there on weekends. That is not the case, though, so I have connected with other Inuit in this land. Now, I advocate for Inuit who come to the South in search of opportunities here.

Canada is becoming more and more a balanced place, where individuals are listening to one another and moving in the right direction. Whether you are from the North, South, East, or West there is value in considering where we have come from as much as where we are going. As our ancestors did, we must make decisions thinking about the place we stand and the place we imagine, and let this guide how we act towards one another and our children. It is important to connect to each other and to our land and ask: How do we support and acknowledge each other? How do we balance our relationships? How do we hear the voices in our home? There are many beautiful stories around us. Do you hear them? Take a moment to breathe, sit, and listen. You will be amazed by what you see and hear.

Stories of Our Past—Honouring Our Elders, Our Strength, and Will to Survive

If you live a life like mine, you grew up in a society where duties are specialized, stores are open seven days a week, and telephones and internet have revolutionized how we communicate. Of course, this has also happened in the North.

---

39 Non-Inuk

Fifty years ago, though, life looked very different there. Life was very traditional. Many people lived on the land. Roles of men and women were well defined and every member contributed to the livelihood of the camp. Society was based on local laws and values. Your life was not separate from the land or the community; you were a part of both in every way.

The land of the north varies from region to region, but is full of mountains, valleys, lakes, oceans, ice, snow, and air as crisp and fresh as a newly picked apple. It is a land where cold not only keeps items fresh and healthy but sustains us spiritually and culturally. It is a place where water is pure and clean, and it used to have so many fish that the water looked white instead of blue.

Even as climate change deeply impacts the Arctic, these lands are still where Inuit come from. My people's struggles and continued presence here reminds us why we must value the beauty of life as we forge through changes in our cultures and geographies—which are sometimes so swift that our attention becomes diverted.

I will share a story that I hope reflects my experience as an Inuk. Amongst my people we have stories of connection and of beauty, stories of struggle and starvation. There are rhymes that challenge the nature of disagreements and teach about reciprocity and relationships. All have a purpose and ring of a truth for all human beings as we walk a life full of beauty, challenges, hurt, and humour.

As I share this story I invite you to imagine a land of ice and snow; a land undisturbed by industry and global economies. A time when you are a part of a tundra filled with Cambrian rock, moss, caribou, whales, berries, seals, so much more. I will do my best to speak of the land, sea, and sky in a respectful manner. Our ancestors remember and value the connection to the land, sea, and sky and acknowledge our role and relationship with life and all its beauty. Stories help connect us and remind us of our relationship to all life so that we may strive for harmony. This story tells of our connection to the stars and expansive universe we are all a part of. It can be considered rude to speak of these things, but as we attempt to bridge understandings, I hope you understand that I only wish for us to remember and share stories so that all live a life of beauty and harmony.

Stories of the Night Sky—The Great White Bear

It is November. The rhythm of the furnace works to keep out the chill as I think of the sun—and how I miss it. The evenings are darker earlier now. As the school bell rings, the sun is setting, reflecting off the ice that has formed on the lakes. Ice has even began to form on the sea, even earlier than previous years.

The house we live in is adequate enough for us. I do not even hear the wind whistling through the stilts. It is different from homes in the south. Here, for example, there is no basement.

As I work in the kitchen, cooking caribou stew and bannock, a youthful sound of boots being thrown off and a falling school bag enter my peaceful space.

"My son, how was school today?"

"Fine, Mom," Adjuk replies. "We learned of a great Greek warrior and hunter named Orion. Did you know there are stars named after him? I am going to be an astronomer one day!"

"Haha. You are very clever Adjuk. I am glad you are learning in school and that you are connecting with the stars. It makes sense; your name, after all, comes from the stars. I do not know much about Orion, but I have heard a story about the same stars. In fact, it is a story of hunters too. Slow down for a minute and I will share this story with you."

"Aw, Mom, I want to go skating on the lake with my friends, and they'll be here any minute. Can you hurry? They're even bringing their new snowmobile."

"Yes, my boy. You will get to skate with your friends. Be careful, though; it is the time of year for polar bears to walk through towns to get to the sea ice. They are quiet and very strong; you do not want to cross to close too their path."

"I know, Mom. We can take Kelsey with us—bears don't like dogs. Uncle Darryl will be with us too, and he'll have his rifle. You worry too much."

"That is my job, son. You should also wear your seal skin mitts today. The wind is chilly and cold. Your other mitts will not be warm enough. Speaking of mitts and polar bears, this story has both."

"I thought you said it was about a great hunter."

"Haha, yes, that too. Sit, my boy, eat some bannock and stew. I will tell you a very old story. It begins with a Grandfather sharing a hunting story with his grandson."

A young boy sat in his igloo one cold day, looking for his toy arrow. Finding his grandfather's old worn out seal skin mitt, he held it up. "What an old ratty mitt, Ataatatsiaq," the young man said. "Why do you keep such an old thing around? You have had several new pairs made for you since then."

"Aw," answered his grandfather (I liked that the old man was slow and melodic as young people often are not). He knew it was time to tell the boy a story. Rising up, he gestured to the young man to come outside.

Once they had dressed and went outside into the evening air, the old man said, "Be careful with that mitt, it is very dear to me. Look closely at those stars. Do you see those three stars in a row? They are hunters whose dogs are with them. In front is a great old white bear. Look closely. Do you see them?"

The boy nodded. The two of them stood there for a long time, looking. Only their breath interrupted the sky.

"Let me tell you the story about how they got there," the old man began, breaking the silence. "I was young when I wore that mitt you hold in your hands. I was maybe only a few seasons older than you are right now. One morning, I was with my three brothers. We were experienced hunters and the land had been very good to us. The sun was still new in the sky when we started out for our hunt that day. We were well fed and ready to go; our skins were well taken care of, and our clothing would keep us very warm. It was a good day to hunt. As we left, there was not a lot of wind, and it was too cold for mosquitoes to bother us. The four of us headed out to catch caribou. Our emotions were high and joyous with the beauty the day offered.

"We had walked for a while and did not spot any caribou on the land. After a while though, we suddenly saw an old great white bear on the horizon. He was fat and his fur was shiny. He was healthy and strong but did not run like most older bears do. He just stood, looking at us. Most older bears know to stay away from hunters. This one watched us, with no fear in his eyes.

"We thought we could catch that bear so we headed in its direction, with our dogs just ahead of us. After a long time, we were not getting closer to it. Something was different about this bear and this chase. The land and the time felt different; almost as if it did not exist. It was like the land was moving while we are not moving at all. Do you understand, my Grandson? That is not how it should feel when you are on the land."

The old man looked up at the stars and down at the boy again.

"I slowed my pace as I became more suspicious of the bear and this situation. I tried to tell the others to stop. I looked up. The sun had moved and we were getting nowhere. I called again. No one listened. They were not going to give up chasing that bear.

"Just then I noticed: I had dropped my mitt. I yelled at my brothers, telling them I was going back for my mitt. They laughed and called to me: *We are still going.* I can still hear their voices, laughing.

"I didn't let their mocking bother me. I felt this situation was suspicious anyways; how could we catch a bear that we couldn't catch? I went back and found my mitt. Then, I turned back, and they were gone. I found footsteps in the snow, following them. Soon, they faded and disappeared. I was stunned. I looked in all directions but could not see anyone, not an animal or person in sight. It was getting dark and colder. The sun disappeared. I had no choice but to head back to camp.

"I immediately went to our Angatkuq[40] to let him know what happened. I asked him if he knew what happened. Our Angatkuq is a very kind and wise man. He is not only a great hunter but helps to find answers when we can't. He helps to heal the sick and the lost.

---

40 Shaman

"After a long time, thinking and praying, Angatkuq chuckled and told me: 'I know where your brothers and that old wise bear you spoke of went. Do you see those three stars in a row in the sky? They were not there before. Look closely. You will see the dogs just ahead of them, and even farther ahead you will see that great white bear. They will chase that bear for all time.'"

"And so, my boy," I concluded, "that is how those stars came to be."

Adjuk smiled. "I didn't know that, Mom."

"Now you do. That old man would not have been there to tell his grandson about the story if he didn't pay attention to what he was taught and trust his instincts. That is your story now; you can share with your teacher who told you about the Orion belt. You can then compare stories and learn from all of the great hunters in the sky."

"Okay. Thanks, Mom," Adjuk said, jumping off the couch. "I hear the snowmobile coming. I have to go."

"I love you, my boy. Don't forget to take Kelsey, and keep your eyes and ears open!"

"Love you too, Mom. Don't worry. We'll be fine, and I'll take the dog."

—*2011*

Columpa C. Bobb

Coast Salish (Tsleil Waututh and Nlaka'pamux First Nations) 1971–

Columpa C. Bobb is a photographer, actor, playwright, poet, and teacher who has been performing and writing plays, and teaching for the past 24 years. She has written over a dozen plays and has been nominated for Dora Mavor Moore awards both as a performer and playwright. As well, she has been nominated for Jesse Richardson Theatre awards, and won one for her portrayal of Rita Joe in The Firehall Arts Centre production of *The Ecstasy of Rita Joe*. She has been a cultural instructor and faculty member of the Centre for Indigenous Theatre in Toronto and currently is the artistic director and instructor at the Aboriginal Arts Training & Mentorship Program at the Manitoba Theatre for Young People in Winnipeg. The program serves over 600 students per year and is free of charge to all participants.

The following monologue is from a multimedia show written, directed, and produced by Bobb, entitled *Will Work 4 Home*, originally produced in 2009 at The Manitoba Theatre for Young People. For the project, Bobb worked with The R.a.Y. Youth Story Collective for two years, gathering stories of the streets and of transitioning back into mainstream society. The character of Maria represents travellers on the streets—family-oriented people in cities who stick together and take care of one another. The excerpt illustrates the beauty of land and how language ties one to place; it reminds us that we are never alone.

From *Will Work 4 Home*

As Maria speaks, a photo montage of the Canadian *landscape appears on the screen; statistics of mental illness in the homeless youth community roll across the images.*

MARIA: You ever wonder what real earth smelled like? Not that caked up dried out ugly city dirt, but real moist sweet earth, the stuff that grows wheat and corn and strawberries. Sounds romantic eh. That's cuz it is. There's no love sweeter than the love you can share with the land. If you can fall in love with the country you live in, you'll never be lonely.

The salt sea rush of waves of the west coast coated in cedar and a green so deep you can almost feel midnight inside it. The jagged angled attitude of the Rockies playing a symphony of life bouncing off Ancient Mountain peaks right into your heart, your mind. The soft hum of wind on wheat tickling your ears; The slow gold whisper of that shy and luscious grain hushing up towards the big blue of the soundless sky; The unforgiving thunderous roar of sea against stone of the east coast waking you from the dead still left inside you from another lifetime ago;

The country we live in is home, is family.

'Specially when it's clear that no one else wants you. When you're all alone stabbing your feet into the cold concrete with thousands of bodies pin-balling you away from them, there's still beauty out there for you; A warmth and love that no human can take from you. The earth itself can bring you closer to your humanity than any person ever could.

You can feel small on the earth and still feel like you matter.

(Landscape montage ends and we are left with an image of the city streets).

You can't feel that way on your own on some dirty city street.

Maria exits.

—2009

Nahanni Fontaine

Anishinaabe (Sagkeeng First Nation) 1971–

Nahanni Fontaine is an activist and writer from the Sagkeeng Anishinaabe First Nation in southern Manitoba. She holds degrees in environmental studies & international development and Native studies, women studies, and critical theory. Her Ph.D. thesis is on narratives of female gang members and issues of race, class, and gender. She is employed as special advisor on Aboriginal women's issues for the Aboriginal Issues Committee of Cabinet of Manitoba, with particular focus on missing and murdered Aboriginal women and girls. Fontaine has been nominated for, and won, numerous scholarships and fellowships for academic excellence and research in Aboriginal issues. She has served the Aboriginal community on a number of boards and committees, including the Winnipeg Police Advisory Board, Canadian Race Relations Foundation, and the United Nations Working Group on the Draft Declaration on the Rights of Indigenous Peoples.

The text reproduced here is a version of a February 2011 speech Fontaine gave in Ottawa to the Status of Women Standing Committee on violence against Aboriginal women. It addresses one of the most important and alarming issues in Aboriginal communities today:

murdered and missing Aboriginal women. As Fontaine describes, there are over 600 cases of missing or murdered Aboriginal women in Canada. Most of these disappearances have happened since 2000. An overwhelming number of these missing women are under the age of 30 and are victims of sexual violence, preyed upon systematically by violent offenders who are often not prosecuted or pursued for their crimes. In her speech, Fontaine calls for justice and imagines a world where our sisters, mothers, aunties, and grandmothers are cherished.

Our Cherished Sisters, Mothers, Aunties, and Grandmothers: Violence Against Aboriginal Women

In attempting better to be conscious of, appreciate, and address violence, in all its forms, in respect of Aboriginal women and girls, one must invariably and rightly begin at the advent of colonialism in Canada—that is to say, to start at the root causes of said violence.

I won't spend time today outlining the colonial policies—residential schools, the Indian Act, etc.—that have marginalized Aboriginal women and girls. Rather, I would simply state that it is imperative that we remember how this collective history has shaped current contexts and I would encourage us to let it guide us in our work.

I would add that, as we operate from within this Residential School post-apology era and its expressed desire to move forward together in a journey of collective healing and reclamation, we now live in a space where we can discuss openly and respectfully a colonial legacy that has deeply impacted Aboriginal women and girls in violent and abusive ways.

Aboriginal women and girls experience violence from within a myriad of manifestations, including racism, sexism, classism, sexual identity discrimination, social and economic marginalization, lack of adequate and safe housing, lack of access to education, lack of access to justice and social services (i.e., lawyers, specialized shelters, and various social service programs)… to name but a few.

Taken together, these manifestations of violence create an overwhelming and inequitable space of marginalization, dislocation, and sense of hopelessness in one's daily life. All too often, Aboriginal women and girls experience crisis through the impacts of intergenerational trauma from colonialism and speak of little opportunity to escape and move toward healing.

Although each of the above manifestations deserves its own, separate volume of discussion, deliberation, and debate, I choose instead to focus my comments specifically on the tragic phenomenon of missing and murdered Aboriginal women and girls in Canada—indisputably the ultimate and most final manifestation on this spectrum of violence.

We know that even moderate figures identify approximately six hundred Aboriginal women and girls as either missing or murdered. We know, too, that each of these women and girls are representative and reflective of the diversity within our Indigenous community. Some were teachers, some students, some workers, some sexually exploited, some with transient mental health disorders—indeed, a microcosmic representation of most (if not all) Canadian women and girls. They were also mothers, daughters, grandmothers, aunties, cousins.

It is with this spirit that communities and people from all across Canada—indeed, the world—affirm the issue of missing and murdered Aboriginal women and children as a regional and national tragedy. It's an issue that demands immediate attention and condemnation by governments, civil society, non-governmental agencies, Aboriginal grassroots associations, and their respective leaders.

Families of missing and murdered Aboriginal women and girls often feel their loved one is not afforded adequate levels of attention or tangible action by both policing and government agencies. While in some areas of the country this has improved, governments and community leaders must commit to ensuring respectful, meaningful, and needed levels of communication between families and partnering agencies in addressing this most critical issue.

· · ·

Current research shows us that truly meaningful social outcomes for Aboriginal communities are achieved when these communities enjoy a sense of ownership and control over their own solutions, and where Aboriginal-led organizations are well supported by governments.

Let us be clear: violence against Aboriginal women and girls is a human rights issue. Aboriginal women and girls have the right to life, the right to freedom, and the right to be safe. In this regard, we, as a collective, must acknowledge that there remains much work and public education that needs to take place in order to secure these basic, fundamental human rights afforded to all Canadians. We, as a collective, must respectfully commit ourselves in spirit and practice in supporting the victims and families of missing and murdered Aboriginal women and girls, and fully commit to working in partnership with the community, government, and policing stakeholders in tangibly and substantially addressing this issue and allowing for the reclamation of Aboriginal voices and spaces.

Finally, from a more personal perspective, I leave the reader with this: every single Aboriginal women and girl who has gone missing or who has been murdered was unequivocally loved and cherished by their families. I have sat countless times with family members and shared in their profound grief and beyond measurable pain as they recount stories of their loved ones, or recall the last time they saw or spoke to their daughter, mother, aunty, sister. The resilience of these families and their love for their missing family member reminds me that we are all incredibly blessed and honoured by knowing about these beautiful and valuable women. The spirit and lives of these victims (Claudette Osborne, Jennifer Catcheway, Velicia Solomon Osborne, Hilary Angel Wilson, Fonessa Bruyere, Cherisse Houle, Sunshine Wood, Glenda Morrisseau—to name a few) continue to be present in the love of their families and reaffirms in me the intrinsic beauty, strength, and spirit of our Peoples. Meegwetch.

—2011

Rosanna Deerchild

Cree (South Indian Lake) 1972–

Rosanna Deerchild is a Manitoba Cree from South Indian Lake. Her birthplace was flooded by Manitoba Hydro, and, in 1974, her family relocated to Thompson. She attended Red River College's creative communication program, majoring in journalism, eventually beginning a career in media for almost 15 years (most recently for CBC). An accomplished poet and a dynamic performer, Deerchild is a favourite with many audiences at literary readings. She was nominated for the 2009 John Hirsch Award for Most Promising Manitoba Writer. Her first book of poetry, *this is a small northern town* (2008), won the Aqua Books Lansdowne Prize for Poetry/Prix Lansdowne de Poésie. She has been published in literary magazines such as *Prairie Fire*, *dark leisure*, and *Contemporary Verse 2*, and in *Post-Prairie: Anthology of New Poetry* (2005).

Deerchild is a member of the Aboriginal Writers Collective of Manitoba, and her works have appeared in their chapbooks *urban kool (2001)*, *Bone Memory* (2004), *xxx ndn* (2011), and on their spoken word CD, *Red City (2003)*.

Deerchild's poetry explores what it means to be Indian in a racially charged, tightly knit northern community. Her work addresses the struggles of community and family, particularly as ties of kinship and relations are challenged by histories of secrets. At their core, Deerchild's poems are about spaces created through language, places where the narrator finds comfort, safety, and escape. Through words and gestures, Deerchild explores identity and the continuation of Cree traditional culture into spaces and places that are remade as new locations of Indigenous life.

back home

mama says we're going back home
for a funeral and even though
we should be sad   we hide smiles
it's been years since we left

when we get off the ferry
a crowd meets us
aunties   uncles
about 20 cousins
press in close   touch
our hair   kiss our faces

at auntie's house
she feeds us moose meat
fried in a cast iron pan
bannock and lard
goose and macaroni soup

our cousins take us down to the lake
we skip rocks   play   watch the sky turn
orange   red   purple   until fat with stars
they ask   *what's town like*
we say confusing

our parents play cards
drink red rose tea in mason jars
tease each other in cree
guffaw say   *tapwe*[41]

this is where mama was born
where pictures of my absent father
hang on family walls   my pictures
in auntie and uncle's memory boxes

me in rubber boots and diapers
sitting next to my cousin
my brothers and sister
dusty faces   messy hair
playing with puppies
in a bush camp

---

41   true

auntie folds her soft brown hands
around mine   holds me in a place
i was lost from   whispers
my girl

uncle asks   *do you remember*
I fed you sucker head soup
we raised you in this house
do you remember natanis[42]

and in my skin
the same colours
as theirs
i do

—2008

crazy horse is a girl

our street is at the top
of the only hill in town
it's steep   curves to the right
a four way stop at the bottom

kids play chicken on their bikes
race down two at a time
until someone breaks
leaves question marks
in the gravel   or fly full speed
through the cross road
like an exclamation point

the possibility of grievous injury
makes their pale skin flush   say
holy shit did you see that

someone double dog dares me
and i get my sister's old bike
my feet don't reach the ground
so i push it to the top   get on
take off   the air and the adrenalin
tingles my skin

---

42 my daughter

halfway down i see
plumes of dust like balloons
heading for the intersection
push back on the pedals
expect the surety of brakes
but the chain whirs uselessly
fear flares in my chest
i can't slow down

my racing rival skids to a stop
near the bottom
open-mouthed   as i speed past
braids flying   elbows up
eyes straight ahead
the sound of dog barking
somewhere behind me

car and bike close in
until the middle aged
woman behind the wheel
finally sees me   surprise
then panic   blares her horn
screeches to a stop   screams
jesus, mary and josiff
but I'm long gone

back at the top of the hill
the boy i raced waits
kids stare   say
you didn't even slow down

i tell them i wasn't scared
that the car missed me
by this > < much

i tell them
i am crazy horse
fearless
                ghostlike

—2008

northern lights

remind me of the powwow dancers
that came to our school once
they looked like new coins
sounded like them when they danced

now i watch a night powwow
grass dancer with his long green
ribbons sway long paths
for fancy shawl dancers to follow
shocks of yellow   red   purple   butterflies
jingle dresses spark off stars
even orion   ursa major
hang bells on his belt
around his neck

dances around the full moon drum

mama told me once not
to whistle at the northern lights
or they would come down
dance me right into the sky

she thought it would scare me
but it's these cracked and narrow
sidewalks that tangle my feet   pull
me down the straight lines
of whichever street   where ever avenue

the northern lights dance
a whistle rises from my lips

—*2008*

paper indians

he draws us out
of dirt roads and rez houses
traces us out of the land
five paper indians
cut   carefully   and folded
in his pocket

pastes our thin bodies
along cement lines of small town
keeps us in box houses

flower print dresses   suits
uncomfortable on brown skin
hard leather shoes hurt
feet ache for moosehide
moccasins

propped up with church steeples
nickel mine smoke stack
pinned down with the sharp
looks of good people

at church dinners he jokes
he went up north to hunt
a moose and got five
laughter tinkles
like cutlery on glass

our spirits squeezed
until we are like bible pages
transparent
against the light

—*2008*

Colleen Simard

Anishinaabe/Cree (Winnipeg) 1972–

Colleen Simard is a Winnipeg freelance writer, researcher, filmmaker, and mother of two. She is Anishinaabe, French, Cree, and Swedish, and both sides of her family can trace their heritage along the shores of Lake Winnipeg and points north. She has been a journalist with the CBC and the Aboriginal Peoples Television Network and has worked with a number of Aboriginal newspapers, including *Urban NDN*, which she published on her own. Simard proudly lives in North End Winnipeg, one of the largest urban settlements of Indian and Métis people in the country. Her column,

"Without Reserve," chronicles the impact of being a foreigner in her own land and opens a window to how the modern world affects the descendents of this country's original inhabitants. Her column has been engaging readers of the *Winnipeg Free Press* all over the world every week since 2004.

Simard's columns often focus on her experiences living in Winnipeg's north end. Her detailed focus on what seems to be the little moments in life are always reflective of larger processes and ideologies at work. Simard is known for pulling no punches in her writing, often speaking directly to a single individual or group, Aboriginal or non-Aboriginal. As these two columns demonstrate, she can be a hard-hitting political writer with a penchant for identifying corruption and hypocrisy or a reflective and considerate observer—and sometimes both.

Listen to the Roar of the Thunderbirds

I'm not really sure what woke me up that night. It was either the squealing of tires or the rumbling of thunder. I'd left my window open to catch the warm spring breeze. Old-school air conditioning.

Still dark, I squinted at the clock. Maybe it's just someone in a bad mood. It sure was nice to hear a storm coming, though.

A minute later I heard the car return, speeding down the street behind my place. Then there was a loud crash, like a car hitting something in its way. After that came a cloud of cheering voices. Great. A stolen car and some joyriders. The sky growled. Thunderbirds.

Long ago, our people told stories of the mighty thunderbird whose flapping wings created rainstorms. Whose eyes of fire could shoot out thunderbolts at will. The thunderbird was to be respected.

Some legends spoke of a kind thunderbird that fed our people during a time of famine. Another tale warned of a thunderbird that would take your wayward child if you gave it a chance.

Again the car sped off to howls of joy, and returned again. The right thing to do is to call the police. These kids will kill somebody, or themselves. This is how it starts. I wondered if they still went to school, or they'd been lured away by the promises of easy money and even easier "good times." Those same good times almost took my cousin's life last spring when his friend stabbed him.

The sky lights up as the thunderbird makes himself known—five loud claps of thunder in a row. I wonder if the boys noticed. Maybe five warnings for five boys, I thought. Did they ever even hear of thunderbirds?

The cops come after the rain has started to dribble down, but by this time the boys have ditched the vehicle on a side street nearby. I don't know if the police arrested those thunderbird boys—but I caught sight of them as they cut through a vacant lot next to my house.

They were wearing hoodies, and sounded more like kids in a schoolyard than criminals. I realized my sister had pointed them out earlier that evening, playing with firecrackers in the twilight. Probably not even 15.

A war reporter friend would often tell me stories of wars he'd been to— Bosnia, Sierra Leone, Iraq. And as we walked down to Selkirk Avenue I told him there was a war going on here, too. Except most people don't see it.

The war is internal you see, hidden inside you. It's hard to escape, my brothers. And sometimes even if you think you've won, you haven't. Don't fall for it. Dirty money and fake brotherhoods. Listen to the thunderbirds.

You shouldn't be out stealing cars. You're supposed to be our fire keepers, our peacekeepers, and the protectors of women and children. Someday you'll have a car, a good job, a safe home of your own. But this isn't the way.

Not many people believe in thunderbirds anymore, but I still do.

—*2006*

Thanks, Mr. Paul, for All Your Help

I remember staring out the school bus window—one part interest, one part fear—as we rambled down the bumpy reserve road: Hollow Water—or Hole River, as most people know it. This was where my grandma was born.

Many homes dotting the landscape were small, but brightly painted in pinks, blues, and even purple. Some looked abandoned and tired. The larger ones stood proudly on hills. I was surprised to see a golden cow grazing along the road as we made our way to Wanipigow School—the huge reserve school kids went to from kindergarten to grade 12.

I was 13 and I'd never been on a reserve much until then. We were living in Winnipeg. But my parents decided work was easier to get in my dad's nearby hometown of Manigotogan. So we moved.

I was an outsider from the start. I got into a fight within days.

Some girls didn't like me. Who was I? On the way home, one of them slapped me before rushing off the bus. I had no choice but to return the favour the next day, or become the newest target for everyone.

I still wince thinking about that. Someone probably bullied her into doing it. But like my old neighbourhood, I had to prove myself. Later on, those same kids changed their minds when they found out I was related to them.

Sure, it was rough, but not nearly half as bad as the accounts some reserve school teachers have had published over the years. Not every reserve is as miserable as those ones were said to be. Those poor souls were likely newly minted teachers unprepared for reserve life and only lasted the year.

At our school a few students took pleasure from picking on new teachers, especially the young ones. One time a kid tried to smoke a cigarette in class. Another afternoon the boys decided to throw frogs at the girls. There was a lot of screaming that day. And the old thumbtack-on-the-chair game lasted right up to Grade 10, for sure.

Then there was Mr. Ralph Paul, my homeroom teacher that first year.

Mr. Paul was a tall, sinewy Dene with short dark hair that wouldn't behave.

He dressed in itchy-looking woolen sweaters. He had high cheekbones and fiery dark eyes behind a pair of strictly utilitarian glasses. Heaven help the kid who got caught in his steely gaze. He yelled a lot, but most students deserved it.

One day he noticed me sitting quietly, trying to escape going up to the blackboard. Dreaded fractions, as I remember. I ended up trying to figure out fractions in front of the whole class. And I was in front of the blackboard the next day, too. But I know fractions now.

Mr. Paul was hard, but he opened some of our eyes. He took our entire class to the Aboriginal Justice Inquiry hearings in Winnipeg. At one point he gave a war whoop and almost got us kicked out. Later, we got to meet judges Murray Sinclair and A.C. Hamilton, the inquiry commissioners.

Mr. Paul taught native studies, too. One of his first lessons was: "You are not an Indian—Indians come from India." Hopefully he can forgive my sometimes carefree use of the word.

While Mr. Paul ruled with an iron fist, his wife was a velvet touch. Mrs. McDonald taught home economics, how to cook and sew. She talked to us about sex education. She was the one we turned to when times were tough, like when one of my friends took a bunch of pills to try end her tragic home life. It was a sadness that infected the whole community at times.

But there were good times on the reserve, too, walking around with friends until dark, sometimes looking for trouble or stopping by the bingo hall for a Coke and a bag of chips. There was almost always laughter, joking, and forever teasing each other.

One day Mr. Paul told me he wanted to see me after morning class. I could feel myself start sweating immediately. Friends cast sympathetic looks my way as they went off for lunch.

But I wasn't in trouble at all. Mr. Paul gave me a dictionary and Chief Dan George's autobiography. He also said I had potential, which was something nobody ever told me, much less a teacher. He made sure I knew what the word meant, too. I read the books he gave me, and thought about what he said. Did I really have potential?

I caught another glimpse of Mr. Paul one warm evening near the end of the school year. Some of my friends and I stopped by his and his wife's house.

Mr. Paul had two children, and a fondness for Gordon Lightfoot. He had the record player on and we listened to those haunting ballads while Mr. Paul talked about his past. He hadn't planned to be a teacher, he told us. He was studying law but an accident put him in the hospital for months, and law school was put aside.

Somewhere along the way, I think Mr. Paul turned from my most feared teacher into my most memorable one. And I wonder if he knew his words would stay with me this long. Any kid on any reserve would only be so lucky to find a teacher like him nowadays.

—2006

Maeengan Linklater

Anishinaabe (Lac Seul First Nation) 1974–

Maeengan Linklater is a poet, filmmaker, storyteller, father, and community volunteer born and raised in Winnipeg, although his family originates from Lac Seul First Nation in Ontario. Linklater's film, *Winnipeg First Nation: Heart of a Home* (2009) and his writings have been featured in *Urban Kool, Bone Memory* (2004), *Red City, xxx ndn* (2011), and *Walk Myself Home: An Anthology to End Violence Against Women* (2010). A featured poet at literary festivals throughout the province, Linklater is working on a manuscript entitled, *Love: Break Ups & Make Ups*.

The following poem reflects a yearning and reverence for Linklater's two "homes" —a quiet, uncluttered forested space, and a busy, occupied, urban one. These two worlds carry messages via complex sounds and scenes, manufactured and unmanufactured, but are still places that make us and that we return to.

Home

Wind gliding smoothly among pine trees and spruce
Feet pressing against the trail
Lit by moonlight
A shadow through the trees branches, leaves

I can see the stars
The untold stories
Forgotten by my people
Replaced, by the cross and the bible
Still this is home

Have we forgotten that place that gave us life
Do we live our lives through a satellite dish

Have we forgotten the smell of fire beside a lake
Digging feet into the beach
Friction of sand between toes
The reflection of Northern Lights on still water
Where land meets sky

I think about home

I live in the city
Hard, uncompromising, mechanical
Twisted by steel and wire
Unforgiving to those lured by syndicated television

The air, filling my nostrils
Clean tender
The wind on my skin
Tickling peaceful
Listening as waves wash the shore
Do you remember home?

—*2011*

Althea Guiboche

Cree/Saulteaux (Duck Bay) 1974–

Althea Guiboche resides in Dauphin, Manitoba. She is a single mother to seven amazing children. After the passing of her father Edward Guiboche, Althea turned to writing to sort out her emotions, thoughts, and feelings and has found it an ideal way to pass on morals, values, and traditions.

Guiboche's poetry explores representations of identity through rhythmic language, arresting images, and skillful use of repetition. In "I Found Myself the Other Day" she narrates a theme of self-discovery by using language that resists stability. "I Dream of Jigging" is an ecstatically energetic poem that evokes a bodily sense of belonging. The reference to "the red river jig" ties the poem closely to Guiboche's Manitoba roots.

I Found Myself the Other Day

I found myself the other day
I don't even know how long I was lost
I don't remember losing myself
I just looked around one day
and I was gone
I don't know where I went
to sleep I suspect
for I am wide awake now
my outlook on life is like
the sunrise in the morning
fresh and full of wonder
radiating sunshine and beauty

inspiration is my morning cup of coffee
happiness, my breakfast
I don't let little things faze me
I am my own clown
my own opinion now matters most to me
my feelings I now always take into account
I am true to myself
nothing can bring me down since
I found myself the other day.

—2009

I Dream of Jigging

i dream of jigging
so hard
my heart is pounding
my limbs are trembling
and i feel so weak
yet i am energized
and strong
exhilarated
and out of breath
on i jig
my feet moving
to the twangy notes
of the fiddle strings
note for note
step for step
sweat pooling
i twirl in a single do-si-do
round and round
legs shaking
pulse thundering
to the fancy steps
of the red river jig
i dream of jigging.

—2009

Niigaanwewidam James Sinclair

Anishinaabe (St. Peter's Indian Reserve/Peguis First Nation) 1976–

Niigaanwewidam James Sinclair is an assistant professor in the departments of English and Native Studies at the University of Manitoba. He is a descendent of removed citizens from the St. Peter's Indian settlement near Selkirk, Manitoba, an illegal act perpetrated by the governments of Manitoba and Canada in 1907. His critical and creative work has been translated into several languages and can be found in journals such as *Prairie Fire* and *Canadian Literature* and in books such as *Troubling Tricksters: Revisioning Critical Conversations* (2010) and *The Exile Book of Native Canadian Fiction and Drama* (2010). He is a co-editor of *Centering Anishinaabeg Studies: Understanding the World Through Stories* (2012), a special issue about indigenous-centred criticisms of indigenous literatures for *The Canadian Journal of Native Studies* (2009), and *NDN Ink: New Writing from First Peoples* (2008).

"Water Scroll" is a story Sinclair wrote to honour the birth of his daughter in 2006. It is a retelling of the traditional flood story, where a muskrat travels to the bottom of a world engulfed in water and delivers a pawful of sand to Naanaboozhoo, who recreates the world. In this modern-day version, the question is asked: What is the world made of? What might destroy it? And, most important, what are the pieces of sand we need to recreate it? Considering our modern-day contexts of climate change, environmental pollution, and, simply, the fractured relationships of peoples across the world separated by racism and divided by wars, Sinclair imagines possibility in the direst of circumstances.

Water Scroll

The humans had been here for only a day, but already had created a stir in amongst the sea creatures. Questions emerged amongst the water clans. *How had they survived the flood? How did they make it out here? Were there others? What did they want?*

Whale spoke first. *I think they should be cast away,* he said. *They needn't come into our homes. It was they who had destroyed theirs. I, and my family, don't want them near us. Let them fend for themselves.*

Seal spoke next. *They cannot be trusted,* she said, *I know this. I lost my family to them. Let them swim, like the rest of us.*

Others agreed, and the voices of many murmured in agreement. Even turtle, who had lived long in amongst the humans, agreed.

Otter spoke next, and many silenced, for he was one of the wisest. *They must explain how they have survived this long,* he said. *We hadn't seen any humans for such a long time, we must know if there are more. Maybe they are smarter than we thought.*

Suddenly, Beaver slapped his tail on the water. *I want to speak,* he said, *I want to speak. You know the history as well as I do,* he said, drawing pictures of Naanaboozhoo in the water. Quickly he wiped it away, erasing the story and sending out waves that would find no shores. *It was one of **them** that helped us create earth*, he said, *that's what the old ones told us. We know that we are not that different from them, not any better. We are not so special that we can't see if they can help us again. Many of us need land to survive too, like you, Muskrat, or you, Duck. Maybe they are here for a purpose. Maybe they are here to answer our prayers. Maybe they are here to help, like Naanaboozhoo did so many years ago.*

We trusted Naanaboozhoo, Spotted fish said. *We knew that he could create the world. He knew what to do. All he needed was a grain of sand and he created land.*

Yes, Muskrat added, *but no one has seen him for a long time.*

Silence fell over the water clan chiefs. All had not seen land since the flood waters, a time too long now to be mentioned. The best and fastest swimmers had left and for the few that had come back, had told stories of only water remaining. The land was deep below now, where no one could swim to. When the flood came so quickly, those who could not swim perished, like the land relatives of the water clans. The birds eventually were lost too. It was difficult to watch them die, but nothing could be done.

The humans were one of the first to disappear. Now, the arrival of two of them instilled fear and anxiety, for they were always the most dangerous. There were more unknown stories to come.

Forget Naanaboozhoo, Beaver said. *I will take them to my lodge. I will take care of them.*

Find out why they are here, Otter replied. *We need to know. They are now your responsibility for all of us. Follow me.*

The animals departed, diving underneath the waves as the sun sunk low in the sky. Beaver followed Otter for a long time, emerging at a space far from where the leaders had spoke. It was nighttime, and the moonlight shone on the small pieces of wood, barely tied together and floating in the water.

Lying there was a woman and a small one, clutching each other, sleeping. They were silent, as if dead. The small movement of the woman's hand in keeping the tiny one in place on her breast showed that that they were, in fact, alive.

Beaver dragged the small raft back to his lodge, which now floated high in the water. He attached the humans' world to his, careful to make sure that they were shielded from the rain underneath the few branches he had left. He checked on them all night as they remained huddled close, silent, alone.

For days they remained that way, the only sounds coming from the baby sucking, then sleeping. Still, Beaver watched, knowing that he had to show compassion for them to live. Leaving only to hunt, he returned quickly with fish. Making soup, he fed the woman gently, making sure to stay in the water and not get too close. He cared for the humans as if they were his own children. He covered them in the downpours, shielded them from the tall waves, kept them as safe as possible from the predators in the sea around them.

But still, they slept. Beaver wondered what questions he would ask them when they awoke. I knew not where to begin for he wanted to ask: *How did you survive? How did you get here? What am I to do with you? Why are you here?*

So, instead, he remained silent.

The sun raised and the moon soon followed. The earth continued in its same, wet condition, with only the sounds of waves lapping over top of one another to mark the time passing by. Sometimes, visitors would come to see the humans, soon leaving disappointed to see them sleeping or remaining still, staring at them in amazement.

It was during one late, hot afternoon, that the baby stirred, crying.

Beaver stopped his work of fortifying his lodge and turned to the creatures. The mother opened her eyes and cradled the little one in her arms, bringing her back to her breast, filling the little mouth with skin. The tiny screams muffled, and gave way to happy groans and grunts. She looked up.

Where am I?, she asked.

You are at my home, Beaver replied. *How did you get here?*

I'm sorry, but I'm so tired. I don't know how long we have been floating. I'm honoured to be at your home, she said.

I have so many questions, Beaver interrupted.

I know. I need to take care of my baby, she said. *Then I will answer your questions. Do you have any food?*

The woman fed her baby continuously that day and into the night. Beaver waited, drifting on the water, diving once to get more food for the humans. He waited by the woman deep into the night, wondering when she would speak. The moon emerged from the clouds, full and bright, and Beaver saw the mother raise her head and stare at the bright circle in the sky. Then, he heard her pray quietly, and sing. Her song was sad but soothing and her voice resounded softly amongst the waves in all directions. Beaver felt the wind die down and listen along with him.

Beaver felt the woman's voice deep inside his spirit. He wished he could heal her pain, touch her, embrace her. Instead, he just stood and watched her sing the words in the dim light, letting his ears fill with soft warmth.

He had never touched a human, nor did he want to. He knew that they only brought death and destruction to his relatives and the land, he had heard the stories. So, even though this one sang so beautifully, he knew not to trust her.

Still, he longed for her to continue singing after she ended.

The sound of the waves lapped upon one another again, taking over the night. With each wave, Beaver felt his curiosity rise about why she was here and what her purpose was fall away. It would come in time, he thought.

The moon hid behind the clouds in the sky again, and the darkness grasped them both again.

Suddenly, her words lit up the silence.

I am ready for your questions, she said.

I have only one, he replied. *Will you help us recreate the earth, like Naanaboozhoo did?*

But I ended the last world, she said.

You brought the flood waters? Beaver exclaimed. *You did? You should be ashamed of yourself!*

Beaver's anger, nurtured from watching so many perish while he dived below the surface of the crashing waves, rose in him.

How could you do such a horrible thing?

Let me tell you the story, she interrupted. *Then you can make your own decision if you want us to help.*

Beaver opened his mouth, and then stopped himself.

I gave birth to her at home, she began, pointing at the baby sleeping on her breast. *She needed to come home, to the earth that was hers.* The women closed her mouth and paused, holding back tears.

I had no where else to go. I was a city girl, removed from my family and raised amongst concrete and plastic. When I got pregnant my mother asked me to come home, and have the baby on our reserve, in our territory. Being from the city, I rarely came home, but I did it to make her happy. I returned to the land of my ancestors, moving into my mother's small house by the lake. I lived there and grew bigger and bigger. Soon, it was time for my baby. My mother called all of the old ladies of the community to her house, and we had a moon ceremony together, near the water. We sang songs and ate berries. Then, the old women spoke. There hadn't been a birth in their community since the missionaries came, almost sixty years previous. Back then all the women of the community would help with births, and they wanted to start this tradition again. Still, the old ladies said they had to do this work. Young girls left many years ago to have their babies in the city, they said, and after they left they never came back. When the young women left, so did the men. Everyone who went to the city, they pointed out, never came back. The community was dying. There were no babies being born here, only the old ones getting older.

It would be hard, they agreed, as many had forgotten the right songs to sing, the right stories to tell. They were nervous, but they agreed it should be done.

The moon peeked out from behind a cloud before hiding again.

When I began my first pains, many times they had to help one another. The old women embraced me, fed me, sang songs of celebration and love all night. That morning, with the first signs of water, my labour began. The old women sat in the kitchen and prayed for me, with tea and tobacco in their hands. Two midwives sat with me. Sometimes I could hear the grandmothers calling to me from the table, where they sang more songs, told stories, and laughed, waiting for me to emerge with my child from the bedroom. The pains were hard, sometimes overwhelming, but it helped knowing that they were there, waiting for me. My mother cradled me in her arms until finally my daughter came, with the same waters that first announced her arrival. The old ladies huddled around me and we together left the house, walking down to the lake, where we washed her and sat on the sands of the shore, basking in the morning sun. She was born with her eyes closed, a good and beautiful sign one of the old ladies said. That meant she wanted to keep looking at that other world, keep learning before she came here. We all sang songs and sat there, on the shore of the water, until evening.

The woman stopped her story, and looked up, staring at the stars in the sky. Beaver heard the drops of water in water, a magical sound that separated land from the soft depths of his new world. For a long time she waited, and Beaver listened. She then continued.

After we washed her, again, my baby opened her eyes. My mother gasped. She has no eyes, she said. She was born with no eyes. I looked at her. She was right. She had no eyes. **She was born with no eyes.** *Look, my mother cried to the other women, calling them. Look, she has no eyes. Look, she screamed and began to cry. My granddaughter has no eyes. The old women came to the sands where I lay with my daughter and saw empty sockets where her eyes should have been. The women grew sad, and also began to cry. We are lost, they said, we are lost. Our medicines are gone. We have forgotten how to bring life into this world, to grow, to nurture, to continue. This is a sign that we are at end. It is over.*

The baby awoke briefly and the woman nuzzled her into her neck. Soon the little one was breathing heavy again.

Soon, the woman added after a while, *the tears of the old women filled the grass, creating pools in the earth. Other women, some Anishinaabe and some not, came to see the baby, finding only my mother and the old women of our community crying on the shore, holding one another. Once they saw my child, they too joined in the sadness of my daughter's birth, adding to the pools. I watched them, confused. Men came, and others, and they cried too. Soon, the grounds flooded with tears because of the hatred, anger, and resentment of all we had lost. Many blamed the white man, some even called it due to colonization. These bad feelings grew to calls for violence at the worlds around the community, and finally at themselves. The people fought with each other, raining fists upon fists over tear drops that sprung from their eyes. Soon, our home flooded the sands and the earth, but no one noticed but me. I called to anyone who would listen, but soon it was too late. The tears continued to flow and fill the earth with sadness and grief and anger and pain. The rivers could not hold the water for very long. Quickly our road was flooded, and the homes around our community submerged. Others cried as word spread, and the lake at the base of our community overflowed with the water that entered into the earth. All this time I held my baby close to me, protecting her from the pain. I fed her, and although she was blind, I kept from crying for her sake. I loved her, no matter her blindness.*

Beaver noticed that the woman was stroking the baby's eyelids, just then.

The story of my little girl with no eyes, the poor, hapless, frail Indian of our reservation's future soon was known throughout the world. It was in the news, on the Internet, written in every language. "Indian Culture Lost!" reporters and writers and scholars said. As people heard of the traumatic stories of our home, each person wept, with each tear added to the ocean of grief felt over the plight of my people. Tears of all invaded the land, covering it, as the final, tragic tale of Indian people was told. My daughter became a symbol, an object for all to feel the loss of the original ones of the land. It enraged me, and I refused to try to understand their ignorance. I did not tell them and they did not notice when their own homes filled with tears, overcoming the cities and the towns. Sometime, during the full moon, the waters rose so high that no one could see land anymore. The waters kept rising and rising. Everyone who had heard my story was too sad to even panic and save themselves or their families. These people were so paralyzed in their grief and fear that they didn't realize that they were to die next. Some didn't care and could do nothing too, perishing with the oncoming waves. The earth filled with water faster than anyone could imagine. Days after my daughter's birth, there was no land left, for the story of my blind daughter had created an overwhelming flood of sadness. I had only time to find some wood, tie together a raft, and save some food before we floated away. We stayed on this raft for a long time, eating what we could find and catch, until you found us. You've been so kind, feeding us and taking care of us. I honour you.

It's my honour, Beaver said. *I am saddened by your story. I wish I could help. You can stay as long as you like. I don't expect you to help us recreate the world.*

The woman said nothing, lying back and soon fell asleep. Beaver, his curiosity piqued, leaned over to see the baby. The woman was right, she had no eyes.

What a cruel future this girl has, he thought to himself as he went back to his bed. *What a sad fate.*

The next morning, when Beaver brought the woman soup, she was gone. The woman had disappeared, and had left no sign. Only the child remained, playing by herself in the early sun. She gurgled and giggled, enjoying the beauty of her hands and feet.

Beaver stopped, confused. Had there ever even been a woman? He could not remember if she had even existed, or if he had imagined her. All he could remember was her song.

The old, wise, water chief awoke from his mind. All that mattered now was the child. He had to care for her.

The blind child began to cry, hungry and cold. Beaver could no longer be afraid of humans. He had to help this baby, hold her, and feed her fish soup until she was old enough to fend for herself. He had to teach her how to help herself. Beaver promised himself he would at least do that. Picking her up and placing her into his lap, he fed her the warm broth.

He paused when he noticed that gripped in her small, soft, hand were several grains of sand and a little palm of earth. The beauty of it shone in the morning light.

Laying back, Beaver looked up, thinking deep inside his memory. He waited for a moment, remembering the stories and songs he would need to teach the others to get the world started again. He smiled.

—2006

Donna Beyer

Cree/Anishinaabe (Peguis First Nation) 1976–

Donna Beyer (née McCorrister) is a Cree and Anishinaabe woman from Peguis First Nation in Manitoba, with an M.A. in Native literature at the University of Manitoba. When she was 16, Beyer moved from Peguis First Nation to Winnipeg to complete high school. Her poetry has been published in several local and national poetry anthologies including *Sing, Poetry from the Indigenous Americans* (2011), *The Willows Whisper: A Transatlantic Compilation of Poetry from Ireland and Native America* (2011), and *Northern Writers: Volume 2* (2010).

She is working on a children's story that was inspired by the imagination of her daughter.

Beyer's poetry is a humorous combination of wordplay and oral speech, but also reflects upon more serious themes of love and violence, and the collision of rural and urban Aboriginal experiences. Every word in Beyer's writing is carefully chosen, creating a balance of critical and creative thought that echoes the complexity of community and growing up as a modern-day Cree/Anishinaabe woman in Manitoba.

nichimos

aaaaaa he's your boyfren
they would say
this cool dude
from last year i snagged at dotc day
he told me i smelled of jam
like his dad made in the mornings for his bannock before anyone was awake
oooooo heck i said
sticking out my tongue, waving my hand and giving my head a real shy shake
he even bought me some earrings
from one of the stands
we went to the powwow
making googly eyes during the round dance
he was from over der
me   over here
we made out in his cheemag ole truck
giving eachother hickies   but that's it I fear
we talked for like hours
and he tole me all about his darn crazy ex
who pulled out the hair
of the last girl who put his heart in a hex
we fell in love, teasing and laughing in our own special way
we ended up getting married   us
nipapa was proud
when he gave me to nichimos

—*2009*

backroads

you become accustomed to their ride
black ice winters, washboard summers
your driving accommodates their form

bearings blown
shocks shot

lonely dogs linger
signs falter

hollow cans line their ditches sporadically
their contents now inside someone's nameless void

their potholes
the size of moon craters
giant bruises turned inward

—*2010*

Clayton Thomas-Müller

Cree (Mathias Colomb Cree Nation/Pukatawagan) 1977–

Clayton Thomas-Müller is from the Mathias Colomb Cree Nation (also known as Pukatawagan) in northern Manitoba, but he also has roots in Winnipeg. He is an activist for indigenous rights and has travelled the world to stop industrial society's assault on indigenous peoples' lands to extract resources and to dump toxic wastes. Based in Ottawa, Thomas-Müller is involved in many initiatives to support fair and respectful economic and environmental development. He serves on boards supporting indigenous rights and protection of Mother Earth. Recognized by *Utne Reader* magazine as one of the top 30 under-30 activists in the United States and as a Climate Hero in 2009 by *Yes!* magazine, Clayton is the tar sands campaign organizer for the Indigenous Environmental Network. He is also a gifted poet and rap artist.

"The Seventh Generation" appeared in *This Is an Honour Song: Twenty Years Since the Blockades* (2010), a collection of writings that honours the anniversary of the 1990 Oka resistance at Kahnesatake. Thomas-Müller documents how an event far distant from him, but fully available on television and radio, inspires him to take an active role in Aboriginal politics and activism. It is a role that has led him to global struggles. His "awakening"—familiar to many—is indicative of how Manitoba Aboriginal people continue to make an impact on the global stage.

The Seventh Generation

One of the greatest turning points in my life was in the summer of 1990—the summer I realized how great our Indigenous nations are and, more importantly, when I realized our power as Indigenous nations. I remember being 12 years old and watching the news on TV, I remember witnessing the largest mobilization of the Canadian military since the Korean War against what looked like a group of people that could be my aunties, uncles, and cousins.

Over the summer I watched along with the rest of the world the ridiculous absurdity of the Canadian government—a government stuck in the past trying to enforce racist and colonial ideologies that were just not acceptable any longer, that were never acceptable. I watch a group of Indigenous people stand up against the government and their security forces with nothing but their spirituality and hope. I watched the Grandmothers and warriors of the Mohawk nation defeat the Federal government of Canada.

From this moment something deep inside of me snapped. I quit trying to be Canadian. I just gave up. I knew from what I was watching that I was something else, something much more. That my roots to this land called Canada meant that I was born into struggle, born with responsibilities. I was Cree.

In my journey, I have confronted many challenges that have helped me come to the current understanding I have about our Indigenous struggle. I have seen how our nations' power was attacked by trying to separate our families most notably through the assimilation policy of Indian residential school.

Although I did not go to residential school, I was one of the first in my family that was integrated into Canada's public school system with no social supports to help Native children confront and overcome racism in that system.

I have many fond memories of my family in the bush during the summer, picking berries watching the older boys and my Moo Shum (Grandfather) get fish from the nets. Watching my Koo Kum (Grandmother) cook bannock by our family's fire.

I have many memories of darkness in the city of Winnipeg, of our people living in the harshest of poverty. I can remember fighting my Auntie Lisa and Uncle Ovide for orange peels on Easter morning.

How did we get from such bounty to such pitiful sorrow and hunger?

Hundreds of years ago the Church and the State were inseparable, and Jesuit Priests in Black Robes came into our communities promising a solution to problems our communities faced as they confronted the violence of colonization, through embracing Christianity and changing the way we spoke with our Creator.

I know this played a part in the answer to my question.

Today, we are still confronting the violence of colonization. It has manifested in many forms that I don't care to list. One thing that is clear to me, however, is that there are still those that would enter our communities promising a quick fix to our socio-economic woes when the answer always has and continues to be sovereignty and self-determination over our lands and life.

I have observed in this time instead of Jesuit Priests in Black Robes we have corporate CEOs in Black Suits representing Toxic Waste, Timber, Mining, and Energy Corporations. They come seducing our people with promises of a quick and easy solution to our poverty and sickness by entering into the industrialization game and changing our relations with the sacredness of Mother Earth, relations we've had since time immemorial.

One thing that is clear to me, is that in my life, the greatest riches I have seen have not been on 5th Avenue in New York City, nor have they been in the halls of Parliament or Congress. They were as a child with my Grandparents and my Mother reaping the riches of our loving Mother Earth.

Our greatest power as the peoples of Mother Earth is in maintaining our sacred responsibility to protect her and to speak for those animal and plant relations that cannot speak for themselves.

My human relatives, I write these words to encourage you to be strong and to continue to seek out justice in our struggle. Do not give in to the quick fix of money and political favors of the state or from the corporations that control these colonial governments, these institutions are inseparable. This can be best expressed through the recent transfer of trillions of dollars of public funds from governments of the world to the private sector to prop up a collapsing free market system.

We must continue to fight to protect the sacredness of our Mother Earth. We must remember that our sacred waters and land are forever and we must preserve their integrity to provide not just for us, but also for all life.

Today out of 1.8 million Aboriginal People in Canada, 75% are under the age of 30, which means that we are in the midst of a profound generational shift of power. By 2016, one out of every four people in Canada's workforce will be a Native person. This represents a fantastic shift in economic power from the ruling class to a population that has been marginalized for some time. The shift of social, political, and economic power will be received by a highly educated and sophisticated population of Indigenous People— a group that has more capacity than any other generation has had before us in terms of colonial analysis and education. Many of our Indigenous prophecies speak about this time we live in, including the prophecy of my own people that speaks about a Seventh Generation that will be born free of the colonial mind. Children born in the Seventh Generation are born ready to step up and assert their right to community self-determination. Many of these Seventh Generation warriors were children when Oka happened, many of us are and will continue to hold the front line in our collective struggle in the place of our Aunties and Uncles. We have many tools to use since Oka that will help us in our rapid ascent to power in this country called Canada.

I want you to know, my relatives, that I will stand with you in this struggle, you are not alone, I will be there if you call. And to those that would sacrifice vast swaths of this land, water, air, and our peoples just so that a privileged few can thrive economically know this:

We will never stop, not for one second, so you better be ready.

—*2010*

Ryan McMahon

Anishinaabe/Métis (Couchiching First Nation) 1977–

Ryan McMahon is a comedian, actor, and writer based in Winnipeg. He has made a name for himself as one of the most dynamic Aboriginal comedians working on Turtle Island today. He was born and raised in Fort Frances, Ontario, and is a member of Couchiching First Nation in Treaty #3. McMahon is one of the first Aboriginal graduates of the prestigious Second City Toronto Conservatory and has a degree in theatre. He performs live comedy all over North America and mixes sketch and improvised comedy into his standup act. He also produces comedy podcasts and web videos. McMahon steers clear of tired, cultural stereotypes onstage and combines standup, improv, and sketch comedy weaving stories and characters in an original style of comedy he calls "Indian Vaudeville." He is, perhaps, best known for his innovative and dynamic character "Clarence Two-Toes."

This set of comedy "bits" is from his performance at the 2011 Winnipeg Comedy Festival in an evening entitled "Hystereotypes." In his performance, McMahon hilariously examines the many stereotypes he encounters as a young Aboriginal person and how he engages and upends them. Of particular note is the value of timing and diction in his comedy—particularly his delivery, which is integral to making people laugh. Beneath the humour, however, deep social and political issues and commentary are embedded. McMahon demonstrates why humour is one of the most important vehicles for examining Aboriginal issues.

Hystereotypes, Eh?

Winnipeg, great to be here. Hystereotypes, eh? I'm the Native part of the stereotype show. Can you believe that? They brought in the least looking Native comedian they could find … I think in hopes that I was a little more palatable than Chief Larry Red Thunder—the angriest, native, observational prop comic this side of the great lakes.

Let's get this out of the way, I know I don't LOOK Native, okay? I know. I don't look like the Native guy they cast on the Crimestoppers commercials, I look more like the white cop that beats him at the end of it don't I? I know. Oh, don't let your white guilt get in the way tonight folks, we're gonna have some fun!

I almost didn't get this show because the festival people talked to my wife accidently, they found out I actually WAS a lazy Indian—I had to convince the festival that was just in regards to fixing stuff around the house—I work hard at the funny.

Stereotypes, eh? Well, let's see … well, I know one thing for sure … I won't be cast in "Last of the Mohicans 2" or "Dances With Wolves—The Musical," anytime soon. Me in a loin cloth looks like the Pillsbury doughboy got caught in some duct tape. "WOO WOO WOO WOO I'm angry … and extremely uncomfortable because of my low self-esteem and body image issues."

Ever notice girls don't believe you when you say, "Nah baby, those aren't stretch marks ... those are scars from when I fought a bear."

A lot of people think we've got it easy. And we don't. Like when us Indians ask for our land back, the government is all like, "NO." It's not easy.

When we go to a restaurant and we're greeted by the hostess, she's all like, "Hi. Welcome. Do you folks have a reservaaaaa ... shun. AH, gosh. I'm, uh, sorry. I'm sorry. Cuz you DO have a reservation ... it's just not here at the restaurant."

And, listen folks, I DON'T get mad anymore when I see non-Native people dressed up as Indians on Halloween. I don't get mad. I used to get mad. I don't anymore. I just throw change at them. Really hard. In the face. "Spare change? You want some spare change? Spare ... change."

But people get mad at me when they find out I'm a status Indian. They get mad, want to fight me. If you want to fight anyone over the way I look—fight my mom. She's the one that slept with a white guy that couldn't afford a condom. Fight her, not me. I'll warn ya though, she's a tough Indian woman—she grew up in the bush man. She used to skin beaver with her teeth.

And I see you white people out there—looking all scared right now, "Indians are white now? NOOOOOO." And that sucks for you, but awesome for me. You could accidently vote me in as Prime Minister and this country would be a lot different. "As Prime Minister of Canada, I'd like to enact into law, THE POWWOW HOUR ... on every radio station across the country, mandated by law, a little mini-powwow for all Canadians at every major intersection in every major city. "Dance it whiteman, you're doing great!"

A lot of people out there give me trouble over the way I look. They tell me I'm lucky I look the way I look. They say I haven't experienced the racism and all of that. I'm here to tell you that's not true—it's NOT FUN FOR ME AT THE POWWOW, in my regalia, sitting at my drum, people walking by me all weekend whispering, "God damn hippies," every time they walk past me.

When it comes right down to it—we're the same, but a LITTLE different. Not much, a few small differences. Like last weekend, I was at the powwow right, and I was all like, "SINGING POWWOW" and everyone was standing around goin, "Exactly bro," you know what I mean? You know what I mean, we all rake our yards and wonder, "Ah shit, I wonder if this hurts Mother Earth?" Right guys? And who hasn't sat on a park bench and thought to themselves, "Ah, man ... I wish I WAS an Indian giver..." The land, am I right guys? Am I?

So, I am an Indian but I look like a cowboy. That sucks. Was rough playing Cowboys and Indians as a kid. Back in the day all the kids in the neighbourhood would start picking teams, I'd be the loser standing by himself at the end of it. Of course, I'd end up on the cowboy team—we'd get to playing and all the white kids had battery-operated guns that actually shot stuff, all my cousins were over here with sticks and rocks, looked like they were going to protest at OKA. We'd get into the game and inevitably the white kids would start winning the game and it'd hit me that I'm actually KILLING my cousins. I'd snap. Start shooting everyone! (LASER GUNS SOUND EFFECTS) "Die you dirty Indian." (MORE SOUND EFFECTS) "Die you John Wayne wannabe!" Finally, they'd all catch on that I wasn't actually on a team, they'd kick me out of the game. My brown side and my white side would get in a heated argument on that long walk home. "Do you even KNOW what a Windigo would do to a leprechaun, bro?" "Leprechauns are magic bro, a Windigo wouldn't be able to catch it, it's mystical. Has magic powers." PFFFT. As if, we'd eat those little green buggers for breakfast, decolonizing our minds the whole time, listening to them cry, "Me want me lucky charms for breakfast."

Man, it must be a big night … I'm wearing my town clothes tonight! You know what town clothes are right? Town clothes. They're the clothes us Native people can only wear twice a year—weddings and court. Growing up we had one good set of clothes on the rez … your town clothes. The clothes you're not allowed to get moose blood on.

Thank god for Walmart, we can all afford to look good eh? Oh, yes. Before Walmart what'd we do if something came up out of the blue and your town clothes were dirty—you'd borrow your cousin's town clothes. But it always seemed to happen to me that my cousin would be going to court WITH ME, so I'd be forced to wear my mom's town clothes. It's hard to convince the kids at school that pink button-up shirts with roses all over actually is IN STYLE.

Man, we love our Walmart in Indian Country. If they'd install smudge bowls in the aisle we'd move in. "Oh, ya, real sacred CD shopping." If you ever see an Indian praying at the foot of an aisle leave us alone—we're talking to "Kitchi Manitou" and asking him to roll back the prices on a DVD player. Do you know why we love our Walmart in Indian Country? Cuz we can drop our kids off in the toy aisle and go to the casino. I was there today getting this shirt, and I walked past that toy aisle—and sure enough there they were—six little Indian kids playing a game of football. They're opening up toys like it's Christmas in there. One kid there, snot all on his face, looking real dirty, asking me to put batteries in this remote-control car.

But those kids were getting in trouble from a white lady that worked there. She was yelling at them and I stopped her and said, "Don't blame the kids, blame the parents." She felt bad, told me I was right. So I grabbed my nephews and got the hell out of there before I had to pay for all the broken toys. "C'mon you guys, uncle doesn't have money for that stuff, let's get outta here. C'mon, we're going to sneak into a movie then dine and dash at the Pizza Hut."

All joking aside, we are a proud people. We're killers, bro. But we are a proudful bunch at times. That pride—we're just born with it. I was at my first, real Indian Protest when I got in touch with my Indian Pride. Awe, it was awesome—I don't even remember what it was about, but we WERE MAD. Oh, just mad. Cuz that's how some of us are, eh? Just protesting it up. You end up at a protest, and you don't even know what you're mad at. "What's this protest for?" "I dunno, grab a sign, and yell what they're yelling, I'm just here for the free bbq after." And what do we do when we get REALLY MAD, eh? What do we do? We walk to Ottawa. OH YA, cuz that'll show the government. And how do those conversations happen, anyway? There's a band meeting and someone goes, "Ya, we should do a walk. We'll walk to Ottawa." "Oh, ya. Okay, let's do it. Who's going?" "Well, not me, I've gotta alter the media here." So it ends up three people get sent out to fight the fight for the people, and they get to Ottawa just wet, hungry, and cold. The politicians peek out the window and say, "There's three homeless Native guys on the lawn asking to use the washroom, Mister Prime Minister."

There were 600 brown faces, all gathered at Queen's Park in Toronto. And the chant started, "Screw the whiteman." I was shocked, couldn't believe what I was hearing. "Screw the whiteman," they were shouting, quietly at first, "Screw the whiteman. Screw the whiteman." Then the crowd erupted, "SCREW THE WHITEMAN. SCREW THE WHITEMAN." And, I lost it. I just started givin' 'er. "SCREW THE WHITEMAN, SCREW THE WHITEMAN, SCREW THE WHITEMAN, SCREW THE WHITEMAN." I was ALIVE. But then I took a look around, no one was chanting anymore. I looks. Everyone staring at me. "C'mon, you guys, let's do this. Screw him. C'mon you guys, screw the whiteman. Do it. Let's screw him."

That's when it dawned on me: 600 brown faces, staring at me, like I was propositioning sex.

—2011

Katherena Vermette

Métis (Winnipeg) 1977–

Katherena Vermette is a Métis writer of poetry and fiction. Her work has appeared in several literary magazines and compilations, most recently *The Exile Book of Native Fiction and Drama* (2011) and *Other Tongues—Mixed Race Women Speak Out*. Vermette was the 2010–2011 Blogger in Residence for thewriterscollective.org and was recently accepted into the prestigious Master of Fine Arts Creative Writing program at the University of British Columbia where she began work in July 2011. A member of the Aboriginal Writers Collective of Manitoba since 2004, Vermette lives, works, and plays in Winnipeg, Manitoba.

"nortendgrrl" was included in the 2006 collection *Tales from Moccasin Avenue: An Anthology of Native Stories.* The story tackles issues of alcohol abuse and physical violence facing urban youth. With a dark sense of humour and jarring honesty, Vermette explores how an unfulfilling education, an uncaring family, and an indifferent community can lead to estrangement, isolation, and poverty for some Aboriginal women.

nortendgrrl

Kandi got her first tattoo today. On her right hand—the chubby bit between her thumb and first finger. It's a homemade, a blurry green like it's all fuzzy. It's a cross. Crucifix. Thick with curved points like triangles at the ends. Pointing down the back of her hand.

She likes it. She thinks it's like if she puts her hand up she belongs to Jesus. But if she puts it down—Satan.

She had a scar there. A burn. On the back of her hand. It was red a long time but turned into a bluish white blotch. Her boyfriend Dutchie said that was the white part of her and laughed.

She was embarrassed.

She got the burn at her first real day at her first real job. She had done babysitting and stuff but this was different. A friend of her mom's got her a busboy job at the Convention Centre downtown. She had to buy a white shirt and wear black pants. She was trying really hard but got so uptight and nervous balancing all those heavy glasses on the tray she ended up accidentally knocking over a coffee maker. Everything smashed and glass got everywhere and hot coffee got all over her new white shirt and her hand. She broke a lot of glasses and yelled before she could help it.

"Fucking hell!"

The lady in charge screamed at her.

"Get in the kitchen." All mad like it was her fault.

Kandi ran into the bathroom and wrapped her stinging hand in soaked toilet paper and then left the stupid convention and never went back. She got a cheque in the mail about a week later, three hours pay, enough for a pack of smokes and a slurpee.

THE BURN SCAR hadn't hurt in a long time. But when her friend Tam told her about this guy over on Boyd she knew who did homemades, that was the first thing Kandi thought about covering up. It didn't hurt. She was pretty drunk just in case, but she was pretty sure it wouldn't've hurt anyway. And after, she just stared at her new hand, her blistering skin stained a new colour. White skin completely covered. Like it had never happened at all.

KANDI ALREADY HAS two kids. Her oldest is five and a boy. He lives with her mom, and Kandi too sometimes. Lives there. But her mom and her don't get along so it never lasts. Each time she moves back in, Kandi swears, "She isn't going to get to me this time, this time, this time, I will stay no matter what." But there is always a "what" and she's off like a bad pair of jeans. Kandi's other kid is a girl and about two now. She was put in care right after she was born. Kandi's mom and a social worker put her up to it. Her mom didn't want to look after another. Her mom has issues. Turned out to be a good thing. Her girl wasn't born right. Had to be in the hospital for months. Still. Kandi was bitter about that one for awhile.

Kandi met Dutchie at Duke's—the old country bar on the other side of the bridge. She likes to go there even though sometimes she has to walk a ways. Sometimes if it's nice out, she likes to walk. Dutchie wore a blue silk shirt with a string tie, silver eagle brooch at his neck. He smelled like shampoo. They danced for hours. He knew all the line dances. He bought her drinks and gave her smokes. She thought he was all that, loaded and fun. And he was. That night anyway.

Dutchie has this thing with his ex. Something about his cheque. Gets more money if he pretends to live there. Kandi hasn't really asked him about it, just knows that at the end of the month he goes over there for a few days. Just a few. Kandi don't ask Dutchie a lot of questions about it. Dutchie's not the kind of guy you ask a lot of questions.

They got a place on Cathedral. Just a shitty little apartment, but it has a fire escape Kandi likes to sit on. It was real nice out there before it got so hot the metal burned her legs. When Dutchie's away though, she doesn't like to stay there anyway. There's a few guys living below she don't like. Sure, they're pals of Dutchie's, but….

When he's gone Kandi usually goes to Tam's. Tam rents out a whole house on Aikins, but there's only two bedrooms and Tam has three boys. Kandi has to sleep on the couch. It's a decent couch but it makes Kandi's back hurt. Plus Tam's kids are real loud. Sometimes they're good and it makes Kandi miss her own kids. But mostly she just wants to yell at them. She don't though. She lets Tam do that. That's a mom's job. Tam really likes her kids though. They laugh and eat food together.

Tam got all their initials tattooed up her arm.

BD

MP

PH

Kandi thought that was stupid. No one else would ever know what they mean.

Kandi feels old. She feels like her bones are old when she gets up in the morning. Her knees have been hurting all summer. She can't dance anymore. She feels fat. Way fat. Dutchie doesn't think she's sexy anymore. He told her so. A couple nights ago. Before he left. He told her she was just a uglyfatslob.

"He's one to talk," she thought. "Such a beer gut."

BUT KANDI DIDN'T SAY anything.

SHE WANTS TO MOVE. And then she doesn't. For awhile, Kandi wanted to get a house like Tam's. But then she didn't want that anymore.

Houses are so big and not attached to anything. They just sit there all alone on the ground. Unconnected. Kandi doesn't like the idea of that. How she'd feel all alone in a big house like that. If Dutchie took off for a couple of days. Kandi don't know what she'd do.

HER SECOND REAL JOB was when she was still in school and joined Work Ed. Kandi worked in a frame factory. They made picture frames and all fucking day she had to cut out long sheets of wood with this big scary saw machine. Then she would have to put them all together with hard, clear plastic and tiny metal clips. Then she had to wrap them in tight plastic wrapping and suck the air out of the wrap with another big scary machine. Each day she did a different thing, the same thing, all day. On her first day, she cut. The next day, she put together. The next, she wrapped. The fourth day she was supposed to pack them in huge boxes but she didn't show up. Her wrists ached. She couldn't move her hands right. They sent a cheque to the school. She had enough to buy her kid a video game, and went out that night. She had a good time that night.

It's good to have money when you have it.

SHE HASN'T SEEN HER girl for over a year. When she was only six months old and so small. It was too sad, Kandi thought, all those tubes and stuff. She didn't look right and Kandi didn't know what to do.

Kandi had named her Heaven when she was first born but she didn't look like the girl Heaven she had in her head. The nurse said they called her their little Angel, like a sweet Heavenly Angel.

Kandi told her they could call her anything they fucking wanted.

All Kandi can drink anymore is Pepsi. She can't barely eat a thing. She wishes Dutchie would come home. She went back to the apartment this afternoon but could tell he hadn't been. And she was so tired she wanted to sleep but they were partying down stairs and it was too loud. She lay on her back on the cool floor trying to hear the voices beneath. To hear if Dutchie was down there. But it was all just murmurs and singing with the music.

So she went back to Tam's. She knows Tam is getting sick of her and doesn't want her there. But Kandi doesn't know what else to do. She has to think. She has to eat. She has to sleep. But it's too hot.

She'd go see her mom but she's too embarrassed now. She don't want to hear her bitching. Her "I told you so's." She might have to, but's gonna put it off as long as she can. Tam has an air conditioner, just a small one in the window. Kandi sits with it blowing on her belly and looks out to the back lane. Burnt out garbage bin. Tags across the unpainted garage. Kids playing in the empty lot. In the old car with no wheels.

Kandi hates being this big. She can't wait for it to be over. She can't move. Can't get comfortable. And all she wants to do is sleep. But she can't. Tam's boys are so loud. She has to get the fuck out of here. Her mom's is way too far to walk and she has no bus fare. Maybe Tam'll lend her. She can't even think about it. She just wants to sleep.

Maybe when the baby comes. Maybe then she'll sleep.

Kandi hopes the baby'll come before next Friday. It's her birthday. At Duke's they give you a free drink when it's your birthday—anything you want. Kandi thinks she wants Rye. Not beer. Rye used to burn her throat but she's getting used to it. She'll be twenty after all. Time to start drinking something cooler and more grown up. Maybe she'll get to do that. Maybe Dutchie'll be there and see her looking so good without a big gut anymore. Then he'll remember that he loves her. And if he got his cheque'll buy her birthday drinks all night. Yeah. Probably. Probably she'll do that. Next week.

Kandi's third and last job was as a Telemarketer. She was really good at it. She had got cut off or some shit. Someone fucked up. And her mom screamed at her.

"Go get a fucking job."

So she did. She called a place in the paper that didn't have a name, just the number. But the guy got her an interview right away. She went to this office building downtown. The guy had a thick moustache and long smile. He has a funny way of talking even then. He brought her into this room with a long table. An old paki with a turban was already waiting in there. And Kandi and this paki listened to the guy with the moustache tell them what they were going to do. They just had to read a speech off a card. Speak slow and clear. And be nice. Over and over. The job was getting donations for the zoo. The first night Kandi made twenty dollars and four hours pay.

Kandi can be nice when she wants to be. She can be a cow too. When she wants.

She worked there three months. Nights. Didn't have to get up early. She only quit because the guy with the moustache whose name was Tom started cheating on her with this new white girl. She went in to yell at him but he ended up yelling at her. He called her a stupid squaw. Pointed at her with his dry lips and laughed. Told her to go back to the north end.

So she did. She never got the rest of her pay for that one. Didn't go get it either.

Tam gave Kandi twenty dollars and told her to go to her mom's. Kandi wishes she could walk there and have twenty dollars. But it's too hot. She can only walk slow. It would take forever. She goes to the store for a Pepsi. Has to sit on the step outside and drink before she can walk again. Some guy pulls up in a truck and shakes his head at her. But she can't help it. All she wants to do is lay down and sleep. She cuts through the park and stops at a bench. Finishes her drink. Kandi wishes she had more. Wishes it were rye. But it isn't. Just an empty bottle filled with nothing but air. She breathes in the Pepsi taste. All she wants to do is sleep. So she lies down. The sun is hot but Kandi doesn't care anymore. She's asleep before she can really think about it.

She doesn't feel her hand fall off her chest, still scabby. Her skin touches the sandy concrete, gently. Facing down.

—2006

David Alexander Robertson

Swampy Cree (Norway House/Winnipeg) 1977–

David Alexander Robertson is a Swampy Cree writer who received his B.A. in English from the University of Winnipeg. His realization that education could combat racism and sexism inspired him to write the graphic novel, *The Life of Helen Betty Osborne* (2008) and the four-part graphic novel series 7 Generations (2009–2011). Robertson lives in Winnipeg with his wife and children, and works in the field of Aboriginal employment.

Robertson's graphic-novel series, 7 Generations, addresses and embodies many diverse and complex parts of Aboriginal cultural and political history in what is now known as Canada. The series tells a story that is different from some mainstream representations of Aboriginal people, engaging readers in alternative ways of knowing and perceiving the world through Aboriginal experience and knowledge. The stories, which are sensitive, emotional, and provocative, provide important ways to explore humanity, addressing issues such as family, community, and spirituality. In this excerpt from the third book in the series, two brothers, James and Thomas, are removed from their home community and placed in a residential school—the first steps of their journey into a new and startling world.

From *Ends/Begins*

Wabanakwut (Wab) Kinew

Anishinaabe (Lake of the Woods) 1981–

Wab Kinew is a Sundancer, member of the Midéwewin, and hip-hop artist whose debut album *Live By The Drum* was released in January 2009. He has won an Aboriginal Peoples Choice Music Award, was nominated for a Future Leaders of Manitoba award in 2010, and was named by the *Winnipeg Free Press* as one of the top artists to watch from Manitoba. He works as a CBC reporter on television and radio. Kinew is known for his "Ojibway Word of the Day" segment on Facebook and YouTube, which seeks to revitalize the Ojibway language.

Kinew's "Good Boy" was featured on his popular 2010 Mide-Sun mix-tape album, and originally included artists Troy Westwood (Little Hawk) and Lorenzo. A music video was produced in collaboration with youth from community centres throughout Winnipeg and is available on YouTube. The song honours the memory of Matthew Dumas, an 18-year old Anishinaabe man, who was shot and killed by Winnipeg police on Monday, January 31, 2005. The shooting, which many in the Aboriginal community decried as driven by racial tensions, continues to be a divisive issue in Winnipeg.

Good Boy

He started as a good boy
But died in the hood boy
The city is the jungle so look out for the woods boy
Criminal appearance
Aboriginal appearance
Took the wrong way home now he's walking with the spirits
I'm just talking with my lyrics
Don't get caught in the hysterics
Just trying to let my kids live without the interference
It's bigger than the boy shot
Or cop who pulled the trigger
It's a product of our history how Canada's configured
What you figure
Well here's one man's opinion
Old habits die hard you wanna kill the Indian
but you can't kill us, the Elders taught us to survive
There's a cop chopper in the sky should we run for our lives?
No never, I'm more clever
Makin tomorrow more better
Jessica like a native Coretta Scott King
We need to stop things
I think we should, boys

Or more Native moms
say good-bye to their good boys

We gotta live together
And learn to give together
Or else we die without giving a shit together
Gangsters know eventually the cops is who they run to
And the cops gotta know that these Natives got some guns too
I'm not a sun to you
I see no art in war
I believe in peace
That's what this pipe is for
You may hear the vision
Think it's an oddity
That police and thugs could be living in some harmony
But follow me
Yes I got the mental fitness
I don't go to court
But still I bear witness
Matthew's sisters teaches cops yes
That's their business
Damn man can you imagine the forgiveness
If she forgives cops we should forgive the criminals
If they change their ways
Then respect the individuals
I stand before my God
Saying I'm so pitiful
Please save the children
Make em all invincible

—2010

Julie Lafreniere

Métis (Camperville) 1982–

Julie Lafreniere is a young Métis woman raised in Winnipeg, with roots in Camperville, Manitoba, and in the United States. She is an author who writes in a variety of media, from her op-ed columns in *Urban NDN* to her hip-hop column in *Uptown Magazine* to her blogs on Native issues. She has also written for radio and television.

Julie has a degree in Native Studies and Psychology and attended the University of Winnipeg in the Masters of English and Cultural Studies program. She currently lives in Ottawa, Ontario, with her young son and works in communications.

"Adventures in Dating a White Guy" originally appeared in the newspaper

Urban NDN and is a humorous take on dating, and in particular, interracial dating. It shows some of the ironies around first encounters and some of the real-life cultural exchanges young Aboriginal people experience. It also shows how important education is and how first opinions can be shaped before someone has even entered the room.

Adventures in Dating a White Guy

I have a date with a white guy.

Call it a rediscovery.

I haven't dated one in a decade.

So, I'm going over all the worst-case scenarios in my head.

If he brings me flowers I will probably laugh and run away…

If he wears a suit, or any sort of blazer…

Oh God, what if he wears a *Che Guevara* or an *Obama* shirt…the irony might get the best of me and I would likely vomit.

After having ran away.

I'm freaking out.

After all, what could a white guy and I possibly have in common?

My people have been oppressed for hundreds of years.

His people have…what? Basked and flourished in power? Immersed themselves in ignorance? Danced with delusions of superiority?

Now I'm getting mad.

Ah, shit. I haven't even met the poor guy and already I'm mad at him.

He doesn't stand a chance.

Why did I even agree to this?

Oh right, because he was really cute.

And he was wearing awesome, old-school, Adidas runners. That gave him credibility. I couldn't discount and judge him then.

And, *he asked.*

Maybe I should give him the benefit of the doubt? I DO know a lot of awesome white people.

But I've also been asked a lot of ridiculous questions by white people. My favorites:

So what would you attribute to the current state of your people?

So like, if you're a Métis you're like half and half?

How much free money do you get?

Your people are always whining, why don't they just get over it already?

… to which I promptly respond with a shake of my head.

I hate giving people history lessons. I mean, you live in Canada, learn the fucking history.

Wow, I'm swearing now… poor white dude definitely doesn't stand a chance.

I'm going to do my best to be open minded. Maybe he will surprise me. Pleasantly.

If all else fails, I always manage to have a good time.

Why am I even giving this that much thought? This much time? I don't normally do this. This is sickening.

I remember in my last relationship wishing my ex would bring me flowers or do something nice for me once in a while. Would it really be that bad if he brought me a rose or something … Hello?

YES. It would be absolutely horrendous.

I have a date with a white guy.

—*2009/2011*

Jennifer Storm

Anishinaabe (Couchiching) 1986–

Jennifer Storm is Anishinaabe from Couchiching First Nation in Ontario and is a recent graduate of Native studies at the University of Manitoba. In 2006, she received a Manitoba Aboriginal Youth Achievement Award and a Helen Betty Osborne Award for her work in leadership and the arts. Storm completed her first novel, *Deadly Loyalties* (2007), at the age of 14—a book that has gained widespread critical acclaim. She is an Aboriginal student recruitment officer at the University of Manitoba and is working on a new novel.

Deadly Loyalties follows a year in the life of Blaise, a 14-year-old Aboriginal teenager who witnesses her friend Sheldon's murder. Blaise is pulled into a gang war, discovering with discomforting detail what life on city streets is like. This excerpt (from chapter 3) exposes the many complex pressures that demonstrate the dual nature of relationships. Relationships are the basis in which Aboriginal people survive and persevere—but also can be what threaten their very lives and livelihoods. Dealing with issues of education, poverty, and sexuality, *Deadly Loyalties* paints a rich, vibrant, and thought-provoking picture about the costs of wanting to belong, the pain of violence, and how choices we make sometimes come with consequences we do not expect.

From *Deadly Loyalties*

When we got back to Damion's apartment, we spent the rest of the night smoking joints, listening to music and imaging what life was going to be like on our own. I was looking forward to no more curfews or chores. I could get high whenever I wanted, even stay up all night and sleep all day.

It felt a little awkward being alone with Damion. This was the first unchaperoned sleepover I'd ever had with a boy—and it wasn't even Sheldon.

I knew Damion was trying really hard to act normal, too. When things got quiet we would both stare at the ground or fiddle with our hands and clothes. I realized all we ever had in common was Sheldon and smoking weed.

"Wanna know a secret?" I asked.

"Yeah," Damion replied raising one eyebrow.

"Tom's mom still beats him."

I don't know why we were being so cruel, but we both started to laugh. Tom had become our enemy.

"He used to tell people he got into fights and used the bruises as proof." We laughed so hard our eyes were tearing. The weed had really kicked in.

Damion told me how Amanda, a popular girl in my class, was no longer a virgin. That made me laugh even harder. My cheeks were starting to hurt. We did this all night. Shared secrets, gossip, smoked weed. It was so relaxing I was able to put the Sheldon incident out of my mind completely. I didn't want to think about it all. I didn't want the image of Sheldon lying bloody on the ground to creep into my vision. I just wanted to stay high, laugh and pretend everything was fine.

When it finally got really late and we were both starting to nod off, I went into the bathroom to change into a t-shirt and shorts for pajamas. I looked in the bathroom mirror. My t-shirt was all wrinkled and my eye's were blood-shot and squinty, but when I saw myself, I felt beautiful.

That was the first night I didn't need to cuddle in a nest of blankets. Sleeping beside Damion could be compared to the first few minutes of a sweatlodge. I felt safe and comfortable. I woke up the next morning remembering I wasn't in my own bed. At first I had a drowsy strange sense of, *where am I?* Then I opened my eyes and my mind caught up to reality. A deep, heavy pain centered in the middle of my chest. *Sheldon.* I pushed back the feeling and the thought of him. But my heart still ached. It was a homesick kind of feeling. I started to think about my mom. I allowed myself to daydream.

I remembered when my mom would get a big paycheck or win at the casino she would be happy all week. She'd take me out on shopping sprees and we'd spend the whole day together. If I was ever lonely or depressed she'd spend all night just watching movies with me in her bedroom. I never thought much before about our good times. It wasn't until I missed her that these thoughts came to mind. I wondered if she was feeling the same way— missing me and remembering all the good times we spent together.

Most of the time I felt like, to her, I was just the annoying, expensive consequence of loving my father. Sometimes I thought the only reason I was there was to be the presence that kept her from being alone. I felt sorry for my mom. She probably heard about Sheldon by now and may be thinking the worst of what happened to me. If she'd taken the time to notice my clothes were gone and my school work was sprawled on the floor, she could've put two and two together.

Last time I ran away from home was because she gave me an earlier curfew for skipping. She never looked for me. I knew because I stayed at Carly's house. That should've been the first place she looked, since we were best friends at the time. Carly was over almost every day and my mom hated her because we always got in trouble. She never liked many of my friends for that reason. It never occurred to her that I was the one who came up with all the brilliant "get into trouble" ideas. Whatever Sheldon taught me I would pass on; it was definitely the kind of stuff to get you in trouble. All my friends thought I was cool for it. It was always like a competition for who could be the first to do something audacious, or who could do it better. My other friends felt I was so lucky to have someone like Sheldon in my life. He was the coolest.

I cuddled into the blanket, thinking about how different things were going to be. Me, Sheldon, Tom and Damion used to do all kinds of things together. We used to walk everywhere together; sometimes we'd walk for no real reason. Tom and I would dance together when Sheldon and Damion weren't around to call us lame. We'd put on his mom's old dance CDs and do goofy moves with each other. This is how I learned my jig. It had no real structure, I just moved my feet around real fast.

"Holy Speedy Gonzales! You can barely see your feet move!" Tom would joke.

I knew Tom's mom from hanging out at his house. She was really nice to me. She always said I looked hungry and fed me snacks that could amount to a whole meal. Most days, she looked like a pillowy comforter that you could dive into. Her skin was soft and she smelt like coffee and cupcakes. I had only ever seen her mad once. Tom and I were skipping school and eating our lunches early at the school park. She happened to drive by and recognize her son's big grey t-shirt. She came stomping up to us, red as a tomato and cursing, "I swear to God, Tom Dubois! You're not gonna be able to sit on a toilet after I'm done with you!"

I sat on the swing, my mouth wide open, forgetting all about the peanut butter and jelly bite still inside. She grabbed Tom off the swing by his hair then dug her long nails into his arm. Tom didn't flinch, didn't resist in any way. He just went easy and limp, like a submissive dog. She slapped him a couple times, whacking his head with her thick arms. She didn't seem to care that I was there watching. She acted like she didn't even notice me. After it was over, the three of us never spoke about it.

Sheldon was everything Tom wished he could be. Sheldon had no fear of adults, he had no fear of consequences. I remembered once how Damion wouldn't let me go biking around town with him and Sheldon because he thought I'd slow them down. I was hurt but tried to act like I didn't care or had lost interest in going with them anyway. Sheldon wasn't fazed that I was a girl and didn't think I would slow them down. He told Damion to shut up and then officially invited me to join them. I felt my heart skipping and I couldn't help but smile like an excited dork. I jumped on my bike and tried extra hard to keep ahead of them just to prove Damion wrong. This was how my first real crush happened. Sheldon had stood up for me, he made me feel special. My crush only lasted a couple weeks, but at the time, I thought for sure we were meant to be together.

Those guys had always called me a "little girl," because for a long time I was always trying to prove I wasn't. It was that particular day, on our bikes, that Damion really started to accept me as an equal friend. He started to accept me more and more as I kept proving I could do anything they could, and sometimes better. I knew that day my life was starting to change, and it scared me. I remember I wanted to talk to someone, and that someone was Sheldon. He understood me without thinking I was being lame.

Lying there beside Damion, my daydreams tapered off. My mind wandered back to Sheldon. For the first time, I cried because I hadn't tried to save Sheldon. If I had only called the cops first, or gone outside, or even called someone to help Sheldon. I should have known that he couldn't take on those three guys by himself. I wanted to wail, but I stifled my crying. I made sure that I didn't make any sounds that would wake up Damion. I wished I could have turned to Damion and curled into him. I had never wanted a hug more than I did right then. *It's okay, Blaise. You're alright Blaise. Blaise, shhhoouushhh baby.* I soothed myself.

I got up and looked over at Damion. He had his back turned to me, still sleeping. I went to the bathroom to get dressed. My eyes were still kind of puffy, but less red than last night. When I went back to Damion's room he was up and dressed already. We were both quiet, making small talk. Neither of us mentioned Sheldon. It wasn't long before we headed downtown because Damion wanted to get some new clothes for the party at Randy's that night.

I had never really hung out downtown on a weekday before. There were business people in suits, acting like they didn't notice us kids or the beggars. Maybe they really didn't. Busy with their own important lives—we didn't exist to them.

I could relate more to the street people than to the business people. In the daytime, I thought it might be a fun life being a bum. They never had matching outfits or bothered to comb their hair. They could say weird things to us and we'd just laugh. Damion and I stopped at a corner when an old guy who was picking up cigarette butts looked at me. I smiled and offered him the last of my smoke. He graciously took it and said to me, "You know … I wish people still put pies out on their window sills."

Damion and I laughed.

"Me too, buddy," I said.

I had no money to shop with, but Damion did. He bought me a skirt. I was really excited about it. It was a denim skirt that made me look like a real teenager. I stood in front of the mirror in the store looking at myself. *I bet Sheldon would've thought I looked more like a teenager in this. He wouldn't be able to call me little girl in this.* My eyes welled up with tears. I shook my head; shook off that dark feeling and went to see what Damion was looking at. He had found himself some pants that were baggy all around. He had to wear his belt with them. We couldn't find anything else in that store, so we left.

"Do you like the skirt?" Damion asked as we walked.

"Yeah," I answered shyly. I felt embarrassed that he had to buy it for me. "Thanks." I said.

Damion put his arm around my shoulder. "No problem, Blaise."

In another store, I found a tight tube top that ended just below my bellybutton. I took a couple of shirts into the change room. I adored the tube top, but when I checked the price tag on my top it read thirty-six dollars! I sighed. I couldn't ask Damion for that. I tore the tag off and buried the shirt in the bottom of my purse.

"Nothing fit me," I said walking out of the change room. Damion was looking at his shirt in the mirror.

"I think I should buy this one, what do you think?" I checked out his shirt. It was like any other shirt but it gave him an extra bit of "cool."

"It's cool." I said, starting to feel my adrenaline rise. The shirt in the bottom of my purse was making my heart beat faster. Tom changed out of the shirt and went to the cashier. I went by the door to wait for him. I watched as they put the receipt in the bag and gave it to Damion. I tried to look casual, but I noticed my palms were beginning to sweat. We walked out of the store and I prayed the alarm wouldn't go off. It didn't. When we were a block away from the store, my heart rate returned to normal. I looked back to make sure no one had followed us. "Damion? You know that white tube top I was trying on?"

"Yeah, it was nice. Too bad it didn't fit," he said.

"Yeah, well it did fit, and that's why I got it!" I said as I opened the purse so he could peer in.

He smiled and put his arm back on my shoulder, "You rebel."

I was happy he didn't get mad at me. I had only ever stolen candy in front of him before. I was too excited to wait until we got back to Damion's place, so we stopped in a public washroom for me to change.

The streets were busy downtown. Cars sped by with music blaring or the drivers would be talking on their cells. Even though it was shady downtown during the day because of all the tall buildings, most people seemed to wear sunglasses. The wind was stronger between the buildings and I was worried my skirt would fly up to my chest, but luckily the denim was too heavy for that. I noticed for the first time grown men were turning their heads to look at me. Not for doing something weird or embarrassing, but because I finally looked pretty enough to deserve it.

It was seven o'clock by the time I had a shower, got dressed and dried my hair. While Damion was in the shower I put on my makeup. By eight o'clock I was ready to go. My makeup was done, my outfit complete, my hair styled straight and put into a ponytail. Damion was ready too; he looked handsome in a dangerous way, like he might shank you for looking at him funny. His eyes had a look of wisdom that most kids our age had not developed. His mouth was a thin straight line that still looked tender. I liked his face. He gave me a big puffy black jacket to wear. It had fur along the rim of the hood. It was new and looked really nice. We left his house and waited for our bus across the street.

When we got on the bus, I slid the black jacket under my butt, I did not want to be in direct contact with the public seat fabric. As I sat there staring out the window and I began feeling nervous about being at the party. *What if the guys who killed Sheldon had seen me in the window? What if they were going to be at the party? What if they were waiting for me, ready to kill the only witness?*

I didn't pay attention to where we were going, to the streets or anything on our way there, so when we got off the bus I was as good as lost. The house was across the street from a government housing complex that looked old and empty. I suppose the house was perfect for a party. It also looked old and run down. The eavestroughs were barely hanging on, the paint looked dirty, white and chipped and the grass was overgrown to the point of being wild. It's not like the party could wreck the house any worse than it already was.

Even when we were standing outside the house I could hear the throb of the music from the party. I could feel the bass pulsing in my stomach. It was cool but scary at the same time. Damion and I walked up the sidewalk stepping over broken glass on the ground. Three guys stood outside the house on the street. They were yelling and swearing at each other, but I couldn't make out what they were saying. They were all obviously drunk. One guy seemed more nervous than the others as he tried to mediate and calm the situation down. But the swearing escalated to pushing and then finally turned into a fight. Suddenly, a few people came running out of the house and circled the fight. I wanted to stop and watch too but Damion only slowed down for a moment, glanced over at them, and continued on to the house.

When we got closer to the front door I noticed one slutty-looking girl standing with two older guys. She had bleached blonde hair, gross makeup, and was giggling and acting really drunk. They had their hands all over her and she seemed to be enjoying the attention. Damion looked at me, "Don't separate," he said, and looked at me with a serious look on his face. I looked back at him and nodded my head in agreement. Now I was worried about the shirt I was wearing. It resembled the outfit the girl outside was wearing. I didn't want to go inside, but I followed Damion closely, practically right on his arm. I was mostly nervous about standing out—not fitting in. These people were older and didn't care about anything but a good time. I wanted to be one of them but I wasn't yet. I felt younger. I wanted to know what it would be like having someone like Damion come up to me and tell me I'm the prettiest girl in the room.

It was crowded walking in the house. There were so many people at the party. I looked around the living room. I saw people drinking, but what really caught my eye were the people passing joints around. Although I smoked weed before, it was always while outside or hiding in bedrooms with my friends. One time my uncle caught me with drugs. He came to our house when my mom wasn't home. I tried to put everything away when he walked in my room but it was too late. I was busted and could tell from the anger in his eyes. In my mind I saw him as a cowboy. His boots were tapping on the ground in rhythm, and he was palming his keys like they were a whip. From then on I never wanted to be caught again, so I became a bit sneakier.

Once we were in the living room I noticed a door left slightly open and some people sitting near a partly open door, snickering. Inside that room it was dark, but I could see the end of a bed. I saw movement and immediately turned my gaze away, feeling like I was violating something meant to be private. I wondered if the couple on the bed were being liberated, oblivious, or purposely trying to shock people.

Damion steered me over to the couch where a group of people from Sheldon's gang were smoking up. I've known about these guys ever since Sheldon killed that guy. We sat down beside them. Normally, this would be weird to do in a house full of strangers, but the truth was that there was no room anywhere else, and Damion wanted to talk to Sheldon's gang. I sat near the end of the couch beside a guy who seemed to be about eighteen-years-old. At first, they looked at us with curiosity. The guy beside Damion pointed at him, "I seen you around before. You're one of Sheldon's friends, right?"

Damion knew who the guy was, but he looked at him hard pretending he was trying to remember his face, "Oh yeah … I think I met you once before."

The guy smiled. Then he looked at me. "I don't know you though," he said as he pointed his finger towards me. Nervously my eyes shifted from him and then to Damion.

"That's my friend, Blaise. She's cool. She was a friend of Sheldon's too."

The guy's name was Fred. He shot Damion a look. "What do you mean by 'was'? Do you guys carry beef with Sheldon or what?"

Damion looked at him in disbelief, "You don't know? You weren't told?" Damion shrugged his shoulders, "Sheldon's dead, man. He got killed by The Reds. Happened about two days ago."

Fred looked at us in horror. As Damion told the story, I sat there dazed and numb. I didn't want to listen to the details and relive it in my mind. But I also didn't want to be disrespectful, so I sat there staring at Fred's face. He had three big freckles on his nose that made up a lopsided triangle. It was the perfect number of freckles, one less and it would look like dirt, one more and it would be the only thing you could see. Damion told him about the bad situation we were in now. That we weren't sure what stories were going around about what happened. Or, if the Reds even knew anyone had witnessed the murder. He loosely suggested we should take Sheldon's place.

After Damion finished telling the story, Fred talked to us slowly and seriously, like a teacher does when they're about to say something that's going to be on a test. "Honest, I thought he just fucked off for a couple days, that maybe he'd show up tonight." He buried his head into his hands and then said, "Do you understand our rule about what happens when one of us dies?" He lifted his head to make eye contact with both of us.

"No." I answered. *Has anyone in this gang died before Sheldon?* I wondered.

"Well, you wanna take his place?"

Damion and me exchanged looks and Damion nodded his head, yes.

"Okay, but you have to get initiated first. That's the rule. Cool?" He asked.

"Is that seriously a rule?" I asked.

"Shut up, Blaise. Of course it is. I told you that." Damion looked annoyed with me. Like my stupid question was going to mess everything up. I didn't say anything else. I guess it was supposed to be a rhetorical question.

"Good, we'll initiate you later tonight … after the party," he said with a smile as he passed Damion a joint. I sat there confused; wasn't I in the plan too? I didn't want to be left out, no matter what.

"What about me? Can I be initiated too?" I asked.

Fred looked me up and down, "I guess there's no harm in that."

What Damion could do, I could do too. Maybe he didn't really invite me because he was waiting for me to ask. I hoped it wasn't because he thought I was just a skank that came along to the party with Damion. Either way, I took it as a challenge to my capability and I wanted to take him up on it. But what if I messed up and didn't do as well as Damion for some reason? Would they take him in and turn me out? *Damion wouldn't let us get separated like that ... would he?*

When the joint got passed to me I took a hoot and kept it passing. When the weed kicked in I felt paranoid. I wanted to be in the corner somewhere with Damion so we could laugh at all the stupid shit we laughed about the night before. But I couldn't do that. These guys didn't seem the least bit high, even Damion. I felt like I was the only one getting buzzed—and way too buzzed. I sank into the couch and wanted it to swallow me up. I hated being the highest one, and being paranoid was ruining my buzz.

People were coming and going. At first I was on the end of the couch but now I was more in the middle. A guy sat down beside me and tried to talk to me several times. I tried to keep it short, sinking myself deeper into the couch. Whenever I wasn't looking he'd rub my leg. At first I pretended not to notice, then he'd slide his hand higher. I slapped his hand fast and he recoiled with surprise. Then I got scared he was going to get pissed off. To my surprise he just kept talking. I sighed in relief and turned back to Damion's conversation with Fred. The guy beside me tried again. His hand started massaging my thigh as he spoke to me casually, slurring and trying to give me sexy eyes that, instead, looked like floating buttons. I nodded my head and said "uh-huh, uh-huh," even though I had no idea what he was saying. I nudged Damion. He swirled around and looked at me, "Yeah?"

I nodded my head towards the guy. He was still talking drunkenly, not catching on. Damion got up and shot a fist into the man's face. I held in my scream. I didn't think he'd handle it like that so fast. I just wanted him to tell him to fuck off or something. Then the guy stood up. Damion raised his head high while still looking down at him, "Don't touch her."

The guy smiled. "I'll touch whatever I want." I could see the anger in Damion's face. He hit him again, and the guy flew backwards. The guys on the couch started laughing. "Go Damion! Show us what you got!"

The guy got up and wiped the blood off his nose. "You bitch!"

He threw a punch back at Damion but it wasn't quick, so Damion blocked it and threw another punch. The guy grew frustrated and pulled out a shank. Damion's eyes widened, but not for long. He looked at Fred, who smiled, grabbed an empty beer bottle from beside him, and threw it to Damion. Damion grabbed it and swung it at the guy's head. The guy went down but came up charging with the switch out again. Jumping out of the way, Damion hit the guy in the back of the head. He went down again, but this time he stayed down. I got worried; did Damion make the same mistake as Sheldon had?

This fight was like fights I'd seen before. Even kids at school would try swinging knives around. But I was still shaken up by what happened to Sheldon and I knew that it could actually happen again.

Fred said, "Ha! Ha! Knocked'im out good! You're a real fighter, Damion!" We both sighed in relief.

"Hey, lets gank some of his stuff!" Fred continued. I looked at Damion and he shrugged. I wanted to be accepted as much as Damion seemed to be, so I was the one who bent over him to search his pockets. I found three grams of weed and a wallet. I passed the marijuana to Fred and took the wallet. The rest of the gang dragged the unconscious guy out of the room and threw him outside. I proudly showed Damion: fifty bucks! It was the first time I was ever fought over. I never felt more like a woman in my life.

Early in the evening time flew by, but as the night wore on it slowed to a crawl. We couldn't stop talking about Damion's fight. Every minute felt like an hour. My new buddies told me that it was because of all the weed. I was wasted, and so was Damion.

Damion started to get rowdy and flirted with any girl that walked by. He was getting cocky from all the attention because of his fight. He started to leave me behind to bask in the light of his new popularity. Some guy came along and kept giving me drinks. We sat on the floor and talked. At first I thought he was a little weird but as time flew by my impression changed. He seemed to listen to everything I had to say. I spilled my guts about Sheldon and told him I was staying with Damion because I ran away from home. I talked about everything I could think of, like how Sheldon had been my best friend, how Sheldon was always the one to see me as more than just a girl. He always tried to treat me like one of the guys and trusted me with the secrets only best friends would know. I didn't tell him about the guy Sheldon had done in.

I told him about how Sheldon always listened to me. I began to tell him about the time that Sheldon stood up for me when some girls at school were making fun of me. I remembered the day that Sheldon skipped school and showed up at mine. I remember sitting alone because Carly was at a dentist appointment. I noticed everyone shift towards the entrance, whispering and gossiping. I turned to see Sheldon and smiled instantly. I jumped out of my seat and ran over to him, excited he had come to my school.

Sheldon almost ignored me, like he was pretending he didn't know me. He asked, "Where's those bitches you were telling me about, Blaise?" I inadvertently looked toward the group of gossipy girls that were always picking on me, but then I quickly turned back to Sheldon.

I got nervous that everyone might have heard him. I prayed that whatever he did, that it didn't make my situation worse. Everyone fell silent and just stared at Sheldon, anticipating would come next.

"You!" he walked passed me and pointed to the prettiest girl in the group, "You're the bitch that gave me chlamydia, you dirty bitch! No one touch her, she's got chlamydia! I'm sending you my doctor's bill you dirty slut!" He left the cafeteria, then he yelled from the hallway, "You best believe you'll be hearing from me again!"

The guy sat there listening to my stories, nodding his head with an understanding smile and kept refilling my drink as I drank. We were both drunk. Out of the corner of my eye I saw a man staring at me. I looked back at him every now and then, and he was still there. He was tall with a muscular build, green eyes, dark skin and dark hair. I liked him noticing me. "The guy who'd been filling my drinks was starting to pass out. I stumbled over to Damion and kind of collapsed on the cushion beside him. He smiled and made room for me. I leaned on his shoulder and soon fell asleep.

I awoke with a jolt; Damion was screaming at me to wake up. When I painfully lifted my eyelids, he grabbed my hand and started running out of the house. Being jolted awake while I was drunk caused me to have a foggy understanding of the situation at first. I felt sick to my stomach. I stumbled along and Damion pulled me as he ran. Everyone was running out of the house. The farther we ran, the smaller our gang got. The group kept splitting in half into smaller groups. Some headed for the street while others took back alleys to jump fences, which me and Damion thought safest as well.

"Where are we going?" I asked, still half asleep and nauseated.

Fred and the rest of the gang started climbing a fence. One gang member, the tallest one, yelled, "Hurry up you two, the pigs are coming!"

Damion helped me climb. I was so dizzy I could hardly see. The gang helped me on the other side. I was standing beside the tallest gang member and he asked me if I was okay. I nodded my head but I felt green in the face. In the distance I could hear the sirens. Damion and another boy were still on the front side of the fence. The sirens grew louder. Damion and the boy jumped the fence quickly and we all bolted down the alley. I ran in a blur through the dark, hauling myself over old ratty fences that could collapse under the weight of a single person, until we made it to the tall guy's house.

—2006

Suzanne Morrissette

Métis (Winnipeg) 1987–

Suzanne Morrissette is an artist, curator, and writer from Winnipeg. In 2009, she graduated from Emily Carr University of Art + Design with a Bachelor of Fine Art degree, which she followed soon after with a Master of Fine Art degree at the Ontario College of Art & Design University in 2011. Her thesis, entitled "Stories of place, location, and knowledge" examines the correlation between First Nations artists and reserve life. Morrissette's writing and artistic practice are informed by issues of identity, place, wilderness, and power. Morrissette currently lives in Thunder Bay, Ontario, where she works as the curatorial resident at the Thunder Bay Art Gallery.

Morrissette's "incomplete thoughts on knowing through place" was featured in an anthology workshopped and presented to residential school survivors at the first national event of the Truth and Reconciliation Commission in June 2010. It represents the return of Morrissette to the home of her Nana, her grandmother, through her memories and—at the end—her body. It shows how this is a place that both is isolated from her but is uniquely her home, the place where she came from. It is a testament to the journey she has come from and where she is going.

incomplete thoughts on knowing through place

I find myself in the prairies often, though I have not permanently lived there in a long time. When I am away I think about when I will be there next. I think about the spaces that I used to frequent and about those places that I have yet to see; the houses that I grew up in, the warm living rooms of friends and family, and the remains of the home where my Nana spent her youth. There are good memories, there are those that are not so good, and then there is everything else. It seems to me that visual memories, lists of various significant objects, and other such recollections, together form a repertoire from which to draw a different kind of knowledge. Here, the things I know are in direct relationship with the things that I do not. But in these travels I still notice the ground underfoot.

There were a few summers in the nineties where my family spent a great deal of time up in the Interlake region of Manitoba, more specifically known as St. Laurent, Manitoba. As I recall, I simply woke up one day and we owned property and had plans to build on it. And we did, for the next five or so years. My Cree father and my Mennonite grandfather, on my mother's side, built our house using remnants from another house that my grandfather was tearing down in the city. In true Mennonite fashion everything was reclaimed and used again. His 1978 Toyota Tercel transported the entire house, piece by piece. Tucked inside three walls of aspen brush a house was built that never became our home.

Over time I learned more about the area, things that both did and did not explain why I was never at home in this place. In the movie store, at the Tempo station, and even on our routine trips to the dump, these spaces so swelled with memory that I, for one, could not distinctly interpret at that time. In social spaces there were glances but rarely were there conversations. These were things that we never discussed but that managed to make themselves known somehow.

I did not know a lot of people there but through time I found that my Nana, my father's mother, knew them—or at least I learned that she had known them at one point in her life. I do not remember, but have been told that she allowed herself to speak Michif in these spaces: however seldom, however reluctantly.

On one particularly memorable occasion I visited the site where my Nana's house once stood. Nana was present. We found a few things: a hole in the landscape where the cellar once was, bedsprings, and various other objects that one might find in a prairie household from the early 1900's strewn and buried under dense prairie earth. They were the types of things that sustain life in very subtle ways—forks, teacups—they are also the types of things that sometimes get left behind. That day I remember we were chased out by wild horses. In relation to this piece of land I do not know where the Residential School was where she attended in her youth. She did not tell me a lot of what she carried. I do think that maybe I have come to know her story only, somewhat differently that she must have. I do know bits and pieces. I have heard and read different versions of the same story too. So I come back frequently, to sift through the landscape for stories.

—2010

Rebecca Kantimere

Anishinaabe (Winnipeg) 1989–

An emerging writer, Rebecca Kantimere was raised in Winnipeg, but her mother's family comes from Manigatogan and her father's family is from Waywayseecappo. She is a graduate of RB Russell High School in Winnipeg. Rebecca is married with two children and is currently a full-time, stay-at-home mom.

"A Mother's Promise" was originally workshopped and presented to residential school survivors at the first national event of the Truth and Reconciliation Commission held in June 2010 in Winnipeg, Manitoba. It is a rich, stark portrayal of the intergenerational legacies of residential schools and the effect they have on families and child-rearing. Kantimere's words sear into one's soul, and her emotions are evident—this is the kind of truth-telling narrative that is needed in order for reconciliation to take place.

A Mother's Promise

Growing up my grandmother was never around
much. Not only for us, her
grandchildren, but her children too. Never do I
remember getting a card on my birthday
or a present at Christmas. The only time she ever
came around or called was when she
needed something or was in trouble. For years I
called her Kookoo and I had much respect for
her. As I got older, "Kookoo" turned into Janet and
the respect faded.

   When I was younger, Janet had come over a few
times extremely intoxicated.
The most vivid memory was when I was seven
years old. My cousin was staying with
us, because his parents were unfit to care for him.
Since my aunt was older, Janet had no worries and decided to go on a
binge. She always asked us to
keep her daughter, who was two years older than I
was.

It was summertime and really hot, so we decided
to sleep downstairs. My aunt
and cousin were on the couches, my sister and I
were on the floor, and my mom, dad
and younger brother were on the pull-out couch.
We were all sleeping when Janet came pounding at the door. My dad
opened it, and she forced her way in.
She went over to my aunt and cousin and starting
grabbing them off the couches. While
this was going on, my dad and Janet were
yelling, swearing, and arguing with
each other. My mom was holding my little brother
and we were all crying, begging Janet
to leave, but she refused. My dad eventually got
fed up and shoved her out the door.
Finally outside, Janet decided to call the cops.
When the cops arrived they saw how intoxicated she was, so they took her
   away and
asked no questions. After a night in the

drunk tank, she came over the next morning and took my aunt home.
She didn't apologize or say
anything about the night before.

I wonder if she knows what she has done to us?
Does she even care? Will she
ever want to make things right? Our Elders are
finally starting to heal, but what about
the children? What about the grandchildren?
Residential schools didn't only affect the
people in them, it affected the families of survivors
as well. It isn't only the survivors'
time to heal. I'm stopping the pain in my life now.
My daughters, will never experience the pain or hurt Janet caused us for
    so many
years. That is the promise my husband and I have made to each, and now
    have made to our daughters.

—2010

Alyssa Bird

Cree/Anishinaabe (Peguis First Nation) 1993–

Alyssa Bird's traditional name is Ah-nah-wainsee-quance, and she is a member of the Wolf clan. Born and raised in Winnipeg, her family is originally from Peguis First Nation. She graduated from photography school and aspires to combine her writing with her photographic skills to eventually work in photojournalism, focusing on covering Aboriginal issues all across North America.

"Frustration" was shortlisted in 2008 in the nationally renowned Canadian Aboriginal Youth Writing Challenge, a competition that calls upon "young Aboriginal storytellers to explore their heritage through creative writing." The piece is about dreaming about a future and the many possibilities this place holds—as well as the many doubts it inspires. It is about looking at the path one has travelled, the ancestors who made it possible, and gaining courage, strength, and resilience to carry on. It is with Bird's piece that *Manitowapow: Aboriginal Writings of the Land of Water* ends, but "Frustration" also represents a possibility—a window—into the beautiful path ahead for Aboriginal people in Manitoba, a place where many more have yet to write their story.

Frustration

He sat there with a few pages of loose leaf in front of him and a pen in his hand, tapping it against his head. He was looking towards the corner of the room in deep thought. "What should I write about?" he thought. He then spoke aloud, "Out of all the things I can come up with, why can't I just choose one?" He had narrowed it down by a small fraction by deciding that he wanted to have an Aboriginal perspective of how he was writing.

He had always pictured himself being a famous writer someday. While he was sitting in classes he always could come up with ideas or thoughts about other people's lives going on and all the different problems or adventures that they would face. He was so imaginative that he could come up with last names, family problems, and even scars that these people had. All of his past English teachers had encouraged him to write all of his ideas into different short stories or even books. But he had always thought that no one would care about what he'd have to say. He had always thought to himself, "Why would anyone want to know my stories?"

So he had always kept most of his thoughts and things that went on in his life written down in a notebook, which he had always carried with him everywhere he went. It was very worn out and one could tell that the book had been through a lot, along with whoever had owned it.

He had been born on a small reserve a few hours out of the city and spent most of his life out there. He and his mom had lived with his very traditional grandparents and they made sure that he was bought up to learn the old ways. So when he had moved off the reserve when he was 14, he left with a strong sense of who he was as an Aboriginal person.

He sat there for a few minutes, still thinking. He was the type of person to think out loud when he was alone. "Hmm, What about... no never mind. Hmm..." He thought about writing about the Oka Standoff with a young man's perspective that was fighting against the people trying to develop on his reserve's land. He could picture the story playing out already.

My brother was always the fighter of our family. I was just his nerdy little brother who tagged along with him wherever he went, but as he got older he made me stay home. Everything had gone downhill after the white people tried to develop that sacred area near our reserve and turn it into a golf course. I was 14 when all of this was happening. Being the fighter that my brother was, he was always right in the middle of all the rallies and protests that were going on. He wasn't going to let them walk all over our people and take what they want.

He then crumpled up the paper and took a shot at the garbage can in the corner. He missed and shrugged his shoulders and thought, "I'll just pick it up later" He was convinced that his Oka story was going nowhere and would just end in a cheesy way. He pictured that the boy's brother would get arrested and then the boy would fill his brother's shoes. He thought that it was too predictable.

So he sat there for a while, thinking of all things that his people had to go through. Then he thought about the stories that his Kookum had told him, about what all happened to her when she went to residential school. He got another idea and started writing about this little six year old girl.

She woke up with the tears from last night still on her cheek. But she quickly rubbed her face and started to prepare herself for the upcoming day. The day time was hardest for her; the sisters of the school were always shouting at her, whenever she did or said anything. They would hit her if she spoke in her language. So she just learned to keep quiet. She hated the time when the sun was up because the sisters and priests were always watching her, yelling at her, and calling her down. At night was the only time she was truly alone. At night before she went to sleep she had always hummed songs that her mother and Kookum had taught her.

He shook his head and folded the paper in half and set it aside. Again he thought that the story wasn't going anywhere, it would just be playing with people's sympathy and the last thing he wanted was for people to look down and feel sorry for Indians.

He sat there yet again, thinking, and then thought, "Maybe going into the past of Indians isn't the way to go." He already started to imagine a young man who was deeply involved with this one native gang. So again he started to write.

I stopped and hid in a doorway, trying to catch my breath. It was dark out, so I don't think anyone had seen me. I poked my head out and took a quick look around. So far the coast was clear, and so I just sat there for a few minutes. "Why did I take that shot? What the hell have I done?" I thought to myself. I sat there with my head in my hands trying to figure out what all just happened and what am I going to do next. I can hear shouting in the distance. So I picked myself up and started to run again. I kept to the back lanes and alleys, so I could quickly hide if anyone else happens to run by. I was down this one street just near main when I heard gun shots. I ducked and started sprinting in the opposite direction from where I heard the shots. I wasn't ready to die, not even for the gang I lived for, not for anyone.

He then sighed in frustration, crumpled up the paper, and threw it into the garbage can, the paper ball jumped out and landed next to the paper from earlier. He got up and started to walk around his room. He shook his head and was tired with himself and his ideas. He sat at the corner of his bed. He thought, "Who would want to hear anything that I had to say anyways?" He lay down and sat there for while. "Why should I even bother? Who's going to actually read and get what I'm trying to say?" he said. "Maybe I shouldn't be writing about other people," he thought.

He then glanced to his backpack, and then just stopped. He saw the corner of his notebook sticking out of a hole from his similarly roughed up backpack. He looked to the floor, then at his hand, which was still holding his pencil. He sat there silently, and then he finally got an idea. He sat back down at his desk, took a fresh piece of paper and wrote his story.

—*2008*

Permissions/Sources

Figs. 1, 2, and 3 replicate the rock petroforms of Manitou Api in Whiteshell Provincial Park.

Figs. 4 and 5 replicate rock paintings, often called pictographs.

Fig. 6. Scroll: Image from *The Rainbow in the North: a short account of the first establishment of Christianity in Rupert's Land by the Church missionary society* by Sarah Tucker. London: James Nisbet and Co., 1851. Glenbow Archives NA-3421-10.

Fig. 7. Map attached to Deed of 12 June 1811 conveying Assiniboia to the Earl of Selkirk. HBCA, Archives of Manitoba, E.8/1 fo.6

Fig. 8. "A letter from a Seioux Indian. His Signature is on the other side" [ca. 1822]. 9 x 18.5 cm. HBCA G.1/330.

Fig. 9. Tapis Breland: From the collection of the Le Musée de Saint Boniface Museum. Printed by permission.

Fig. 10. Buckskin coat: from the collection of the British Museum. ©Trustees of the British Museum. All rights reserved.

Fig. 11. Syllabics: Excerpts from *Sagkeeng Legends: Sagkeeng Aadizookaanag.* ed. Craig Charbonneau Fontaine. Copyright ©2010 by Craig Charbonneau Fontaine. Reprinted by permission.

Peguis: Excerpts from *Peguis: A Noble Friend* by Donna G. Sutherland. Winnipeg: Chief Peguis Heritage Park, 2003.

Pierre Falcon: "Li Lord Selkirk au Fort William," and English translation from *Pierriche Falcon: The Michif Rhymester,* ed. and trans. by Paul Chartrand. Copyright ©2009 by Gabriel Dumont Institute Press. Reprinted by permission.

Cuthbert James Grant and the Sioux Chiefs: Excerpts from *The Red River Settlement: Its Rise, Progress, and Present State.* London: Smith, Elder and Co., 65 Cornhill, 1856.

Peter Jacobs (Pahtahsega): Excerpts from *Journal of the Reverend Peter Jacobs, Indian Wesleyan missionary, from Rice Lake to the Hudson's Bay territory, and returning; commencing May, 1852: with a brief account of his life; and a short history of the Wesleyan mission to that country.* Toronto: Anson Green and the Conference Office, 1853.

Henry Budd (Sakachuwescam): Excerpts from *The Diary of the Reverend Henry Budd, 1870-1875.* Winnipeg: Manitoba Record Society Publications, 1974.

Louis Riel: "Song of the Métis Maiden" translation in Margaret Arnett MacLeod, ed., *Songs of Old Manitoba.* Toronto: Ryerson, 1959. Copyright ©L. Verrault. "Shudder, my Spirit" English translation ©2011 by Warren Cariou. Printed by permission.

Gabriel Dumont: Excerpts from *Gabriel Dumont Speaks,* trans. Michael Barnholden. Copyright ©1993 by Talon Books. Reprinted by permission.

Harriett Goldsmith Sinclair Cowan: Excerpts from *Women of Red River,* ed. W.J. Healy. Winnipeg: The Women's Canadian Club, 1923.

Charles Alexander Eastman (Ohiyesa): Excerpt from *Indian Boyhood,* New York: McClure, Philips & Co., 1902.

Kuspatchees: Excerpts from *Swampy Cree Legends*, as told to Charles Clay. Toronto: Macmillan Company of Canada, 1938.

William Berens (Tabasigizikweas): Excerpts from *Memories, Myths, and Dreams of an Ojibwe Leader*, as told to A. Irving Hallowell, eds. Jennifer S.H. Brown and Susan Elaine Gray. Montreal: McGill-Queen's University Press, 2009.

Maurice Sanderson: "Mill Stones at Fairford" selected from *Manitoba Pageant*, Jan. 1958, Vol. 3, Nr.2 by The Manitoba Historical Society. "Reminiscences of St. Paul's Industrial School" selected from *Manitoba Pageant*, Sept. 1958 Vol. 4, Nr.1. "Recollections of an Indian Missionary" selected from *Manitoba Pageant*, Sept. 1959, Vol. 5, Nr. 1.

Alex Grisdale: Excerpts from *Wild Drums: Tales and Legends of the Plains Indians*. Copyright ©1972 by Peguis Publishers.

The Dene Elders Project: Excerpts from *They Will Have Our Words: The Dene Elders Project Vol. 2*, produced by Lynda Holland and Mary Ann Kailther, from research by Larry Hewitt. Copyright ©2003 by Holland-Dalby Education Consulting.

George Barker: Excerpts from *Forty Years A Chief*. Copyright ©1972 by Peguis Publishers.

James Redsky (Esquekesik): Excerpts from *Great Leader of the Ojibway: Mis-quona-queb* by James Redsky. Copyright ©1972. Published by McClelland & Stewart. Used with permission of the publisher. All rights reserved.

Albert Edward Thompson: Excerpts from *Chief Peguis and His Descendants*. Copyright ©1973 by Peguis Publishers.

Thomas Boulanger: Excerpts from *An Indian Remembers: My Life as a Trapper in Northern Manitoba*. Copyright ©1971 by Peguis Publishers.

Elders from Norway House: Excerpts from *Norway House Anthology: Stories of the Elders, Vol. 1 & 2*. Copyright ©1991 and 1992 by Frontier School Division, Winnipeg. Reprinted by permission.

David Courchene Sr.: "Message of the Grand Chief" in *Wahbung: Our Tomorrows*, Winnipeg: Manitoba Indian Brotherhood, 1971. Copyright ©1971 by the estate of David Courchene. Reprinted by permission. "Problems and Possible Solutions" in *Indians Without Tipis: A Resource Book by Indians and Metis*, ed. D. Bruce Sealy and Verna J. Kirkness for Project Canada West. Copyright ©1973 by the estate of David Courchene. Reprinted by permission.

Alice Masak French: Excerpt from *My Name is Masak*. Winnipeg: Peguis Publishers, 1992. Copyright ©1992 by Alice Masak French. Reprinted by permission.

Louis Bird (Pennishish): Excerpts from *The Spirit Lives in the Mind: Omushkego Stories, Lives and Dreams,* ed. Susan Elaine Gray. Copyright ©2007 McGill-Queens University Press. Used with permission of the publisher. All rights reserved.

Elders of Moose Lake: Excerpts from *Cree Stories From Moose Lake*, ed. Dan Ehman. Winnipeg: Native Education Branch, Manitoba Department of Education, 1980.

Tobasonakwut Kinew: Excerpt from *Sacred Lands: Aboriginal World Views, Claims, and Conflicts*, eds. Jill E Oakes et al. Transcribed by Kathi Kinew. Copyright ©1998 by Tobasonakwut Kinew. Reprinted by permission.

Elders of Grand Rapids: Selections from *Grand Rapids Stories Vols 1 & 2*, ed. Raymond M. Beaumont. Copyright ©1996 and 1997 by Frontier School Division, Winnipeg. Reprinted by permission of the publisher.

Joanne Arnott: "Manitoba Pastoral" from *Wiles of Girlhood*, Vancouver: Press Gang Publishers, 1991. Copyright ©1991 by Joanne Arnott. "Migration" from *absinthe*, 7:2 (1994). Copyright ©1994 by Joanne Arnott. Reprinted by permission.

Brenda Isabel Wastasecoot: "Down the Flats" in *Eclectica* February 2005. Copyright ©2005 by Brenda Isabel Wastasecoot. Reprinted by permission.

Jordan Wheeler: "Sap" from *Voices: Being Native in Canada*, eds. Linda Jaine and Drew Hayden Taylor. Copyright ©1992 by Jordan Wheeler. Reprinted by permission.

Cheryl Smoke: "The Hills," from *Who Put Custer's Bloomers on the Pony?* Brandon: Bearpaw Publishing, 1998. Copyright ©1998 by Cheryl Smoke.

Trevor Greyeyes: "Jupiter and Mars" from *Prairie Fire*, 22.3 (2001). Copyright ©2001 by Trevor Greyeyes. Reprinted by permission.

David McLeod: "I write" and "statement of account #346" from *Prairie Fire* 22.3 (2001). Copyright ©2001 by David McLeod. Reprinted by permission. "boy I can't wait to get my cheque" from *Bone Memory*, Winnipeg: Aboriginal Writers' Collective of Manitoba, 2005. Copyright ©2005 by David McLeod. Reprinted by permission.

Paul DePasquale: "At the Edge of the Woods is a Fire" and "School of Hard Knocks." Copyright ©2011 by Paul DePasquale. Printed by permission.

Shayla Elizabeth: "chief miskwa mukwa" from *Bone Memory*, Winnipeg: Aboriginal Writers' Collective of Manitoba, 2005. Copyright ©2005 by Shayla Elizabeth. Reprinted by permission.

Gregory Scofield: "Prayer Song for the Returning of Names and Sons," "Women who Forgot the Taste of Limes" and "The Repatriation of Mrs. Ida M. Scofield" from *Singing Home the Bones*. Copyright ©2005 by Gregory Scofield. Reprinted by permission.

Warren Cariou: "Going to Canada" from *Across Cultures/Across Borders: Canadian Aboriginal and Native American Literatures*, eds. Paul DePasquale, Renate Eigenbrod and Emma LaRocque. Copyright ©2010 by Broadview Press. Reprinted by permission.

Gilbert James Fredette: "Visions or Screams" and "A Lifetime Ago" from *Northern Writers, Volume 1*. Norway House: Goldrock Press, 2009. Copyright ©2009 by Gilbert James Fredette. Reprinted by permission.

Randy Lundy: "deer-sleep," "ghost dance" and "ritual" from *Under the Night Sun*. Regina: Coteau Books, 1999. Copyright ©1999 by Randy Lundy. Reprinted by permission.

Ian Ross: Excerpts from *The Book of Joe*. Winnipeg: J.G. Shillingford Publications, 1999. Copyright ©1999 by J.G. Shillingford Publications. Reprinted by permission.

Nichola Tookoome Batzel: "Our Stories Belong Here Too: Manitoba Inuk." Copyright ©2011 by Nichola Tookoome Batzel. Printed by permission.

Columpa C. Bobb: Excerpt from *Will Work 4 Home*. Copyright ©2011 by Columpa C. Bobb. Printed by permission.

Nahanni Fontaine: "Our Cherished Sisters, Mothers, Aunties, and Grandmothers: Violence Against Aboriginal Women." Copyright ©2011 by Nahanni Fontaine. Printed by permission.

Rosanna Deerchild: "back home," "crazy horse is a girl," "northern lights" and "paper indians" from *This is a Small Northern Town*. Copyright ©2008 by The Muses' Company. Reprinted by permission.

Thematic Index